Building Android Projects with Kotlin

Use Android SDK, Jetpack, Material Design, and JUnit to Build Android and JVM Apps That Are Secure and Modular

Pankaj Kumar

www.bpbonline.com

Copyright © 2023 BPB Online

All rights reserved. No part of this book may be reproduced, stored in a retrieval system, or transmitted in any form or by any means, without the prior written permission of the publisher, except in the case of brief quotations embedded in critical articles or reviews.

Every effort has been made in the preparation of this book to ensure the accuracy of the information presented. However, the information contained in this book is sold without warranty, either express or implied. Neither the author, nor BPB Online or its dealers and distributors, will be held liable for any damages caused or alleged to have been caused directly or indirectly by this book.

BPB Online has endeavored to provide trademark information about all of the companies and products mentioned in this book by the appropriate use of capitals. However, BPB Online cannot guarantee the accuracy of this information.

Group Product Manager: Marianne Conor
Publishing Product Manager: Eva Brawn
Senior Editor: Connell
Content Development Editor: Melissa Monroe
Technical Editor: Anne Stokes
Copy Editor: Joe Austin
Language Support Editor: Justin Baldwin
Project Coordinator: Tyler Horan
Proofreader: Khloe Styles
Indexer: V. Krishnamurthy
Production Designer: Malcolm D'Souza
Marketing Coordinator: Kristen Kramer

First published: 2023

Published by BPB Online
WeWork, 119 Marylebone Road
London NW1 5PU

UK | UAE | INDIA | SINGAPORE

ISBN 978-93-5551-082-2

www.bpbonline.com

Dedicated to

My beloved Parents:
Shri Ranjeet Kumar Singh
Smt. Dr Manju Verma
&
My wife Sangeeta Kumari and My Daughters Shanvi Pankaj and Pankhudi Pankaj

About the Author

Pankaj Kumar holds a master's degree in computer science and has worked as a lead Android application developer for more than a decade. He has expertise in various domains including banking, enterprise security, multimedia, e-commerce and real estate. He also knows about AOSP development.

He presently serves as the mobile tech lead and mentors for developers at PropertyGuru Singapore. He contributes frequently to a few development communities and has earned more than 81,000 Stackoverflow reputation.

He wrote stories and poems for a few local and national magazines while still a teenager. His debut book is this one. He spends time with his daughters when he is not working.

About the Reviewers

- **Alexey Mostovoy**

    An android developer from Ukraine with 5 years of experience in building mobile applications. Have been successfully involved in the development of various banking, communications, news and entertainment applications.

    Believe that nothing is impossible with well-coordinated team

- **Milap**

    He believes that any fellow can write code that a computer can understand. "Good programmers" write code that humans can understand.

    Milap holds a master's degree in computer science. He has worked on the Android platform since Android 2.2(Froyo), and he has more than nine years of experience as a skilled Android developer. He is working with Accenture India as a tech lead.

    He has extensive industry experience, including those in banking, health, digital, multimedia, e-commerce, and many others. For him, it's always been about breaking out of his comfort zone.

    He also makes a contribution to his current organization as the innovation lead.

    He also contributes frequently to tech communities and has earned more than 10,000 reputations on Stackoverflow. He's also active on Github, where he has published a library of reusable Android components.

Acknowledgements

There are many whom I want to thank for the continued and ongoing support they have given me during the writing of this book.

To my wife Sangeeta,

Dear backbone of my family, without you nothing is possible. Thank you for your continuous encouragement. I could have never completed this book without your support.

To my daughters,

The day when you will be old enough to read this book, you will be happy to understand that most of our playtime was invested in something awesome. Shanvi (my photocopy), thank you for being caring and waking up late nights with me to just giving me company while writing this book. And Pankhudi, without your hard work and support I could have completed this book before 5-6 months. I will not share this secrete with anyone. Lots of love my princesses.

I am grateful to my teacher Mr Jay Sinha, my teammates, my juniors, my seniors, and mentors from each organization where I worked or work now. You gave me support throughout the learning process, your support and belief in me allowed me to explore everything in Android and take risks while developing something new in Android. These all things open doors to see the Android world in depth, and I tried to express all my learning to explain topics in the book, which can help readers to understand Android differently. Prabhat Singh, thank you for reviewing initial chapters and your valuable feedback, so I continued writing this book.

My gratitude also goes to the team at BPB Publication (including Nrip, Surbhi, Lubna, Shalli and the team) for being supportive enough to provide me with a long time to finish the book. You all helped me to write good quality content with very good quality reviews.

And I want to mention Alexey Mostovoy and Milap Tank for their technical reviews of the book and for helping to enhance the contents with their valuable feedback.

Preface

This book covers everything you need to learn for developing an amazing Android application. It explains the basics of Android, components of Android and their uses. This book also introduces the importance of clean code and architecture patterns. It also explains the use and benefits of using modularized code. This book introduces important tools which can be used while developing an Android application, it let the reader understand how to evaluate a layout performance, how to choose a better image type and the basics of multiscreen application development.

This book explains the development of chat applications, video sharing applications and a game. While developing and explaining functionalities for these projects, the book will explain best practices, libraries, functional requirement gathering and developing features. It covers a real-time industry example while explaining the implementation of any feature. This book also explains the backend, it explains a bit about it and gives you an idea about choosing the right server for your application. And it also covers Firebase and implements a few features of Firebase in those three projects which will be discussed in the book.

This book is divided into 10 chapters. These chapters will cover Android basics, optimizing layouts and images, use of important tools for development, writing clean code, developing the app for multiscreen, and developing a chat app, video sharing app and a game. Each chapter is written considering three things "what are options for doing a particular task", "why an option is better to perform a particular task" and "how to do a particular task by using that better option". So, the reader/ learners can get more interest in Android. The details are listed below.

Chapter 1 will let you know to create your first Android application using an Android template. It will explain about Android project structure, modules and creation of launcher icons and emulators. It will also cover a few important things like Layout Inspector, Memory Profiler and Database Inspector.

Chapter 2 will cover basic components of Android like Activity, Fragment, Service, Broadcast receiver, Content Provider and the lifecycle of Activity and Fragment. It will also explain a few important tools like GPU Overdraw, Systrace, and Perfetto which help us to measure the performance of the layout, so you can write an optimized layout design for your application.

Chapter 3 will explain Architecture patterns. It will cover commonly used architecture patterns like MVP and MVVM, and it also explain usecases. It will also cover writing scalable, testable, and maintainable code using these architecture patterns and writing clean code.

Chapter 4 will explain everything about developing chat applications. It will explain requirement gathering and choosing backend technology. It will also cover Firebase and its services, and Jetpack libraries like RecyclerView and ViewPager2.

And this chapter will cover to design and develop each screen of the chat application.

Chapter 5 will explain the process for publishing an Android application to Play Store. It will cover build variants, creating release Keystore, pricing strategies and preparing a checklist for app release. It will also cover account creation on Play Store, updating information about the app, publishing the update for the app, and analysing a few statistics like the number of installs and uninstalls.

Chapter 6 will explain about developing a video-sharing application. It will cover data storage options in Android, Material design library and UI components like BottomNavigationView. It will explain the Repository pattern, and it also explains about Exoplayer library to implement video features.

Chapter 7 will cover the basics of game development. First, it will explain game engines which are commonly being used to develop Android applications and then it will explain the basics of Unity, like creating the first project in Unity, adding some game objects and playing with a few properties of those game objects. It will explain about writing C# scripts for the game objects, and it will also cover creating Android build for the game.

Chapter 8 will explain about developing a game using Unity. It will cover adding all components for the game and adding C# scripts for it. It will explain about adding game objects dynamically. It will also explain about adding support for multiple screens, so users can run your game on any screen.

Chapter 9 will explain about adding support for big screens in your application. It will cover qualifiers for Android resources. It will cover designing and developing the application for tablets, wearables, and TV. It will explain about optimizing image resources for better performance and minimizing the size of the application.

Chapter 10 the last chapter let you know about commonly used tools, and libraries. It covers Jetpack Compose, App bundles, SafetyNet and Hilt. It also covers writing test cases in Android using Junit, Espresso and Robolectric. It explains best practices and some awesome 3rd party libraries.

Code Bundle and Coloured Images

Please follow the link to download the
Code Bundle and the *Coloured Images* of the book:

https://rebrand.ly/9ff9fd

The code bundle for the book is also hosted on GitHub at **https://github.com/bpbpublications/Building-Android-Projects-with-Kotlin**. In case there's an update to the code, it will be updated on the existing GitHub repository.

We have code bundles from our rich catalogue of books and videos available at **https://github.com/bpbpublications**. Check them out!

Errata

We take immense pride in our work at BPB Publications and follow best practices to ensure the accuracy of our content to provide with an indulging reading experience to our subscribers. Our readers are our mirrors, and we use their inputs to reflect and improve upon human errors, if any, that may have occurred during the publishing processes involved. To let us maintain the quality and help us reach out to any readers who might be having difficulties due to any unforeseen errors, please write to us at :

errata@bpbonline.com

Your support, suggestions and feedbacks are highly appreciated by the BPB Publications' Family.

> Did you know that BPB offers eBook versions of every book published, with PDF and ePub files available? You can upgrade to the eBook version at www.bpbonline.com and as a print book customer, you are entitled to a discount on the eBook copy. Get in touch with us at :
>
> **business@bpbonline.com** for more details.
>
> At **www.bpbonline.com**, you can also read a collection of free technical articles, sign up for a range of free newsletters, and receive exclusive discounts and offers on BPB books and eBooks.

Piracy

If you come across any illegal copies of our works in any form on the internet, we would be grateful if you would provide us with the location address or website name. Please contact us at **business@bpbonline.com** with a link to the material.

If you are interested in becoming an author

If there is a topic that you have expertise in, and you are interested in either writing or contributing to a book, please visit **www.bpbonline.com**. We have worked with thousands of developers and tech professionals, just like you, to help them share their insights with the global tech community. You can make a general application, apply for a specific hot topic that we are recruiting an author for, or submit your own idea.

Reviews

Please leave a review. Once you have read and used this book, why not leave a review on the site that you purchased it from? Potential readers can then see and use your unbiased opinion to make purchase decisions. We at BPB can understand what you think about our products, and our authors can see your feedback on their book. Thank you!

For more information about BPB, please visit **www.bpbonline.com**.

Table of Contents

1. Creating Hello World Project 1
   Structure 1
   Objectives 2
   Creating a project from Android Studio Template 2
   Introducing templates 5
   Understanding files in the created project 6
      AndroidManifest.xml 6
      Java/ 7
      res/ 7
      build.gradle 8
      gradle-wrapper.properties 10
      gradle.properties 10
      proguard-rules.pro 11
      settings.gradle 11
      local.properties 12
   Creating a custom launcher icon 12
   Creating android virtual device (AVD) 13
   Running the Hello World application 16
   Important tools to develop, debug, and improve Android application 17
      Gradle 17
      Logcat 20
      Writing Logs 23
      Android Lint 24
      How to use Lint from Android Studio 25
      Using Lint from command/terminal 26
      Layout inspector and layout validator 28
         Using Layout Inspector 28
      Introducing Layout Validator 30
      Memory profiler 30
      Database Inspector 35
         Modifying table from Database Inspector 36
         Run query from Database Inspector and DAO 37
   Conclusion 38

Points to remember 39
Multiple Choice Questions 39
    Answers *40*
Questions 40
Key Terms 40

2. Basics of Android Components 41
Structure 41
Objectives 42
Basic components of Android 42
    Activity *43*
    Service *45*
    Broadcast receiver *48*
        Static broadcast receivers *48*
        Dynamic broadcast receivers *49*
    Content provider *51*
        Content resolver *52*
Introducing Fragment and View 52
    View *52*
    Fragment *53*
        Ways to show Fragments *54*
Lifecycle of an Activity 58
Lifecycle of a Fragment 61
Introducing dimensions and screen sizes 63
    Dimensions *63*
    Handling of screen sizes *66*
Understanding different types of Layouts 68
    LinearLayout *69*
    RelativeLayout *71*
    TableLayout *73*
    FrameLayout *75*
    ConstraintLayout *77*
Choosing a better Layout for a design 82
    GPU overdraw *82*
    Perfetto/Systrace *83*
Basics of material design 83

Conclusion	84
Points to remember	85
Multiple Choice Questions	86
Answers	*86*
Questions	87
Key Terms	87

3. Architecture Patterns 89

Structure	89
Objectives	90
Understanding the need for an architecture pattern	90
Understanding clean architecture	91
Understanding SOLID principle	*91*
Single responsibility principle	92
Open-closed principle	93
Liskov's substitution principle	95
Interface segregation principle	96
Dependency inversion principle	98
Understanding MVP	103
Points to remember:	104
Understanding MVP with code	*104*
Advantages of using MVP	*115*
Disadvantages of MVP	*115*
Understanding MVVM	115
Understanding MVVM with code	*117*
Using databinding	125
Advantages of using MVVM	*129*
Disadvantages of MVVM	*129*
MVVM with UseCases	*129*
Conclusion	137
Points to remember	138
Multiple Choice Questions	139
Answers	*139*
Questions	140
Key Terms	140

4. Developing Chat Application 141

Structure 141
Objectives 142
Gathering functional requirement 143
Creating user flow diagrams 143
Introducing server 144
    Choosing better backend technology 145
    Introducing BaaS 146
Introducing Firebase and its services 146
    Adding Firebase to application 146
        Step 1: Creating a Firebase project 146
        Step 2: Registering the Android application with the Firebase project ... 147
        Step 3: Adding Firebase configuration file to the Android project 148
        Step 4: Adding Firebase SDKs to the app 149
    Identifying and introducing Firebase services 150
        Introducing Firebase Authentication 151
        Introducing Firebase real-time database 153
        Introducing Cloud Storage 155
        Introducing FirebaseUI 155
Introducing Android Jetpack 158
    Introducing RecyclerView 158
        Understanding important classes of RecyclerView 158
        Understanding how RecyclerView works 159
    Introducing TabLayout and ViewPager 161
Understanding project structure of Chat app 163
Writing code for the first screen 164
Developing login screen 167
Developing of chat home screen 173
Developing contacts screen 177
Developing chat screen 183
Developing profile screen 191
Using of notifications 197
Conclusion 197
Points to remember 198
Multiple Choice Questions 198

    Answers 199
  Questions 199
  Key Terms 200

5. Publishing the Application 201
  Structure 201
  Objectives 202
  Introducing build variants 202
    Customizing build configurations 204
      Build types 204
      Product flavors 208
      Build variants 210
  Creating release Keystore 211
  Introducing R8 and Proguard 213
    Renaming identifiers 217
    Enabling of R8 217
    Adding custom rules 219
  Creating a distributable file (release application) 220
  Creating a Google Play Store developer profile 221
  Pricing the application 223
    Understanding pricing strategy 224
      Free 224
      Freemium 224
      Paid 225
      Subscription plan 225
  Getting screenshots for the application 226
  Preparing Android app release checklist 228
  Uploading application to the Play Store 228
    Settings for paid applications 229
      Creating App at Google Play console 229
      Setting up your app 230
      Publishing/releasing the application 232
  Watching the number of installs 233
  Updating application at Play Store 234
  Conclusion 235
  Points to remember 235

- Multiple Choice Questions 236
  - *Answers* *236*
- Questions 236
- Key Terms 236

6. Developing Video Sharing Application 239

- Structure 240
- Objectives 241
- Gathering functional requirement 241
- Creating user flow diagram 242
- Introducing material UI components 244
  - *Introducing BottomNavigationView* *244*
- Introducing data storage in Android 248
  - *Introducing files* *249*
  - *Storage Access Framework (SAF)* *249*
  - *Preferences* *251*
  - *Database* *253*
    - *Room* *253*
- Creating CRUD for video sharing application 254
  - *Creating database* *254*
- Introducing repository pattern 258
  - *Introduction* *258*
  - *Package structure for repository pattern* *260*
  - *Implementing the repository pattern* *260*
- Introducing ExoPlayer 264
  - *Dependencies for ExoPlayer* *264*
- Understanding project structure 269
- Developing home screen 269
- Implementing the likes feature on clips 278
- Implementing the share feature for clips 281
- Implementing the comment feature on clips 283
- Developing add clips screen 284
- Conclusion 291
- Points to remember 291
- Multiple Choice Questions 292
  - *Answers* *292*

Questions	292
Key Terms	293

7. Introduction to Game Development ... 295

Introduction	295
Structure	295
Objectives	296
Introducing game engine	296
Unity	*297*
Unreal engine	*298*
Buildbox	*298*
Solar2D	*298*
GameMaker Studio 2	*298*
Introducing Unity	299
Installing Unity	*299*
Creating Hello Unity project	*301*
Introduction to Unity workspace	*303*
Adding game objects to the project	*304*
Adding texture to objects	*305*
Adding Cube to the Scene	*305*
Adding bricks image file	*306*
Adding material object	*307*
Applying bricks image to material object	*307*
Applying bricks material object to the Cube	*309*
Introducing important terms in Unity	*310*
Introducing C# script	*312*
Creating an Android build	*317*
Conclusion	322
Points to remember	323
Multiple Choice Questions	323
Answers	323
Questions	324
Key Terms	324

8. Development of the First Game ... 327

Structure	327

Objectives	328
Introducing the project requirement	328
Creating the project	329
Adding game objects	330
Adding floor	*331*
Adding target objects	*334*
Adding blocks	334
Adding diamond	336
Adding the ball	*337*
Adding the bouncing effect to the ball	*338*
Creating ball pin object	*341*
Adding C# script	345
Adding ball to the game dynamically	349
Creating Prefab for ball	*349*
Modifying script to use ball prefab	351
Adding support for multiple screens	*359*
Conclusion	362
Points to remember	363
Multiple Choice Questions	363
Answers	*363*
Questions	363
Key Terms	364
9. Adding Support for Big Screens	**365**
Structure	365
Objectives	366
Introducing resources in Android	366
Understanding resources	*367*
Introducing different qualifiers	*368*
Qualifiers for drawables	369
Qualifiers for layouts	371
Qualifiers for values	372
Working with resources	*373*
Choosing the optimized image resource type	377
Raster Image	*377*
PNG	378

  WebP *378*
  Vector image *379*
   Vector drawables *379*
 Designing and developing an app for Tablets 381
  Introducing tablet-specific dimensions and layout qualifiers *381*
  Optimizing layouts for tablets *381*
  Preparing checklist for Tablet app quality *383*
 Developing apps for wearables and TV 384
  Creating project for wearables *384*
   Creating an AVD for wearables *389*
  Creating project for TV *389*
   Declaring Leanback support *393*
   Declaring touchscreen not required *393*
   Creating an AVD for TV application *394*
 Conclusion 394
 Points to remember 395
 Multiple Choice Questions 395
  Answers *395*
 Questions 395
 Key Terms 396

10. Introducing Important Tools/Libs for Android 397
 Structure 397
 Objectives 398
 Introducing Jetpack compose 398
  Introducing Row *400*
  Introducing Column *401*
  Introducing Box *401*
  Introducing ConstraintLayout *402*
 Introducing App Bundles 404
  Understanding benefits of App bundles *404*
 Introducing SafetyNet 407
  SafetyNet Attestation API *407*
  SafetyNet Safe Browsing API *408*
  SafetyNet reCAPTCHA API *408*
  SafetyNet Verify Apps API *408*

Introducing Hilt	409
Exploring dependency injection	*409*
Understanding benefits of dependency injection solutions	*411*
Adding dependency for Hilt	*411*
Introducing annotations in Hilt	*412*
Writing test cases with JUnit/Robolectric	417
Introducing test cases	*417*
Writing good test cases	*417*
Writing local test cases using JUnit	*419*
Introducing Espresso	*421*
Introducing Robolectric	*423*
Best practices to follow	425
Third-party libraries you should know	427
Choosing the right Android library	*427*
List of a few libraries	*427*
Conclusion	428
Points to remember	429
Multiple Choice Questions	429
Answers	430
Questions	430
Key Terms	431
Index	**433**

CHAPTER 1
Creating Hello World Project

Before going ahead, the recommendation is to do the setup of Android Studio on your development machine. Any latest version would work for each chapter in this book.

In this chapter, we are going to create our first Hello World application for Android by creating a project using Android Studio Templates. We will see the project structure and know about each file added by default to the Hello World project.

We will also read about Templates, Modules, the creation of the launcher icon, setting up emulator, and at last, we will know about some important tools that would be used while developing and debugging Android applications.

Structure

- Creating a project from Android Studio Template
- Introducing templates
- Understanding files in the created project
- Creating a custom launcher icon
- Creating android virtual device (AVD)
- Running the Hello World application

- Important tools to develop, debug, and improve android applications
    - Gradle
    - Logcat
    - Android lint
    - Layout inspector
    - Memory profiler
    - Database inspector

Objectives

The objective of this chapter is to let you know how to create a new project using the Android Studio template, the basics about files that are part of the Android project, creating a launcher icon, and creating an emulator.

You will also know about important tools which would help develop and debug Android applications.

Creating a project from Android Studio Template

To start the development of an Android Application, we need to create a project with the basic setup. Android Studio helps you do this. It provides you with the basic setup of the project with different types of commonly used projects. Those are known as templates. We need to choose the template depending on our requirement or whichever would be closer to our requirement. We will read more about the template later in this chapter.

So first, we will create a project using Android Studio Template. To do that, perform the following steps to create a new project:

1. Run Android Studio.
2. Click on **+ Create New Project** on the Welcome Window as shown in *figure 1.1*:

Figure 1.1: Welcome window of Android Studio

3. Create a **New Project** window, which will be shown in *figure 1.2*. Go to the **Phone** and **Tablet** tab, select **Empty Activity** template, and press **Next**:

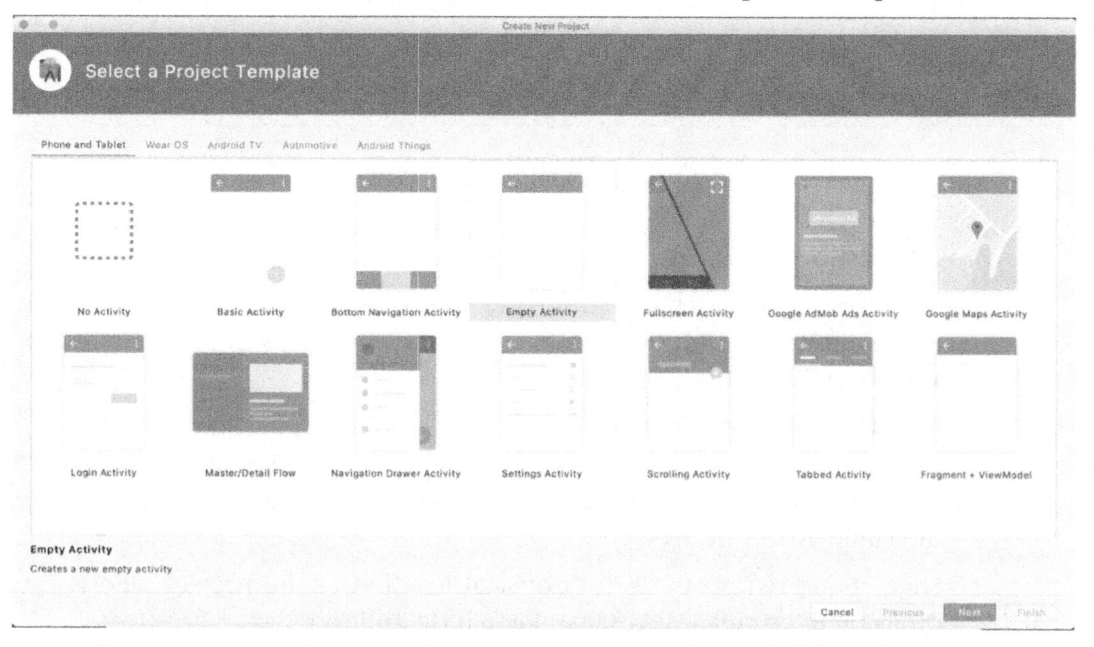

Figure 1.2: Choosing a template from the Project Template list

4. On the **Project Configuration** window, you will require to add the following configurations, as shown in *figure 1.3*:

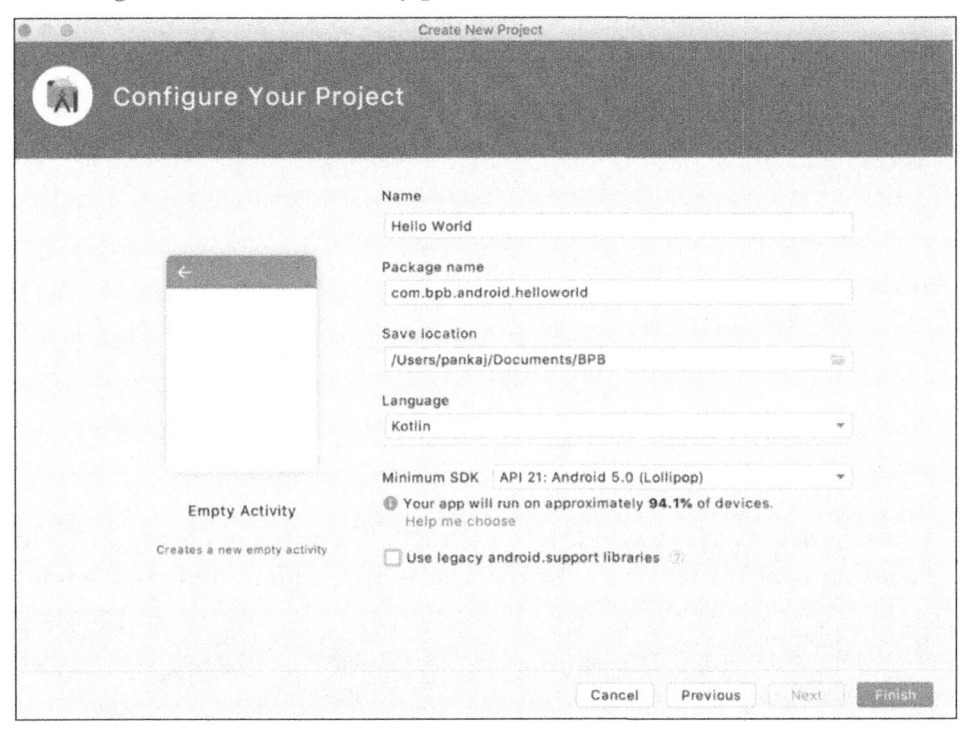

Figure 1.3: Configuring the project

Let us see these parameters in detail, which requires while creating the project, as shown in the preceding *figure 1.3*:

- **Name**: The name which you see on the phone for each application. Android will identify your application by this name. As of now, let us put "**Hello World**" in this field.
- **Package Name**: Best practice is to create a unique package name. To do that, you can put your company domain with the project name, like **com.uniquecompany.app_name**. Let us put **com.bpb.android.helloworld** for the Hello World project.
- **Save location**: Choose the physical location of the project where the project will be created. You can keep it default too.
- **Language**: There are two options, Java/Kotlin, and we are here to learn Kotlin; choose **Kotlin** as language.
- **Minimum SDK**: This option is a filter for the Play Store and Android system to allow your application to be installed on only those devices which are running on either the given min SDK version or newer.

Android studio will show the percent of devices in the world that can use your world depending on the version you choose. So, for our Hello World project, let us choose API21.

5. Click on **Finish**.

Introducing templates

Templates are a set of files for common uses and are added to your application automatically when you choose one of them. They follow design and development best practices to get you on the right track to create your awesome application.

Android Studio gives you some commonly used templates, which can be added to your app in two ways:

- **From create project wizard (starter templates)**: These templates can be chosen when you are creating a new project as shown in the preceding *figure 1.2*, for example, template for Login Screen, Screen with Tabs, and so on.
- **Templates for the existing project**: If you already have created a project and you need to add any template (let us say you want to add any screen), Android Studio gives you this ability too. From Tool Bar, click on `File` -> `New` -> and choose the category of template -> and choose a template, as shown in *figure 1.4*.

  For example, if you want to add a Login Screen to our Hello World Project, then it can be added by following these steps, `File | New | Activity | Login Activity`:

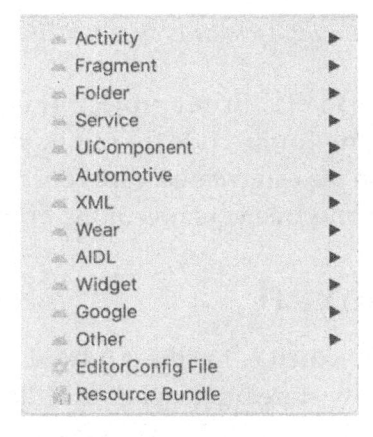

Figure 1.4: Templates for existing project

You should explore all templates and make practice using these templates in your application. There are benefits of using these, like you need to write less code and get prewritten code that follows the best practices of Android.

Understanding files in the created project

When Android Studio opens the project in the workspace, you will see a workspace similar to *figure 1.5*:

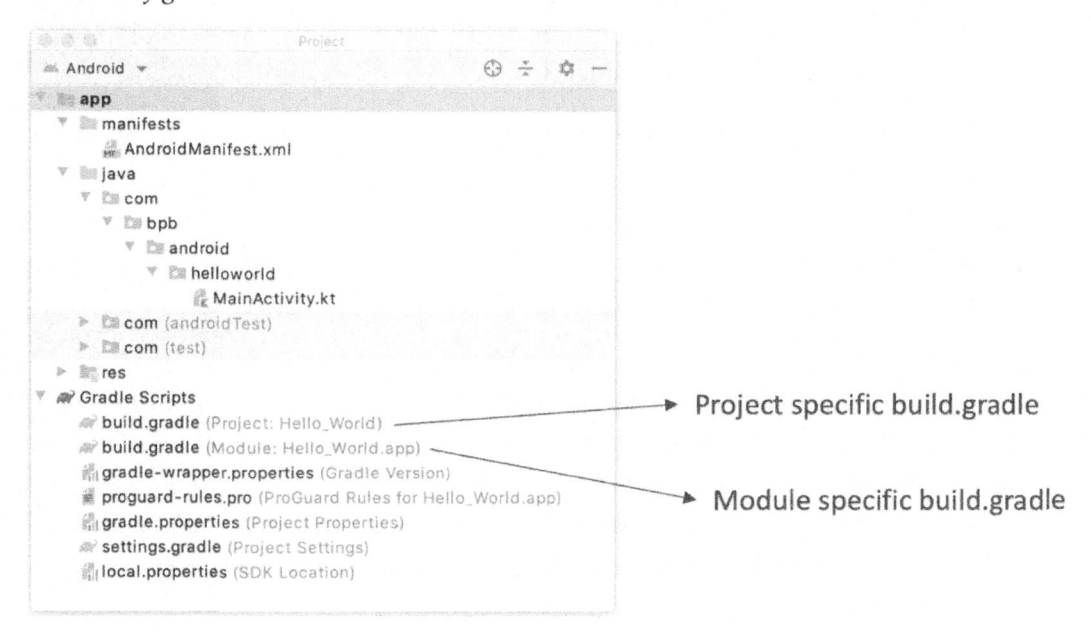

Figure 1.5: Default Project structure

Each file has an important role to play in our project. These files help us in creating a build, designing UI, and writing Kotlin code for our application. Some of these files help us to customize builds so we can create a different type of application from the same code base, like the paid and free versions of the application.

AndroidManifest.xml

This file contains information which is for the Android operating system, Android build tools, and the Google Play store. In general, this file has information about:

- Each Android component (activity/broadcast receiver/content provider or services).
- Which hardware or software feature is required to use your application? For example, Camera, NFC, and so on.

- Permissions that are required by your application. For security reasons, Android has a set of permissions that need to be requested from an application if doing any such task which needs permission.

You will know more about this file in *Chapter 4: Development of Chat Application*, *Chapter 6: Development of Video Sharing Application*, and *Chapter 8: Development of First Game*.

Java/

This directory keeps **Java/** Kotlin code for the application. **Java/** is the default structure, and we can rename it too, like **kotlin/**. For the Hello world project, the code of **MainActivity.kt** is as follows:

```
package com.bpb.android.helloworld

import android.os.Bundle
import androidx.appcompat.app.AppCompatActivity

class MainActivity : AppCompatActivity() {

    override fun onCreate(savedInstanceState: Bundle?) {
        super.onCreate(savedInstanceState)
        setContentView(R.layout.activity_main)
    }
}
```

res/

This is the most interesting directory in an Android Project. You will know more about this directory in *Chapter 4: Development of Chat Application*, *Chapter 6: Develop Video Sharing Application*, *Chapter 8: Development of First Game,* and *Chapter 9: Adding Support for Big Screens*. Till then, just remember that this is the directory that keeps images (drawable), screen designs (layouts), texts used in the app, fonts, and so on. As the UI file is present in this directory, let us see what is inside a layout which shows Hello World text:

```
<?xml version="1.0" encoding="utf-8"?>
<androidx.constraintlayout.widget.ConstraintLayout
    xmlns:android="http://schemas.android.com/apk/res/android"
```

```
        xmlns:app="http://schemas.android.com/apk/res-auto"
        xmlns:tools="http://schemas.android.com/tools"
        android:layout_width="match_parent"
        android:layout_height="match_parent"
        tools:context=".MainActivity">

        <TextView
            android:layout_width="wrap_content"
            android:layout_height="wrap_content"
            android:text="Hello World!"
            android:textColor="@color/black"
            app:layout_constraintBottom_toBottomOf="parent"
            app:layout_constraintLeft_toLeftOf="parent"
            app:layout_constraintRight_toRightOf="parent"
            app:layout_constraintTop_toTopOf="parent" />

</androidx.constraintlayout.widget.ConstraintLayout>
```

In this XML, you see **ConstraintLayout**, which is a type of **ViewGroup** that acts as a container of Views, and **TextView** in a View, which is used for showing texts in Android Applications. In our Hello World project, we are using this View to show the text **Hello World**.

build.gradle

You can see two different **build.gradle** files in preceding *figure 1.5*:

- The first file is for project-specific configurations. In general, configurations added to this file will be applied to each module used in the application. You can use **allprojects {}** or **subprojects {}** to define settings for all other modules, as follows:

```
allprojects {
    repositories {
        google()
        jcenter()
    }
}
```

- The second build.gradle file in the preceding *figure 1.5* contains **configuration/** dependencies for a module. Dependencies can be added using implementation with library identifier and the version available on Google, Jcenter, or Maven repositories. For our Hello World project, these dependencies can be written as follows:

  ```
  dependencies {
      implementation "org.jetbrains.kotlin:kotlin-stdlib:$kotlin_version"
      implementation 'androidx.core:core-ktx:1.3.2'
      implementation 'androidx.appcompat:appcompat:1.2.0'
      implementation 'com.google.android.material:material:1.2.1'
      implementation 'androidx.constraintlayout:constraintlayout:2.0.4'
      testImplementation 'junit:junit:4.+'
      androidTestImplementation 'androidx.test.ext:junit:1.1.2'
      androidTestImplementation 'androidx.test.espresso:espresso-core:3.3.0'
  }
  ```

Here `testImplementation` and `androidTestImplementation` act the same as implementation, but these make libraries available only in the test and **androidTest** source set.

NOTE: **Modules are the concept of separation of concerns, where you divide application features into modules. Creating features as modules enables reusability of the feature into different applications and a few awesome features of Android like App Bundle and Instant Apps. Let us assume you are creating a messenger application that provides three different ways to communicate, call, message, and video call. In this case, call, message, and video features can be created as separate modules. One thing to remember is that each module can be debugged, build, and tested independently.**

In preceding *figure 1.5*, **the app is the module. In later chapters, you would be learning to add configurations into Gradle files.**

gradle-wrapper.properties

You can specify the Gradle version in this file. The following is the code of **gradle/wrapper/gradle-wraper.properties** file:

distributionBase=GRADLE_USER_HOME

distributionPath=wrapper/dists

zipStoreBase=GRADLE_USER_HOME

zipStorePath=wrapper/dists

distributionUrl=https\://services.gradle.org/distributions/gradle-6.5-bin.zip

The preceding code sets the Gradle version 6.5 by setting the value for **distributionUrl**. Note that this file will be created with default values when you create a new project. You only need to modify this file when you want to change the Gradle version.

gradle.properties

Project-wide Gradle settings, you will find in any Android project. The purpose of using this file is to provide start-up options for Gradle such as Gradle daemon's maximum heap, use of AndroidX package structure, code style, and so on, as follows:

Project-wide Gradle settings.

IDE (e.g. Android Studio) users:

Gradle settings configured through the IDE *will override*

any settings specified in this file.

For more details on how to configure your build environment visit

http://www.gradle.org/docs/current/userguide/build_environment.html

Specifies the JVM arguments used for the daemon process.

The setting is particularly useful for tweaking memory settings.

org.gradle.jvmargs=-Xmx2048m -Dfile.encoding=UTF-8

When configured, Gradle will run in incubating parallel mode.

This option should only be used with decoupled projects. More details, visit

```
# http://www.gradle.org/docs/current/userguide/multi_project_builds.
html#sec:decoupled_projects

# org.gradle.parallel=true

# AndroidX package structure to make it clearer which packages are bundled with the

# Android operating system, and which are packaged with your app"s APK

# https://developer.android.com/topic/libraries/support-library/
androidx-rn

android.useAndroidX=true

# Automatically convert third-party libraries to use AndroidX

android.enableJetifier=true

# Kotlin code style for this project: "official" or "obsolete":

kotlin.code.style=official
```

The preceding codes are from our Hello World project, and these codes are added by default when you create the project. This file is optional, and these values can be overwritten by Gradle command-line arguments or a file located at **USER_HOME/.gradle/gradle.properties**.

You can also set environment variables for the build in this file, where **systemProps** would be prefixed, as follows:

```
systemProp.gradle.wrapperUser=myuser

systemProp.gradle.wrapperPassword=mypassword
```

proguard-rules.pro

ProGuard is a tool to shrink, optimize, and obfuscate the code of the application. This file contains rules for the tool. You will read more details about this tool in *Chapter 5, Publishing the Application*.

settings.gradle

This file would be one file per project, so you will find only one copy of this file for a project, even if you are using more than one module in the project. The main role of **settings.gradle** is to define all submodules, as follows:

```
include ':app'

rootProject.name = "Hello World"
```

In our Hello World project, we have only one module app, so you see only one entry of includes **:app**. In case you use more than one module for the project, there will be more than on include statements as follows:

```
include ':app'

include ':module1'

include ':module2'
```

local.properties

This file is autogenerated and contains local environment properties for the build system, like the path of SDK/ NDK, and so on, as follows:

```
sdk.dir=/Users/your_name/Library/Android/sdk
```

You should not modify this file as this file is autogenerated and your changes will be erased. Most importantly, this file should not be added to your code repository.

After reading the overview of each file in the project structure, let us change the launcher icon.

Creating a custom launcher icon

When you go to the application list on an Android device, it shows the application icon and name for all installed applications. That icon is known as the Launcher icon. While creating a new project, Android Studio adds the default launcher icon, which works well. But if you want to release your application, you must change it to the custom icon representing it.

To create a launcher icon, go to **File | New | Image Asset**. You will see **Configure Image Asset** dialog, as shown in *figure 1.6*:

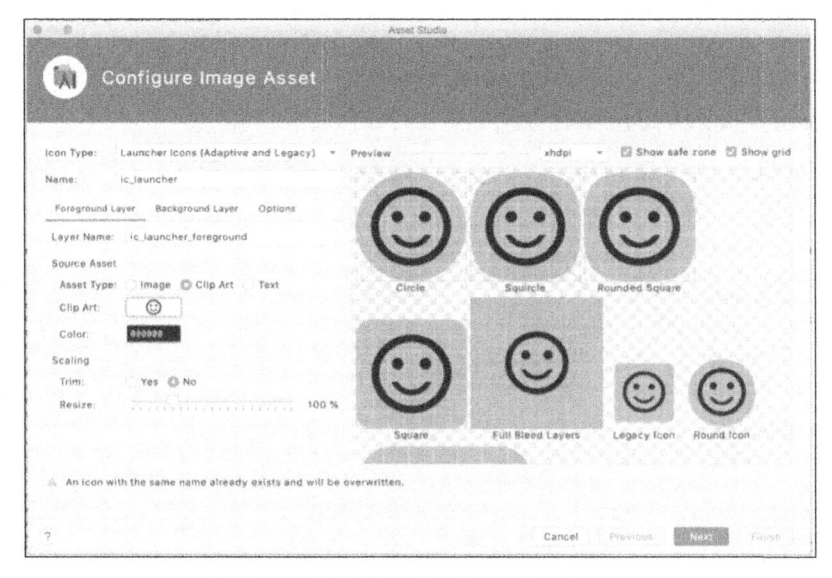

Figure 1.6: Creating launcher icon

At this screen, the icon type, which is the launcher icon is our case, name for the icon, three different types under asset type so you can choose any type to create an icon (as in preceding *figure 1.6*, Smiley has taken from Clip Art. Other settings can be changed, but these settings are as is, as these are recommended and follow standards.

Now, click on **Next**. You will see the `Confirm Icon Path` screen and click **Finish**.

Creating android virtual device (AVD)

As shown in *figure 1.7*, if you see **No Devices** in Toolbar, you do not have an emulator or device connected:

Figure 1.7: Running AVD from Toolbar

So, you need to create AVD or connect the device. Let us see how you can create AVD (Emulator) using the following steps:

14 ■ Building Android Projects with Kotlin

Open the AVD Manager by clicking **Tools | AVD Manager** or by clicking on Icon from Tool Bar as shown in the preceding *figure 1.7*.

1. Click on **Create Virtual Device** on AVD Manager Dialog.
2. On the **Select Hardware** screen, select category as **Phone** and **Hardware** screen as Pixel 2 as of now, as shown in *figure 1.8*:

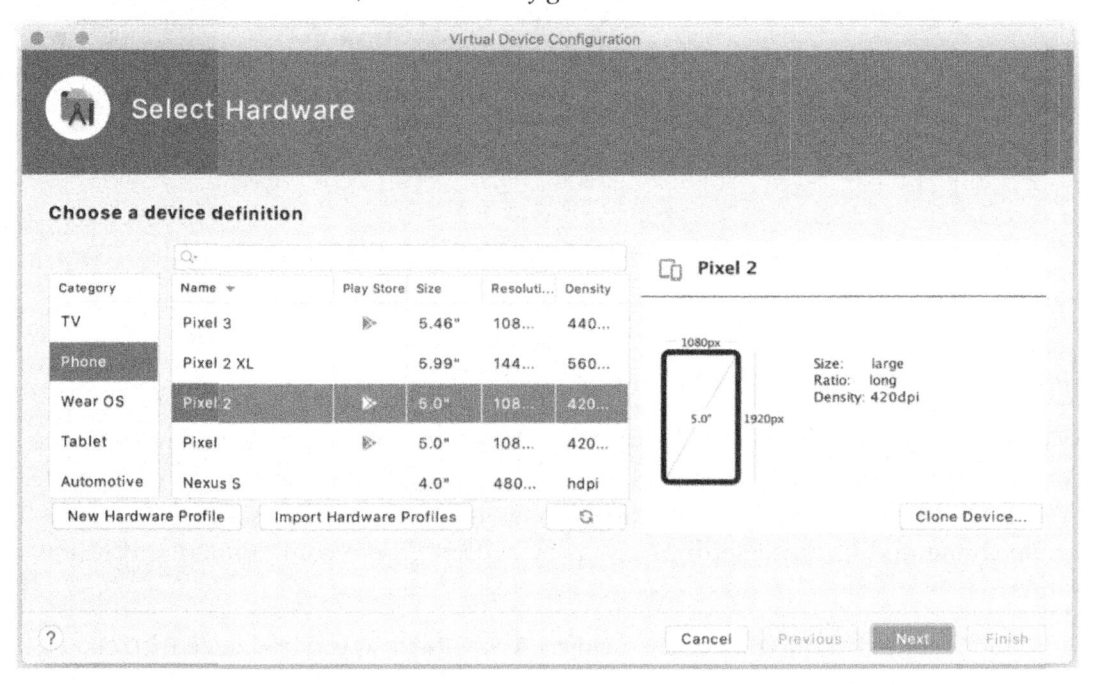

Figure 1.8: Choosing hardware for emulator

You can choose any hardware profile here, but profiles which include the Play Store are fully CTS compliant, and AVD will have play services features, including the Play Store application.

Now click on **Next**.

3. On the **System Image** screen, select the system image for a specific API level, and click on **Next**, as shown as *figure 1.9*:

Creating Hello World Project ■ 15

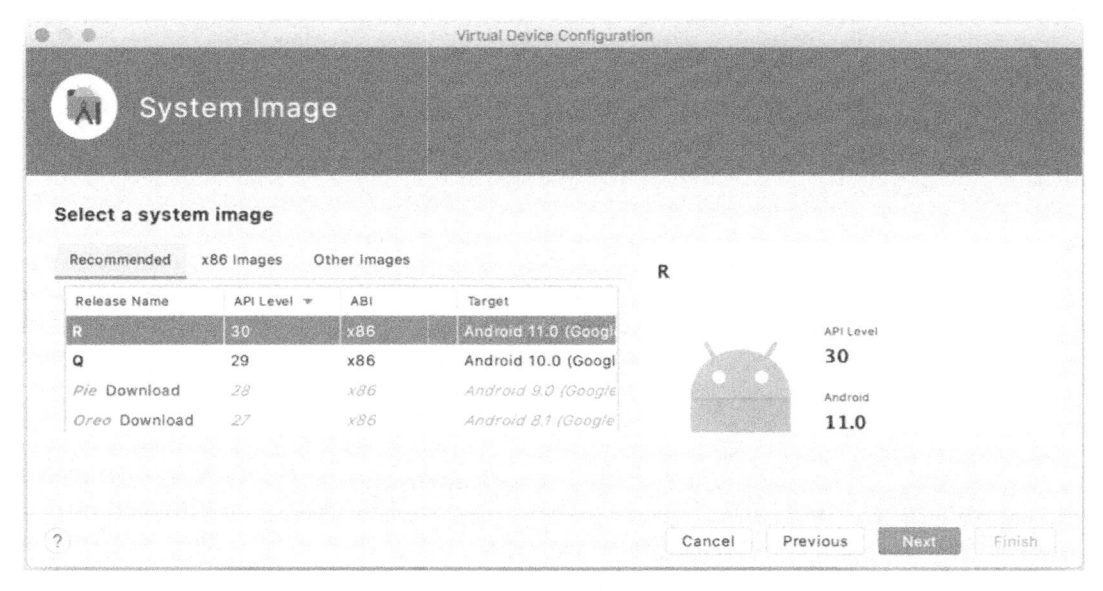

Figure 1.9: Choosing API level

TIP: While choosing API level, you need to check the value of minSdkVersion from the manifest or Gradle file and make that value of minSdkVersion is either equal to or less than API level.

You can see three Tabs in preceding *figure 1.9*, recommended tab shows you default recommendations. The other two tabs have the complete list of system images. So you can play with them and try to understand their uses.

4. On **Verify Configuration** screen, you can change the name of AVD or more settings by clicking on **Show Advance Settings**, as shown in *figure 1.10*:

Building Android Projects with Kotlin

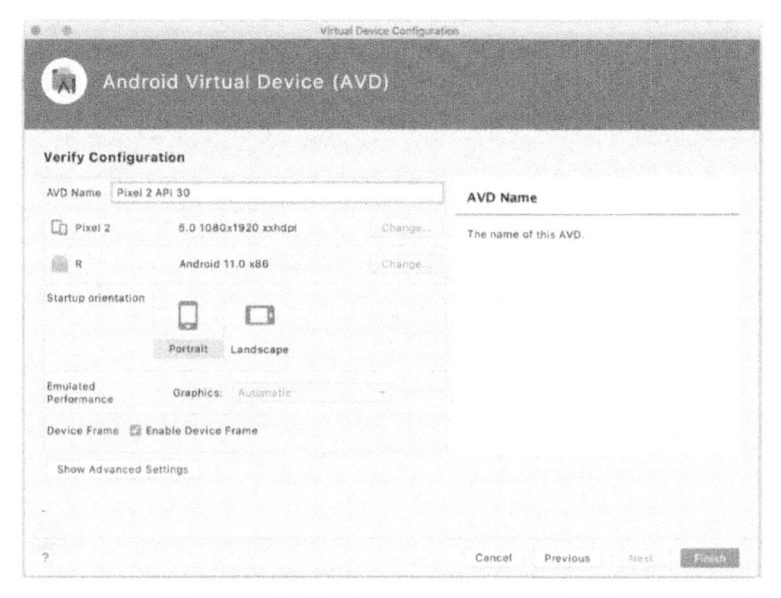

Figure 1.10: Final steps to create an AVD

And click on **Finish**.

Congratulations, now you know how to create Android Virtual Device.

Let us run our Hello World application.

Running the Hello World application

To run the application, click on **Run | Run 'app'** from Tool Bar or click on the run icon on Tool Bar.

On first lunch, Android Studio will take some time to launch the application, as it will sync your application with Gradle files. After a successful build, you will see an amazing application running on the emulator, saying "**Hello World!**", as shown in *figure 1.11*:

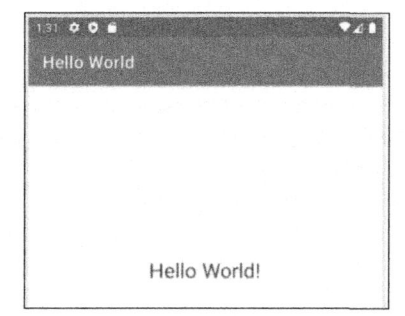

Figure 1.11: Output of Hello World app

Now you know how to create a project using the template, how to create an emulator, and how to run the application.

Important tools to develop, debug, and improve Android application

Let us read more about a few important tools that help while developing and debugging the application and need to know before you start an awesome project. The following are those tools:

- Gradle
- Logcat
- Android Lint
- Layout Inspector and Layout Validator
- Memory Profiler
- Database Inspector

Let us know more about these tools in the next section.

Gradle

Gradle is an open-source build automation tool that can be used to build almost any type of software. Keeping definition more simple, Gradle is software for building software.

In terms of Android, Android Studio uses Gradle to create Android builds, and Gradle plugins add many features that are specific to building Android applications. It helps you to customize the build easily. For example, if you want to:

- Create free and paid versions of your application from the same project
- Create a country/region-specific application from the same source code
- Use different configurations like server URL for your debug application or release application
- Use any library in debug application, but you do not want to include that library in the release application.

These all-custom configurations can be configured easily using Gradle. We will see how to do these configurations in a later chapter.

While looking into a project structure, as shown in preceding *figure 1.5,* you saw a few files used for Gradle configurations, and you read a little bit about those files. In this section, we will learn more about the **build.gradle** file of app module in detail.

So first of let us see the **defaultConfig**:

```
android {

    ...

    defaultConfig {

        applicationId "com.bpb.android.helloworld"

        minSdkVersion 21

        targetSdkVersion 30

        versionCode 1

        versionName "1.0"

    }

    ...

}
```

In the preceding code, we set the following:

- **applicationId** is the unique identification of the application. In a normal case, this id would be the same as the package name you set while creating a new project. But this can be changed, and it is not required to keep it the same as the package name. In the URL https://play.google.com/store/apps/details?id=com.ulektz.BPB, com.ulektz.BPB is the application id.
- **minSdkVersion** [see create project section for more information]
- **targetSdkVersion** refers to the API level on which you have tested your application, and the Android system used to not enable any forward-compatible behavior to run your application well on a newer version than **targetSdkVersion**.
- **versionCode** This positive integer number is used as the version number of your application, so different versions of the application can be identified, like which version is newer or older. And most importantly, by using version code, the Android system prevents downgrading of your application by disallowing the installation of applications that have a lower value of version code.

- **versionName** used to be a string that describes the application version <major>.<minor>.<point> like 1.0.1. The only purpose of it is to display the version to the user.

Let us see **buildTypes** section of **build.gradle**:

```
buildTypes {

        debug {

            debuggable true

        }

        release {

            minifyEnabled false

                proguardFiles getDefaultProguardFile('proguard-android-optimize.txt'), 'proguard-rules.pro'

        }
}
```

buildTypes contains configurations per build type. In the preceding code, you see debug and release build types with few configurations for each. You can add more build types like beta (we release the beta version to let the public test the app and then provide feedback to the developer). We will learn more about this file while explaining build flavors in *Chapter 5*: *Publishing the Application*.

And at last, let us look into **dependencies** field:

```
dependencies {

    // Dependency on local JARs
    implementation fileTree(dir: 'libs', include: ['*.jar'])
    // Dependency on a local library module
    implementation project(':mylibrary')
    // Dependency on a remote binary
    implementation 'androidx.appcompat:appcompat:1.4.2'

}
```

In the preceding code, you set different types of dependencies, like if your module depends on a local jar file, you will add a dependency similar to Line 3. Line 5 can be used when your module depends on another local module **myLibrary**. And Line 7 is used to provide dependency to the module, which is online and placed on any online repository, like Maven.

Logcat

A tool, which shows your android device logs, including crash logs and the logs that you have written for your application. VERBOSE, DEBUG, INFO, WARNING, ERROR, or FATAL are logging levels that can be used to log errors, warnings, or some other text. As Logcat is a command-line tool, here are a few important commands which you can use to see logs on the command window. [Assuming you have added SDK path as an environment variable, or logcat can be found into platform-tools/ of Android SDK].

- To view log output, it will show the device log, including your application log:

    `adb logcat`

- To clear the device logs, you can use either of the following commands:

    `adb logcat -c`

    `adb logcat --clear`

- To filter logs with Log level. Given command will print logs with log level DEBUG and higher:

    `adb logcat *:D`

- To know about more commands and uses:

    `adb logcat --help`

You should also read the official documentation https://developer.android.com/studio/command-line/logcat for logcat commands.

Android Studio provides a logcat window, which is an easy way to view log messages, so we will not go into more details for logcat commands. Apart from the log view, this window gives a few other interesting features. Let us go back to Android Studio and open **View | Tool Windows | Logcat** or click on `6: Logcat` at the bottom toolbar. You see a Logcat Window, as shown in *figure 1.12*, where you can see logs for the Hello World application:

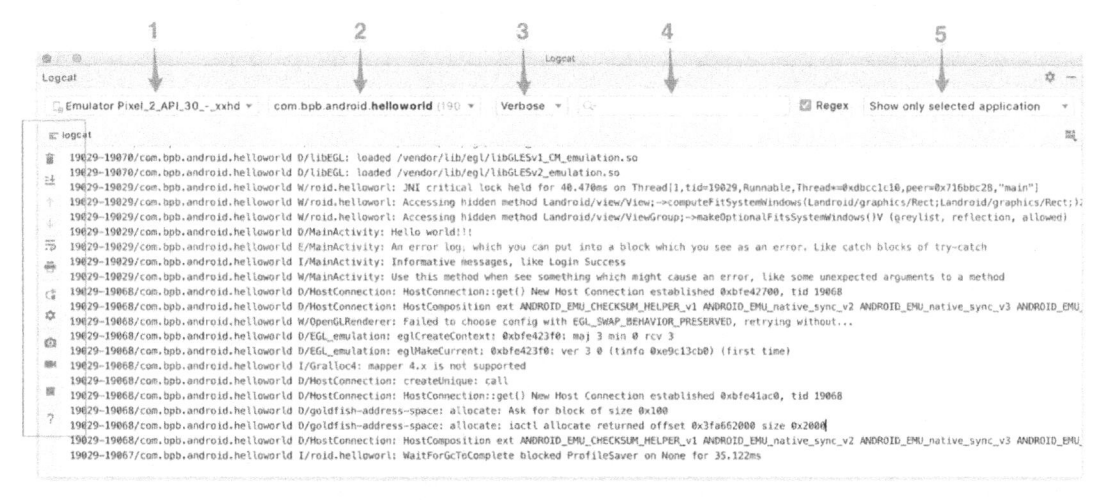

Figure 1.12: The logcat window

In the preceding *figure 1.12*, you can see a few options at the top, which are marked with numbers. These are filtering options to filter log messages. Let us see what these are as follows:

1. This option shows you attached emulators and devices to ADB. You see log messages from the device which is selected in this option. You can switch to different devices by using the drop-down.

2. This dropdown keeps all debug-able applications for the selected device. By choosing a different application from this drop-down, you can see logs of the chosen application.

3. You can filter logs by Tag using this drop-down. In the preceding *figure 1.12*, Verbose is selected, which means you will see each type of log message that is Verbose, Debug, Info, Warning, and Error. Similarly, if you select Warning, then you will see the log messages, which are tagged with Warning or Error.

4. The search box with regex gives you an option to filter log messages by some text. Logcat window will show only those messages which contain the text added into the search box.

5. The last drop-down has options to show logs only for selected applications (Point 2) or complete device logs. It gives an option to create a custom filter too, where you can filter log messages by Process Id, Package Name, Log Tag, and more.

There are some buttons(tools) on the Logcat Window, highlighted in the rectangular area in the preceding *figure 1.12* and also shown in *figure 1.13*. These tools help us to perform some action on the logcat window, take a screenshot of a running application, take a video of the application, and so on. Let us look into these tools (as shown in *figure 1.13*) in more detail:

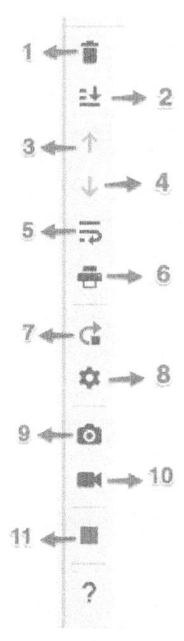

Figure 1.13: Tools at Logcat window

1. **Clear Log**: Choose to click this button when you want to clear the log messages on logcat Window.
2. **Scroll to the end**: Clicking on a particular line stops scrolling and keeps that line visible.
3. **Up the stack trace and Down the stack trace**: These buttons are useful when you get a crash in the Application. By using these two buttons, you can navigate up or down in stack trace and open files that are in the stack trace.
4. **Soft wrap**: Sometimes, you get long messages on the logcat window, and you need to scroll horizontally to see that long message. If you want to break this type of long message in multiline, you can use this button.
5. **Print**: Print the logcat messages.
6. **Restart**: Restart the Logcat. You can use this button if logcat becomes unresponsive. It does not clear the previous log.
7. **Logcat Header**: You can configure the appearance of the log message, such as daytime, process id, and Log tags should be included in each log message or not.

8. **Screen Capture**: By clicking on this button, you can take a screenshot of the Emulator screen or Device screen.
9. **Screen Record**: You can record up to three minutes of video. If you want to make a demo of your application, you can use this option to record the application flow.
10. **Terminate application**: Choose this button to terminate the application, which is currently running and attached to the logcat window.

Writing Logs

We already know about the logcat Window and the options available on this window. Let us see how to write code to show logs on the logcat window. For writing the logs, you need to use **android.util.Log** class and **Log.w()**, **Log.e()**, **Log.i()**, **Log.d()** or **Log.v()** depending on type of message you want to log. Let us add the following code snippets into **MainActivity.kt**. The file is located at **app** | **src** | **main** | **java** | **com** | **bpb** | **android** | **helloworld** | **MainActivity.kt**:

```kotlin
class MainActivity : AppCompatActivity() {

    // TAG for logs of MainActivity, so filtering of logs for
    // this activity by TAG would be easy.
    private val TAG = MainActivity::class.java.simpleName

    override fun onCreate(savedInstanceState: Bundle?) {
        super.onCreate(savedInstanceState)
        setContentView(R.layout.activity_main)

        // Write a debug log
        Log.d(TAG, "Hello world!!!")
        // Similarly you can use other methods of this class to show
        // different type of messages. Like
        Log.e(TAG, "An error log, which you can put into a block which" +
                " you see it as an error. Like catch blocks of try-catch")
```

```
        Log.i(TAG, "Informative messages, like Login Success")
        Log.w(TAG, "Use this method when seeing something which "
            + "might cause an error, "
            + "like some unexpected arguments to a method")
    }
}
```

And when you run the application, you see logs at the logcat window, as shown in *figure 1.14*:

Figure 1.14: Application logs at logcat window

You can see each log message is being shown in a different color, depending on its type. You can change these colors too, but until you be an expert in analyzing logs, keep defaults only.

That is it for logcat and logcat window.

Android Lint

This is a code scanning tool that helps you to improve the quality of code. It is used to identify problems as follows:

- Deprecated code used in your code
- Unused code
- Unused imports
- Incorrect use of access specifiers for members of the class
- Code snippets that can cause the application to crash on different Android versions
- Unhandled exceptions

Lint gives suggestions also as follows:
- If a newer version of any library is available at the repository
- A better way to write a code snippet
- Notify you if you are not using the internationalization of text used to show on UI and many more

In short, Lint checks your source files for codes that can produce bugs and improvements for security, internationalization, usability, accessibility, performance, and correctness.

Android Lint creates reports with the severity level of each problem found. So, you can prioritize these improvements depending on their criticality.

There are two ways to run Lint.

How to use Lint from Android Studio

From Android Studio, click on **Analyze | Inspect Code**. And you will see a window, as *figure 1.15*:

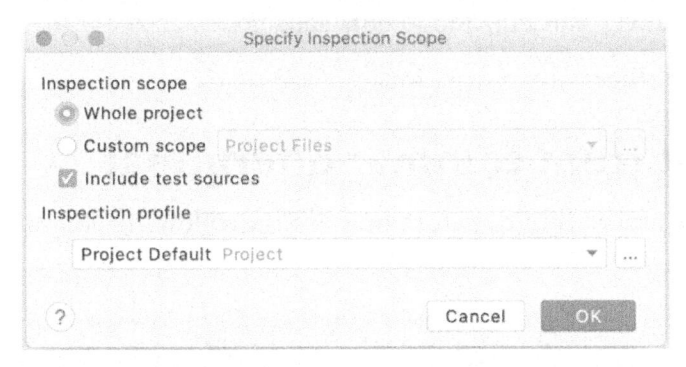

Figure 1.15: Choosing scope for Lint check

Here, you can choose `Whole project` or `Custom scope`. For now, let us choose `Whole project` and press `OK`.

You will see the Inspection Result window, as shown in *figure 1.16*:

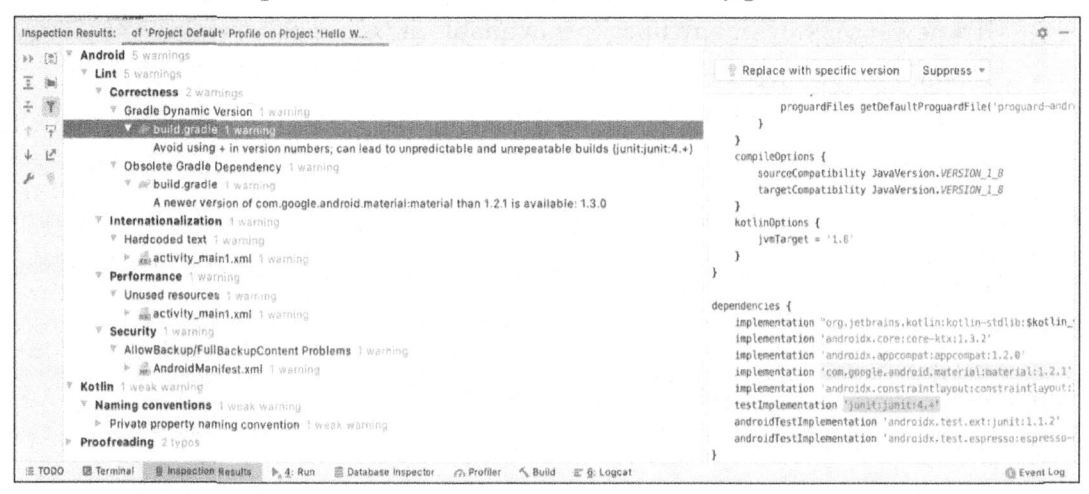

Figure 1.16: *Lint check result*

In the report shown in the preceding *figure 1.16* is for our Hello World Project. You can see that Lint created categories such as **Correctness**, **Internationalization**, **Performance**, **Security**, **Kotlin**, and **Proofreading**.

Now, let us see another way to use Lint.

Using Lint from command/terminal

Navigate to your project root directory and use the following command:

On Linux or Mac:

`./gradlew lint`

On Windows:

`gradlew lint`

After execution of this command, Lint will create a report in HTML file and XML file and gives you summarised report information, as follows:

`> Task :app:lint`

`Ran lint on variant debug: 7 issues found`

`Ran lint on variant release: 5 issues found`

`Wrote HTML report to` Error! Hyperlink reference not valid.`Users/pankaj/Documents/BPB/app/build/reports/lint-results.html`

```
Wrote XML report to Error! Hyperlink reference not valid.Users/pankaj/
Documents/BPB/app/build/reports/lint-results.xml
```

When you open the HTML file `../lint-results.html`, you will see output similar to *figure 1.17*:

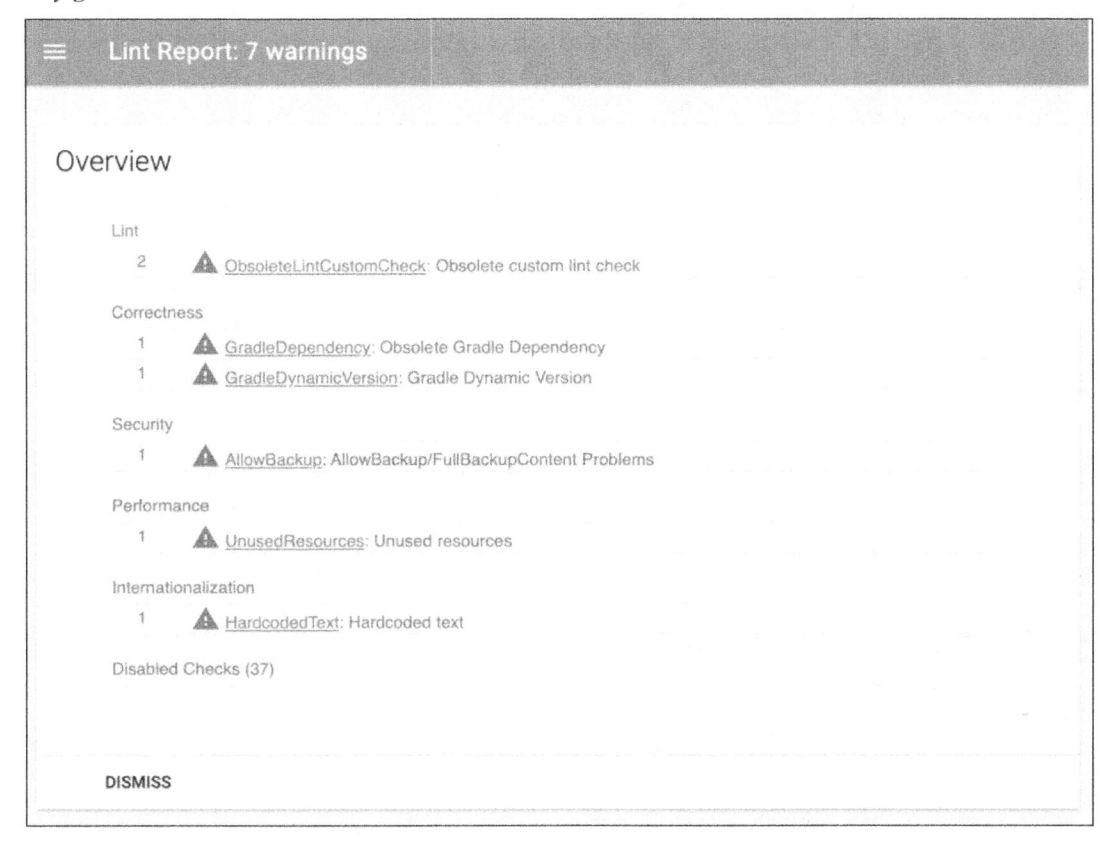

Figure 1.17: Warnings in Lint check report

This report is the same as the report which we got from the Android studio. You can look into the report and fix the problem. This tool can be your best guide which guides you toward writing a good code that follows best practices. You should always run this command for your project.

This tool can be customized checks; for example, if you want to enforce a rule to your project that no deprecated code should be in the project, then you can turn warning to error and many more. You should read more about this tool and take maximum benefits of it into your project.

Layout inspector and layout validator

Let us assume you are working on a beautifully designed application, where each pixel in your design matters. You get designs/mock-ups from the UX team, and you used to work on those to create a beautiful screen. Now how do you validate that each view added by you is perfectly aligned with the design/mock-ups? Here Layout Inspector comes into the picture. But wait, this is a small use of Layout Inspector. As the name suggests, you can inspect the layout of a screen and can validate that:

- your layout is optimized, and you are not using unnecessary view hierarchy/nesting of view groups, specifically when you create a screen design at runtime.
- the layout is being rendered as expected when you are creating it on runtime. (Creating a layout runtime means when you create a layout using Kotlin code, not using XML.)
- layout specifications are similar to design/mock-ups

Apart from these, this tool may help you to debug some UI issues when any view is not showing on the device screen, but it should be. In that case, you can quickly check if that view is actually added to UI or not by this tool, and then you can start fixing that.

Using Layout Inspector

First, run your application on a device or emulator. Choose **View | Tool Windows | Layout Inspector** or, from **Toolbar**, click on **Tools | Layout Inspector**. You will see a screen similar to *figure 1.18*:

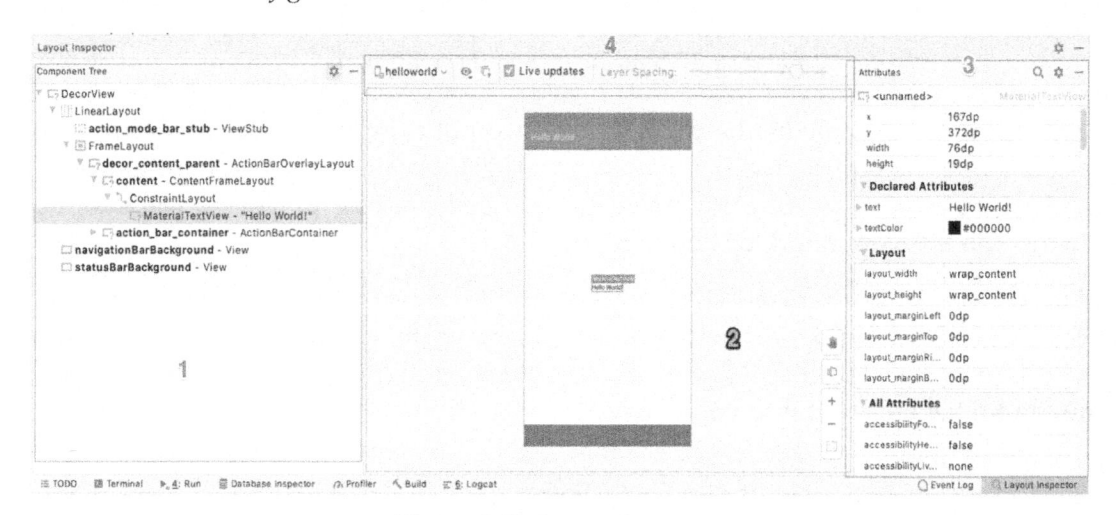

Figure 1.18: Layout Inspector

In the Layout Inspector window, you see the following four different parts:

1. **`Component Tree`**: It shows you the hierarchy of views for a screen. Views in this pane are selectable and expandable till the last child. Whatever you will select from it, the Attributes pane will show attributes of that view, and the **`Layout Display`** pane will select that view. You can utilize this window to make sure that you do not have any container which is not required, and you can optimize your design.

2. **`Layout Display`**: It shows the same screen which appears on your emulator or device. You can select views at this pane, same as **`Component Tree`**.

3. **`Attributes`**: This pane shows you the attributes and applied values of the selected view from the **`Component Tree`** or **`Layout Display`**.

4. **`Layout Inspector Toolbar`**: This is a toolbar for Layout inspector, which gives you the following tools to perform the following tasks:

    - `helloworld` **Select process tool**: Using this tool, you can select a device/emulator if running more than one, and you can choose the different running applications from the selected device/emulator in case more than one application is running on your device/emulator.

    - **View options tool**: This tool gives you options to **`Show Borders`** and **`Show View Label`**. You can toggle the visibility of both. In the preceding *figure 1.18*, the rectangle which you see around "**`Hello World`**" in the display pane is Border, and just above it, you see **`MaterialTextView`** in a blue background, that is View Label.

    - **Load Overlay**: This tool allows you to compare application layout to reference image (design/ mock-ups). When you select the image to be compared, it shows the selected image on top of the layout design as an overlay. You can set the transparency of this overlay to analyze your UI with the referenced image.

    - `Live updates` **Live updates**: When you enable it, the Layout inspector refreshes itself when any change happens on the application layout running on your emulator/device. In other words, it shows you real-time changes in application layout. This feature is available if you are running your application on API 29 or newer versions.

    - `Layer Spacing:` **Layer Spacing**: This tool enables 3D visualization of views in your layout by sliding this slider. This will help you to understand the view hierarchy of your layout better.

Introducing Layout Validator

A layout validator is a tool that helps you to validate your layout and identify any problem in your layout in terms of accessibility. Choose **View | Tool Windows | Layout Validation**. When you tap on it, it will open the **Layout Validator** pane. On this pane, you will get two tools as dropdowns, as shown in *figure 1.19*:

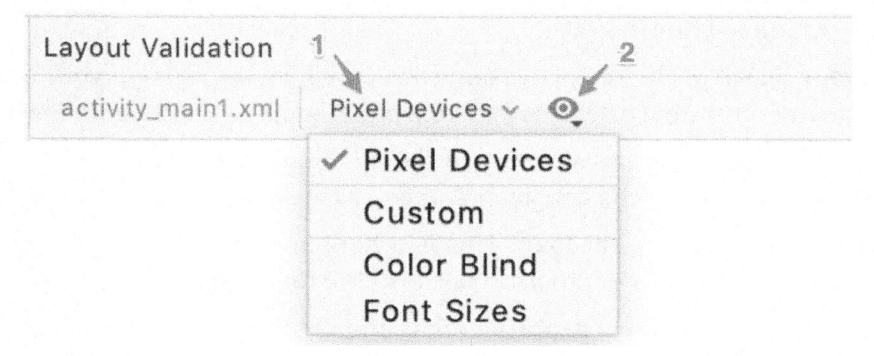

Figure 1.19: Layout validator

Let us know about these two tools of Layout Validator:

1. **Configuration Set**: This tool gives you the following options in the drop-down:
   - **Pixel Devices**: When you choose this option, it shows how your screen layout would be shown on Pixel devices.
   - **Custom**: It previews your layout on screens, same as Pixel devices, but here you customize the device to be used to show the preview.
   - **Color Blind**: It validates your layout with a few common color blindness simulations and shows output too
   - **Font Sizes**: This tool helps you to validate your layout with different font scales.
2. **View Options**: You can toggle on/ off the system view by choosing this option.

So, that is from **Layout Inspector** and **Layout Validator**. You should explore more about these tools.

Memory profiler

While developing any application, there are a few things that you should consider, how you can reduce the use of memory, no memory leaks are there, and how you can improve the performance of your application. And due to limited memory on mobile devices, memory is always a major thing to consider while developing an application.

Here memory profiler comes into the picture, and it helps you to identify the code snippet which is using more memory or can identify the code snippet which you can modify to use less memory by looking into heap and memory allocation.

To open **Memory Profiler**, the following are steps:

1. **View** | **Tool Windows** | **Profiler**, or you can click on the **Profile** icon on Tool Bar.
2. Select the emulator or device (if more than one device is running) and select the application (process) which you want to analyze:

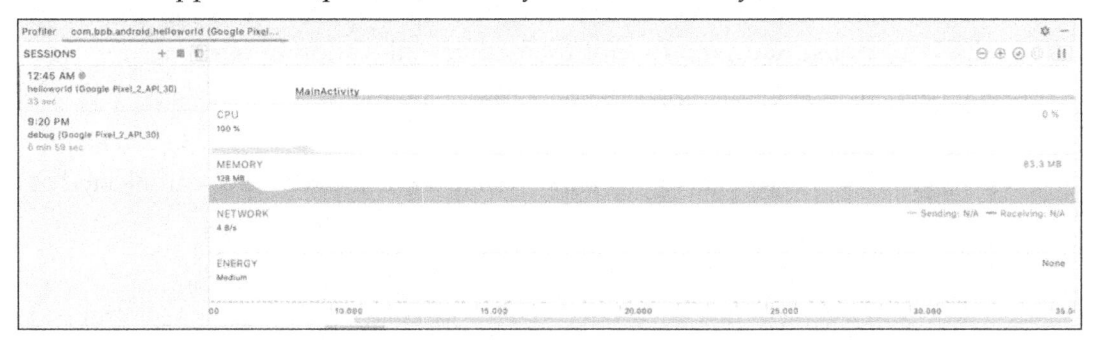

Figure 1.20: Profiler window

3. Click on Memory timeline, as shown in the preceding *figure 1.20*, to open the **Memory Profiler**.

You will see a window pane like in *figure 1.21*:

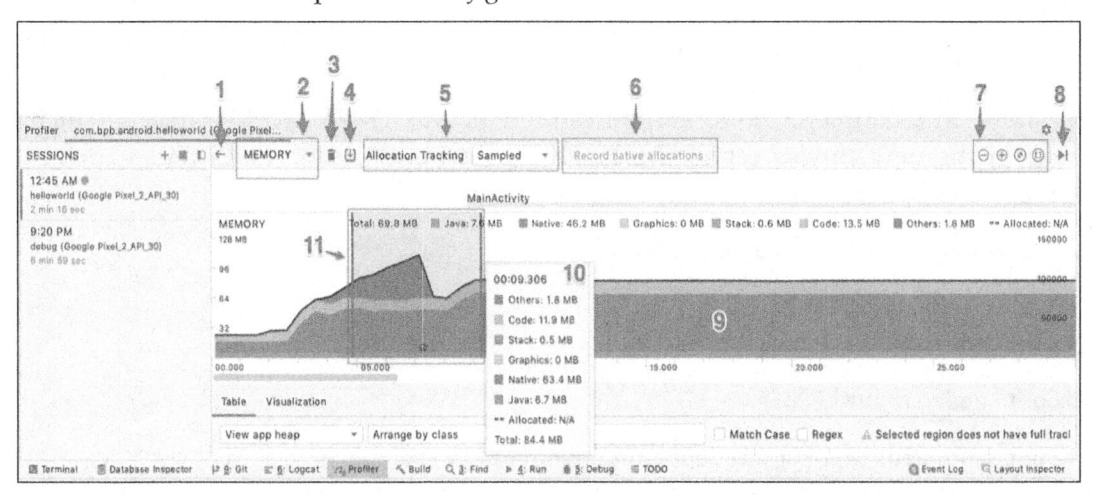

Figure 1.21: Options available in the profiler window

Let us see the options given on this window, as shown in preceding *figure 1.21*:
1. A button to **Go Back** to the Profiler page, as shown in *figure 1.19*.
2. The profiler has four options **CPU**, **Memory**, **Network**, and **Energy**, and you can choose any option to see the profiler for that particular selection. (Here, we are talking about Memory only.)
3. You can choose this option to forcefully call a Garbage collector
4. This tool is to capture Heap Dump. Where Heap Dump shows you all objects being used by your application, and you can identify memory leaks
5. **Allocation Tracking** dropdown helps you to capture the memory with options like Full or Sampled. Like its name, Full is used to capture all memory allocations, which slowdowns your application while profiling, and you choose Sampled to capture memory allocation in intervals.
6. The tool Native allocations are to capture memory allocations of C/C++ code.
7. This group of controls is for memory timeline (whatever type you selected at Point 2).
8. This tool helps you to start or pause the tracking of live memory.
9. The stacked graph shows memory uses in each category, as you can see legends of this graph in Point 10 in the picture. This graph also shows Garbage collection events.
10. Legends of Memory uses graphs.
11. To analyze memory uses in detail, you can select a section by clicking on the memory uses timeline (graph) and drag the start and the end. The first blue vertical line is the start, and the second is the end of the section which you want to analyze.

To show an example, a code snippet added to our Hello World project, which runs on the new thread when the Hello World application starts, and it prints **HelloWorldMemoryEater** class which holds one string:

```
package com.bpb.android.helloworld

import android.os.Bundle

import android.util.Log

import androidx.appcompat.app.AppCompatActivity
```

```kotlin
class MainActivity : AppCompatActivity() {

    // TAG for logs of MainActivity, so filtering of logs for
    // this activity by TAG would be easy.
    private val TAG = MainActivity::class.java.simpleName

    override fun onCreate(savedInstanceState: Bundle?) {
        super.onCreate(savedInstanceState)
        setContentView(R.layout.activity_main)

        // This code block has been added to show you an example
        // for memory profiler
        Thread(Runnable {
            for (i in 0..20000) {
                Log.d(
                    TAG, HelloWorldMemoryEater(stringVal = "temp")
                        .toString()
                )
            }
        }).start()
    }
}

// This data class has been added to show you an example for
// memory profiler
data class HelloWorldMemoryEater(val stringVal: String)
```

34 ■ *Building Android Projects with Kotlin*

As you see in *figure 1.22*, allocation count for two objects `java.lang.String` and `com.bpb.android.helloworld.HelloWorldMemoryEater` is more than 6K each:

Figure 1.22: Memory allocation details

Now, you can find the code block which is creating more than 6K objects of `HelloWorldMemoryEater` or String. To do that, select any of these rows. You will see the `Instance View` pane on the left of the `Profiler` window. Let us click on the `HelloWorldMemoryEater` row. You will see a window similar to *figure 1.23*:

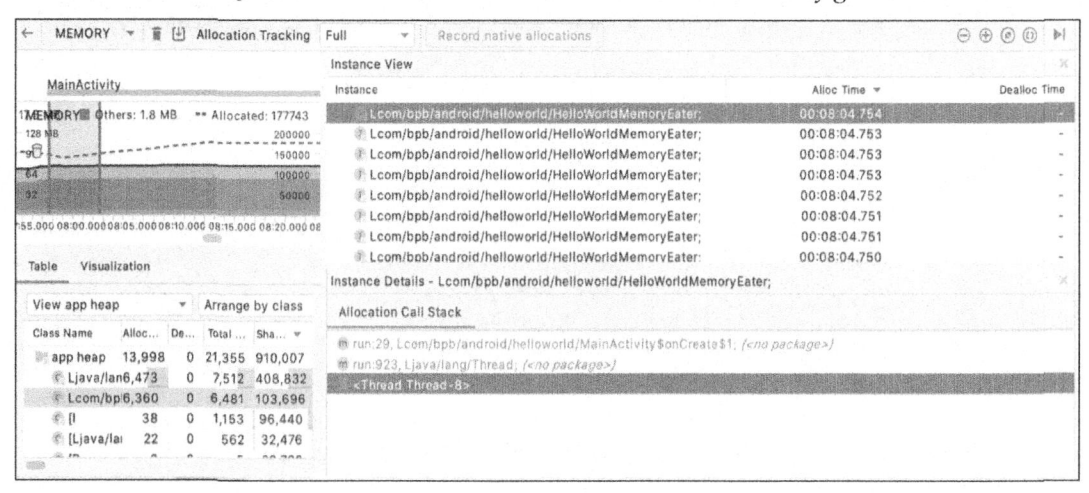

Figure 1.23: Allocations for HelloWorldMemoryEater

Creating Hello World Project ■ 35

On selection of any instance of `HelloWorldMemoryEater`, you will see the `Allocation Call Stack` pane. This pane shows you the call stack which is creating the selected object. As you see in the preceding *figure 1.23*, the selected object is being created/used from `MainActivity` | `onCreate()` | `Thread`.

So this was an introduction to `Memory Profiler` with example. Each profiler CPU, Network, and Energy (including Memory) is important when you make an amazing application with better performance. Making a practice of using these Profilers helps you to be a good developer, too, because you know how/when to allocate/deallocate memory, a better code that saves phone battery, minimizes network calls, and so on.

Database Inspector

Almost every mobile application is used to store some data in the database, and even we will use a database when we develop our chat application. Before this tool, looking into the database was not so easy. `Database Inspector` is not only a tool to look into databases, but you can do some more interesting tasks, which help you in day-to-day work on Android projects. This has been available since Android Studio 4.1 and works with SQLite library.

As the Hello World project is not using any database, let us use Android's official sample project with some customization to see the uses of Database Inspector.

To open this tool, click on `View` | `Tool Windows` | `Database Inspector`. You will see the `Database Inspector` tool, as shown in *figure 1.24*:

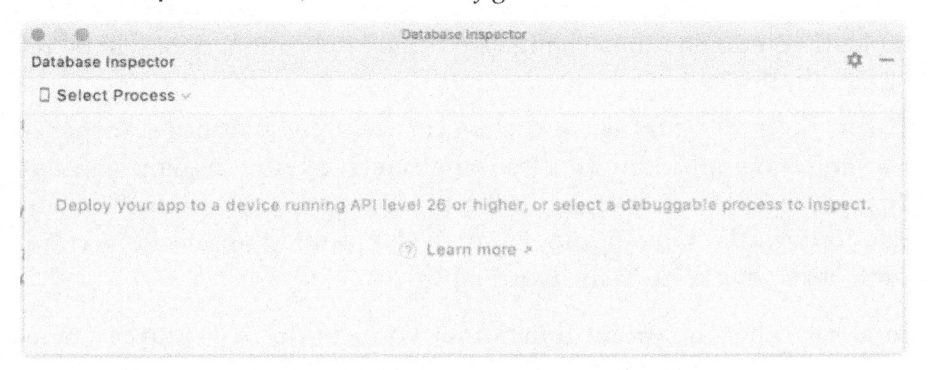

Figure 1.24: Database Inspector tool

Now you need to click on `Select Process` | `Select Running Device` | `Select running application`; you see the selected process and database of the application as shown in *figure 1.25*:

36 ■ *Building Android Projects with Kotlin*

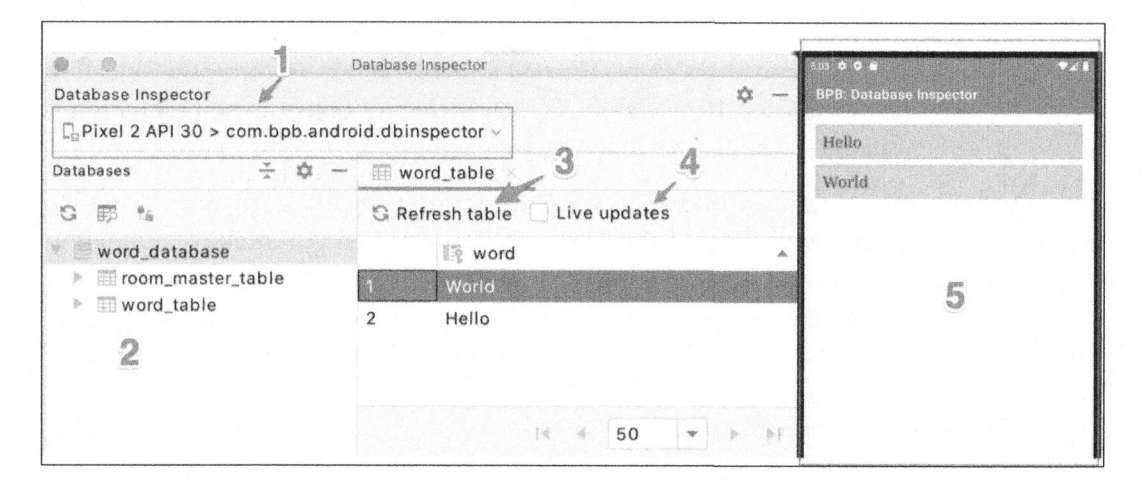

Figure 1.25: Using of Database Inspector

Let us see a few tools available in this window:

- The selected process shows the application ID of the app which is being debugged.
- Database pane, where you see the database and all tables of your application
- To sync table data at Database Inspector with actual, you need to Refresh the table
- Live updates are to sync data automatically. If this option is on, data on actual and Database Inspector will be in sync, and you need not do Refresh table. If you do any data change from the application, data will be reflected automatically.
- This is not part of **Database Inspector**. To show **Database Inspector** and running the application together, the screen of running app and **Database Inspector** has been merged in the preceding *figure 1.25* to show you both windows in the same figure. Here, in the running application, you see the same texts which are in the word table.

There are a few other important things that you can do in **Database Inspector**, which are as explained in the next section.

Modifying table from Database Inspector

Let us consider one use case. We want to check the appearance of the text field if we set text for more than a line. One option is to enter the long text from the application code. But you can quickly do it from here too. Double click on the row which you want to modify, as shown in *figure 1.26*, and after modification, press **Enter**:

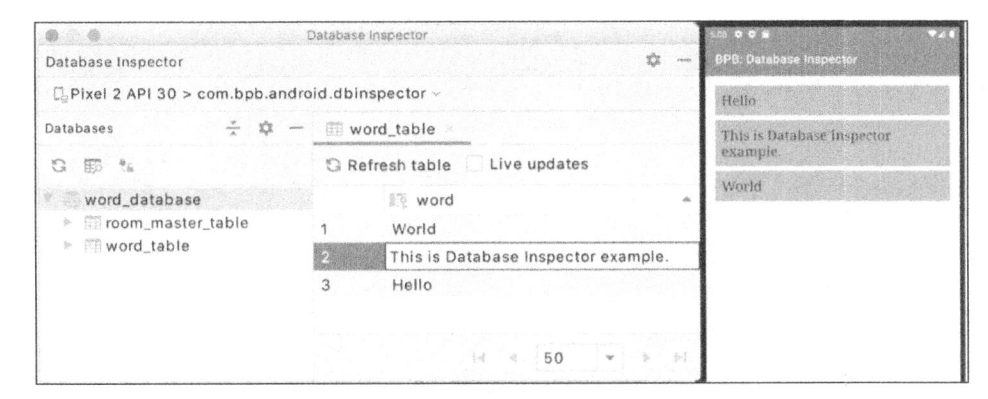

Figure 1.26: Live updates on Database Inspector

If your code can update UI on database change, changes done from a table will also be reflected in the application, as shown on the right side of the preceding *figure 1.26*. So this way, you can directly check the UI responsiveness of your application.

Run query from Database Inspector and DAO

When you write any SQL query, you want to validate it to make sure of its correctness. What are the options? To execute queries and see the result, you will write code and print the result on the log may be.

When you use Database Inspector, it is just one click to see the result of any query. To do that, go to DAO class (DAO is the class where you write queries, we will see more while writing chat application) and click on the Run button available before each query, the red circled option in *figure 1.27*:

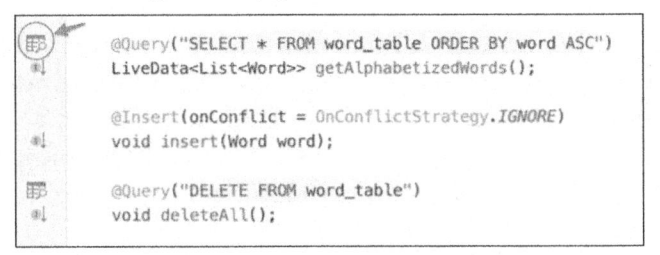

Figure 1.27: Running queries from DAO class

You will see the result immediately in **Database Inspector**. You can see *figure 1.28* for how the result is being shown when we click on the red circled run option in the preceding *figure 1.27*:

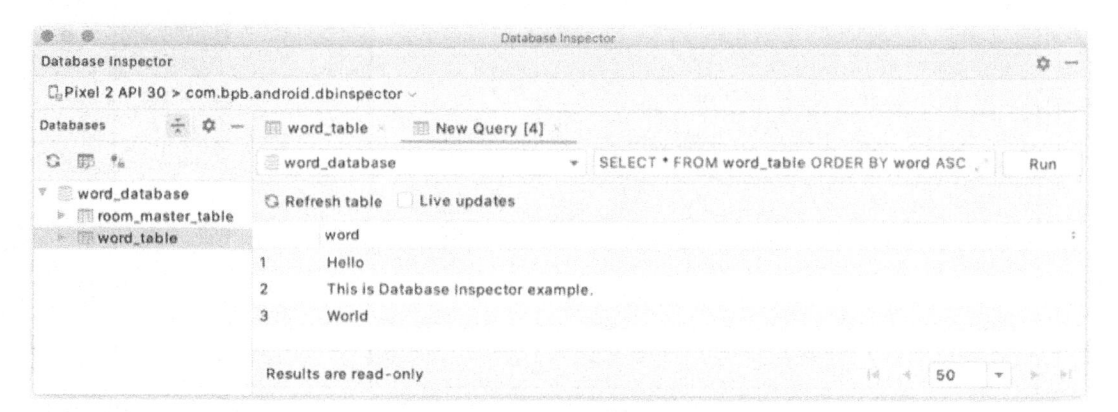

Figure 1.28: Result of the query

NOTE: You can see a query field in the preceding *figure 1.28*. As this field is editable, you can write custom SQL queries without writing them into DAO class. So this option will help you to test SQL queries before writing into DAO class.

Conclusion

In this chapter, we have learned how to create an Android Project, what are Android Studio Templates and how to use them. We understood each file of an Android application, such as layouts, manifest, Gradles, and resources (strings/drawable). We also learned about modules, which help us to modularise our application by features or layers. We learned about how to create custom launcher icons, how to create Android Virtual Device (Emulator), and run our first "Hello World" application.

We learned about Gradle, which is a build creation tool, Logcat window, which is a GUI tool in Android Studio to show device/application logs, Android Lint, which is a code inspection tool, and Memory profiler, which we use for analyzing memory uses and leaks, and Database Inspector which helps us to look into the database of the application. These all help us in developing, debugging, or improving our Android application.

In the upcoming chapter, we will know about the Basics of Android components Activity, Services, Broadcast receiver, and Content provider, and we will also learn about Fragment and View. We will know about the lifecycle of Fragment and Activity and the uses of these lifecycle methods. We will know about layout types, and we will learn how to choose a better layout for any screen by learning how to analyze the performance of these layouts. We will also learn about material design and the material library of Android.

Points to remember

- Templates follow Android best practices, so you should use these templates if they fit your requirement.
- Android used to update libraries frequently. So always use the latest version of the library.
- Lint reports helping you to improve code quality and performance of your application, making a practice to reduce Lint warnings as much as possible.
- You should always focus on removing the nesting of layouts. To identify nesting, Layout Inspector can be used.
- As Gradle is a tool that creates Android builds, we can utilize it to create different versions of an Application. We can configure it to create a Full version of our app and a Lite Version of our app. We can create an application for debugging as well as release. We can use a different set of files for each building type. Similarly, we can do many customizations in Android build using gradle.

Multiple Choice Questions

1. Which of the following tool analyze your code and find deprecated code or unused code?

    A. Logcat   B. Database Inspector

    C. Android Lint   D. Layout Inspector

2. Which file has information about Android components used in our application or information about the hardware required for the application?

    A. build.gradle   B. project.properties

    C. proguard-rules.pro   D. AndroidManifest.xml

3. Modules can be used for

    A. App Bundles

    B. Instant Apps

    C. To achieve separation of code by features

    D. All of above

4. Which tool you can use for writing SQL queries and verifying results?

    A. Logcat   B. Database Inspector

    C. Android Lint   D. Layout Inspector

5. Which task you cannot do using Layout Inspector?

    A. Analyze view hierarchy

    B. Accessibility validation of layout

    C. Analyze performance of screen/application

    D. Validate layout with mock-up

Answers

1. C
2. D
3. D
4. B
5. C

Questions

1. What is a Template in Android Studio?
2. What is a Module, and why should we have multiple modules in an Android application?
3. How to analyze the database of any Android debug application?
4. How to write SQL queries in Database Inspector?
5. What is Gradle?

Key Terms

- Template
- Module
- Launcher Icon
- Android Virtual Device
- Gradle
- Logcat
- Lint
- Database Inspector
- Layout Inspector
- Profiler

CHAPTER 2
Basics of Android Components

In the previous chapter, we learned about creating a new project. Now, in this chapter, we will learn about the basic components of Android and some other components that we use in an Android application extensively, such as Activity, Fragment, the Lifecycle of Activity and Fragment, and an introduction to services, receivers, and content providers.

We will also read about the handling of different screen sizes, which will help us to design layouts for multiple screens. We will learn about frequently used layouts, and we will learn how to choose the better layout for our design. While choosing a better layout, we will learn about GPU Overdraw, Systrace, and Perfetto, which will help us to measure the performance of the layout (as well as the whole application).

At the end of this chapter, we will learn about Material designs and the library, which will help us to design good-looking apps.

Structure

In this chapter, we will cover the following topics:
- Basic components of Android
    - Activity

- o Service
- o Broadcast receiver
- o Content provider
- Introducing Fragment and View
- Lifecycle of an Activity
- Lifecycle of a Fragment
- Dimensions and screen sizes
- Understanding different types of Layouts
- Choosing a better Layout for a design
- Basics of Material design

Objectives

The objective of this chapter is to let you know about the basic components of Android and some other components that we use in the Android application. After completing this chapter, you will have a clear understanding of Activity, Fragments, and the Lifecycle of Activity and Fragment, so you will have a better idea about when to initiate a task, when to pause/resume a task, or when to close a task for the current screen with the help of choosing best fit lifecycle event. Introduction to Services, Broadcast Receivers, and Content Providers will help you to choose the right component for a screen/task/Application.

We will also learn how to choose the layout for the design and how we can design a layout that can perform better and can work well on different screen sizes of Android devices.

Basic components of Android

Application components are required/essential components of any Android Application. Each component is an entry point of your application, by which the user or Android System itself can enter into your application. Like in *Chapter 1: Creating Hello World Project*, we saw `MainActivity.kt` class, which was an entry point of our Hello World application. Each type of component has a specific use; we will be looking into more in this chapter. So, the components are as follows:

- Activity
- Service
- Broadcast Receiver

- Content Provider

Activity

A component that represents the user interface of the application to the user and the user can interact with our application. In our Hello World application in *Chapter 1: Creating Hello World Project*, `MainActivity.kt` is an Activity class that shows "**Hello World**". In an Application, there can be more than one Activity. There are two ways to create UI, either to create XML (similar to `activity_main.xml` in *Chapter 1: Creating Hello World Project*), or to create UI at runtime using Kotlin code. In both ways, you need to use a variant of the `setContentView()` method. Apart from multiwindow mode, usually, Activity takes the whole available area of the device, as shown in *figure 2.1*:

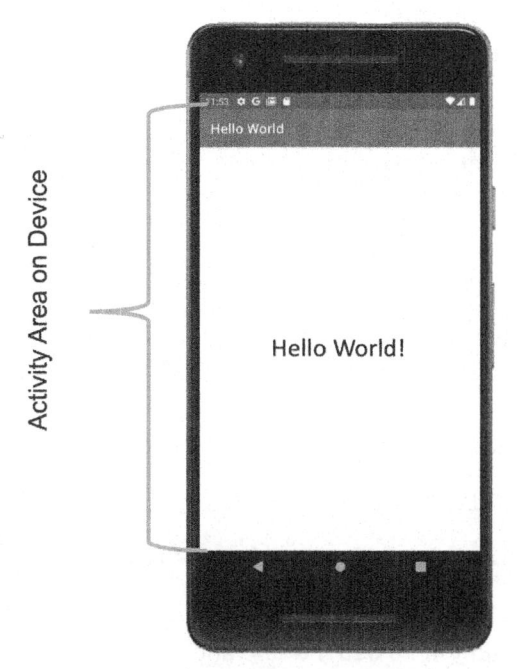

Figure 2.1: Hello World Application

There are a few methods of Activity class that need to be implemented in subclasses; those methods are known as lifecycle methods of an Activity. This is not mandatory to implement all methods, but depending on the requirement, we implement these methods. There is the only method that almost all Activities use to implement is `onCreate(savedInstanceState: Bundle?)`, and the reason is that we create UI for particular Activity in this method, as shown in the following code:

```
class MainActivity : Activity() {
```

```
override fun onCreate(savedInstanceState: Bundle?) {
    super.onCreate(savedInstanceState)
    // Setting the layout activity_main.xml as UI
    setContentView(R.layout.activity_main)
    ...
    }
}
```

In the preceding code, we are using a static way to create UI for **MainActivity**, using **setContentView()**. We will know more about lifecycle methods in the *Lifecycle of an Activity* section in this chapter.

Each Activity component must be added to manifest with an activity tag, as shown in the following code:

```
<?xml version="1.0" encoding="utf-8"?>
<manifest xmlns:android="http://schemas.android.com/apk/res/android"
    package="com.bpb.android.helloworld">
    <application
        ...>
        <activity android:name=".MainActivity">
            <intent-filter>
                <action android:name="android.intent.action.MAIN" />

                <category android:name="android.intent.category.LAUNCHER" />
            </intent-filter>
        </activity>
    </application>

</manifest>
```

As you see in the preceding code, **android:name** keeps the name of the **Activity**

".MainActivity" in the `<activity>` tag. And inside `<intent-filter>` tag, we defined that ".MainActivity" is a launcher Activity. It means when you tap on the application icon to launch the app, this ".MainActivity" will be called first. In general, `<intent-filter>` is not required for Activities if that Activity is not a launcher activity. But in some use cases like deep-linking, where the system or some other application tries to open your application, we use the `<intent-filter>` tag.

NOTE: **AppCompatActivity is the type of Activity, which can be used to use newer platform features on older Android versions/devices. In our projects, we would be subclassing activities from AppCompatActivity, to use new features on older versions too. If you see in the preceding *figure 2.1*, Hello World at the top of the screen, that area is known as ActionBar, and that is one of the things that we can achieve by using AppCompatActivity in older versions.**

Task and Back stack is the important thing that you should be aware of. In short, Android uses the stack to keep Activities in it, that is how it manages back navigations, and the user sees previous activity when the user presses back from the device. The recommendation is to read about Task and Back Stack at: https://developer.android.com/guide/components/activities/tasks-and-back-stack and play with Task and Back Stack.

Service

Service is an Android component that runs in the background without any UI. The most important thing to remember is that even if it runs into the background of the application, it runs on the application's main thread. So writing a long-running task into Services will freeze your application, and you will see the "Application Not Responding" error. To handle such errors, we create a thread from the service and move the long-running task into a newly created thread.

There are a few common uses of Services given as follows:

- Audio player application.
- Doing a long-running task that does not have to do anything with UI.
- Access location information.
- Client-Server interface between applications. Or Inter-Process Communication (IPC) between processes can be implemented.

Writing a Service class, as follows:

```
class BpbExampleService : Service() {
    override fun onCreate() {
```

```kotlin
        // Can start a new thread which can perform long running
        // task on background Thread (can use HandlerThread).
        …
    }

    override fun onStartCommand(
        intent: Intent,
        flags: Int,
        startId: Int
    ): Int {
        // Pass this intent to thread which we started on onCreate(),
        // so that can be completed by that thread on background
        // thread.
        ...
        // Restart, if we get killed.
        return START_STICKY
    }

    override fun onBind(intent: Intent): IBinder? {
        // When we want to expose some functionality to other
        // application through Interprocess communication (IPC),
        // we use bound services. Here in example, we are not
        // using bound service so we are returning null.

        return null
    }
```

}

As you see at preceding code, we need to extend **android.app.Service** class and override **onCreate()**, **onStartCommand()**, and **onBind()**.

NOTE: Service runs on the main thread, so writing any long-running task in Service will block the main thread and can cause Application Not Responding error (ANR).

To handle this situation, we create a separate thread using HandlerThread, which can handle our long-running task. We can even use a normal Java thread to handle the long-running task.

We need to add this component into the manifest using the service tag, so the code inside the manifest would be as follows:

```
<manifest xmlns:android="http://schemas.android.com/apk/res/android"
    package="com.bpb.android.helloworld">

    <application ...>
        ...
        <service android:name=".BpbExampleService" />
    </application>
</manifest>
```

And **BpbService** can be started as follows:

```
Intent(contextObject, BpbExampleService::class.java).also { intent ->
    startService(intent)
}
```

NOTE: Since Android API 26, Android imposed restrictions on background services, so Services may not fit better into your requirement. So, it is advisable to learn about WorkManager and Coroutines. Most of the time, these two can be a better pick for a long-running task.

For any reason, if you want to use Service, read about JobIntentService. It is a subclass of Service and a better replacement of plain old Service.

Broadcast receiver

As its name, it receives broadcasted messages from the Android system, from other applications, or your application. Similar to the Publish-Subscribe pattern, receivers are similar to the subscriber. If you want to listen to an event either from the Android system or from any application and perform some task, we need to register a `BroadcastReceiver` to listen to that event.

Following are a few examples of System events that you can listen to using Broadcast receivers:

- Device Boot
- Device screen on and screen off
- Date and Locale specific changes
- Installation or removal of applications from the device
- Device connected/ disconnected to Bluetooth, and so on

Apart from system events, the following are a few use-cases where you can use Broadcast Receivers:

- Push Notifications
- Communicate with other application

NOTE: While communicating with a different application, you may expose sensitive data. So do not use Broadcasts to send sensitive data to other applications or even within your application. For any reason, if you have only this way to use, then add custom permission with an appropriate protection level like a signature or system.

LocalBroadcastManager is a better choice when you want to broadcast and listen to that broadcast in the same application.

There are two ways to register for broadcasts that are explained in the next section.

Static broadcast receivers

When you register a receiver in `AndroidManifest.xml` (as we already discussed this file in *Chapter 1: Creating Hello World Project*), it is known as the static way of registering the receiver. For example, if we want to listen to a device boot event, the code can be written as follows:

```
import android.content.BroadcastReceiver
```

```
import android.content.Context
import android.content.Intent

class SystemEventReceiver : BroadcastReceiver() {
    override fun onReceive(context: Context, intent: Intent) {
        // This method will be called on the broadcast you are
        // listening for.

        // To avoid doing long running task here, you can choose
        // androidx.core.app.JobIntentService to do the task.

        // See the code of manifest to know about how to register
        // this receiver to listen to an event.
    }
}
```

And to register the receiver, the code in the manifest would be as follows:

```
<receiver android:name=".SystemEventReceiver">
    <intent-filter>
        <action android:name="android.intent.action.BOOT_COMPLETED" />
    </intent-filter>
</receiver>
```

Dynamic broadcast receivers

The dynamic way is to register receivers using the Context object, where your application can listen to events till the object of context is valid. In general, Activities are components that we use to register for dynamic broadcast. For example, if we want to listen for the events when the device becomes interactive or non-interactive, we need to use **registerReceiver()**. The code would be written as follows:

```
import android.content.Intent
import android.content.IntentFilter
```

```kotlin
import android.os.Bundle
import androidx.appcompat.app.AppCompatActivity

class MainActivity : AppCompatActivity() {

    var systemEventReceiver: SystemEventReceiver? = null

    override fun onCreate(savedInstanceState: Bundle?) {
        super.onCreate(savedInstanceState)
        setContentView(R.layout.activity_main)

        // Initialize Receiver and register is to listen
        // for the events when the device becomes non-interactive
        // or interactive.
        val filter = IntentFilter(Intent.ACTION_SCREEN_ON)
        filter.addAction(Intent.ACTION_SCREEN_OFF)
        systemEventReceiver = SystemEventReceiver()
        registerReceiver(systemEventReceiver, filter)
    }

    override fun onDestroy() {
        super.onDestroy()
        unregisterReceiver(systemEventReceiver)
    }
}
```

So, for dynamically registered receivers, we need to unregister them when we do not need them. If the activity, which was doing some action on a broadcast, is not alive, then there is no point to listen to the event. This causes memory leaks if you do not unregister for broadcast. To unregister for broadcasts, we need to use **unregisterReceiver()**. See **onStop()** in preceding code.

Content provider

Content providers are components that provide you with a way to access the data stored by itself or stored by other applications. It means it provides a way to share data between applications, and you can configure a content provider to allow other applications to securely access and modify your application data, as shown in *figure 2.2*:

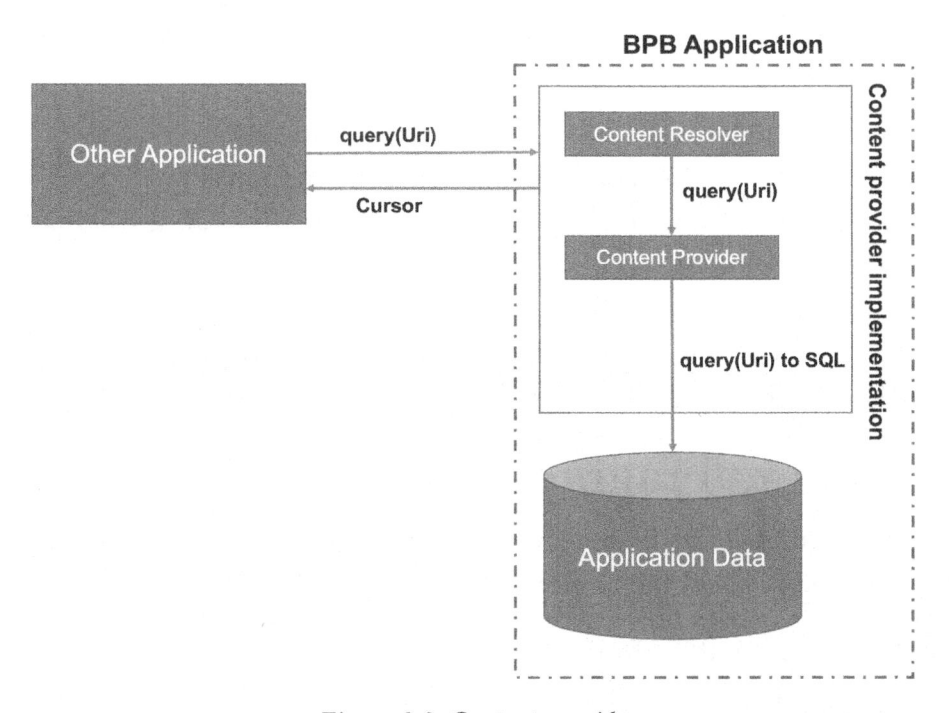

Figure 2.2: Content provider

So when application **A** requires data from BPB Application, the following steps will be taken:

1. An application **A** that needs BPB Application's data calls `getContentResolver().query(Uri, String, String, String, String)`. It calls the query method of the Content resolver.
2. Content resolver determines which `ContentProvider` handles the given Uri by parsing authority and arguments of URI.
3. Content provider converts incoming Uri into SQL query and returns the result of SQL query as Cursor.

As we can see, the Content provider works with `ContentResolver`. Let us read about Content resolver.

Content resolver

As its name suggests, Content Resolver is used to resolve requests for data access from other apps or the same app by choosing the right Content provider by looking into unique content authority. To perform this task, the Content resolver stores a mapping from authorities to Content providers.

Let us see how ContentUris looks like when an application wants to read data from our Hello World application (assuming we have a database and a table named as `HelloWorldTable`):

content://com.bpb.android.helloworld/HelloWorldTable/1

- `content://` is scheme and indicates that it is a `ContentUri`.
- `com.bpb.android.helloworld` is a Content authority, and `ContentResolver` uses it to resolve to a unique provider (in this case, `ContactProvider`).
- `HelloWorldTable` is the path that identifies some subset of the provider's data (in our example, table name)
- `1` is the ID used to uniquely identify a row within the subset of data.

Introducing Fragment and View

Fragment and View help us to create reusable UI/ ViewGroup or Widget. Fragments are life cycle aware. It means when you use Fragment in Activity, the Lifecycle of Fragment will be in sync with Activity, whereas View is lightweight, and its Lifecycle and not in sync with Activity by default.

Let us read more about these two in detail.

View

The View is the base class for Widgets and ViewGroups, where widgets are like `TextView`, `Buttons`, and `ViewGroup` is layout types like `LinearLayout`, and `RelativeLayout`. The View represents a rectangular area on the screen, see *figure 2.3* for more details.

While developing the android application, we get some common view which is being used on more than one screen, and the default set of widgets provided by Android does not fit into the requirement we use to create a custom view by extending the View class or Compound View by extending and ViewGroups such as `ViewGroup`, `LinearLayout`, `RelativeLayout`, and so on.

For example, if we need to show an image in a circular view, we can extend the default `ImageView` class and do customizations to show the image in a circular view. Note that, even if the View looks circular, it is still representing a rectangular area on the screen, as shown in *figure 2.3*:

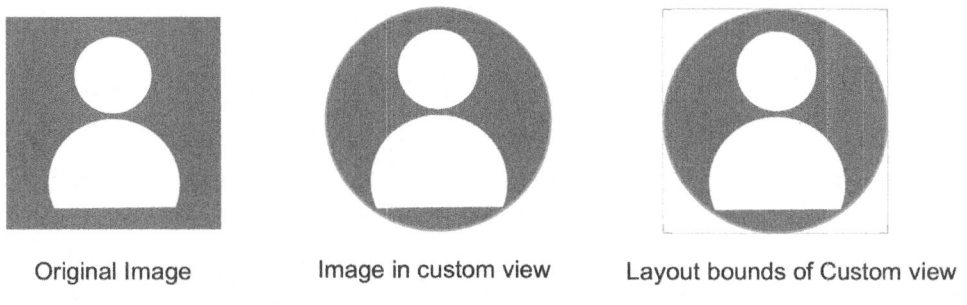

Figure 2.3: View representation on the screen

As another example, we can think of a NEWS application that has a view to show news highlights. Considering this application shows NEWS by categories or by regions, and whenever the user changes category or region, this highlights-view shows highlights of selected category or region. It means highlights-view can be reused on multiple screens. Usually, such a view can be a group of views to show the title of NEWS, important lines of that NEWS, and an Image. In this case, we can create a custom ViewGroup (known as Compound View) by extending the appropriate layout.

Uses of Custom View or Compound View are opportunities to reuse your code and faster development.

Fragment

The Fragment has a similar use case as of View, but it also provides us a better way to handle UI. The fragment has its Lifecycle and works in sync with the Activity, which shows the Fragment, so when we divide the screen using Fragment, handling of each division works very well without adding more code to recycle unused View. On a larger scale, Fragments allows us to ndroidze UI and reusable activity UI.

A famous use case of **Fragment is Master-Detail Flow**. Consider the Gmail Android app for an example. When you open Gmail on your phone, it shows a list of emails, and when you tap on any email, it shows the details/content of the email. When you open the Gmail application on Tablet, you see the screen in two parts. On the left, you see a list of emails, and on the right side, you see the content of the selected email. This is an example of responsive UI, and we use Fragments to achieve such kind of UI.

Ways to show Fragments

There are two ways to show Fragments:

    (1) Adding Fragment in XML (Static way)

    (2) Using FragmentManager to show Fragment at Runtime (Dynamic way)

Let us see these two ways in more detail.

Showing Fragments statically

We can add fragments in the XML layout file. We use **FragmentContainerView** and its name attribute as **android:name="com.bpb.android.fragmentlifecycle.FragmentC"**, like following code:

```
<?xml version="1.0" encoding="utf-8"?>
<androidx.fragment.app.FragmentContainerView xmlns:android="http://schemas.android.com/apk/res/android"
    android:id="@+id/container"
    android:name="com.bpb.android.fragmentlifecycle.FragmentC"
    android:layout_width="match_parent"
    android:layout_height="match_parent" />
```

Showing Fragments dynamically

Most of the time, we will need this approach to show fragments, as it allows us to decide which Fragment to be shown at runtime. Following is the code snippet to create a container for Fragment.

Note that the container is the area in Activity, where our Fragment will be shown:

```
<?xml version="1.0" encoding="utf-8"?>
<androidx.fragment.app.FragmentContainerView
    xmlns:android="http://schemas.android.com/apk/res/android"
    android:id="@+id/container"
```

```
android:layout_width="match_parent"

android:layout_height="match_parent" />
```

And code in Kotlin to show Fragment in the preceding container is as follows:

```
val fragmentManager: FragmentManager = supportFragmentManager

val ft: FragmentTransaction = fragmentManager.beginTransaction()


// Can be used replace() or add() to show fragment with either

// using addToBackStack() or without addToBackStack()

ft.add(R.id.container, fragment).addToBackStack(null).commit()

// ft.replace(R.id.container, fragment).addToBackStack(null).commit()
```

While showing Fragments we got to know about three methods: **add()**, **replace()**, and **addToBackStack()** to show a Fragment. Let us know more about **add()** and **replace()** methods first.

So, for example, we have four fragments with four different UI, and they need to be shown in an Activity as shown in *figure 2.4*:

Fragments with their UI

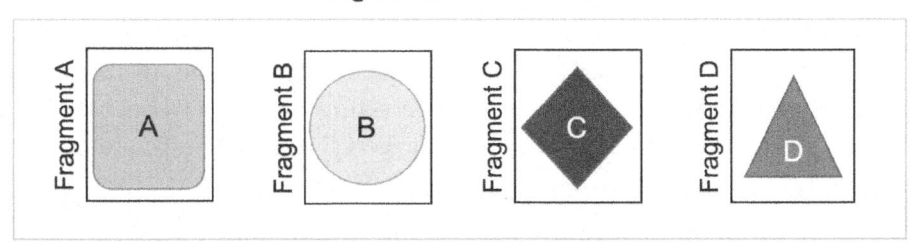

Figure 2.4: Fragments A, B, C, and D

In *figure 2.5*, let us see how **add()** and **replace()** works when we use these two methods to show these four fragments shown before in preceding *figure 2.4*:

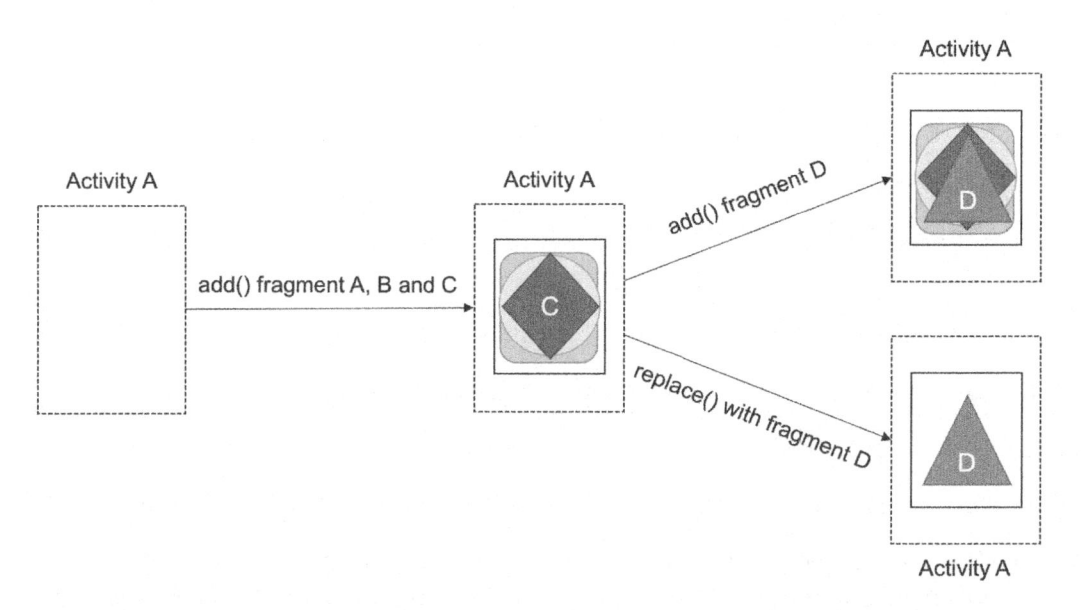

Figure 2.5: Working of add() and replace() methods

As shown in preceding *figure 2.5*, **add()** method add Fragment on top of the container. You can see in the preceding *figure 2.5* that when we use **add()** for Fragments A, B, and C, then Fragments A and B are still visible behind Fragment C.

And **replace()** first removes previously added views from the container and then adds the Fragment. In other words, it uses **remove()** to remove all fragments and then uses **add()** to show the fragment. In preceding *figure 2.5,* you can see when we show Fragment D using **replace()**, it removed Fragment A, B, and C and then added Fragment D.

Android does not provide a default back stack for Fragments, which means there is no default back navigation for Fragments. It means you cannot go to Fragment C by pressing back navigation from Fragment D. If you want a back stack for Fragments, addToBackStack() comes into the picture.

addToBackStack() adds fragment transactions to the back stack, so when you press back navigation, you will return to the previous Fragment. Let us see how navigation work with and without addToBackStack().

Figure 2.6 shows how the back navigation works without using `addToBackStack()`:

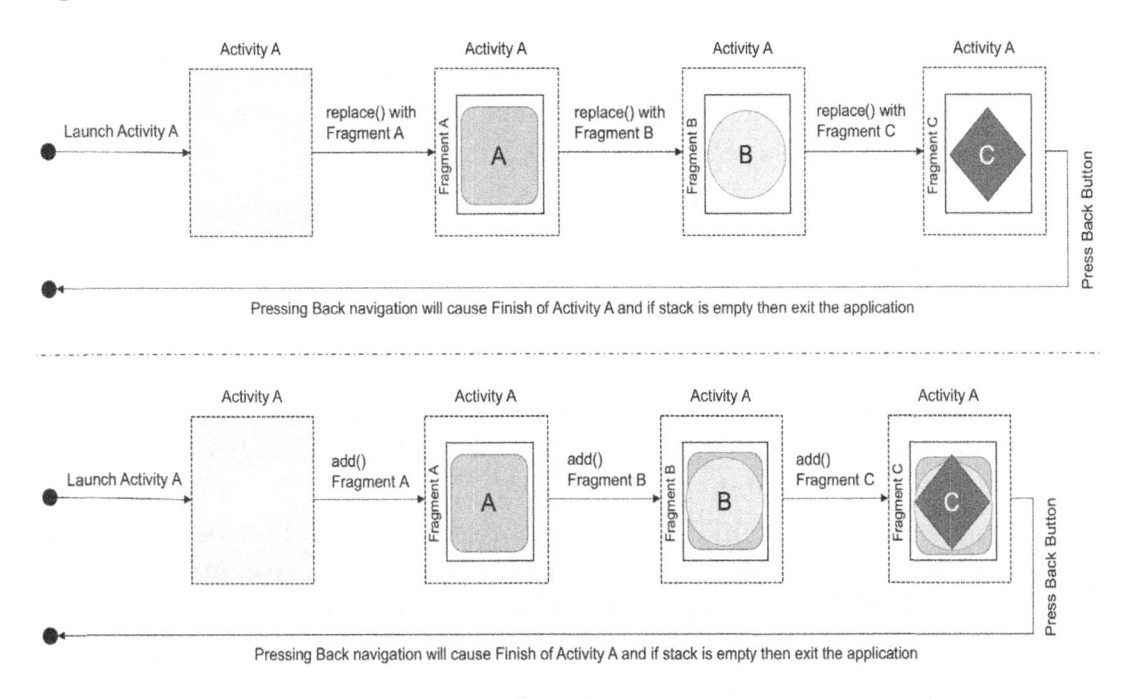

Figure 2.6: *The back navigation of Fragment without addToBackStack()*

And *figure 2.7* shows how the back navigation works if using `addToBackStack()`:

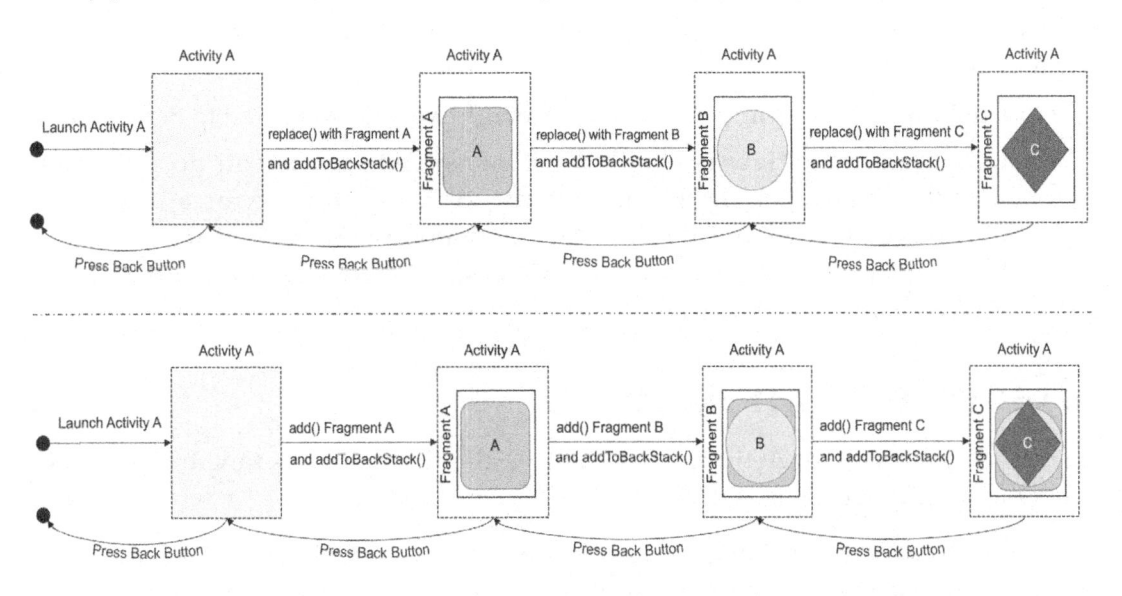

Figure 2.7: *The back navigation of Fragment with addToBackStack()*

So, the `addToBackStack()` plays an important role in lifecycle method call-backs. We will see about it while looking into the Lifecycle of Fragment.

NOTE: **Custom views or Fragments both can be used to represent common views of your application, and almost every common View can be written as a Custom View or fragment.**

Following are a few points that can help you to choose Fragments over custom views:

- Fragments were introduced by Android as a way to help us to decompose our applications into different parts (can say different features). Features like app bundles and instant apps are the best example of it.
- Fragments can be used to logically divide the screen into multiple parts, for example, Master-Details Flow, which was discussed before while discussing Fragment in this chapter.
- Fragments are more like Activities and can represent the whole area on the screen of the device, similar to Activities. And using fragments in such cases is an easy and more optimized way than Custom Views.
- Android gives a method to handle back Navigation for Fragments.
- Features like Navigation components, tab bar, and bottom sheets can be implemented using Fragments.
- If the required View is going to cover the whole screen, choose Fragments.

Following are a few points that can help you to choose a custom view over Fragments:

- Custom views or compound views are lightweight compared to Fragments.
- If the required View is coupled with host Activity or you do not need lifecycle events for the required View, or until you are forced to write complex code for handling the state or changing the state of the required View, you can give priority to Custom View/Compound View over Fragments.

Lifecycle of an Activity

We learned the basics of Activity before in this chapter; now it is time to know the basics of the Lifecycle of an Activity.

When a user navigates through the application, such as opening your application/screen, going outside from your application, receiving phone calls, and so on. In all these cases Android System is used to notify your application about the current state of an Activity using a few methods, which you need to override in your Activity class. These lifecycle call-back methods help us to define the behavior of the Activity. For example, if you are developing a game, you might pause the game when the user gets the call and start from the same place when the user comes back to your application.

While developing your application, you should ensure that:

- Your application is not crashing when it goes into the background because of any reason, that is, the user pressed Home or got a phone call.
- Your application is not crashing when the user rotates the device. You have to take care of keeping the state of the Activity when the user rotates the device.
- Your application is not using valuable system resources when the user is not active on your application.

These are a few examples that can be handled by the proper use of lifecycle call-back methods. Let us see these lifecycle call-backs of an Activity in *figure 2.8*:

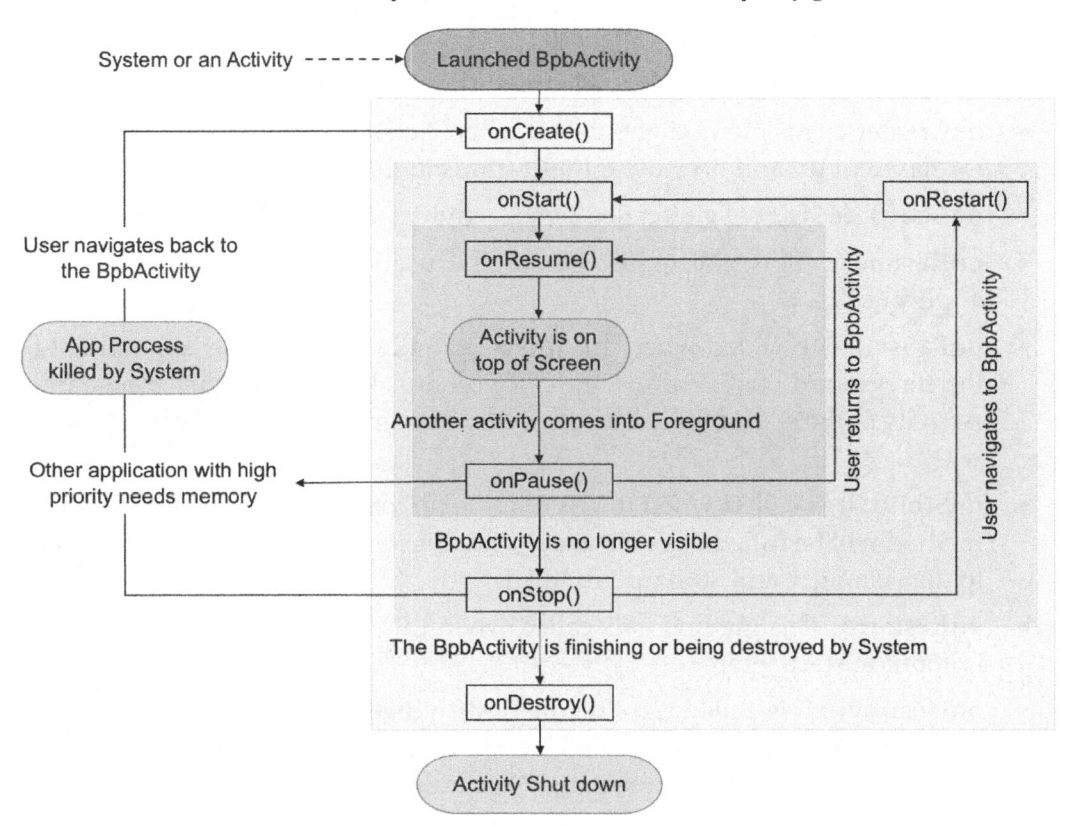

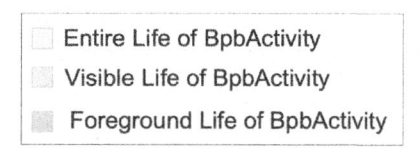

```
Entire Life of BpbActivity
Visible Life of BpbActivity
Foreground Life of BpbActivity
```

Figure 2.8: Lifecycle of an Activity

The preceding *figure 2.8* is a generic example that shows the sequence of these method calls and shows how these methods get called in a few state changes like, if the user navigates to a different activity, or the user presses Home and System kills your application from the background if a high priority application needs memory.

NOTE: onCreate() is the method where we use to define UI for that Activity, so for an Activity, the minimum call-back method you should use is onCreate(). Apart from these lifecycles methods that are shown in *figure 2.8*, there are other lifecycle call-backs too. All those can be used in specific requirements. The recommendation is to learn about all these call-backs and learn when to use these. Remember that handling transitions properly makes your application more robust and performant.

Let us see when these call-backs get called and the use-cases of these methods:

- **onCreate()**: This method gets called when Activity is first created. We set UI for the Activity and do view initializations in this method.
- **onStart()**: `onStart()` gets called when activity is becoming visible to the user.
- **onResume()**: It is called just before the user starts interacting with the application.
- **onPause()**: It is called when the app is partially visible on screen and not in the foreground state. For example, if you are showing another transparent Activity or the size of the second Activity is not matching with screen height/width.
- **onStop()**: It is called when the Activity is no longer visible to the user. This method will be called after `onPause()`. In this method, you can stop listening to data changes and stop updating UI.
- **onRestart()**: This method gets called when the Activity in the stopped state is about to start again.
- **onDestroy()**: It is called right before destroying the Activity if the Activity is cleared from the application stack or you called `finish()` of the Activity. This method will be called after `onPause()` and `onStop()`.

Lifecycle of a Fragment

We now know about Activity lifecycle methods and a few use cases of them. Now let us see about the Fragment lifecycle, which works in sync with the Activity lifecycle. As shown in *figure 2.9*, Fragments life starts after **onCreate()** of Activity and ends with **onDestory()** of Activity:

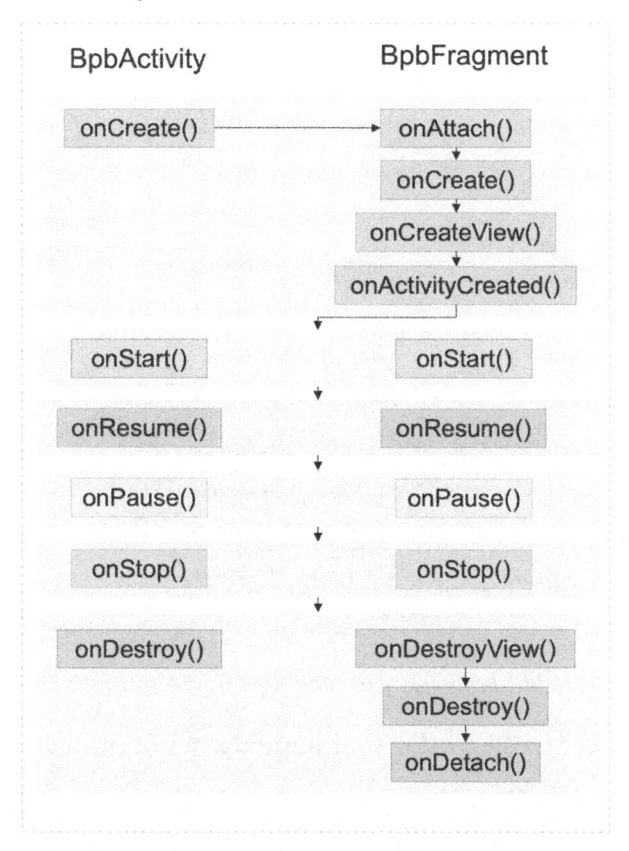

Figure 2.9: Fragment life cycle methods

Similar to an Activity, fragment lifecycle methods are almost the same. **onCreateView()** is the method where you define UI for Fragment, similar to **onCreate()** of an Activity. In the preceding *figure 2.9*, we see the Lifecycle of Fragment, which is tied with Activity, which means it shows lifecycle call-backs of Fragment when the Lifecycle of Activity gets changed.

But, most of the time, you would be adding/replacing Fragments in an Activity. In that case, the lifecycle state of the current Activity will not change, but Fragment will have changes in the lifecycle state.

Let us see how these lifecycle methods get called for Fragments with **add()**, **replace()**, and without **addToBackStack()** and with **addToBackStack()**.

- When **add()** use to show Fragments, without **addToBackStack()**, see *figure 2.10*:

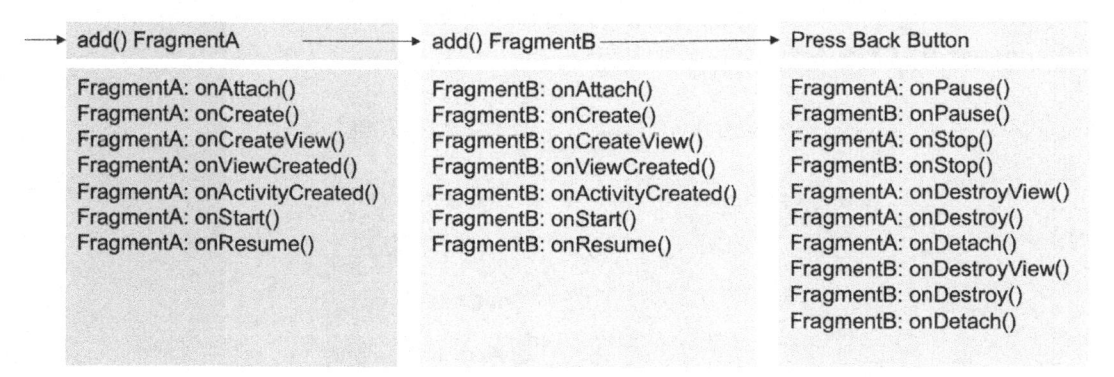

add() FragmentA	add() FragmentB	Press Back Button
FragmentA: onAttach() FragmentA: onCreate() FragmentA: onCreateView() FragmentA: onViewCreated() FragmentA: onActivityCreated() FragmentA: onStart() FragmentA: onResume()	FragmentB: onAttach() FragmentB: onCreate() FragmentB: onCreateView() FragmentB: onViewCreated() FragmentB: onActivityCreated() FragmentB: onStart() FragmentB: onResume()	FragmentA: onPause() FragmentB: onPause() FragmentA: onStop() FragmentB: onStop() FragmentA: onDestroyView() FragmentA: onDestroy() FragmentA: onDetach() FragmentB: onDestroyView() FragmentB: onDestroy() FragmentB: onDetach()

Figure 2.10: add() behavior without adding a fragment to the back stack

- When **add()** use to show Fragments, with **addToBackStack()**, see *figure 2.11*:

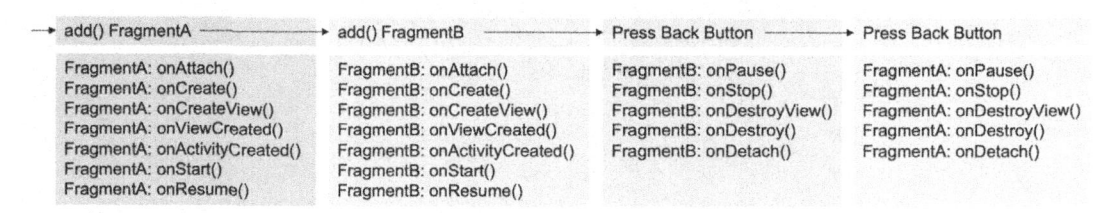

add() FragmentA	add() FragmentB	Press Back Button	Press Back Button
FragmentA: onAttach() FragmentA: onCreate() FragmentA: onCreateView() FragmentA: onViewCreated() FragmentA: onActivityCreated() FragmentA: onStart() FragmentA: onResume()	FragmentB: onAttach() FragmentB: onCreate() FragmentB: onCreateView() FragmentB: onViewCreated() FragmentB: onActivityCreated() FragmentB: onStart() FragmentB: onResume()	FragmentB: onPause() FragmentB: onStop() FragmentB: onDestroyView() FragmentB: onDestroy() FragmentB: onDetach()	FragmentA: onPause() FragmentA: onStop() FragmentA: onDestroyView() FragmentA: onDestroy() FragmentA: onDetach()

Figure 2.11: add() behavior when adding a fragment to the back stack

- When **replace()** use to show Fragments, without **addToBackStack()**, see *figure 2.12*:

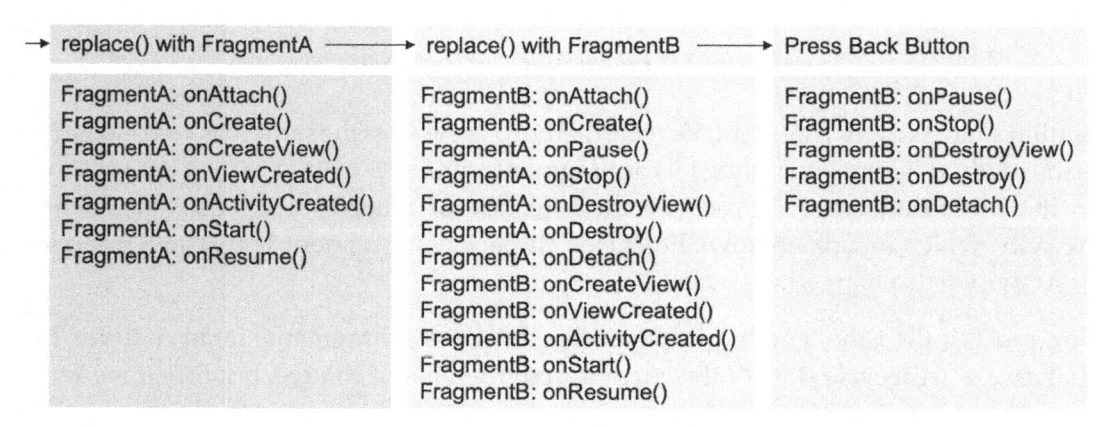

replace() with FragmentA	replace() with FragmentB	Press Back Button
FragmentA: onAttach() FragmentA: onCreate() FragmentA: onCreateView() FragmentA: onViewCreated() FragmentA: onActivityCreated() FragmentA: onStart() FragmentA: onResume()	FragmentB: onAttach() FragmentB: onCreate() FragmentA: onPause() FragmentA: onStop() FragmentA: onDestroyView() FragmentA: onDestroy() FragmentA: onDetach() FragmentB: onCreateView() FragmentB: onViewCreated() FragmentB: onActivityCreated() FragmentB: onStart() FragmentB: onResume()	FragmentB: onPause() FragmentB: onStop() FragmentB: onDestroyView() FragmentB: onDestroy() FragmentB: onDetach()

Figure 2.12: replace() behavior without adding a fragment to the back stack

- When `replace()` use to show Fragments, with `addToBackStack()`, see *figure 2.13*:

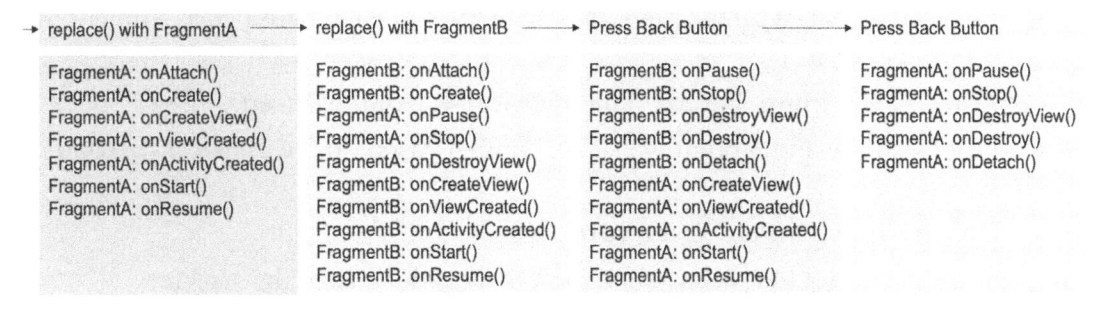

replace() with FragmentA	replace() with FragmentB	Press Back Button	Press Back Button
FragmentA: onAttach()	FragmentB: onAttach()	FragmentB: onPause()	FragmentA: onPause()
FragmentA: onCreate()	FragmentB: onCreate()	FragmentB: onStop()	FragmentA: onStop()
FragmentA: onCreateView()	FragmentA: onPause()	FragmentB: onDestroyView()	FragmentA: onDestroyView()
FragmentA: onViewCreated()	FragmentA: onStop()	FragmentB: onDestroy()	FragmentA: onDestroy()
FragmentA: onActivityCreated()	FragmentA: onDestroyView()	FragmentB: onDetach()	FragmentA: onDetach()
FragmentA: onStart()	FragmentB: onCreateView()	FragmentA: onCreateView()	
FragmentA: onResume()	FragmentB: onViewCreated()	FragmentA: onViewCreated()	
	FragmentB: onActivityCreated()	FragmentA: onActivityCreated()	
	FragmentB: onStart()	FragmentA: onStart()	
	FragmentB: onResume()	FragmentA: onResume()	

Figure 2.13: *replace() behavior when adding a fragment to the back stack*

Understanding lifecycle methods is important, so you should read and research more about the Lifecycle of Activity and Fragments.

NOTE: There are a few points that you should remember:

- **To show Fragments, we can use FrameLayout as the container, but now there is a better option for it. FragmentContainerView is a new container provided by Android and specially designed for Fragments.**
- **As we saw how to show fragments using add() or remove(), there is one more interesting way to show Fragments. Navigation Component is an easy way to show Fragments and handle navigations between fragments, and it requires less code to write.**

Introducing dimensions and screen sizes

Android devices come in different screen sizes and with different pixel sizes. While one device has 160 pixels per square inch, another device fits 640 pixels in the same 1 square inch. If we do not consider these variations in pixel density, the Android system might scale your images (and scaling can turn images into blurry images), or the images might appear at the completely wrong size. Android provides different units for sizes that are used to scale text, images, and widgets depending on screen sizes.

Dimensions

A dimension value is defined in XML. These dimensions are specified with a number followed by unit type (unit of measure), for example, 8dp, 16px, 14sp, and 2in. The following are the units that can be used in Android for size, that is, size of text, size of an image, and margins of a view:

- **Pixels [px]**: Point per scale corresponds to actual pixels on the screen. In other words, it represents one physical dot on the screen.
- **Inches [in]**: Based on the physical size of the screen, where 1-inch equals 2.54 centimeters.
- **Milli-meters [mm]**: Based on the physical size of the screen.
- **Points [pt]**: A single point is 1/72 of an inch based on the physical size of the screen.
- **Density-independent Pixels [dip/ dp]**:
  o A pixel unit that is based on the physical density of the screen.
  o In general, this is the most used unit to define the size of views, margins, paddings, and so on.
  o It scales as per device screen density, where 1dip is equivalent to 1 pixel on a 160DPI screen.
  o We can use dip and dp both as unit types in Android. In this book, we would be mostly using dp.
- **Scalable Pixels [sp]**:
  o It is similar to dip but used for font sizes.
  o It scales as per device screen density (same as a dip) and user's font size preferences. We should always use sp to define font size, so they will be adjusted for the screen density and the user's font size preferences.

Figure 2.14 shows how these units impact UI on different sizes and densities of devices:

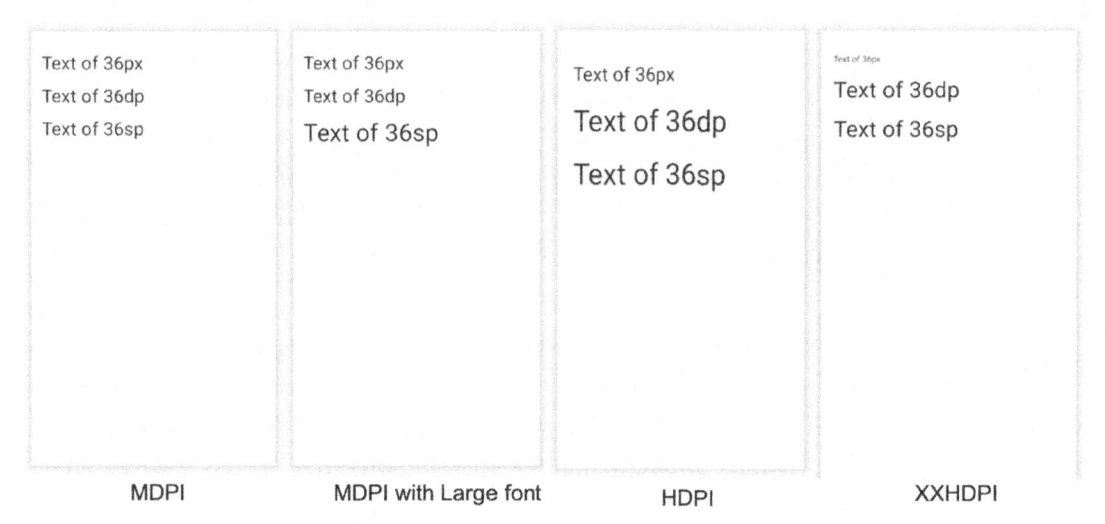

MDPI	MDPI with Large font	HDPI	XXHDPI
Text of 36px Text of 36dp Text of 36sp	Text of 36px Text of 36dp Text of 36sp	Text of 36px Text of 36dp Text of 36sp	Text of 36px Text of 36dp Text of 36sp

Figure 2.14: Dimension units on different screen resolutions

As you can see in preceding *figure 2.14*, in MDPI 3 units, PX, DP, and SP are almost the same in size, but in the other three screens, these units are giving different results. DP and SP units provide the same result in normal font size settings, but in case the user change font size settings, DP and SP will give a different result. Let us see it by comparison as shown *Table 2.1* to understand how these units work:

Unit	Units per Physical Inch	Density Independent	Works with user's Font settings	Same Physical size on every device
px	Varies	No	No	No
in	1	Yes	No	Yes
mm	25.4	Yes	No	Yes
pt	72	Yes	No	Yes
dp	~160	Yes	No	No
sp	~160	Yes	Yes	No

Table 2.1: Working of units

In the preceding *figure 2.14*, you see MDPI, HDPI, and XXHDPI; these are known as density buckets. Let us find out why we should use dp as a measuring unit in Android

DP to Pixel conversion with Density Bucket

Screens of Android devices come under a density bucket, where the density bucket defines the Dots Per Inch (dpi) of the screen. For example, if the screen of the device comes under XXHDPI, the logical density for that device would be 480dpi. See how Android converts DP on different density buckets, and so on:

Density bucket	Logical density	Scale	1dp will be scaled as	32×32dp will be scaled as
ldpi	120 dpi	0.75×	0.75 × 0.75 px	24×24 px
mdpi	160 dpi	1×	1 × 1 px	32×32 px
hdpi	240 dpi	1.5×	1.5 × 1.5 px	48×48 px
xhdpi	320 dpi	2×	2 × 2 px	64×64 px
xxhdpi	480 dpi	3×	3 × 3 px	96×96 px
xxxhdpi	640 dpi	4×	4 × 4 px	128×128 px

Table 2.2: DP to Pixel conversion with density buckets

As shown in the preceding *Table 2.2*, you can see how dp is used to be converted into pixels so that it can produce almost the same output on devices of different density buckets (different screen sizes and screen resolutions). There is one formula to calculate dp from pixel or vice versa for a particular DPI, formula is *[dp = px * 160 / dpi]*.

Figure 2.15 shows another example to know how DP works on different screen resolutions:

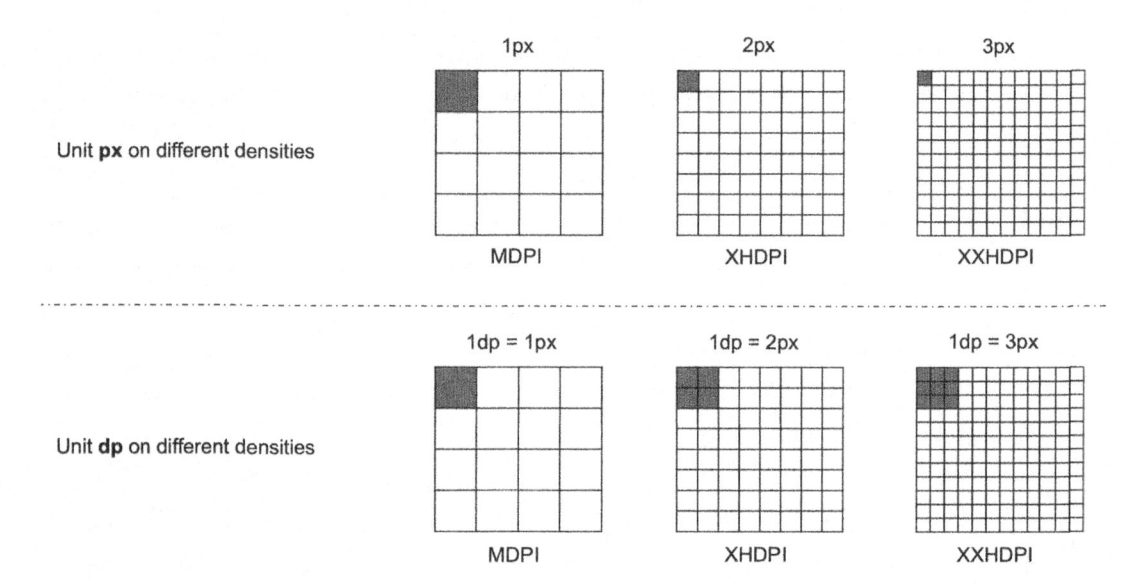

Figure 2.15: Pixel and dp representation on different densities

As shown in the preceding *Figure 2.15*, the representation of px is 1px on each screen, so the visual representation of unit px is different on each screen. As you see in *Table 2.2*, the Android system scales dp into px concerning the density bucket; that is why you see the representation of dp is almost the same on each screen in preceding *figure 2.15*.

Handling of screen sizes

Making our application compatible with different screen sizes (that is, Handset, Tablet, Handset landscape, and Tablet landscape), Android provides few qualifiers for values, drawable, and layouts. So let us see how these qualifiers can be defined to handle multiscreen.

- **Qualifiers for dimensions**: Defining different dimensions for view can be done in **dimens.xml** files using different qualifiers for the values directory, as follows:

  res/
      values/

```
            dimens.xml
    values-mdpi/
            dimens.xml
    values-xhdpi/
            dimens.xml
    values-xxxhdpi/
            dimens.xml
    values-sw600dp/
            dimens.xml
    values-sw720dp
            dimens.xml
```

Note that these directories are optional, and you should not create them until required. However, values/**dimens.xml** is default and crated while creating a project.

Let us see how we define a dimension for multiple screens:

```
# Dimensions declared in values/dimens.xml

<dimen name="logo_height">40dp</dimen>

<dimen name="logo_width">100dp</dimen>


# Dimensions declared in values-sw720dp/dimens.xml

<dimen name="logo_height">70dp</dimen>

<dimen name="logo_width">160dp</dimen>
```

In the preceding code example, **logo_height** and **logo_width** are dimensions for an **ImageView**. Android will automatically pick values depending on screen size for these dimensions and scale the ImageView. Note that the dimension's name must be the same in each qualifier directory.

- **Qualifiers for layouts**: We can create different layout files (file name must be the same) to show different UI depending on the device resolution. For it, we can create a directory with qualifiers as follows:

```
res/
    layout/
        main_activity.xml
    layout-land/
        main_activity.xml
```

```
layout-sw600dp/
    main_activity.xml
layout-sw600dp-land/
    main_activity.xml
```

- **Qualifiers for drawables**: These directories contain images that we show in our application. This is the most important directory when you work for multiple screens. Using proper qualifiers and proper size for an image can make a better visual for the image, and you can avoid scaling of images. These directories can be:

```
res/
    drawable/
        icon.png
    drawable-hdpi/
        icon.png
    drawable-xhdpi/
        icon.png
```

Here **icon.png** is added three times with three different sizes so that one image from the applicable qualifier will be picked and shown at UI.

NOTE: **There are many qualifiers that you can use to support multiscreen. The preceding examples do not show all of them. The recommendation is to read official documentation so that you can add the perfect resource qualifier for your requirement. We will read about "Choosing the optimised image resource type" in Chapter 9 "Adding support for the big screen", which is very important to understand about image resource available in Android and choose the best image type for your application.**

Understanding different types of Layouts

ViewGroup is known as layouts, such as LinearLayout and RelativeLayout. These layouts define the structure for the UI of screens in our application. A layout acts as an invisible container for widgets (View objects, like TextView, Button) and other layouts (ViewGroup objects).

We can create a layout either by using XML or creating objects of Views and ViewGroups at runtime. The recommended way is to create a layout using XML, and it makes it easy to provide different layouts for different screen sizes and orientations (already discussed in the previous topic, Handling of Screen Sizes).

The following are commonly used layouts:
- LinearLayout
- RelativeLayout
- TableLayout
- FrameLayout
- ConstraintLayout

LinearLayout

LinearLayout can align its children in only one direction, either vertically or horizontally. Children are stacked one after one in the given direction. In other words, if the direction of LinearLayout is vertical, then it can show only one child per row, and if the direction is horizontal, then LinearLayout can have only one row with multiple Views.

In *figure 2.16*, the left-most section explains how LinearLayout works in both orientations; in the vertical blueprint, you can see some views are aligned left, some are at right, and some are in the middle, which can be done in LinearLayout. You can align views in other layouts too:

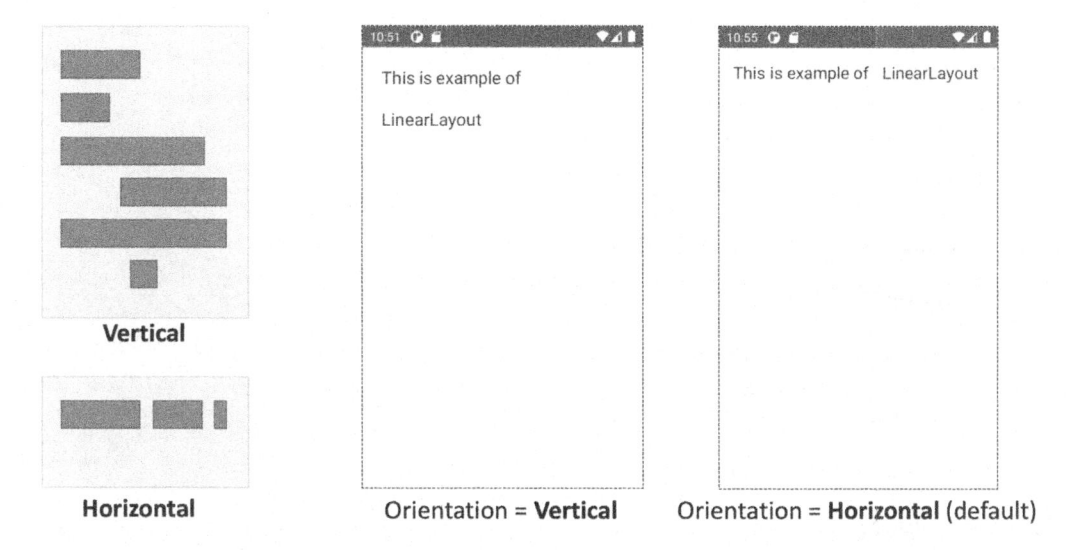

Figure 2.16: Example of LinearLayout and its orientation

XML code for the preceding *figure 2.16* is as follows, where the code added is for Vertical only. You can change **android:orientation="vertical"** to **android:orientation="horizontal"** for horizontal alignment:

```xml
<?xml version="1.0" encoding="utf-8"?>
<LinearLayout xmlns:android="http://schemas.android.com/apk/res/android"
    android:layout_width="match_parent"
    android:layout_height="match_parent"
    android:orientation="vertical"
    android:padding="16dp">

    <TextView
        android:layout_width="wrap_content"
        android:layout_height="wrap_content"
        android:padding="5dp"
        android:text="This is example of "
        android:textColor="@color/black"
        android:textSize="20sp" />

    <TextView
        android:layout_width="wrap_content"
        android:layout_height="wrap_content"
        android:layout_marginTop="10dp"
        android:padding="5dp"
        android:text="LinearLayout"
        android:textColor="@color/black"
        android:textSize="20sp" />

</LinearLayout>
```

RelativeLayout

As its name, RelativeLayout displays children in relative positions to the parent or other Views inside RelativeLayout. For example, a TextView can be shown to the left-of or right-of another View or can be shown at the top or bottom of the parent (RelativeLayout). Using RelativeLayout we can keep the layout hierarchy flat (see *Chapter 1: Creating Hello World Project* for layout hierarchy), which improves the performance of a layout.

Let us see what can be achieved using RelativeLayout using mock-up and output sample code as shown in *figure 2.17*:

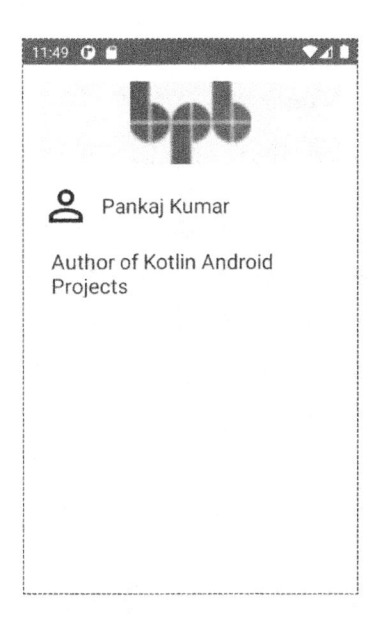

Figure 2.17: Example of RelativeLayout

The preceding layout is designed using two objects of an **ImageView** and two objects of **TextView**. Let us see the code for it:

```
<?xml version="1.0" encoding="utf-8"?>

<RelativeLayout xmlns:android="http://schemas.android.com/apk/res/android"
    android:layout_width="match_parent"
    android:layout_height="match_parent"
    android:padding="16dp">
```

```xml
<ImageView
    android:id="@+id/logo"
    android:layout_width="match_parent"
    android:layout_height="80dp"
    android:layout_alignParentTop="true"
    android:background="#f6f6f6"
    android:src="@drawable/bpb_logo" />

<ImageView
    android:id="@+id/person_img"
    android:layout_width="48dp"
    android:layout_height="48dp"
    android:layout_below="@id/logo"
    android:layout_alignParentLeft="true"
    android:layout_marginTop="16dp"
    android:src="@drawable/baseline_perm_identity_black_48" />

<TextView
    android:id="@+id/title"
    android:layout_width="wrap_content"
    android:layout_height="48dp"
    android:layout_below="@id/logo"
    android:layout_marginStart="10dp"
    android:layout_marginTop="16dp"
    android:layout_toRightOf="@id/person_img"
```

```
        android:gravity="center_vertical"
        android:text="Pankaj Kumar"
        android:textColor="@color/black"
        android:textSize="20sp" />

    <TextView
        android:id="@+id/sub_title"
        android:layout_width="wrap_content"
        android:layout_height="48dp"
        android:layout_below="@id/person_img"
        android:layout_alignParentLeft="true"
        android:layout_marginStart="10dp"
        android:layout_marginTop="16dp"
        android:gravity="center_vertical"
        android:text="Author of Kotlin Android Projects"
        android:textColor="@color/black"
        android:textSize="20sp" />
</RelativeLayout>
```

TableLayout

As its name suggests, any UI that needs to be shown in rows and columns can be developed using **TableLayout**. You can use any view as a direct child of **TableLayout**, but we should use **TableRow** as a direct child, which provides better control for rows and columns.

Let us see an example with code and output as shown in *figure 2.18*:

Figure 2.18: Example of TableLayout

Layout bounds (red lines around texts as a border) are enabled to understand how **TableLayout** renders its children as rows and columns. Let us see the code for it:

```
<?xml version="1.0" encoding="utf-8"?>
<TableLayout xmlns:android="http://schemas.android.com/apk/res/android"
    android:layout_width="match_parent"
    android:layout_height="match_parent"
    android:stretchColumns="1">

    <TableRow>
        <TextView
            android:padding="5dp"
            android:text="First Name"
            android:textColor="@color/black"
```

```
                android:textSize="20sp" />
            <TextView
                android:gravity="left"
                android:padding="3dp"
                android:text="Pankaj"
                android:textColor="@color/black"
                android:textSize="20sp" />
    </TableRow>
    <TableRow>
        <TextView
            android:padding="5dp"
            android:text="Last Name"
            android:textColor="@color/black"
            android:textSize="20sp" />
        <TextView
            android:gravity="left"
            android:padding="5dp"
            android:text="Kumar"
            android:textColor="@color/black"
            android:textSize="20sp" />
    </TableRow>
</TableLayout>
```

FrameLayout

The **FrameLayout** is designed to display a single view, so it should be used to hold a single child view. Although it can have more than one child, the alignment of children without overlapping can be difficult. Children of **FrameLayout** are drawn in a stack where the most recently added child View will be on top, so it can be helpful to create an overlay UI.

Uses of **FrameLayout** can be:

- Using **FrameLayout** as the container of Fragment and can show Fragments inside it.
- Add a label on view. For example, adding a timestamp on the photo.

Let us see how we can show a label preceding an image to show the captured date of a picture, as shown in *figure 2.19*:

Figure 2.19: Example of FrameLayout

Code for the preceding output (*figure 2.19*) is as follows:

```
<?xml version="1.0" encoding="utf-8"?>
<FrameLayout xmlns:android="http://schemas.android.com/apk/res/android"
    android:layout_width="match_parent"
    android:layout_height="match_parent"
    android:orientation="vertical">

    <ImageView
        android:id="@+id/backgroundImage"
```

```
        android:layout_width="match_parent"

        android:layout_height="wrap_content"

        android:src="@drawable/image_frame" />

    <TextView

        android:id="@+id/descTextView"

        android:layout_width="wrap_content"

        android:layout_height="wrap_content"

        android:layout_gravity="bottom|right"

        android:layout_marginBottom="75dp"

        android:background="#60000000"

        android:padding="10dp"

        android:text="Added on 5th April 2021"

        android:textColor="@android:color/white"

        android:textSize="22sp" />

</FrameLayout>
```

ConstraintLayout

A ViewGroup allows you to position and size Views in a flexible way by creating constraints. Where a constraint defines a relationship between two Views in the layout and controls the position of Views within the layout, it can set relative positions of views (like RelativeLayout) and also can set weights for dynamic UI (similar to LinearLayout).

As we read earlier, the nesting of Views is a costly operation, and it can slow down layout/app performance; ConstraintLayout can be used to optimize and flatten the view hierarchy of your layouts by applying some rules to each view to avoid nesting. Any UI that can be created into LinearLayout, RelativeLayout, or other ViewGroup can be created using ConstraintLayout and even in a better way in many cases.

Let us try two simple examples where we will design the layout which we designed earlier for LinearLayout vertical orientation and RelativeLayout using

ConstraintLayout. *Figure 2.20* shows output and gives little idea about how Views relate themselves with other Views using Constraints:

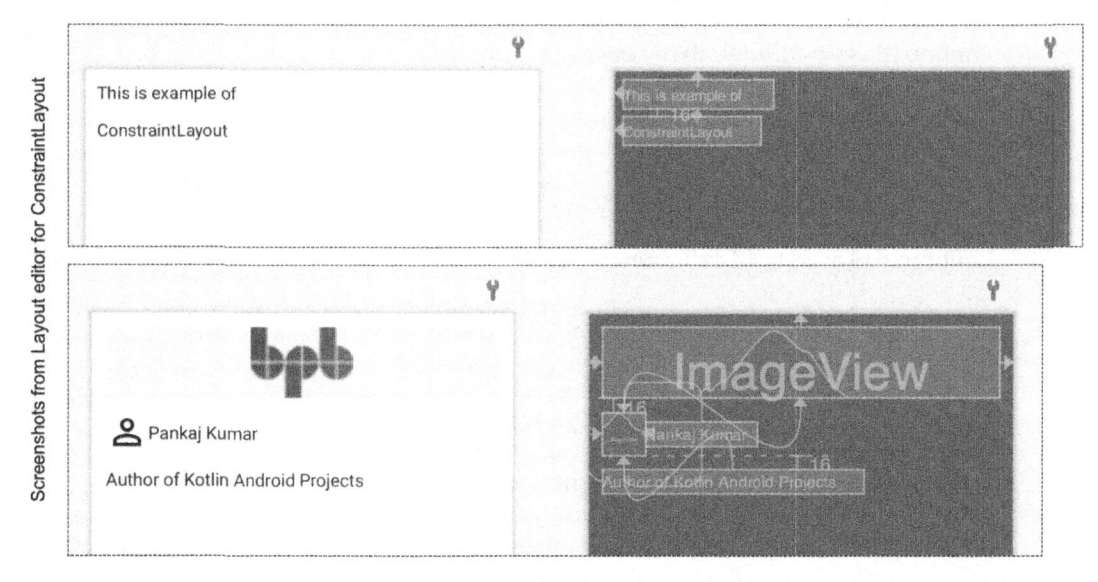

Figure 2.20: Example of ConstraintLayout

And XML code for these two layout designs is as follows:

Similar layout design as LinearLayout example (see preceding example for LinearLayout) can be designed using ConstraintsLayout, as the following example:

```
<?xml version="1.0" encoding="utf-8"?>
<androidx.constraintlayout.widget.ConstraintLayout
    xmlns:android="http://schemas.android.com/apk/res/android"
    xmlns:app="http://schemas.android.com/apk/res-auto"
    xmlns:tools="http://schemas.android.com/tools"
    android:layout_width="match_parent"
    android:layout_height="match_parent"
    android:padding="16dp"
    tools:context=".MainActivity">

    <TextView
```

```xml
        android:id="@+id/textView"
        android:layout_width="wrap_content"
        android:layout_height="wrap_content"
        android:padding="5dp"
        android:text="This is example of "
        android:textColor="@color/black"
        android:textSize="32sp"
        app:layout_constraintLeft_toLeftOf="parent"
        app:layout_constraintTop_toTopOf="parent" />

    <TextView
        android:id="@+id/textView2"
        android:layout_width="wrap_content"
        android:layout_height="wrap_content"
        android:layout_marginTop="16dp"
        android:padding="5dp"
        android:text="ConstraintLayout"
        android:textColor="@color/black"
        android:textSize="32sp"
        app:layout_constraintLeft_toLeftOf="parent"
        app:layout_constraintTop_toBottomOf="@+id/textView" />

</androidx.constraintlayout.widget.ConstraintLayout>
```

And we can design the same layout in ConstraintLayout, which was designed by RelativeLayout (see the preceding example for RelativeLayout), as follows:

```xml
<?xml version="1.0" encoding="utf-8"?>
<androidx.constraintlayout.widget.ConstraintLayout
    xmlns:android="http://schemas.android.com/apk/res/android"
```

```xml
    xmlns:app="http://schemas.android.com/apk/res-auto"
    xmlns:tools="http://schemas.android.com/tools"
    android:layout_width="match_parent"
    android:layout_height="match_parent"
    android:padding="16dp"
    tools:context=".MainActivity">

    <ImageView
        android:id="@+id/logo"
        android:layout_width="match_parent"
        android:layout_height="80dp"
        android:background="#f6f6f6"
        android:src="@drawable/bpb_logo"
        app:layout_constraintEnd_toEndOf="parent"
        app:layout_constraintStart_toStartOf="parent"
        app:layout_constraintTop_toTopOf="parent" />

    <ImageView
        android:id="@+id/person_img"
        android:layout_width="48dp"
        android:layout_height="48dp"
        android:layout_below="@id/logo"
        android:layout_marginTop="16dp"
        android:src="@drawable/baseline_perm_identity_black_48"
        app:layout_constraintStart_toStartOf="@+id/logo"
        app:layout_constraintTop_toBottomOf="@+id/logo" />
```

```xml
<TextView
    android:id="@+id/title"
    android:layout_width="wrap_content"
    android:layout_height="wrap_content"
    android:text="Pankaj Kumar"
    android:textColor="@color/black"
    android:textSize="20sp"
    app:layout_constraintBottom_toBottomOf="@+id/person_img"
    app:layout_constraintStart_toEndOf="@+id/person_img"
    app:layout_constraintTop_toTopOf="@+id/person_img" />

<TextView
    android:id="@+id/sub_title"
    android:layout_width="wrap_content"
    android:layout_height="wrap_content"
    android:layout_marginTop="16dp"
    android:text="Author of Kotlin Android Projects"
    android:textColor="@color/black"
    android:textSize="20sp"
    app:layout_constraintStart_toStartOf="@+id/person_img"
    app:layout_constraintTop_toBottomOf="@+id/person_img" />
</androidx.constraintlayout.widget.ConstraintLayout>
```

ConstraintLayout is awesome, and due to better support from the layout editor, you can design the layout by drag-drop and setting constraints from the design view of the layout editor. So, it is easy to use. If this is so awesome, should we use ConstraintLayout for any type of layout design? No, we should not. There are cases where another layout performs better than ConstraintLayout. We will look more about it immediately next topic.

Choosing a better Layout for a design

We learned about almost all layouts that are frequently being used. In most cases, a layout design can be developed in any layout (except `FrameLayout`). But questions you should ask yourself are, "Is this layout design optimized?" or "Can this design perform better than other options?", before making a final decision. And how can you find the answer to these questions?

Two tools will help you to find answers to the preceding questions:

- GPU Overdraw
- Perfetto/ Systrace

Let us read more about these tools.

GPU overdraw

This tool is available on your device. You can enable it by following these steps, "`Developer options` | `Debug GPU overdraw` | Select `Show overdraw areas`".

This tool identifies the amount of overdraw, and it shows some colors on the screen for each overdraw.

- **True colour**: No overdraw
- **Blue**: Overdrawn once
- **Green**: Overdrawn twice
- **Pink**: Overdrawn thrice
- **Red**: Overdrawn 4 or more times

Note that some overdraw is unavoidable, but you should try to prevent this overdraw (re-painting). Following are a few points that can help you to minimize/prevent these overdraw.

- Create a flat hierarchy as much as possible
- Remove unnecessary background, Common background (added same background colour for ViewGroup and View, which can work only by setting to ViewGroup)
- Remove transparent background

Perfetto/Systrace

Perfetto is a tracing tool (similar to the legacy tracing tool Systrace). It allows you to record arbitrarily long traces than Systrace. Perfetto UI is used to open and analyze traces. Using this tool, we can analyze many things related to application performance, including "layout inflation". We can use this tool for analyzing the performance of the layout and decide if that design is better.

It is recommended that to follow Android official documentation for Systrace and Perfetto and make a habit to analyze your application to improve its performance.

Now coming back to our main topic, "How to choose a better layout for the design". Apart from analyzing the layout using the preceding tools, we should always remember the following points:

- The target for flat hierarchy for layout design.
- If you are designing a complex UI, it is recommended to use ConstraintLayout to achieve a flat hierarchy. Although most of the cases, ConstraintLayout can be used if, for some reason, it blocks you, then at least try to reduce the nesting of the View hierarchy.
- For simple designs where Views are placed horizontally or vertically, LinearLayout is the better choice to use.
- `RecyclerView` (as a single child of its parent) in LinearLayout performs better than `RecyclerView` inside ConstraintLayout.
- Use `FrameLayout` if the design has a single View centered on the screen.

Basics of material design

Material design is a guideline for visual, motion, and animations across all platforms, such as Android, iOS, and the Web. In other words, it is a design language/set of guidelines to help designers to design the application in a better way and enhancement of user experience, and to help end-users to be familiar with a similar view, actions, transitions, and so on. The main goal of material design is to set a common fundamental design principle for the development of any application. It also gives detailed guidelines for the proper size of icons, text, margins, touchable areas, and more, which enhances the user experience of an Android/iOS/Web application.

In Android, there is material components library that contains View/Widgets, animations, and more, which are part of Material design guidelines. To get the support of material components, we need to add dependency as follows:

```
dependencies {
    // ...
    implementation 'com.google.android.material:material:<version>'
    // ...
}
```

In the preceding code, replace <version> with the current version of this library. Visit https://maven.google.com/web/index.html#com.google.android.material:material to get the latest version. This dependency will be added to **build.gradle**, in the case you missed reading about this file, go back and read the **build.gradle** section of *Chapter 1: Creating Hello World Project*.

As a developer, we get the following benefits from using Material Library:
- Widgets for complex views such as lists and cards
- A material design application theme to style all your UI widgets
- Custom animations, shadows, and transitions
- Views/widgets such as Text view, buttons, Chips, Banners, Bottom Navigation, and many more
- And the most amazing update on this library is Jetpack Compose. We will be learning about composition later in *Chapter 10, Important tools/libs*, which you must try.

NOTE: Following material design guidelines is not mandatory, but it is recommended to use for any Android application. Read more about these guidelines; even if you are not a designer, one thing you are going to defiantly learn is "how to think for better UX".

Similarly, you should learn more about Material components with an amazing set of features/ widgets.

Conclusion

In this chapter, we have learned about the basic components of Android, Fragment, and View. Now, we have a better understanding of the uses of these three, and we also know why we use Fragments over custom views. We learned about how **add()** and **replace()** work for showing Fragment and enabling the back stack for Fragments using **addToBackStack()**.

We learned about the Lifecycle of Activity and Fragment, which helps us to use resources in a better way with the help of lifecycle call-backs of Activity and Fragments. Proper handling of lifecycle call-backs allows us to control the state of the screen and ongoing tasks for the screen.

By exploring how dimensions work in Android, we have now a better understating to handle different sizes of screens for layout design. And by knowing the different types of layouts available in Android and the use-case of each Layout type, we have a clear idea about choosing the right layout for our screen design. Tools such as GPU Overdraw, Systrace, or Perfetto help us to measure the performance of a layout (as well as the performance of an application).

We learned about Material design and the uses of the Material library, which will help us to design and use nicely designed/developed widgets of the Material library in our application.

In the upcoming chapter, we will know about Architecture patterns such as MVP, MVVM, and best practices, which will help us to design and develop an application with good architecture.

Points to remember

- Think about a single Activity concept for your application if your application allows you to do. This concept helps us to modularize our application easily, and you can create modules with features that can help to achieve many features of Android like App Bundle and Instant Apps, or you can create a free and paid version of your application easily.
- Layouts should be developed by considering common style guidelines for your application. For example, margins from left and right for layout content, header text, icon size, button style, font, and so on should be the same and should be handled using styles as much as possible. The benefit of it is that your app UI will look consistent, and if any change is required for a widget or style will be applied throughout the application by doing changes at a single code snippet.
- You should always try to minimize the nesting of layouts. Most of the time ConstraintLayout can be used.
- There is no default back stack for Fragments, so if you need back navigation, you should always use **addToBackStack()**. Navigation components is another way of showing Fragments, and it allows you to set navigation by doing

just drag and drop (behind the scene, it writes codes for you automatically). Follow official documentation for more details and its uses.

- Use DP for view margins and SP for font sizes.

Multiple Choice Questions

1. Which Android component is used to show UI on screen?
   A. Activity
   B. Service
   C. Broadcast Receiver
   D. Content Provider
2. In which lifecycle call-back method we use to set the layout of an Activity?
   A. onResume()   B. onStart()   C. onCreate()   D. onPause()
3. How can a Fragment be added to the back stack
   A. Android handles the back stack for Fragments by default
   B. Using add()
   C. Using replace()
   D. Using addToBackStack()
4. Which layout can show views only in one direction, either vertically or horizontally?
   A. FrameLayout
   B. TableLayout
   C. LinearLayout
   D. RelativeLayout
5. Which method is used to set the layout for a Fragment?
   A. onCreate()
   B. onActivityCreated()
   C. onCreateView()
   D. onAttach()

Answers

1. A
2. C
3. D
4. C
5. C

Questions

1. How to analyze the performance of a layout?
2. Why should we use SP over DP for font size?
3. What are Service and JobIntentService?
4. What are the options to perform background tasks in Android?
5. How can we securely share the data of an application with other applications?

Key Terms

- Activity
- Service
- Broadcast Receiver
- Content Provider
- View
- Fragment
- Lifecycle of Activity
- Lifecycle of Fragment
- Dimensions
- Qualifiers
- PX vs. DP vs. SP
- Multiscreen Support
- LinearLayout
- RelativeLayout
- FrameLayout
- TableLayout
- ConstraintLayout
- GPU Overdraw
- Perfetto
- Systrace

CHAPTER 3
Architecture Patterns

In the previous chapter, we learned about the basic components of Android, handling of different screen sizes, and different types of layouts available in Android, and we also learned about the Material library.

In this chapter, we will learn about architecture patterns. We will learn to organize the code and write scalable, testable, and maintainable code using architecture patterns. There are a few most used architecture patterns in Android, such as MVP and MVVM. Here, we will look into these patterns and understand how we organize our code using these patterns.

Structure

In this chapter, we will cover the following topics:
- Understanding the need for an Architecture Pattern
- Understanding Clean Architecture
- Understanding MVP
    o Introduction to MVP
    o Advantages of using MVP
    o Disadvantages of MVP

- Understanding MVVM
    - Introduction to MVVM
    - Using Databinding
    - Advantages of using MVP
    - Disadvantages of MVP
    - MVVM with use cases

Objectives

The objective of this chapter is to let you know about Architecture patterns being used in Android and the requirement of Architecture patterns in our project. After completing this chapter, you will have a clear idea about what problems you may face while not using a proper Architecture pattern and how to organize your code to follow clean architecture. You will also have a clear idea about the benefits and drawbacks of each Architecture pattern, so it can help you to decide which Architecture pattern you should use in your project.

We will also have an introduction to the Architecture pattern, which the Android community adopted from other platforms, such as VIPER and MVI.

Understanding the need for an architecture pattern

Think about a team where each developer writes code the way he likes. The result would be the repository will have multiple code styles, principles, or rules that make your code unmaintainable, unreadable, and may be buggy too. When you choose Architecture, you follow a set of rules/guidelines for designing or developing your application. And when you follow a defined set of rules/guidelines, your code will be consistent, readable, maintainable, and less error-prone.

Understanding the need for Architecture by one more example would be, assume that we are developing an application, and we wrote code for UI state change, deciding on user action, database call, and network call, all inside the Activity. Now, let us find out answers to a few question will that Activity be readable, maintainable, or easy to update? The most important question is: Is that Activity class testable? The answer is "No" for both questions. Sometimes you may end up rewriting the whole application for an update of a feature. And the reason is tightly coupled code.

To resolve these problems, clean architecture came the solution. It is most important to write clean code for your application, which requires effort and experience. Writing clean code means you are writing a code that should be easy to understand, flexible, maintainable, and testable.

After applying clean architecture to the application, UI code, decision-making code, database call, and network calls will be written into separate classes, and those will have dedicated responsibility as per chosen Architecture pattern.

The following points explain more about why we need a cleaner approach:

- The separation of code in modules or different layers with specific responsibilities makes our code easier to maintain and easier for modification.
- High level of abstraction
- Loose coupling between code
- Easy testable code
- Easy to understand
- Cost effective (modifications/extensions requires less cost)

Understanding clean architecture

The architecture of an application means the overall design of the project. It helps us to organize our code into different classes/layers with their responsibility. An architecture defines how the application performs its core functionality and how that functionality interacts with other layouts like UI/database.

Clean architecture follows some guidelines that help us write maintainable, extendable, testable, and readable code. These guidelines are known as SOLID principles.

Understanding SOLID principle

The SOLID principles guide us to create maintainable, flexible, and readable/understandable code for the software. So as the software grows, you can easily add more features and maintain it, and one can easily understand the code of the software.

These principles were first introduced by Robert Cecil Martin (Uncle Bob) in his 2,000 papers *"Design Principles and Design Patterns"*, and in 2004, Michael Feathers prepared a subset of these principles and introduced them as the SOLID acronym to the software world.

The following are SOLID principles:
- **Single responsibility principle**
- **Open-closed principle**
- **Liskov's substitution principle**
- **Interface segregation principle**
- **Dependency inversion principle**

Let us understand these concepts in detail.

Single responsibility principle

Single responsibility says that a class should have a single responsibility. In other words, a class should have a single reason for the change. Assume that we have created a **Vehicle** class as follows:

```kotlin
class Vehicle {
    fun start()
    fun stop()
    fun wash()
    fun drive()
    fun changeTyre(tireToChange: Tire)
    fun checkOilMeter()
    fun changeEngineOil()
    fun getMake()
}
```

In the preceding code, there are five methods that should be responsibilities of a **Vehicle** class, so it does not follow the Single Responsibility Principle. Let us see how we can rewrite this code to follow the Single Responsibility Principle:

```kotlin
class Vehicles {
    fun start()
    fun stop()
    fun getMake()
}
```

```kotlin
class Driver {

    fun checkOilMeter(vehicle: Vehicle)

    fun drive(vehicle: Vehicle)

}

class CarWasher {

    fun wash(vehicle: Vehicle)

}

class Mechanic {

    fun changeTyre(vehicle: Vehicle, tireNumber: Tire)

    fun changeEngineOil(vehicle: Vehicle)

}
```

We have created **Driver**, **CarWasher**, and **Mechanic** classes and moved methods into these classes, which should be the responsibilities of these three classes, not of the **Vehicle** class:

Open-closed principle

The open-closed principle says that a class should be open for extension and closed for modifications. It means extending a module/class with additional behavior without modifying it. Abstraction is the key to this principle. Let us see with an example:

```kotlin
interface Shape {

    fun area(): Double

}


class Circle(val radius: Double) : Shape {

    override fun area(): Double {

        return 3.14 * radius * radius
```

```kotlin
        }
    }

    class AreaCalculator {
        fun calculateArea(shapes: Array<Shape>) {
            shapes.forEach { shape ->
                // Calculate area of shape
                val area = shape.area()
                // Do something with calculated area
            }
        }
    }
```

Here, **AreaCalculator** has a utility that can calculate the area for any shape class and perform a given task. In the future, if we need to extend the implementation to other shapes like Square, Rectangle shapes, we only need to extend the class Shape and write the implementation for the **area()**. So Square class will be as follows:

```kotlin
class Square(val area: Double) : Shape {

    override fun area(): Double {
        return area * area
    }

}
```

And **Rectangle** class would be as follows:

```kotlin
class Rectangle(val width: Double, val height: Double) : Shape {

    override fun area(): Double {
        return width * height
    }

}
```

As you see, we extended the **Shape** class to **Square** and **Rectangle** but did not change anything in **AreaCalculator** class or **Shape** class. This is how we achieved *"Open for extension/ closed for modifications"*.

NOTE: **Remember that a function that checks object type is a violation of the Open-closed principle.**

You should be able to extend the class without worrying if the base class can support our extension. But inheritance can lead to limitations where subclass would depend on the base class (and as you can extend only one class in Kotlin/ Java, you might face limitations). So interfaces are recommended choices over classes. And the choice of interface leads to loose coupling.

Liskov's substitution principle

This principle says that subtypes must be substitutable from their base type. Let us see an example:

```
open class Bird {
    fun fly() {}
}


class Duck : Bird()


class Ostrich : Bird()
```

In general, ducks can fly, but what about Ostrich? Even Ostrich is a bird, but it cannot fly. So it should not be able to use/access the **fly** method. So the preceding code is breaking Liskov's Substitution Principle. So, how it can be corrected? Let us see the following example:

```
open class Bird


open class FlyingBirds : Bird() {
    fun fly() {}
}
```

```
class Duck : FlyingBirds()
```

```
class Ostrich : Bird()
```

In the preceding example, we have created one new class, **FlyingBirds**, which is now being extended by Duck which can fly, and Bird is being extended by Ostrich, which cannot fly.

Interface segregation principle

The interface segregation principle says that an interface should not have methods that implementing classes do not require. We should not force a class to implement methods which are not required. Let us see an example:

```
interface Animal {

    fun feed()

    fun groom()

}


class Cat : Animal {

    override fun feed() {

        // Add code to feed the Cat

    }


    override fun groom() {

        // Add code to Groom the Cat

    }

}


class Lion : Animal {

    override fun feed() {

        // Add code to feed the Cat

    }
```

```
    override fun groom() {
        // Can't groom Lion (wild animals)
        // Add dummy implementation to make compiler happy,
        // as you are forced to do so by Animal contract.
    }
}
```

In the preceding example, `feed()` and `groom()`, both methods are relevant to `Cat`, but `groom()` is irrelevant to the `Lion`. And this design is bad as we are forced to implement the irrelevant method to `Lion` class.

So we should segregate an interface into smaller and highly cohesive interfaces, known as *role interfaces*, and each *role interface* can have one or more methods depending on type/specific behavior. So the classes can only implement those interfaces which are relevant to that class. Let us rewrite the preceding code in terms of the Interface Segregation Principle as follows:

```
interface Animal {
    fun feed()
}

interface WildAnimal : Animal

interface PetAnimal : Animal {
    fun groom()
}

class Cat : PetAnimal {
    override fun feed() {
        // Add code to feed the Cat
    }
```

```
    override fun groom() {
        // Add code to Groom the Cat
    }
}


class Lion : WildAnimal {
    override fun feed() {
        // Add code to feed the Lion
    }
}
```

We segregated the **Animal** interface into two interfaces. The animal can have the **groom()** method as it is relevant to any type of **Animal**, and **feed()** is moved to **PetAnimal**. Now, **Cat** can implement **PetAnimal**, and **Lion** can implement **Animal**.

We can rewrite it to be more extensible by creating a **WildAnimal** interface by extending the **Animal** interface and can add wild animal-specific methods, and **Lion** can implement the **WildAnimal** interface instead-of **Animal**.

Dependency inversion principle

Dependency inversion concerns the relationship between classes/modules. It follows two points:

(1) High-level modules should not depend on low-level modules. Both should depend on abstractions.

(2) Abstraction should not depend on details. Details should depend on abstractions.

Let us understand it by an example. Assume that we are required to write a code that can create a **Book** object and assign an **ISBN** to the **Book**:

```
data class Book(val title: String, val generateNumber: String)


class IsbnGenerator {
    fun generateNumber(): String {
        // Generate 13 digits ISBN Number
```

```
            return "ISBN " + Math.abs(
                kotlin.random.Random.nextLong(
                    1000000000000, 9999999999999
                )
            )
        }
    }


    class PublicationService {
        private val isbn = IsbnGenerator()


        fun createBook(title: String): Book {
            return Book(title, isbn.generateNumber())
        }
    }
```

In the preceding example, **title** and **ISBN** are required for creating an object of **Book**, **PublicationService** is the class that generates ISBN using **IsbnGenerator**, and puts it into a **Book** object. No problem till now, this works as per our requirement.

After some time of this implementation, you get a new requirement to add another type of book ID, which is ISSN. Can the current implementation of **PublicationService** handle this change without modification? The answer is, No. You need to modify **PublicationService** class, and probably, you will be creating one if-else block in **createBook()** to check which type of book ID you need to create. We will be adding more and more if-else blocks for similar requirements in the future too. And this is defiantly not a good way.

The major problem in the preceding code is the strong dependency between **PublicationService** class and **IsbnGenerator** class. The following is the code that follows the Dependency Inversion Principle and solves the problem, which is in the preceding code:

```
interface BookNumberGenerator {
    fun generateNumber(): String
```

```
}

class IsbnGenerator : BookNumberGenerator {
    override fun generateNumber(): String {
        // Generate 13 digits ISBN Number
        return "ISBN " + Math.abs(
            kotlin.random.Random.nextLong(
                1000000000000, 9999999999999
            )
        )
    }
}

class PublicationService(
    private val bookNumberGenerator: BookNumberGenerator
) {

    fun createBook(title: String): Book {
        return Book(title, bookNumberGenerator.generateNumber())
    }
}
```

We created an interface **BookNumberGenerator** and implemented it by **IsbnGenerator**. And we pass the implementation of **BookNumberGenerator** to the constructor of **PublicationService**. So now **PublicationService** depends on the interface, not on the implementation, and instead of creating an object of **IsbnGenerator** by itself, it is asking the caller to pass the **BookNumberGenerator** object. This solved the dependency problem too.

Coming to our requirement, let us add code to create ISSN for Books:

```
class IssnGenerator : BookNumberGenerator {
    override fun generateNumber(): String {
        // Return 8 digits ISSN number
        return "ISSN " + Math.abs(
            kotlin.random.Random.nextInt(
                10000000, 99999999
            )
        )
    }
}
```

As you see, we only need a new class, **IssnGenerator**, that is it. The two types of **BookNumberGenerator** can be used as follows:

```
val isbnService = PublicationService(IsbnGenerator())
val book1 = isbnService.createBook("Book with ISBN")


val issnService = PublicationService(IssnGenerator())
val book2 = isbnService.createBook("Book with ISSN")
```

Implementation of **BookNumberGenerator** is passed as a parameter of the constructor of **PublicationService**, so if we need a service that generates ISBN, we will just pass **IsbnGenerator** implementation to the constructor. If we need a service for ISSN, we will pass the implementation of **IssnGenerator**. This is known as Inversion of Control.

Now, we know how the SOLID principle helps us to write a well-structured code that is easy to understand and easy to modify.

Coming back to clean architecture, let us understand it via a picture as shown in *figure 3.1*, which is a modified version of the original diagram from Robert Cecil Martin (Uncle Bob), inventor of clean architecture:

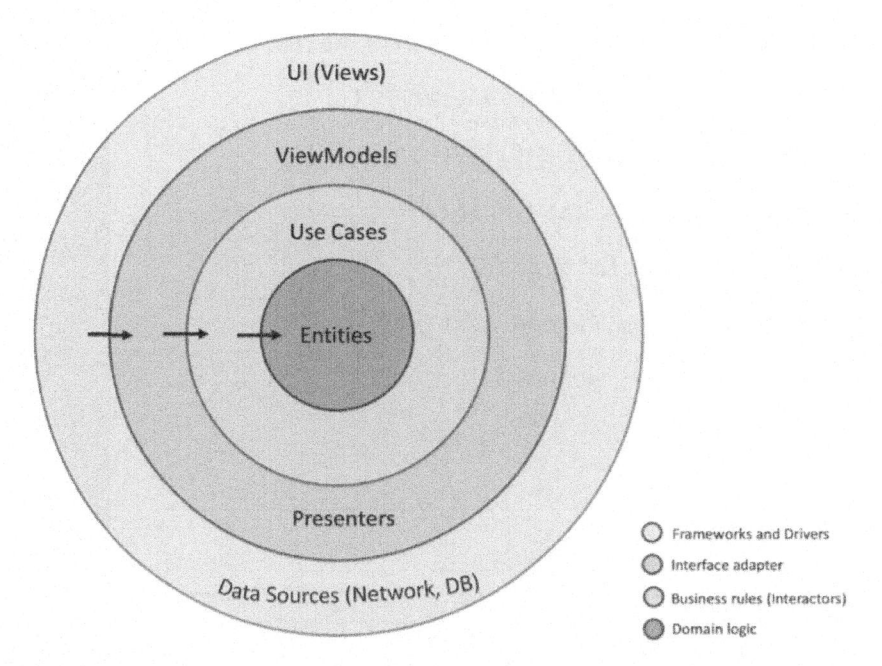

Figure 3.1: Clean architecture

As shown in the preceding *figure 3.1*, clean architecture divides code into a few layers depending on characteristics, and communication between these layers is defined as arrows in the preceding *figure 3.1* show it. Let us understand these layers:

- **Entities**: These are model classes (business objects) of the application.
- **Use cases**: Contains business rules, and these use cases coordinate the flow of data to entities and from the entities. These are also known as Interactors.
- **Interface adapters**: Presenters, Controllers, and View Model are defined at this layer. These adapters prepare data to be used by use cases and entities. This layer also informs UI about data changes.
- **Frameworks/UI**: All UI component (like Activities/Fragments) exists at this layer. Also, tools and frameworks are used to define here.

The following are a few important benefits we observe after looking at the preceding *figure 3.1*:

- Separation of UI from the rest of the layers. It means we can change UI without changing the rest of the layer.
- Separation of the data layer. It gives us the flexibility to change the database and change data sources such as remote calls or local database calls.
- It makes code more testable. Business logic can be tested without the UI or DB layer.

In the next sections, while understanding MVP and MVVM, we will see how we create layers and implement code that follows clean architecture.

Understanding MVP

MVP stands for Model View Presenter. In MVP, we separate our code into these three layers, and each has defined responsibilities.

Let us understand the flow in MVP using saving a note in the Note Application example. When you tap on the **Save** button from View, the View passes the title and description of the note to the Presenter to save the note. The Presenter prepares the note information (an object of the Note class) to be saved into the local database or to the API if you are using a remote database via API to save notes. And at last, Presenter passes the note model to the data layer/ network layer to save the note. After the saving of note is done, the presenter will get notified by the data/network layer via call-back, and then it will prepare a success message and asks the View to show the success message and update the list of notes. *Figure 3.2* shows the layers in MVP and the flow between layers in MVP:

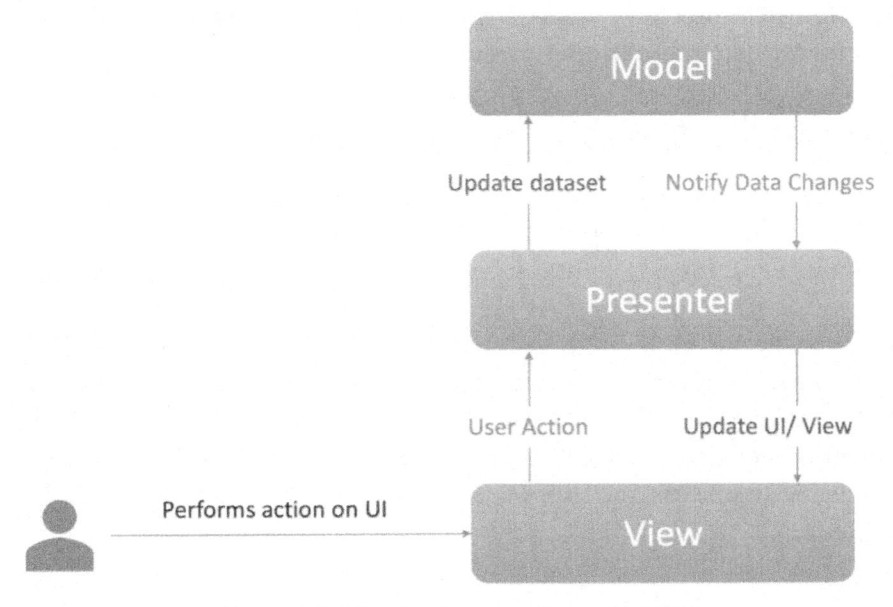

Figure 3.2: The flow between layers in MVP

Let us know more about these layers (see the preceding *figure 3.2*):
- **Model**: The model is only the gateway to the domain or business layer. It provides data that need to be shown on View or process data after changes made by View.

- **View**: This is the user interface layer, and Activity or Fragments are kinds of the View. It keeps a reference of the presenter, and by using the reference, it requests to get data to show on UI and asks the presenter to update data if changes are made on UI and if they need to be saved somewhere (local/ remote).

- **Presenter**: The presenter is a mediator between View and Model. It decides what will happen when any interaction happens on the View, such as `on button click`, `screen-swipe`, and so on. And it retrieves the data from the model and applies the UI logic to decide what to display (like if login success, it can ask the view to show the post-login page.

Points to remember:

- **Communication between View to Presenter and Presenter to Model happens via interfaces (callback patterns).**
- **There is a one-to-one relationship between the Presenter and the View. It means One Presenter can manage one View at a time.**
- **Communication chain is like View -> Presenter -> Model. It means a View cannot talk with the Model directly.**

Understanding MVP with code

Figure 3.3 shows the project structure for MVP, where we are using the login feature to understand the flow between Model-View-Presenter. In *figure 3.3*, the `LoginRequest` is a class that is being used to send a login request to API, and `LoginResponse` is the class that is being used to convert API response (JSON) to model. And as the name suggests, `LoginPresenter` is the presenter class, and `LoginActivity` is the view of MVP, where `LoginContract` keeps interfaces for each layer to make communication happen between layers in MVP. Note that Repository is not part of MVP; it represents the data layer or network layer. In this chapter, we will get to know repository via code, and we will understand Repositories more in *Chapter 6: Developing Video Sharing Application*:

Architecture Patterns ■ 105

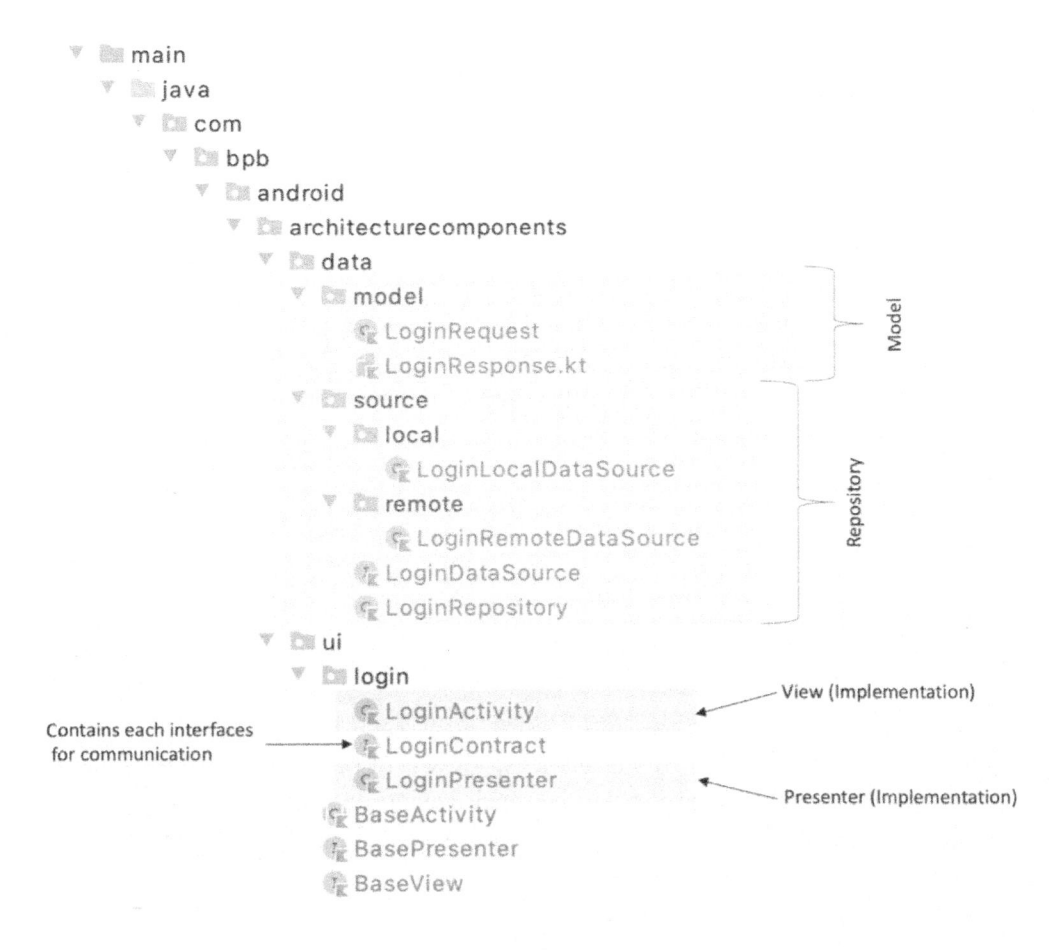

```
▼ main
   ▼ java
      ▼ com
         ▼ bpb
            ▼ android
               ▼ architecturecomponents
                  ▼ data
                     ▼ model
                           LoginRequest              ⎤
                           LoginResponse.kt          ⎦ Model
                     ▼ source
                        ▼ local                      ⎤
                              LoginLocalDataSource   ⎥
                        ▼ remote                    ⎥ Repository
                              LoginRemoteDataSource ⎥
                        LoginDataSource             ⎥
                        LoginRepository             ⎦
                  ▼ ui
                     ▼ login
                           LoginActivity    ← View (Implementation)
                           LoginContract    ← Contains each interfaces for communication
                           LoginPresenter   ← Presenter (Implementation)
                        BaseActivity
                        BasePresenter
                        BaseView
```

Figure 3.3: *Project structure for MVP*

After looking into the project structure, as shown in the preceding *figure 3.3*, let us look into the code:

- **LoginContract.kt**:

    Let us first define **LoginContract**, where we will define contracts for the layers of MVP:

    ```
    interface LoginContract {

        interface View : BaseView<Presenter> {
            fun showProgress(show: Boolean)
            fun showPostLoginPage(userName: String)
            fun showLoginFailed()
    ```

```
    }

    interface Presenter : BasePresenter {
        fun performLogin(userName: String, password: String)
    }
}
```

You see two classes, **BaseView** and **BasePresenter,** that act as base classes for interfaces View and Presenter. These base classes are not really important, but if you need to add some common methods for each View or Presenter, having base classes can be useful. The following is the code for these interfaces:

```
interface BaseView<T> {
    var presenter: T
}


interface BasePresenter {
    fun start()
}
```

LoginContract contains two interfaces, View and Presenter, where View will be implemented by **LoginActivity**, and Presenter will be implemented by **LoginPresenter**. Creating interfaces, in this case, helps us while writing test cases.

- **LoginActivity.kt**:

    LoginActivity represents the View. As you see the following code of **LoginActivity**, it uses **presenter.performLogin(...)** to ask the presenter to validate the input. It also have few methods such as **showProgress()**, **showLoginFailed()**, or **showPostLoginPage()**, which will be called from presenter. Let us look into the following code:

    ```
    class LoginActivity : BaseActivity(), LoginContract.View {

        override lateinit var presenter: LoginContract.Presenter
        override var isActive: Boolean = false

        override fun onCreate(savedInstanceState: Bundle?) {
            super.onCreate(savedInstanceState)
            setContentView(R.layout.activity_login)
    ```

```
        setUp()
    }

    override fun setUp() {
        isActive = true
        presenter = LoginPresenter(
                LoginRepository(LoginLocalDataSource()),
                this
        )

        btnLogin?.setOnClickListener {
            doLogin()
        }
    }

    override fun showPostLoginPage(userName: String) {
        // We can show next activity after login success.
    }

    override fun showLoginFailed() {
        // Notify user about Login Failure.
    }

    override fun showProgress(show: Boolean) {
       progressBar.visibility = if (show) View.VISIBLE else View.GONE
    }

    override fun onDestroy() {
        super.onDestroy()
        isActive = false
    }

    private fun doLogin() {
```

```
......
presenter.performLogin(
        edtUserName?.text.toString(),
        edtPassword?.text.toString()
    )
    }
}
```

If you look closely while creating an object of the Presenter, we are passing **this** keyword means current activity reference. It means View and Presenter know about each other by keeping a reference of each other. This is how View and the presenter will talk to each other.

- **LoginPresenter.kt**:

    Now let us write the Presenter **LoginPresenter** class to handle actions from the view and talk to the data/network layer and then update the view according to the result from the data/network layer:

```
class LoginPresenter(
        private val repository: LoginRepository,
        val loginView: LoginContract.View
) : LoginContract.Presenter {

    init {
        loginView.presenter = this
    }

    override fun performLogin(userName: String, password: String) {
        loginView.showProgress(true)

        // Prepare data format required by model layer.
        // Like here, we are creating LoginRequest object with
        // required data.
        val loginRequest = LoginRequest(userName, password)

        // Asking model using repository to validate credentials,
```

```kotlin
        // and expecting result by callback. See implementation
        // of callback
        repository.validateLogin(loginRequest, callback)
    }

    private val callback = object : LoginDataSource.LoginCallback {

        override fun onCredentialsValidated(loginResponse:
        LoginResponse) {
            // Login succeed. Notify View about it.

            // Check if the view is able to handle
            // UI updates or not.
            if (!loginView.isActive) {
                return
            }

          // Ask View to update itself with given data for success
            loginView.showProgress(false)
            loginResponse.userInfo?.let { user ->
                loginView.showPostLoginPage(user.name)
            }
        }

        override fun onCredentialInvalid() {
            // Check if the view is able to handle
            // UI updates or not.
            if (!loginView.isActive) {
                return
            }

          // Ask View to update itself with given data for failure
            loginView.showProgress(false)
```

```
            loginView.showLoginFailed()
        }
    }
}
```

As you can see in the preceding code of **LoginPresenter**, **performLogin()** in the previous presenter implementation, we are preparing the object of **LoginRequest** with credentials and asking the repository to validate it.

Look at **onCredentialsValidated()** and **onCredentialInvalid()**, these are callbacks which gets result from data-source. In these two callbacks, we are using a few methods of **loginView** to notify about login status to View (that is **LoginActivity** in our case).

One more thing to notice here is that as View and Presenter keep the reference of each other, this is not the same for Presenter and Data layer (Model). The presenter keeps a reference of the repository, but the repository does not. We sent the object of callback to the repository, and by using that callback, the repository was used to notify the presenter. In other words, the repository does not need to know our presenter. So repository can be used for more than one Presenter at a time if required.

Now, let us look into data layer code that follows repository patterns.

- **LoginRequest.kt**:

    LoginRequest is a model class to be used to send data to the login API:

    ```
    data class LoginRequest(
        val userName: String,
        val userPassword: String
    )
    ```

- **LoginResponse.kt**:

    LoginResponse is a model class to be used to parse the data which we get as JSON from login API:

    ```
    data class LoginResponse(
        val success: Boolean,
        val userInfo: UserInfo?,
        var error: String?
    )
    ```

```
data class UserInfo(
    val name: String
)
```

- **LoginDataSource.kt**:

LoginDataSource is an abstraction for the local and remote data source. This abstraction helps us to implement behavior for local and remote, and it also helps us to switch between local and remote data sources:

```
interface LoginDataSource {
    /**
     * Contract for presenter.
     * Presenter will get notified by these callbacks.
     */
    interface LoginCallback {

        fun onCredentialsValidated(response: LoginResponse)

        fun onCredentialInvalid()
    }

    fun validateLogin(loginRequest: LoginRequest, callback:
    LoginCallback)
}
```

LoginDataSource is a contract for local and remote data sources. **LoginLocalDataSource** and **LoginRemoteDataSource** will implement these methods and write implementation for **validateLogin(...)**.

- **LoginRepository.kt**:

LoginRepository is the class that does actual data-source calls. It decides to look for data at local or remote:

```
class LoginRepository(
    private val dataSource: LoginDataSource
) : LoginDataSource {
    override fun validateLogin(
        loginRequest: LoginRequest,
        callback: LoginDataSource.LoginCallback
```

```
        ) {
            dataSource.validateLogin(
                loginRequest,
                object : LoginDataSource.LoginCallback {

                    override fun onCredentialsValidated(response:
                    LoginResponse) {
                        callback.onCredentialsValidated(response)
                    }

                    override fun onCredentialInvalid() {
                        callback.onCredentialInvalid()
                    }
                }
            )
        }
    }
```

Notice about data-source type passed in **LoginRepository** while creating an object of **LoginPresenter** in **LoginActivity** (see code of **LoginActivity.kt**). The data-source type was **LoginLocalDataSource**. In general, we can change it to **LoginRemoteDataSource** as well, and this is how we can decide when to use local data-source (process data on local DB/preferences or files, and so on) or remote data-source (in case of processing data on remote DB). In some MVP templates, you will see that the repository class (**LoginRepository** in our case) will have both types of data sources, and depending on the case, it uses each type of data source. For example, if we are caching data at local, the repository will first check data availability on local using a local data source, and in case of data unavailability, the repository will use a remote data source.

And at last, let us look into the implementation **LoginLocalDataSource**:

```
class LoginLocalDataSource : LoginDataSource {

    override fun validateLogin(
            loginRequest: LoginRequest,
            callback: LoginDataSource.LoginCallback
```

```kotlin
) {
    // A dummy wait to showcase how long running tasks
    // in data-sources perform the given task and
    // passes result back to repository.
    Handler(Looper.getMainLooper()).postDelayed({

        // Dummy validation to showcase the example only.
        val nameLength = loginRequest.userName.length
        val pwdLength = loginRequest.userPassword.length
        if (nameLength != pwdLength) {
            callback.onCredentialInvalid()
        } else {
            val response = LoginResponse(
                success = true,
                userInfo = UserInfo(loginRequest.userName),
                error = null
            )
            callback.onCredentialsValidated(response)
        }

    }, 3000)
  }
}
```

NOTE: The Android does not allow other threads to communicate directly with the UI thread, so one of the ways is to use Handler. A Handler allows communication back with UI thread from other background thread. There are methods like post(Runnable runnable) and postDelayed(Runnable runnable, long delayMillis) can be used. Where post(Runnable runnable) runs the runnable on the thread to which the Handler is attached. The method postDelayed(Runnable runnable, long delayMillis) does the same work as the post(Runnable runnable), but it causes runnable to be run after the specified amount of time elapsed. Read more at https://developer.android.com/reference/android/os/Handler.

114 ■ *Building Android Projects with Kotlin*

In general, `LoginLocalDataSource` will have a local database call (or preferences or files). To keep our example small and simple, we are using a dummy implementation in `LoginLocalDataSource`.

Similarly, we can implement `LoginRemoteDataSource`, which would be doing network calls to validate credentials.

This was an example to show how we separate code at different layers using MVP Architecture Pattern. This project is available at the BPB GitHub repository.

We saw how View and Presenter interact with each other and how Presenter interacts with the Model and get results from the Model; at last, let us see the sequence diagram to understand the flow in MVP as shown in *figure 3.4*:

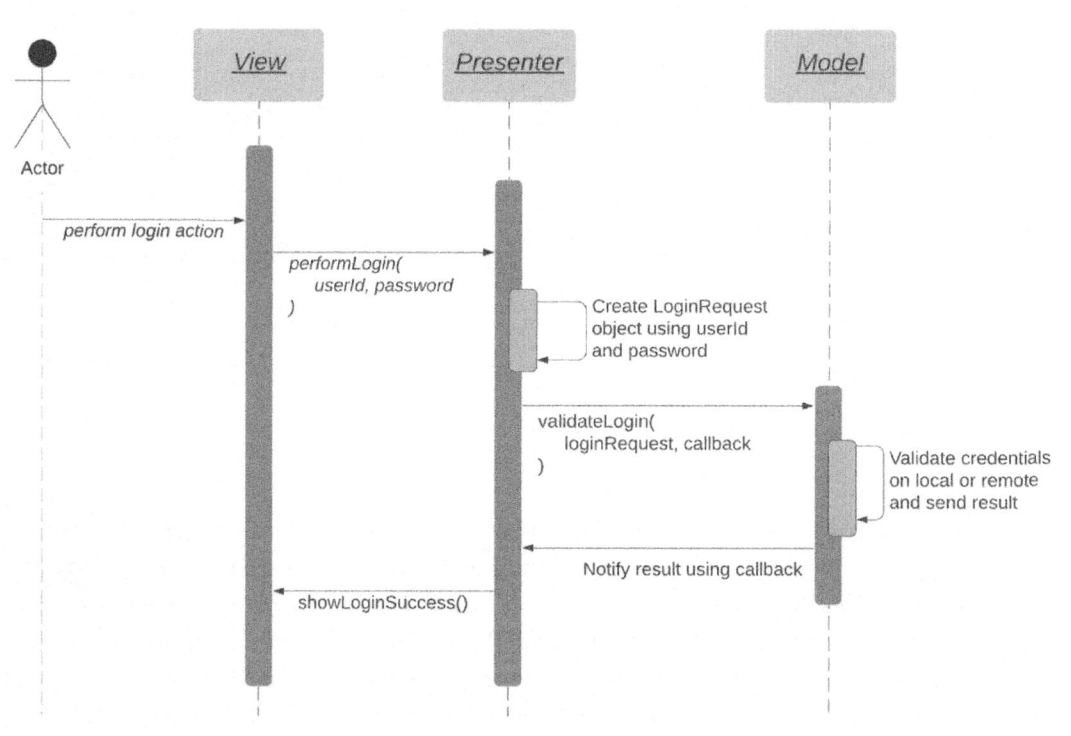

Figure 3.4: Sequence diagram to understand the flow in MVP

The preceding *figure 3.4* shows a sequence diagram of the code example of MVP, which we saw in this section before.

Advantages of using MVP

The following are advantages of MVP:

- Module responsibilities are divided. So now, code is easier to read and maintain.
- The View layer is light (contains very little code) as it has code only to update the UI as it does not perform any data operations.
- Code reusability and flexibility increased
- Business logic is separated from the UI layer, which makes mocking simple, and as a result, we can write more test cases and get better Test case coverage.

Disadvantages of MVP

The following are disadvantages of MVP:

- The presenter keeps a reference of View (Activity); it is a tight coupling between these two. This approach leads to less-generic code as the presenter cannot be used for other Views.
- The presenter keeps a reference of View, which may lead to an Activity leak if not used correctly.
- View (Activity/Fragment) may not be active when the presenter tries to update View, so we need to check if View is alive to handle the update. See uses of `loginView.isActive` in `LoginPresenter` class.
- It requires a lot of interfaces for interaction between layers.

Understanding MVVM

MVVM for android was introduced with Android architecture components. It stands for **Model View ViewModel**. In MVP, we used Presenter, and in MVVM, we used ViewModel. This replacement solves many problems which exist in MVP. The following are a few important points about MVVM:

- The View and ViewModel are not tightly coupled as View and Presenter were in MVP. ViewModel does not keep the reference of View, and only View has a reference of ViewModel.
- The recommendation is to keep one ViewModel for a View, but you may have more than one ViewModel with a View to follow the "Single Responsibility" of the SOLID principle.

- We use LiveData in ViewModel, which is a lifecycle-aware observable data holder. So no check is required now for view active to show UI update or not. See uses of the isActive variable of **LoginActivity** in the MVP code example.

Let us understand MVVM using *figure 3.5*, which shows about components and communication flow in MVVM:

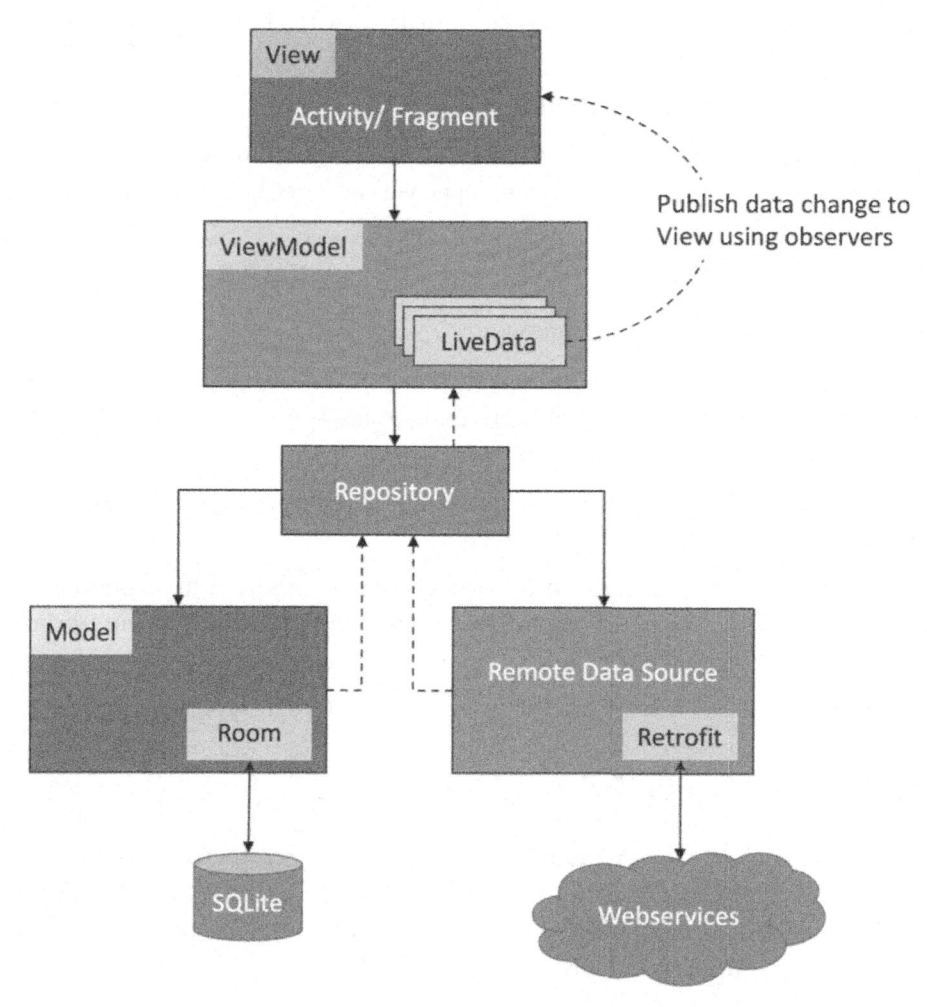

Figure 3.5: *Components and communication flow in MVVM*

The communication happens as same as MVP but with some improvement. Let us take the same example of saving notes as we saw while looking at MVP. In MVVM, when you click on the **Save** button, the view sends the title and description to ViewModel to save a note. Then ViewModel talks to the repository to save notes at the local or remote database. After getting the result of saving notes from the data layer, ViewModel publishes the result to View via LiveData.

Let us know more about the layers of MVVM:

- **Model**: Same as the Model of MVP, it handles application data. It is used to expose data for the ViewModel after retrieving requested data from the local or remote data source.
- **View**: View (Activity/Fragment) in MVVM binds to observables (LiveData) present in ViewModel, so no interface (callback pattern in-between View and ViewModel) is required for communication.
- **ViewModel**: It provides the data for specific UI components and contains data-handling business logic to communicate with the Model. The ViewModel does not know about View (Activity/Fragment), so it does not get affected by configuration changes, and it does not get recreated in case of recreating activity on orientation/config change.

NOTE:

- **Communication happens between View to ViewModel using the reference of ViewModel. LiveData in ViewModel emits data changes which View uses to observe and update UI. No callback/ interfaces involve in communication.**
- **A View can have more than one ViewModel.**
- **Similar to MVP, the Communication chain is like View -> ViewModel -> Model. It means a View cannot talk with the Model directly.**

Understanding MVVM with code

Figure 3.6 shows the project structure for MVVM. We are using the same login feature for an example for MVVM too, so it will be easier to compare MVP and MVVM and understand code differences between these too architecture patterns:

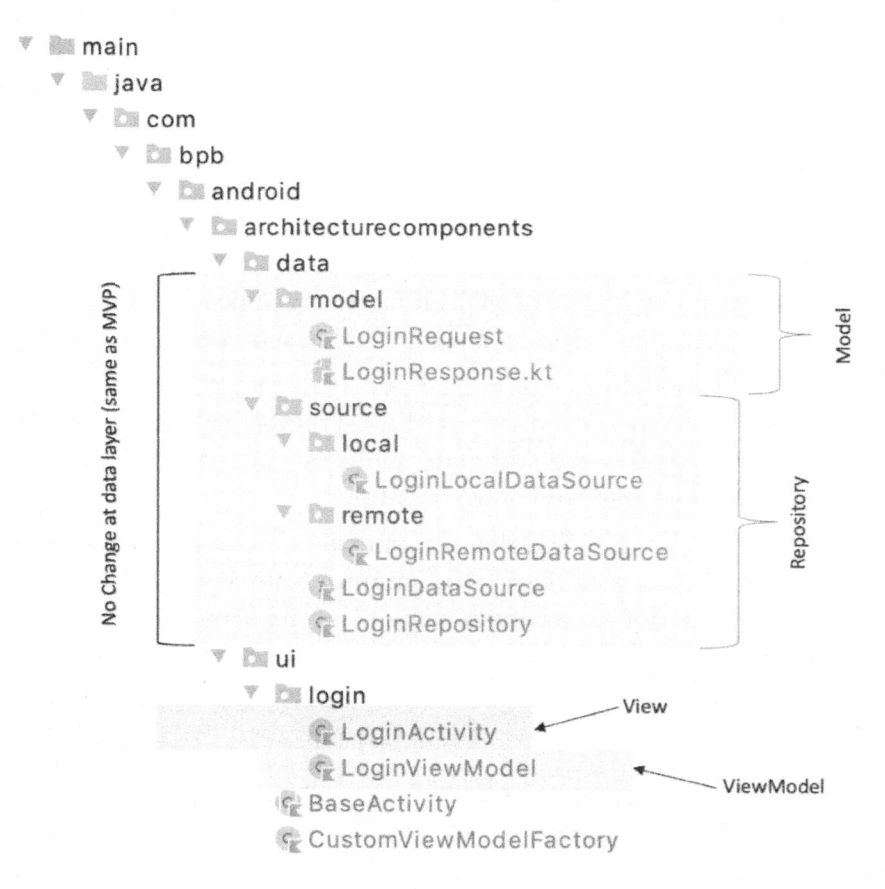

```
▼ ■ main
    ▼ ■ java
        ▼ ■ com
            ▼ ■ bpb
                ▼ ■ android
                    ▼ ■ architecturecomponents
                        ▼ ■ data
                            ▼ ■ model
                                    LoginRequest
                                    LoginResponse.kt
                            ▼ ■ source
                                ▼ ■ local
                                        LoginLocalDataSource
                                ▼ ■ remote
                                        LoginRemoteDataSource
                                    LoginDataSource
                                    LoginRepository
                        ▼ ■ ui
                            ▼ ■ login
                                    LoginActivity          ← View
                                    LoginViewModel         ← ViewModel
                                BaseActivity
                                CustomViewModelFactory
```

On the left side: "No Change at data layer (same as MVP)" bracketing data. On the right: "Model" bracketing model folder, "Repository" bracketing source/LoginDataSource/LoginRepository.

Figure 3.6: *Project structure for MVVM*

As you can see in the preceding *figure 3.6*, the data layer (Model and Repository) is the same as MVP, but a new class, **LoginViewModel** has been added to the project, and **LoginContract** and **LoginPresenter** have been removed. In MVVM, we use ViewModel, so **LoginPresenter** is removed, and ViewModel does not know about View, so **LoginContract** is removed.

Let us look into View and ViewModel code to understand how communication happens between these two components and how we removed tight-coupling between View-Presenter of MVP in MVVM with ViewModel:

- **LoginViewModel.kt**:

    Let us write ViewModel, which uses LiveData to keep results from the data layer and publishes changes that can be observed by View. Note that ViewModel survives configuration changes, so you do not need to care about the data refresh on configuration changes, as ViewModel does not gets recreated as Activity gets created on configuration change:

```kotlin
class LoginViewModel(private val repository: LoginRepository) : ViewModel() {
    private val _loginState = MutableLiveData<LoginResponse>()
    val loginState: LiveData<LoginResponse>
        get() = _loginState

    private val _loginInprogress = MutableLiveData<Boolean>()
    val loginInprogress: LiveData<Boolean>
        get() = _loginInprogress

    fun performLogin(userName: String, password: String) {
        // Post update for data processing is in-progress. If
        // View want to show progress can show on update.
        _loginInprogress.postValue(true)

        // Prepare data format required by model layer.
        // Like here, we are creating LoginRequest object with
        // required data.
        val loginRequest = LoginRequest(userName, password)

        // Asking model using repository to validate credentials,
        // and expecting result by callback. See implementation
        // of callback
        repository.validateLogin(loginRequest, callback)
    }

    private val callback = object : LoginDataSource.LoginCallback
    {
        override fun onCredentialsValidated(loginResponse: LoginResponse) {
            // Post update for login success. If View is still
            alive or still
```

```
            // observing for data change will get update.

            // Post update the in-progress task is done. So View
            // can hide progress indicator view.
            _loginInprogress.postValue(false)
            // Post data for login success
            _loginState.postValue(loginResponse)
        }

        override fun onCredentialInvalid() {
            // Post update for login success.
            // If View is still alive or still
            // observing for data change will get update.

            // Post update the in-progress task is done. So View
            // can hide progress indicator view.
            _loginInprogress.postValue(false)

            // We can use either custom message created here or
            // can utilize response from server, in that
            // can data-source would be passing
            // status as argument of onCredentialInvalid().
            _loginState.postValue(
                LoginResponse(
                    false,
                    null,
                    "Invalid Credentials"
                )
            )
        }
    }
}
```

NOTE: The difference between LiveData and MutableLiveData is the ability to edit the stored value. LiveData has no publicly available methods to update the stored data. The MutableLiveData class has two public methods, setValue(T) and postValue(T), which we use to edit the value stored in a LiveData object.

Usually, MutableLiveData is used in the ViewModel, and then the ViewModel only exposes immutable LiveData objects to the observers. Like in our LoginViewModel class, the variable _ loginState is the type of MutableLiveData, and it is privately accessible, whereas loginState is the type of LiveData and publicly accessible.

The benefit of this approach is that the ViewModel (that is, LoginViewModel) can edit the value of LiveData as it has access to _loginState (an object of MutableLiveData), but outside of the ViewModel, no one can change the value of LiveData as loginState (an object of LiveData) is exposed outside of ViewModel.

In the code of **LoginViewModel**, we are using two LiveData **loginInprogress** and **loginStat**e. These two livedata keep the state of progress of login-request and result of login-request. View (**LoginActivity**) is used to observe these LiveData objects for updates. If you remember, we were keeping the object of View into Presenter to update View (See **LoginPresenter** code in MVP section). But here in MVVM, ViewModel (**LoginViewModel**) does not have any reference to View (**LoginActivity**); that is why we say that ViewModel does not know about View.

ViewModel is used to post the update, and the View has the power to decide whether it wants to (still) listen for data change or not, using subscribe and unsubscribe methods.

- **LoginActivity.kt**:

Let us write **LoginActivity**, which will use **LoginViewModel** to do login call and observes data (live data) changes to handle the result of the login action:

```kotlin
class LoginActivity : BaseActivity() {

    private lateinit var loginViewModel: LoginViewModel

    override fun onCreate(savedInstanceState: Bundle?) {
        super.onCreate(savedInstanceState)
        setContentView(R.layout.activity_login)
        setUp()
```

```kotlin
    }

    override fun setUp() {
        // As you see the LoginViewModel has dependency
        // on LoginRepository, we need our own
        // ViewModelProvider.Factory to create an object of
        // LoginViewModel. The CustomViewModelFactory class
        // in the following code, does the same and it
        // creates an instance of LoginViewModel and
        // provides an instance of LoginRepository created
        // at line 17.
        val factory = CustomViewModelFactory(
                LoginRepository(
                        LoginLocalDataSource()
                )
        )
        // In case if LoginViewModel does not have dependency
        // (it does not need any argument) then the object
        // of LoginViewModel can be created as
        // ViewModelProvider(this).get(
        // LoginViewModel::class.java
        // )
        // As of now we will create an object using
        // CustomViewModelFactory.
        loginViewModel = factory.create(LoginViewModel::class.java)

        loginViewModel.loginInprogress.observe(this){ inProgress->
            showProgress(inProgress)
        }

        loginViewModel.loginState.observe(this) { response ->
```

Architecture Patterns

```kotlin
            if (response.success) {
                response.userInfo?.let { userInfo ->
                    showPostLoginPage(userInfo.name)
                }
            } else {
                showLoginFailed()
            }
        }

        btnLogin?.setOnClickListener {
            doLogin()
        }
    }

    private fun showPostLoginPage(userName: String) {
        // We can show next activity after login success.
    }

    private fun showLoginFailed() {
        // Notify user about Login Failure.
    }

    private fun showProgress(show: Boolean) {
        progressBar.visibility = if (show) View.VISIBLE else View.GONE
    }

    private fun doLogin() {
        when {
            edtUserName?.text.toString() == "" ->
                tilUserName.error = getString(R.string.err_msg_
                user_name)

            edtPassword?.text.toString() == "" ->
```

```
                        tilPassword.error = getString(R.string.err_msg_
                        password)

                else -> loginViewModel.performLogin(
                        edtUserName?.text.toString(),
                        edtPassword?.text.toString()
                    )
                }
            }
        }
```

The code of `LoginActivity` is similar to the code which we used in MVP. But notice that, in `LoginActivity.kt`, `setUp()` is the method where we created the object of `LoginViewModel` and started observing `loginViewModel.loginInprogress` and `loginViewModel.loginState`, so UI can be changed whenever `LoginViewModel` posts the update on these LiveData.

TIP: LiveData is a lifecycle-aware observable, which means LiveData makes sure that only those components (like Activities/Fragments) can get updates that have an active lifecycle state. We used to follow the following steps for using of LiveData in MVVM:

- Create an object of LiveData with the type that LiveData can hold.
- Start observing this LiveData in Activity/Fragment, where we get updates in the onChanged() method.
- While observing LiveData, we pass an object of LifecycleOwner (Activity/Fragment/viewLifeCycleOwner, and so on). This smart implementation of LiveData with LifecycleOwner makes sure that we should not care about if View is alive to handle updates from LiveData or not. This is the reason we are not using code to check the View state (like we used loginView.isActive in MVP).

Instead of observing LiveData in View to do some changes on UI, we can also use Databinding in MVVM, which was the initial recommendation from Android, and ViewModel was introduced with Databinding. Let us see how we can use Databinding.

Using databinding

The databinding library is part of the architecture component that is used to bind UI components in layouts (layout XML files) to data sources using declarative format instead of programmatically.

First, we need to configure the project to use data binding. Add the following code to the app/build.gradle:

```
android {

    .....

    dataBinding {
        enabled = true
    }

    .....

}
```

Need to add a few codes in **activity_login.xml**:

```
<?xml version="1.0" encoding="utf-8"?>
<layout xmlns:android="http://schemas.android.com/apk/res/android"
    xmlns:app="http://schemas.android.com/apk/res-auto"
    xmlns:tools="http://schemas.android.com/tools"
    tools:context=".ui.login.LoginActivity">

    <data>

        <import type="android.view.View" />

        <variable
            name="loginLiveData"
            type="com.bpb.android.architecturecomponents.ui.login.LoginViewModel" />

    </data>
```

```xml
<!-- Root layout of Login screen. Exact the same as MVP or
    previous example of MVVM.

    Notice code of <ProgressBar> android:visibility handles Livedata
    changes
-->
<androidx.constraintlayout.widget.ConstraintLayout
    android:layout_width="match_parent"
    android:layout_height="match_parent">

    <ProgressBar
        android:id="@+id/progressBar"
        style="?android:attr/progressBarStyle"
        ....
        android:visibility="@{(loginLiveData.loginInprogress ==
        true) ? View.VISIBLE : View.GONE}"
        ...
        />

</androidx.constraintlayout.widget.ConstraintLayout>

</layout>
```

We added the **<data>** section with variable and import statement, and you can relate these two with normal variable declaration and import statement of Kotlin/Java code.

Notice that we are handling visibility of progress bar using **android:visibility="@{(loginLiveData.loginInprogress == true) ? View.VISIBLE : View.GONE}"**. And now we do not need to observe livedata in **LoginActivity** to update the visibility of progressbar.

The following is the code of **LoginActivity.kt**:

```kotlin
class LoginActivity : BaseActivity() {

    private lateinit var loginViewModel: LoginViewModel
    ......
    override fun setUp() {
        val factory = CustomViewModelFactory(
            LoginRepository(
                LoginLocalDataSource()
            )
        )
        loginViewModel = factory.create(LoginViewModel::class.java)

        val binding: ActivityLoginBinding = DataBindingUtil.setContentView(
            this,
            R.layout.activity_login
        )
        binding.loginLiveData = loginViewModel
        binding.lifecycleOwner = this

        loginViewModel.loginState.observe(this) { response ->
            if (response.success) {
                response.userInfo?.let { userInfo ->
                    showPostLoginPage(userInfo.name)
                }
            } else {
                showLoginFailed()
            }
        }

        btnLogin?.setOnClickListener {
            doLogin()
```

```
        }
    }
    .....
}
```

So you can see we removed **`loginViewModel.loginInprogress.observe(…)`** code because now this task is done by DataBinding in **`activity_login.xml`**.

Note that we can do a lot of things using databinding, like we can add click handlers for the widget in XML itself, can change state, or can do cosmetic changes.

We saw how MVVM can be used for the project. We also saw how we can observe and do UI changes or use databinding. At last, let us see a sequence diagram to understand the flow of MVVM as shown in *figure 3.7*:

Sequence Diagram
MVVM

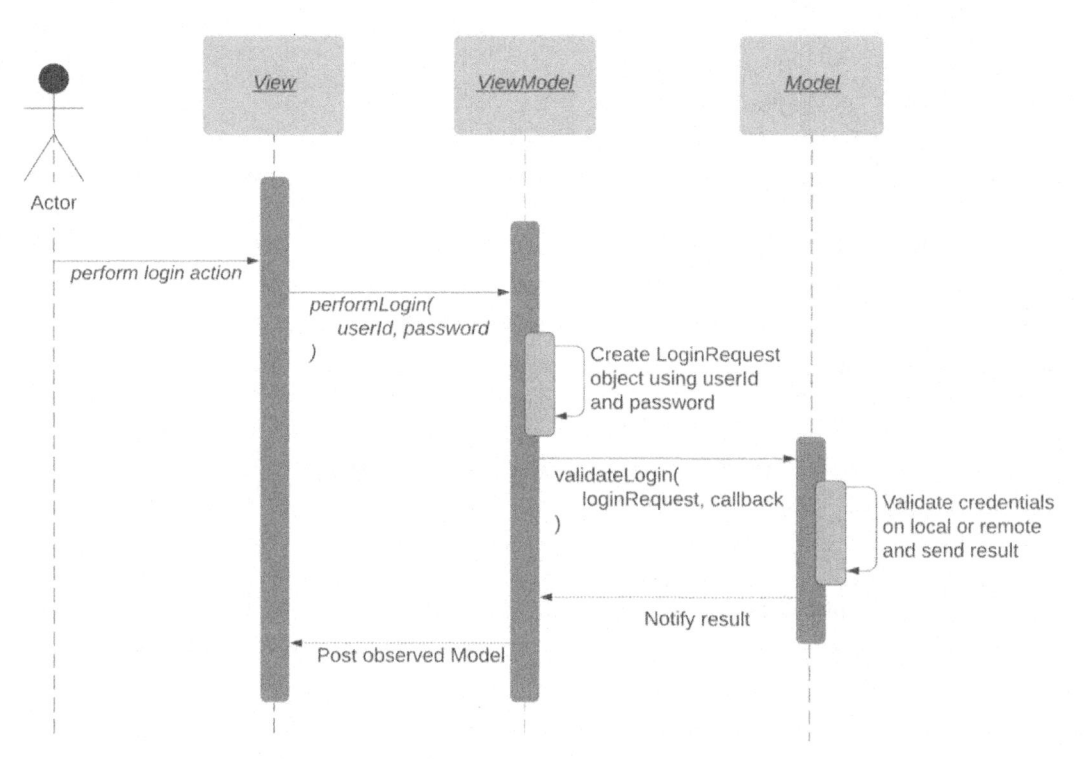

Figure 3.7: Sequence diagram to understand the flow of MVVM

Advantages of using MVVM

The following are advantages of MVVM:

- MVVM is recommended by Android, so we get many libraries (known as Architecture components) that better fit with MVVM.
- Data Binding enables automatic updates. When ViewModel changes, then View will be updated automatically. And if the binding is done in both directions and if View gets changed, ViewModel will also get changed automatically.
- As in MVVM, ViewModel does not control the UI (like the presenter does in MVP); we do not need to write code in ViewModel to update View. So, it makes ViewModel cleaner and lighter.

Disadvantages of MVVM

The following are disadvantages of MVVM:

- While using data binding, the code can be seen in the form of XML. Sometimes this confuses the developer, and it also makes debugging process complicated.
- Debugging bugs can be hard when we use Data binding.
- Large modules or models are not efficient for the release of memory.

MVVM with UseCases

While using MVVM, we may end with writing large codes into ViewModel, which may not follow the "Single Responsibility" of Clean architecture, and if a few features at a screen are being used on more than one screen, you might end up with code duplicity in different ViewModels. Let us think about an application for online shopping, where we use to show Cart on almost all screens. So the question is, should we write code for showing the count of items in Cart in each ViewModel? If we write this code in each ViewModel, do all ViewModel follow Clean Architecture ("Single Responsibility")? The answer is "No".

Here, UseCase comes into the picture. First, look into *figure 3.8* to understand how it will be added to MVVM:

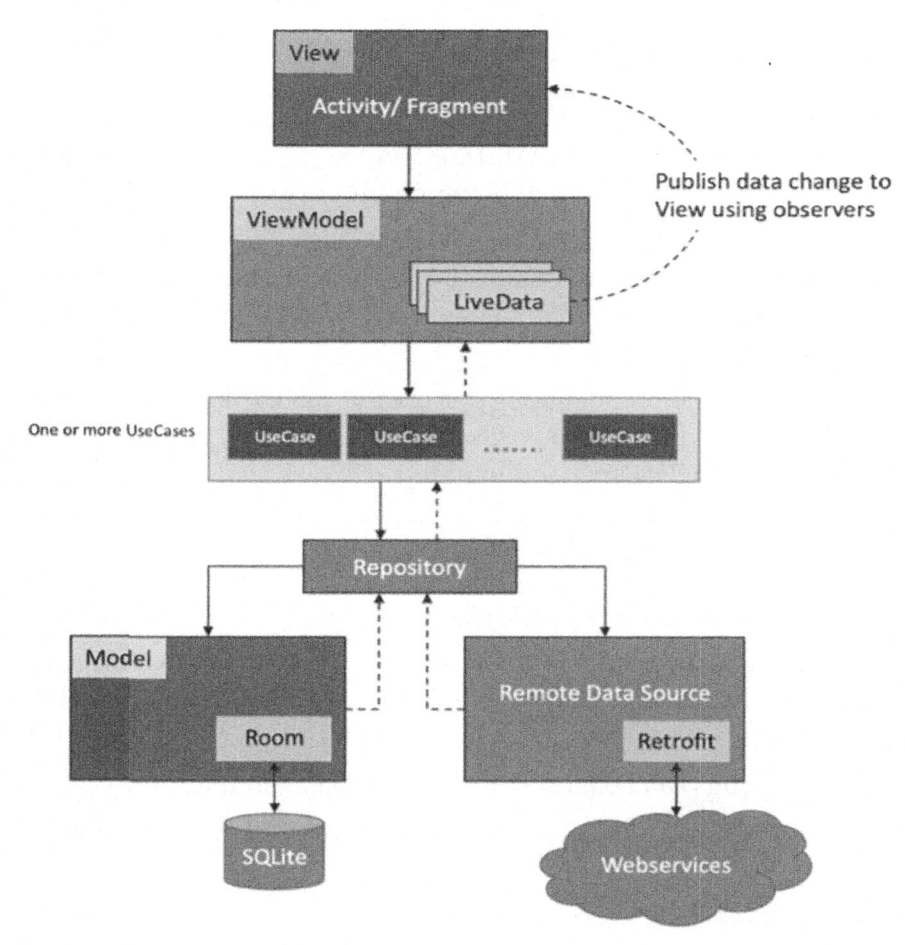

Figure 3.8: MVVM with UseCases

In the preceding *figure 3.8*, we have added UseCases in between ViewModel and Repository. Note that we can use UseCases into MVP as well, which goes in between Presenter and Repository.

NOTE: **The use-case refers to the class/component that contains the business rules/ business logic. The dependency rule defines that the use case (the business logic) should not have (compile) dependencies to the view, any external framework, or IO.**

These use cases Orchestrate the flow of data to and from the entities and direct those entities to use their critical business rules to achieve the goals of the use case.

Coming back to our Cart example for an online shopping application. For example, let us take a screen that shows the best deals from each product category and the count of items in the Cart. So going with UseCases, we create at least two UseCases, one for Cart and the second for getting the best deals for each product category. So let us take an example code that keeps everything in a single ViewModel, and after that, we will look at the same ViewModel with UseCases.

Let us look into the code of Repository for Cart and Best Deals:

- **BestDealDataSource.kt**:

    Let us write the Data source for the best deals:

    ```
    interface BestDealsDataSource {

        interface BestDealsCallback {

            fun onBestDealsFetched(response: BestDealsResponse)
        }

        fun getBestDeals(callback: BestDealsCallback)
    }
    ```

- **CartDataSource.kt**:

    Let us write the data source for the cart:

    ```
    interface CartDataSource {

        interface CartItemsCallback {

            fun onCartItemsFetched(response: CartResponse)
        }

        fun getCartItems(callback: CartItemsCallback)
    }
    ```

- **BestDealsRepository.kt**:

    Let us write the repository class for best deals, where we would be using **BestDealsDataSource** to get the best deals:

    ```
    class BestDealsRepository(
            private val remoteDataSource: BestDealsDataSource
    ) : BestDealsDataSource {

        override fun getBestDeals(
                callback: BestDealsDataSource.BestDealsCallback
    ```

```
        ) {
            remoteDataSource.getBestDeals(
                object : BestDealsDataSource.BestDealsCallback {

                    override fun onBestDealsFetched(
                        response: BestDealsResponse
                    ) {
                        callback.onBestDealsFetched(response)
                    }
                }
            )
        }
    }
```

- **CartRepository.kt**:

    Let us write the repository class for the cart, where we would be using **CartDataSource** to get cart items:

```
class CartRepository(
        private val remoteDataSource: CartDataSource
) : CartDataSource {

    override fun getCartItems(
            callback: CartDataSource.CartItemsCallback
    ) {
        remoteDataSource.getCartItems(
                object : CartDataSource.CartItemsCallback {

                    override fun onCartItemsFetched(
                            response: CartResponse
                    ) {
                        callback.onCartItemsFetched(response)
                    }
                }
        )
```

}
}

Till now, we have written code for the repository which follows the SOLID principle. We skipped adding code here for Local or Remote data source implementation. You can assume we have implementation for data sources to fetch cart or deals data from local or server, similar to previously seen **LoginLocalDataSource** or **LoginRemoteDataSource** in login flow example.

Now, let us see how ViewModel can break the SOLID principle and how we can use UseCases to correct it.

- **BestDealsViewModel.kt**:

Let us write ViewModel without the uses of UseCases and see the problem:

```kotlin
class BestDealsViewModel(
        private val dealsRepository: BestDealsRepository,
        private val cartRepository: CartRepository
) : ViewModel() {

    private val _bestDeals = MutableLiveData<BestDealsResponse>()
    val bestDeals: LiveData<BestDealsResponse>
        get() = _bestDeals

    private val _cart = MutableLiveData<CartResponse>()
    val cart: LiveData<CartResponse>
        get() = _cart

    private val _dataLoading = MutableLiveData<Boolean>(false)
    val dataLoading: LiveData<Boolean>
        get() = this._dataLoading

    fun getCartItems() {
        _dataLoading.postValue(true)
        cartRepository.getCartItems(cartCallback)
    }

    fun getBestDeals() {
```

```kotlin
            _dataLoading.postValue(true)
            dealsRepository.getBestDeals(dealsCallback)
        }

        private val dealsCallback = object : BestDealsDataSource.BestDealsCallback {
            override fun onBestDealsFetched(response: BestDealsResponse) {
                _dataLoading.postValue(false)
                _bestDeals.postValue(response)
            }
        }

        private val cartCallback = object : CartDataSource.CartItemsCallback {
            override fun onCartItemsFetched(response: CartResponse) {
                _dataLoading.postValue(false)
                _cart.postValue(response)
            }
        }
}
```

As you see, this **BestDealsViewModel** class has more than one reason to update (that is, cart and best deals). And as some other pages are also showing cart information, so you have to write **getCartItems()** and Cart-related functions in each ViewModel. This means the same code again and again, and if any change is required, you may need to do changes at all ViewModel.

So let us rewrite **BestDealsViewModel** again with UseCases:

```kotlin
class BestDealsViewModel(
        private val cartUseCase: CartUseCase,
        private val bestDealsUseCase: BestDealsUseCase
) : ViewModel() {
    // Common code with previous BestDealsViewModel skipped.
    ....
```

```kotlin
fun getCartItems() {
    _dataLoading.postValue(true)
    cartUseCase.getCartItems(cartCallback)
}

fun getBestDeals() {
    _dataLoading.postValue(true)
    bestDealsUseCase.getBestDeals(dealsCallback)
}

private val dealsCallback = object : BestDealsCallback {
    override fun onBestDealsFetched(response:
    BestDealsResponse) {
        _dataLoading.postValue(false)
        _bestDeals.postValue(response)
    }
}

private val cartCallback = object : CartItemsCallback {
    override fun onCartItemsFetched(response: CartResponse) {
        _dataLoading.postValue(false)
        _cart.postValue(response)
    }
}
}
```

Notice that instead of passing repository as an argument in ViewModel, we are passing two UseCases **CartUseCase** and **BestDealsUseCase**. Let us look into the UseCases code.

- **BestDealsUseCase.kt:**

Let us write Best deal UseCase to write only deals-specific repository code:

```kotlin
class BestDealsUseCase(
    private val repository: BestDealsRepository
```

```
    ) {

        fun getBestDeals(
                callback: BestDealsDataSource.BestDealsCallback
        ) {
            return repository.getBestDeals(callback)
        }
    }
```
- **CartUseCase.kt**:

    Let us write cart UseCase to write only cart-specific repository code:
    ```
    class CartUseCase(
            private val repository: CartRepository
    ) {
        fun getCartItems(
                callback: CartDataSource.CartItemsCallback
        ) {
            return repository.getCartItems(callback)
        }
    }
    ```

Notice that we moved repository code into UseCases, and UseCases follow the "Single Responsibility" principle (deals-related method moved to BestDealsUseCase, and CartUseCase have now cart-related methods). Now, ViewModel of other screens can reuse CartUseCase if the cart feature is required.

So, if you want to strictly follow Clean Architecture, then you should use UseCases. UseCases are used for creating a more scalable project and reusing the code. The following are a few cases where we can use UseCases:

- If more than one ViewModel contains common logic for processing data (local or remote). Common logic can be moved into a UseCase, and UseCase can be used in different ViewModels.
- If we want to avoid God objects (an object that knows too much or does too much) that deal with both UI logic and data-flow logic. UseCases enable data-flow logic to be reusable across different ViewModels.
- If we are required to write caching logic or logic for switching between threads (for example, to read cache on the main thread or switch to a

background thread to perform a network call). In other words, if we want to do some tasks which should not be the responsibility of either ViewModel or Repository.

NOTE: **If you look into our previous code examples such as UseCases, ViewModel, and Repositories, we are passing objects into the constructor. This is known as a constructor-based injection, where we are providing dependency to the class. This is the way how we solve the dependencies problem. We already discussed the "Dependency Inversion Principle" while understanding SOLID principles.**

The constructor-based injection is fine for small-sized applications, but as application size grows, it can be problematic. So we can use any dependency injection library. Hilt and Dagger are two libraries that we can use in our application.

So you learned about MVP, MVVM, and UseCases, and while developing a project, you can decide which architecture pattern best suits the project. Note that using architecture pattern is not mandatory, but it is the recommendation to use, as it is going to make your many tasks easy in the long term.

NOTE: Apart from MVP and MVVM, there are other architectures too which can be used for our Android projects.

MVI and VIPER. "Model View Intent" is newly introduced with Android, which is a unidirectional and reactive pattern based on Finite State Machine and originated from Redux (Java Script Library).

And "View Interactor Presenter Entity Router" is originally from iOS. This five-layered architecture aims to assign different tasks to each layer by following the Single Responsibility Principle.

As we discussed earlier, an Architecture pattern sets some rules to organize our code. Depending on the expertise of our team or the size of the project, we should choose one of these Architectures which suits better in our requirements.

Conclusion

In this chapter, we have learned about Clean Architecture. We learned about the requirement and benefits of an architectural pattern. We also got to know about SOLID principles, where we learned about "Single Responsibility", "Open Closed", "Liskov's Substitution", "Interface Segregation", and "Dependency Inversion" principles by example code.

We got to know about MVP, where we learned about the separation of code and applying SOLID principles to each layer. We also read about MVVM and learned how MVVM handles data changes without tight coupling between View and ViewModel. We learned about LiveData and learned its benefits.

We also got to know about UseCases and learned how UseCase help to achieve the *Single Responsibility* principle and increase reusable code. You can perform the extra task on data without changing code ViewModel, caching or switching between threads, and so on.

While reading about all these architecture patterns, we learned about Repository Pattern, which is a pattern to design our data layer. It makes it easy to switch between local or remote data sources, clean code, and easy to modify.

In the upcoming chapter, we will develop a Chat Application and learn about the uses of Fragments, RecyclerView, resources, material library, Notifications, and Basic knowledge of Firebase.

Points to remember

- Writing code without any defined architecture is usually unreadable and unmaintainable. You should always have an architecture for your project.
- While writing code, you should always consider SOLID principles and make sure your code follows them.
- MVP uses callbacks/interfaces for communication, which leads to tight coupling between layers.
- In MVVM, ViewModel is a key component that is lifecycle-aware, so handling of data becomes easier, and now you do not need to check every time if View is alive before updating View.
- MVVM removed tight coupling between View and Presenter (in MVP) by replacing Presenter with ViewModel. ViewModel does not know about View.
- Repository patterns are for the data layer. It gives you more flexibility for data sources. You can switch local/remote data sources and change the database without affecting other layers. And you can create a separate module for the data layer for the application.

Multiple Choice Questions

1. What are the benefits of clean architecture?
   A. Cost-effective code in the long run
   B. Easily testable code
   C. High level of abstraction
   D. Loose coupling between code
   E. All of the above

2. Which SOLID principle is about "Open for extension Closed for modification"?
   A. Open closed principle
   B. Single Responsibility
   C. Dependency Inversion
   D. Interface Segregation

3. What is LiveData?
   A. A UI component
   B. Used to get data from the data source
   C. A data holder
   D. None of the above

4. Which is/are the characteristics of ViewModel?
   A. It is Lifecycle aware
   B. It does not have a dependency on View
   C. It does not get recreated on config changes (like orientation change)
   D. All of the above

5. UseCases follow the "Single Responsibility" principle
   A. True
   B. False

Answers

1. E
2. A
3. C
4. D
5. A

Questions

1. Why do we need an architectural pattern?
2. What are SOLID principles?
3. How does MVP increase tight coupling between view and presenter?
4. Why MVVM is better? What are the architecture components provided by Android SDK?
5. What is the repository pattern? What are the benefits of using it?

Key Terms

- Clean architecture
- SOLID principles
- Single responsibility principle
- Open closed principle
- Liskov's substitution principle
- Interface segregation principle
- Dependency inversion principle
- MVP
- MVVM
- ViewModel
- LiveData
- UseCases
- Repository pattern

CHAPTER 4
Developing Chat Application

In the previous chapter, we read about Architecture Patterns in Android and understood about choosing the right architecture for your application.

In this chapter, we will create our first chat application. While creating and developing this project, we will learn a few Android View, choosing server technology, and Firebase.

We will learn requirement gathering for chat application and finalize the list of features that we are going to add to our first chat application, and then we will understand how to develop all those features.

Structure

In this chapter, we will cover the following topics:
- Gathering functional requirement
- Creating user flow diagrams
- Introducing server
    - Choosing better backend technology
    - Introducing BaaS

- Introducing Firebase and its services
    - Adding Firebase to application
    - Identifying and introducing firebase service
- Introducing Android Jetpack
    - Introducing RecyclerView
    - Introducing TabLayout and ViewPager
- Understanding project structure of Chat app
- Writing code for the first screen
- Developing login screen
- Developing of chat home screen
- Developing contacts screen
- Developing chat screen
- Developing profile screen
- Using of notifications

Objectives

The objective of this chapter is to let you know about developing a chat application, and our focus will be to understand the process in terms of Android applications. This chapter will explain a bit about system design, where we will be finding functional requirements for a chat application and developing those requirements by choosing the right backend technology. After completing this chapter, you will also have a clear understanding of converting requirements into code.

We will also learn about Jetpack libraries, like RecyclerView, and notifying users of new messages if a user gets a message but the user is not online or not using the application at that time.

Gathering functional requirement

Functional requirements are the list of features for the specific application. It explains about input/output and behavior of an application.

So first, let us find out the functional requirement for the chat application:
1. Users can login or register. Basic login features should be there, like login by phone/email/or Google, and so on.
2. Show a list of registered users, so users can select to chat.
3. Users can see the profile page. The profile can be either of a logged-in user or a profile of friends.
   a) Logged-in user can change their profile picture and name and can log out from the application.
   b) Users can select a photo from the phone gallery or can take a photo.
   c) Users can view the profile of contacts from the contact list of the application.

These are functional requirements for a messaging application, and we will be developing our chat application for these requirements.

Note that these are not the complete list of requirements for any messaging application. There can be more features for a messaging application. It depends on what features you want to add to your chat application, as follows:
- There can be a group chat feature.
- Users can share media files such as photos, videos, audios, or documents.
- You can also support voice or video calls, where users can do one-to-one or group calls and can manage calls like mute/unmute or hold the call.
- Users can invite their friends who are not registered on the application.

Creating user flow diagrams

Let us create a flow diagram as shown in *figure 4.1* for our chat application. It will give you an idea about the overall chat application flow:

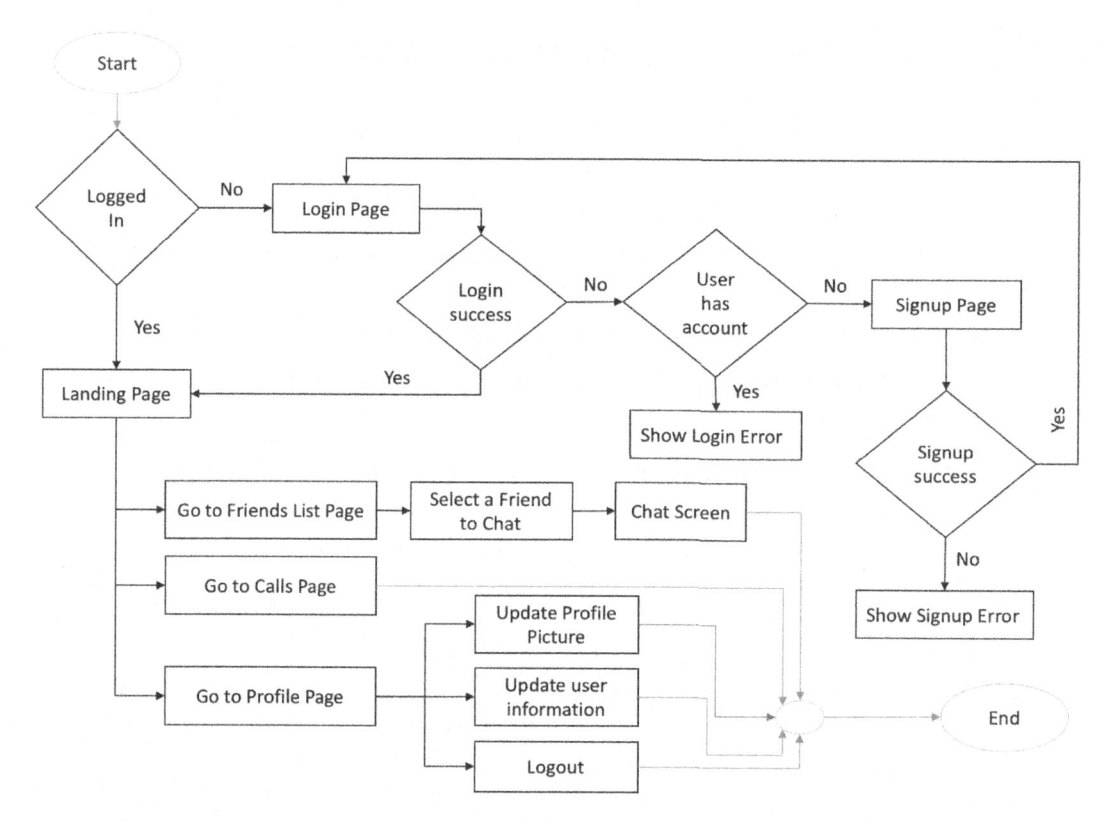

Figure 4.1: User flow diagram

Introducing server

Servers are dedicated computers that provide services on behalf of the client. It is a centralized machine where multiple clients can connect to the internet on a local area network. The server provides a specific service to the client, like a server can be used for accessing data, accessing emails, and accessing websites.

Usually, large organizations use multiple servers for delivering specific tasks to each server, like one server can handle the website, one can handle database requests, and one can handle emails. In small organizations, only one server can be used to handle all types of requests.

NOTE: **Servers used to be powerful machines but we can use our daily uses computers too as a server.**

Choosing better backend technology

Backend development is used to create an **Application Programming Interface (API)**, which serves data to the user interface. API can serve data to any platform.

For backend development, we commonly use two types of programming languages:

- **Server-side programming language** that helps build the API. Generally, we use Python, Java, JavaScript, Ruby, and PHP, which help us to build the API.
- **Structured Query language (SQL)** is used to fetch the data from the database.

The preceding two require skills in writing code that serves UI faster and synchronized data. Now, the question is how to decide on better technology? Secrete is that there is no best programming language in general. Technology is better if it serves your requirements. Each has its characteristics and drawbacks.

We can create a checklist for our requirements and can evaluate each language; whoever fits better, that is a better language for us. The checklist can be as follows:

- **Technical expertise**: While choosing the right language, the technical capability of the team plays an important role. It requires very good knowledge of the language while designing the framework. Sometimes organizations choose to hire experts if they do not have expertise in the chosen language. So, choosing such a language in which you do not have expertise can cost you more.
- **Identifying Domain and Technology**: Depending on the domain of the business, the right technology may differ. For example, if you are building a data analysis solution, Python may fit better. If you are building an enterprise solution, you can think of Java and .NET.
- **Choosing Language**: As you see above both points, choosing a language depending on expertise or domain is important, but choosing language depending on the characteristics of a language is equally important. It is always better to hire someone if you do not have technical expertise than to choose a language if you have the expertise, even if the chosen language does not fit better in your requirement.

These commonly used languages are Python, Java, Ruby, ASP .NET, and PHP. So, depending on the requirement, always evaluate these languages/community support, and so on.

For our chat application, instead of writing backend, we will look any BaaS solution that can do our backend-related tasks. Before going ahead, let us explore a little bit about BaaS.

Introducing BaaS

BaaS stands for Backend-as-a-Service. It provides services such as Authentication, database management, cloud storage, hosting, push notifications, and so on. In other words, it can act as the backend of our application, and you, as a developer, have to develop only the frontend (as in our case, a mobile app only). And you save a lot of time and resources to design and implement the backend.

For our chat application, we will be using BaaS, as it serves all of our requirements. There are many BaaS providers, such as Firebase, Parse, AWS Amplify, Back4App, Kinvey, and many more. For our chat application, we will use Firebase as a BaaS provider.

Introducing Firebase and its services

Firebase is a cross-platform BaaS from Google. It supports all features written previously for a BaaS, including Google search index and many more. Many big brands use Firebase, such as NY Times, The Economist, Alibaba.com, and so on.

It is supported on Android, iOS, and the Web, and you can start using it for free. It is free for limited uses, and after the limit, you need to pay. So, first of all, we will learn how to add Firebase to our application.

Adding Firebase to application

There are two ways to add Firebase to your application. One is to add it via https://console.firebase.google.com/ and the second way is to add Firebase from Android Studio. Adding Firebase via console is recommended way, so we will read more about the first option, and we will add the Firebase project in three simple steps:

Step 1: Creating a Firebase project

In this step, we create a project on the Firebase console, which will be used to configure our Android application at Firebase:

1. Go to Firebase console https://console.firebase.google.com/ and click on **Add Project**.
2. Enter a project name. Note that you can edit the project id also; adding your project id is optional and cannot be changed once the project is created.
3. Review and accept the terms of Firebase if prompted.
4. Click on **Continue**

5. In the next window, we will be asked to set up Google Analytics. This is optional.
6. Click on **Create Project**.
7. After the process is completed, you will be redirected to the Project overview page.

Step 2: Registering the Android application with the Firebase project

In this step, we will register our Android application at the Firebase project:

1. Open to Firebase console https://console.firebase.google.com/ and click on the newly created project in Step 1. In our case, it would be BMessaging.
2. You will be navigated to the Project overview page. Click on the Android icon (🤖).
3. You will be navigated to the screen as shown in *figure 4.2*.

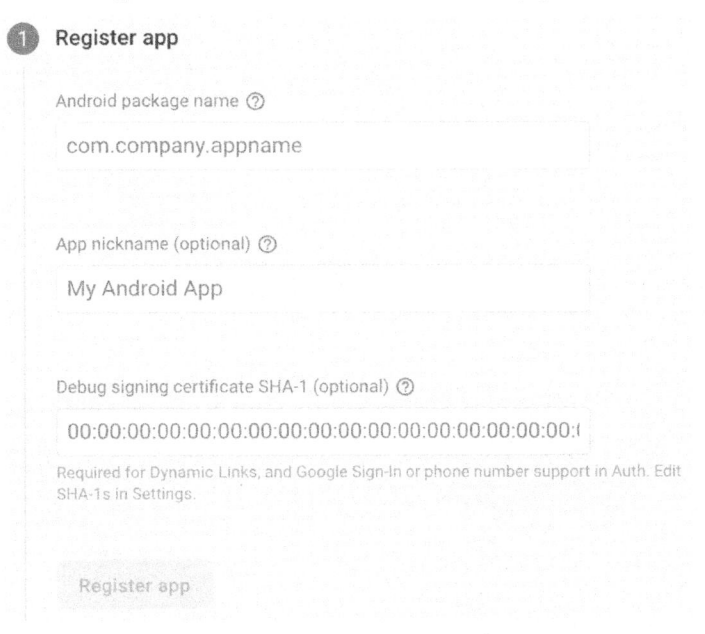

Figure 4.2: Registering app on Firebase console

4. Enter the package name in the Android package name field. Value of **applicationId** into build configs of **app/build.gradle** file is the package name of your application.
5. In the App nickname, you can add the name of your application. This is optional.

6. In Debug Signing certificates, we add the SHA-1 key of debug certificate. In most cases debug certificate that we use is provided by Android SDK itself. Although it is optional to add this key, we need to add it because of Google Sign-in or Phone authentication, which we are going to use in our chat application

7. Click on **Register app**.

Step 3: Adding Firebase configuration file to the Android project

After configuring our project at the Firebase console, now it is time to configure Firebase into our Android application. Let us configure it using the following steps:

1. After completing *Step 2*, you will be navigated to *Step 3*, as shown in *figure 4.3*:

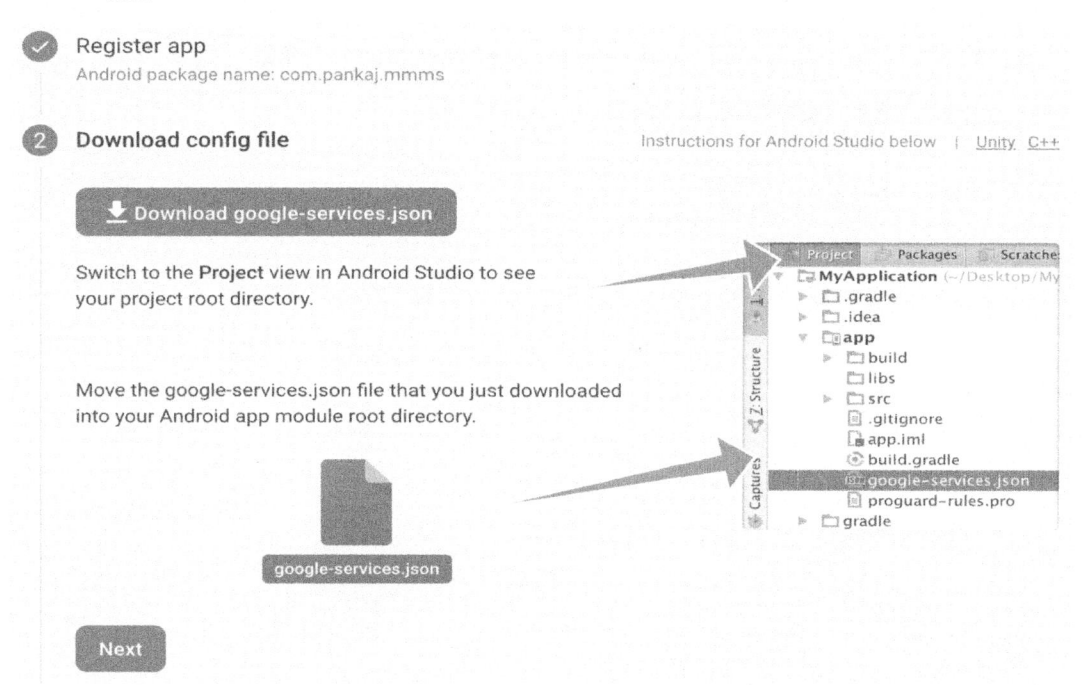

Figure 4.3: Adding Firebase config file to Android project

2. Download **google-services.json** and copy it to the app module, as shown in the preceding figure.

3. Now, we need to add rules for the Google Services Gradle plugin. So open project-level **build.gradle** file and add the following code:

```
// Top-level build file where you can add configuration
// options common to all sub-projects/modules.
Buildscript {
    // ...
    dependencies {
        classpath 'com.google.gms:google-services:4.3.10'
        // ...
    }
}
```

Here, 4.3.10 is the current version of Google Services. Android Studio gives you a hint about the latest version of any plugins.

4. And in the app-level **app/build.gradle** file, we need to apply the Google Services plugin as follows:

```
plugins {
    // ...
    id 'com.google.gms.google-services'
}
```

Now, we have enabled Firebase in our application. To use Firebase, we need Firebase SDK, so take the following steps.

Step 4: Adding Firebase SDKs to the app

In the app-level **app/build.gradle** file, write the following code:

```
dependencies {
    // ...
    // Import the BoM for the Firebase platform
    implementation platform('com.google.firebase:firebase-bom:28.4.2')
```

```
        // Declare the dependencies for the desired Firebase products
        // without specifying versions
        // For example, declare the dependencies for Firebase Authentication
        // and Cloud Storage library
        implementation 'com.google.firebase:firebase-auth'
        implementation 'com.google.firebase:firebase-storage'
}
```

The preceding code can be written as follows:

```
dependencies {
        // ...
        // Declare the dependencies for Firebase Authentication and
        // Cloud Storage library with specific versions
        implementation 'com.google.firebase:firebase-auth:21.0.1'
        implementation 'com.google.firebase:firebase-storage:20.0.0'
}
```

NOTE: **The benefit of using Firebase Bill of Materials (BoM) in your app is that the BoM automatically fetches the individual library versions mapped to BoM's version. Versions of those individual libraries will be compatible with each other. When we update the version of BoM, all the Firebase libraries which we are using in our application will be updated to the versions mapped to the updated BoM version.**

We are now all set to use Firebase in our chat application or in fact, in any application where you want to use Firebase services.

Now, let us find out which Firebase services can be used in our chat application and learn how we can use those services in the application.

Identifying and introducing Firebase services

For our chat application, we need auth service to provide login, a database to store chats and user's basic info specific to our application.

So as a backend of our chat application, we would be using the following Firebase features:
- Firebase Authentication
- Firebase Realtime Database
- Firebase Cloud Storage
- FirebaseUI for Android

Let us see how these services can be used.

Introducing Firebase Authentication

Firebase Authentication provides an end-to-end identify solution that supports authentication via email and password, phone, Google, Facebook, Twitter, GitHub, and so on. It integrates tightly with other Firebase services and can be easily integrated with your custom backend, as it supports industry standards like Oauth 2.0 or OpenID Connect. It also manages user sessions so the logged-in user can be logged in after the application restart.

Firebase Authentication integrates tightly with other Firebase services, and it can be easily integrated with your custom backend, as it supports industry standards like Oauth 2.0 or OpenID Connect.

When we use Firebase Authentication to sign users into our application, we need authentication credentials like email id and password or an Oauth token. Then we pass these credentials to the Firebase Authentication SDK, and Firebase backend services verify the given credentials and return the result (response) to our application (client). If the login is successful, we can access the user's profile information and can use other Firebase services.

TIP: We can use the authentication token to verify the identity of users in our backend services (in case we are using our own backend).

To enable Firebase authentication, we need to go to the project at Firebase and click **Authentication | Get started**. The authentication page will be shown. On the authentication page, enable sign-in providers **Email/Password**, **Phone**, and **Google,** as shown in *figure 4.4*:

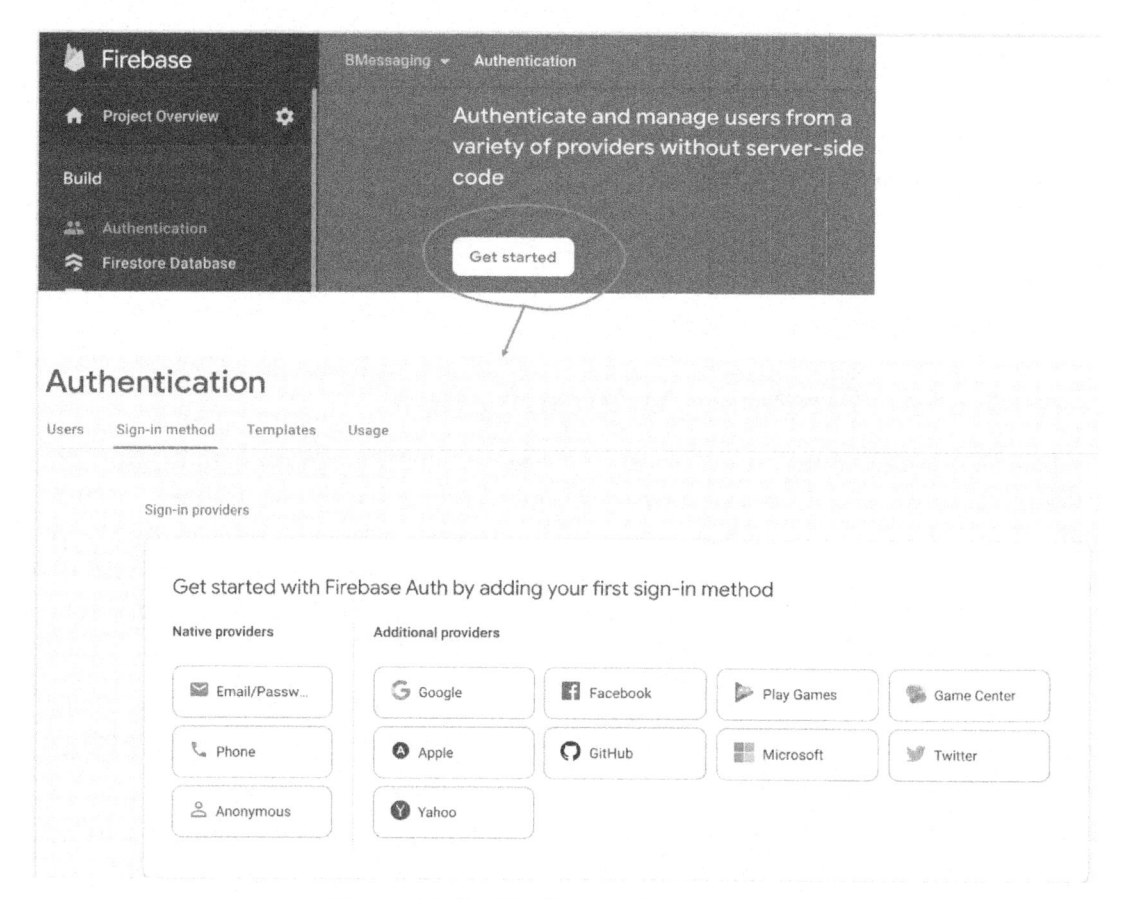

Figure 4.4: Enable Firebase Authentication

We are going to use these three sign-in providers in our chat app, but if you want, you can add many or all available providers. Note that apart from the selected three providers, most of the providers need some more configuration to enable them into client applications.

NOTE: **By default, authenticated users can read and write data to the Firebase Realtime Database and Cloud Storage. We can control the access of these users by modifying security rules for Firebase Realtime Database or Firebase Cloud Storage.**

While reading FirebaseUI and developing a login screen, we will learn how to use Firebase Auth in our chat application.

Introducing Firebase real-time database

The Firebase real-time database lets us store and sync data between our users in real-time. This makes it easy to access user's data from any device or platform. Whenever you update data in the real-time database, it stores the data in the cloud and simultaneously notifies all devices (who wants that update). Data is stored as JSON.

This is also supporting offline uses. So, when a device loses internet connection, the database STK uses the local cache on the device to serve or store changes. And when the device connection gets restored, the local data use to synchronize. And most importantly, it provides us security on the database, and we can write custom rules for that.

The security rules determine who can read or write to our database, how our data will be structured, and what indexes exist. These Firebase real-time database rules live on the Firebase servers and are always enforced automatically on each read/write request. By default, these rules are set to not allow anyone to read/write to the database.

The following are two examples for the writing of security rules:

(1) Allow read for all users and write for none:

```
{
  "rules": {
    ".read": true,
    ".write": false
  }
}
```

(2) Allow read and write to the authenticated user:

```
{
  "rules": {
    ".read": "auth != null",
    ".write": "auth != null"
  }
}
```

These are only two examples, but we can write rules and validate many things. You can write rules to validate users from a specific domain, block delete operations, apply indexes, and so on.

154 ■ *Building Android Projects with Kotlin*

Now let us learn how to enable it on the Firebase console to use it in our application. To enable Firebase real-time database, we need to go to the project at Firebase and click **Realtime Database** | **Create Database**, as you can see in *figure 4.5*:

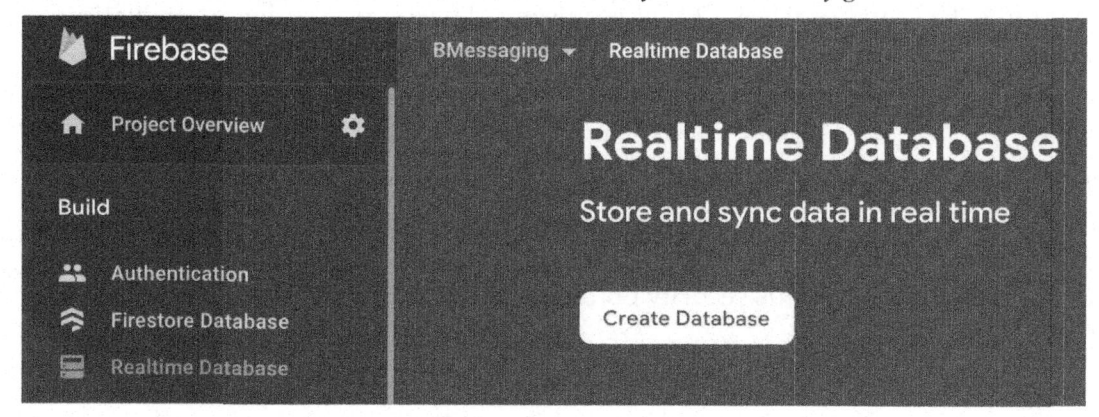

Figure 4.5: Create database

You will be navigated to set up the database screen. Choose any available database location (you can choose the location which is geographically nearer to your user base) and click on **Next**. On the next screen, you will be asked to set up rules, choose any rule and click on **Enable**. Our database will be created, and we will be navigated to the real-time database screen. Here at this screen, we can change the rule for our database after navigating to the **Rules** tab, as shown in *figure 4.6*:

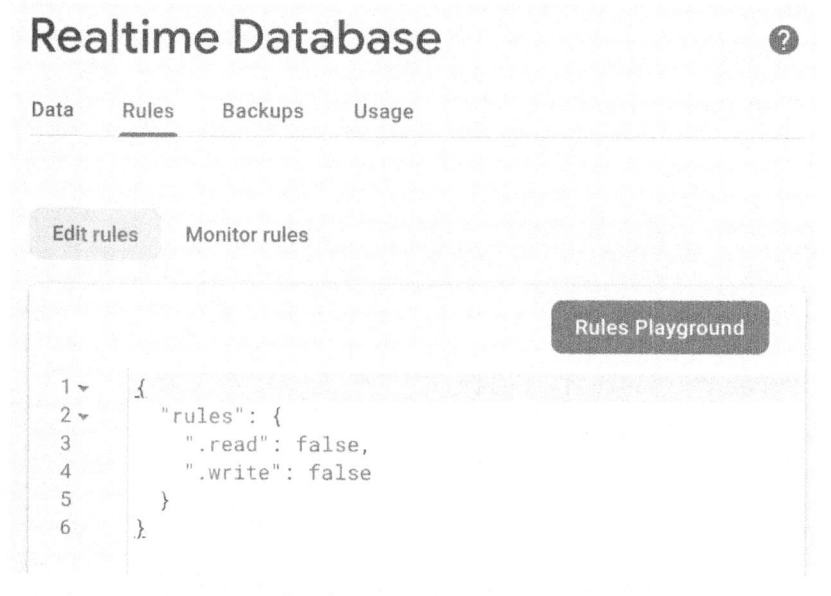

Figure 4.6: Configuring rules to access database

For our chat application, we will keep the rule as follow to allow the reading and writing to the authenticated user:

{

  "rules": {

    ".read": "auth != null",

    ".write": "auth != null"

  }

}

We will use Firebase real-time database to store chats and user info. Later in this chapter, we will see how we can read and write from our application.

Introducing Cloud Storage

Firebase Cloud Storage is used to store content such as audio, videos, photos, or any other content. The SDK provides security on content to upload and download.

To enable it from the Firebase console, choose **Storage** and click on **Get started**. You will see the setup wizard. Set rules for a bucket (in simple language, a bucket is like a directory where content will be stored) and click on **Next**. Choose cloud storage location and click on **Done**. A bucket will be created, and you will be navigated to the Storage window. On this screen, like Firebase real-time database, you can see data, update rules, or see its uses of it.

Now the question is, why do we need it in our chat application? Note that Realtime Database supports JSON structure only, so we will store the user's profile picture at Cloud Storage and keep the URL of the profile picture in Realtime Database. Later in this chapter, we will see it in detail.

Introducing FirebaseUI

FirebaseUI is a collection of open-source libraries for Android, which allow us to quickly connect common UI elements to Firebase APIs. For example, we can use FirebaseUI for Firebase Authentication, and we can use another FirebaseUI for Firebase real-time database and another FirebaseUI for Firebase Cloud Storage. Each FirebaseUI library has a transitive dependency on the appropriate Firebase SDK, so there is no need to include dependencies for Firebase SDK in our application.

We will be using FirebaseUI libraries for Firebase Authentication and Firebase Realtime Database.

NOTE: **FirebaseUI helps us to reuse user interface elements. There are use cases where we still need Firebase SDK to do our task. For example, to upload user's profile picture on Cloud Storage, we will use com.google.firebase:firebase-storage instead of com.google.firebase:firebase-ui-storage because we will create our own UI to show profile pictures and implement our own methods to update profile pictures.**

After adding each dependency of Firebase services, dependencies in our **app/build.gradle** will be similar to the following code:

```
dependencies {
    // ...

    // FirebaseUI for Firebase Authentication
    implementation 'com.firebaseui:firebase-ui-auth:7.2.0'
    // FirebaseUI for Real-time database
    implementation 'com.firebaseui:firebase-ui-database:6.2.0'
    // Firebase Realtime Database KTX
    implementation 'com.google.firebase:firebase-database-ktx:20.0.2'
    // Firebase cloud Storage KTX
    implementation 'com.google.firebase:firebase-storage-ktx:20.0.0'
}
```

Now, we know about each service of Firebase that we are going to use in our application, and we have done the required setup for each of them. So we are ready to use these services in our application. We will see each of these while writing code for screens in this chapter.

After finalizing the backend of the application, let us focus on the user interface. *Figure 4.7* shows screens of our chat application which we will be developing:

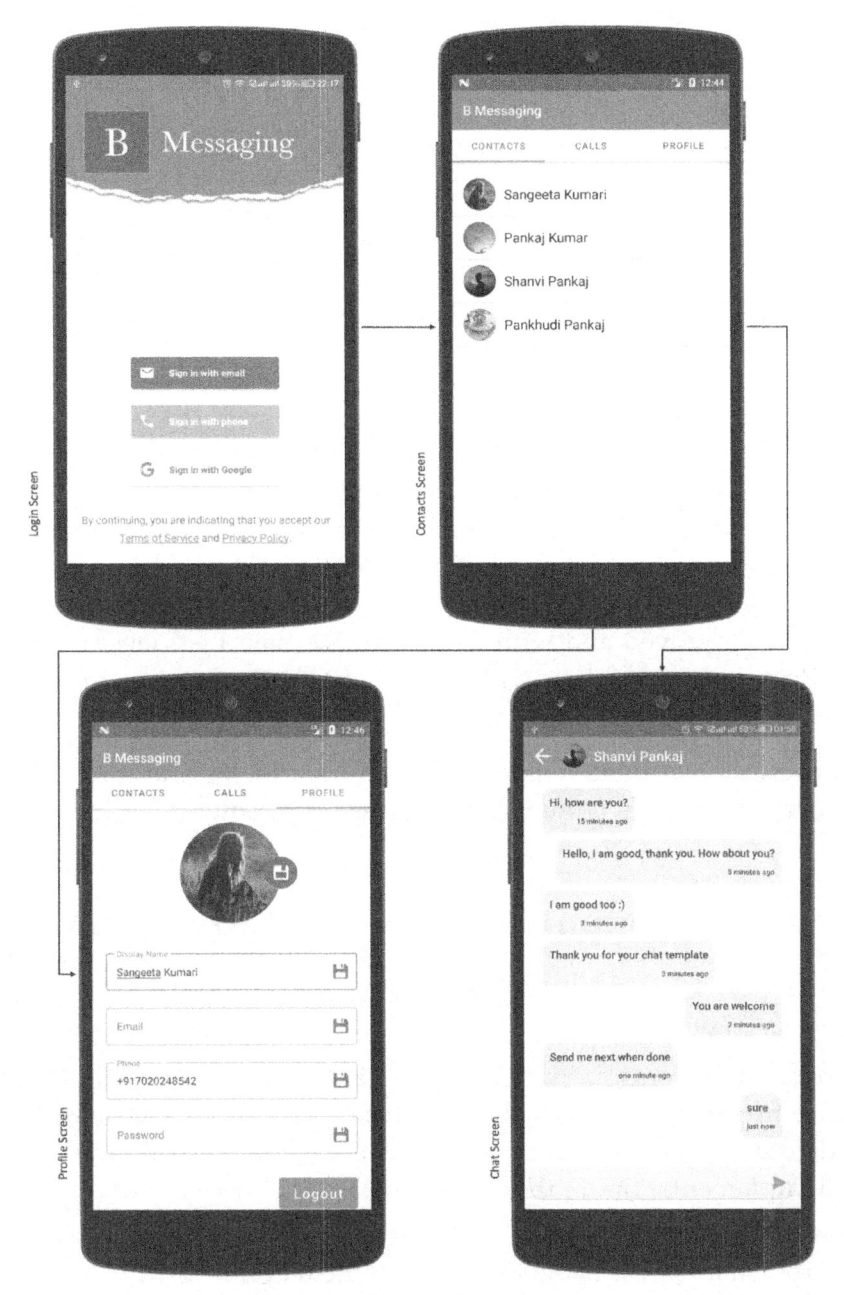

Figure 4.7: Chat application screens

After looking at the preceding screens, we observe that mostly there are two types of views that we will be using in our chat application. One view is to show lists of chats or users, and the second is to show Tabs for **Contacts**, **Calls**, and **Profile** options. So let us read about these two types of Views first.

Introducing Android Jetpack

Jetpack is a collection of libraries to help us to follow best practices, reduce boilerplate code, and write less code that works consistently on different Android versions and devices.

Many libraries are part of it, but as of now, we will learn about libraries that we are going to use in our Chat application. To show a list of contacts or a chat screen, we will use RecyclerView. We will use `TabLayout` and `ViewPager2` to show `Chats`, `Calls`, and `Profile` options.

Introducing RecyclerView

A view like our chat screen or contacts screen shows the list of similar data. The chat screen shows messages and the time of those messages; similarly, the Contacts page shows the image and name of the contact in a list. To show such a view in Android, there are two ways, ListView and RecyclerView, which show a list of similar data. RecyclerView is improved and with more features than ListView, so we will read only about RecyclerView, and we will use it in our chat app or other projects, which we will discuss further in this book.

We need to set a list of data, define how each item looks, and how items will be arranged on the screen; that is, items will be listed horizontally, vertically, or in Grids on the screen.

Understanding important classes of RecyclerView

To use RecyclerView in an Android application, we need at least the five main parts:
- RecyclerView.
- An Adapter to control what data will be tied to which view in the recycler view. There are three main methods `onCreateViewHolder()`, `onBindViewHolder()`, and `getItemCount()`, which we need to override into our adapter class and add implementations of these methods.
- One ViewHolder (or more ViewHolder in case of multiple view types) to control what view is being used within the recycler view.
- View Layout, which is a layout resource for item view and used in ViewHolder.
- The LayoutManager to determine how each view in RecyclerView will be shown.

The relationship between the preceding five components is as *figure 4.8*:

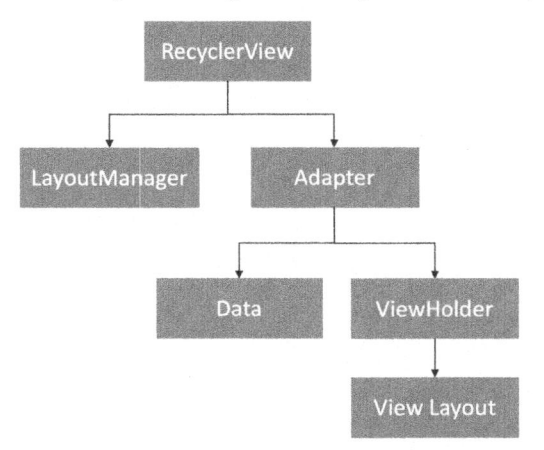

Figure 4.8: RecyclerView components

If you look at the preceding figure, a RecyclerView needs at-least two components, a LayoutManager and an Adapter. Then adapter uses a data set to be shown on UI and a ViewHolder (or maybe more than one ViewHolder in case of multiple view types). And the ViewHolder uses an underlying layout resource to inflate the view.

The dependency for RecyclerView will be added into **app/build.gradle** as the following code:

```
dependencies {
    // 1.2.1 is the latest version while writing this book. You should
    // always use latest stable version of jetpack libraries.
    Implementation "androidx.recyclerview:recyclerview:1.2.1"
    // ...
}
```

Understanding how RecyclerView works

In RecyclerView, when an item scrolls off the screen, the view of that item does not destroy. RecyclerView recycles those individual elements and reuses the view (ViewHolder) for new items that have scrolled onscreen recently. Reusability of view improves the performance and responsiveness of our application. And as it does less processing, it reduces power consumption as well. Let us see *figure 4.9* to understand it:

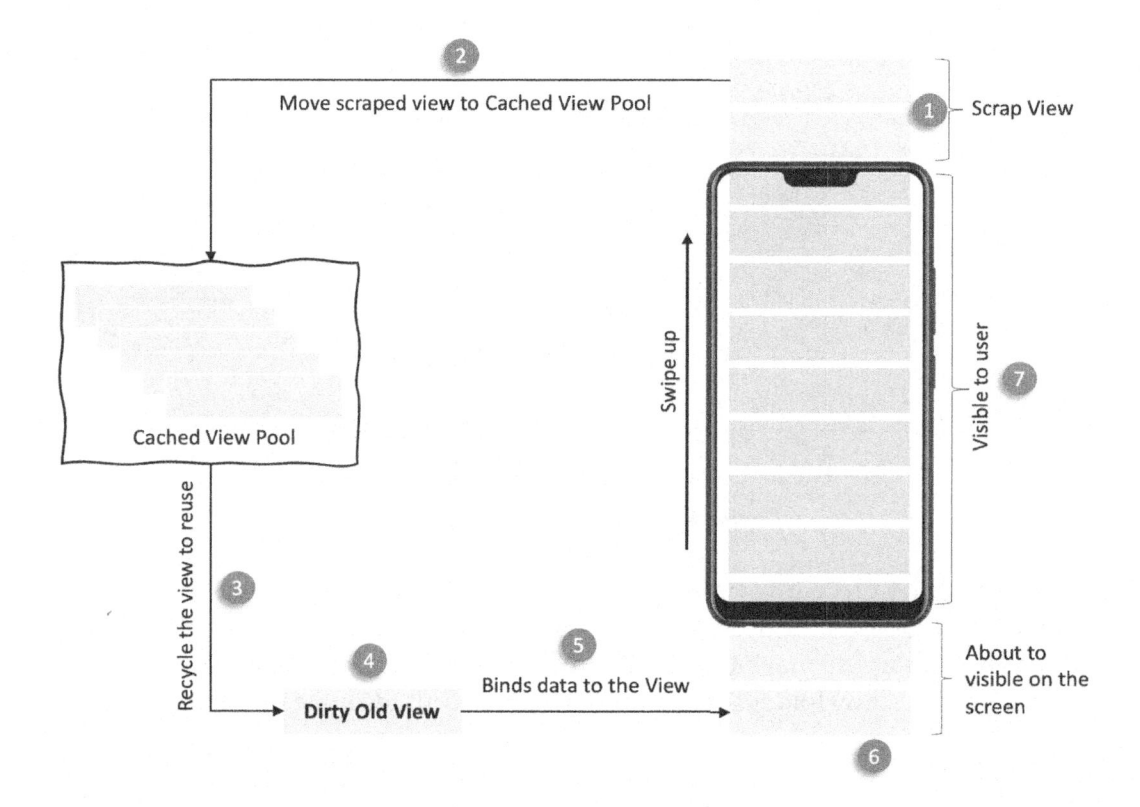

Figure 4.9: How RecyclerView works

Let us understand the preceding *figure 4.9*:

- The view becomes a scrap view when that view scrolls out of sight and is no longer visible on the screen.
- The scrap view is placed in a cached view pool.
- When a new item is to be displayed in RecyclerView, a view is taken from the cached view pool for reuse. The view taken from the cached view pool is known as the dirty view.
- The dirty view is recycled and ready to bind with new data.
- The adapter finds the data for the next item to be displayed and copies that data to the views for this item using **onBindViewHolder()**. Note that while doing this, RecyclerView reuses references of views present into one item (list row) using the ViewHolder pattern and improves the performance of the list.
- The recycled view is added to the list of items in the RecyclerView that are about to be visible on the screen.

- The recycled view becomes visible on the screen as the user scrolls the RecyclerView. And at the same time, another view scrolls out of sight and is recycled (becomes scraped view), and the same login will be executed as from Point 1.

Now, we know about the RecyclerView. We will write the code for RecyclerView while developing the **Contacts** and **Chat** screens.

Introducing TabLayout and ViewPager

When we want to show a view like in the top view of the page that you see after login, we use **TabLayout**. **TabLayout** works with **TabItem**, which represents an individual item of the Tab.

To show tabs in Android, we use **TabLayout**, which provides a horizontal layout to display tabs. **TabLayout.Tab** represents a single tab in **TabLayout**, where you can set the icon and title for the Tab. Following is an example code to add tabs:

```
tabLayout.addTab(tabLayout.newTab().setText(R.string.tab_text_1))

tabLayout.addTab(tabLayout.newTab().setText(R.string.tab_text_2))

// Can set icon too using below code

tabLayout.addTab(
    tabLayout.newTab().setText(R.string.tab_text_3)
        .setIcon(R.drawable.ic_save_info)
)
```

We can use tabs using via XML as well, so let us rewrite the preceding code as follows:

```
<com.google.android.material.tabs.TabLayout
    android:layout_width="match_parent"
    android:layout_height="wrap_content">

    <com.google.android.material.tabs.TabItem
        android:layout_width="wrap_content"
        android:layout_height="wrap_content"
        android:text="@string/tab_text_1" />
```

```
<com.google.android.material.tabs.TabItem

    ...

    android:text="@string/tab_text_2" />


<com.google.android.material.tabs.TabItem

    ...

    android:icon="@drawable/ic_save_info"

    android:text="@string/tab_text_3" />
```

`</com.google.android.material.tabs.TabLayout>`

ViewPager is used to implement transitions like screen slides between one entire screen to another screen. Note that the transitions can be customized, and you can add your own animation for changing screens in ViewPager.

When you use TabLayout with ViewPager, the user can change the screen by either tapping on a different tab on the screen or can perform a swipe left-to-right or right-to-left to change the screen. Note that, like RecyclerView, the ViewPager also requires an adapter to show pages (Fragments).

To use ViewPager with TabLayout, we need to pass references of these two to TabLayoutMediator, and the rest of the work will be handled by TabLayoutMediator class.

So, keeping both TabLayout and ViewPager together, let us see how we can use these two in Android. Instead of an example, let us write code for the home page of our chat application in the following "Developing of Chat home screen" section.

So, keeping both TabLayout and ViewPager together, we will see how we can use these two in our application to achieve the home page design later in this chapter (see the section "Developing of Chat home screen". Before writing code for our application, let us first see the project structure.

Understanding project structure of Chat app

Figure 4.10 represents the project structure of our chat application:

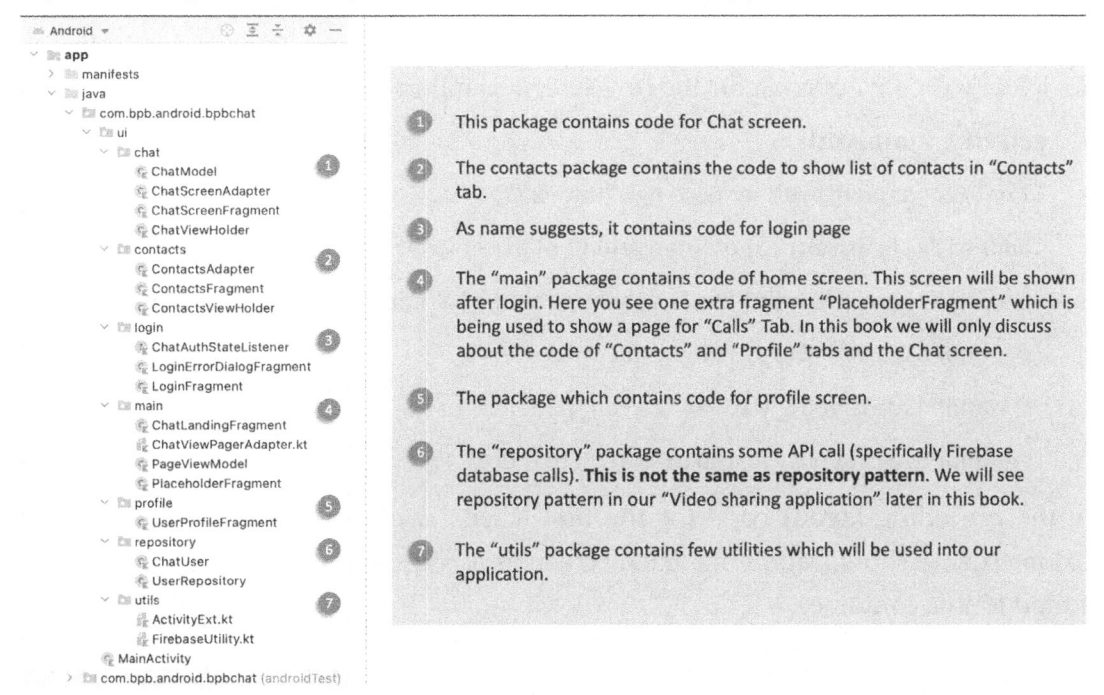

①   This package contains code for Chat screen.

②   The contacts package contains the code to show list of contacts in "Contacts" tab.

③   As name suggests, it contains code for login page

④   The "main" package contains code of home screen. This screen will be shown after login. Here you see one extra fragment "PlaceholderFragment" which is being used to show a page for "Calls" Tab. In this book we will only discuss about the code of "Contacts" and "Profile" tabs and the Chat screen.

⑤   The package which contains code for profile screen.

⑥   The "repository" package contains some API call (specifically Firebase database calls). **This is not the same as repository pattern.** We will see repository pattern in our "Video sharing application" later in this book.

⑦   The "utils" package contains few utilities which will be used into our application.

Figure 4.10: Project structure of chat application

You can see in preceding *figure 4.10* that we have divided our features into packages. Similarly, you can create different modules for these features and show/hide them depending on the requirement. Like, for the free app, you can show the **Chat** feature to the user, and for the paid application, you can also add **Video calls** as a dynamic module.

Now, let us write code for the home page of our chat application in the following *Developing of Chat home screen* section.

Writing code for the first screen

At our first screen, we will write code to make a decision to show either the login page or chat home page. To do that, we will use Firebase Auth to check if a user is logged in or not. If a user is logged-in, then show the chat home page; else, navigate the user to the login page.

So, let us write layout code for the first screen as follows:

- **activity_main.xml**:

    ```
    <?xml version="1.0" encoding="utf-8"?>
    <androidx.fragment.app.FragmentContainerView
        xmlns:android="http://schemas.android.com/apk/res/android"
        android:id="@+id/fragmentContainer"
        android:layout_width="match_parent"
        android:layout_height="match_parent" />
    ```

In the preceding layout code for the first screen, we have added **FragmentContainerView** to show fragments. Each screen as a Fragment of our chat app will be added to this container.

Now let us see the Kotlin code for our first screen as follows:

- **MainActivity.kt**:

    ```kotlin
    class MainActivity : AppCompatActivity(), ChatAuthStateListener {

        override fun onCreate(savedInstanceState: Bundle?) {
            super.onCreate(savedInstanceState)

            setContentView(R.layout.activity_main)
            showFragment()
        }

        // Overridden from ChatAuthStateListener
        override fun onAuthStateChanged() {
            if (FirebaseAuth.getInstance().currentUser != null) {
    ```

```kotlin
            showFragment()
        }
    }

    private fun showFragment() {
        // If user is not logged-in then show login page,
        // then show login page, else show home page.
        If (FirebaseAuth.getInstance().currentUser == null) {
          replaceFragment(R.id.fragmentContainer, LoginFragment())
        } else {
            replaceFragment(R.id.fragmentContainer,
            ChatLandingFragment())
        }
    }

    override fun onBackPressed() {
        // To handle back press to avoid blank screen after last fragment.
        If (supportFragmentManager.backStackEntryCount == 0) {
            finish()
        } else {
            super.onBackPressed()
        }
    }
}
```

In the preceding code of **MainActivity.kt**, we are using **showFragment()** when our **MainActivity** gets launched. This method **showFragment()** checks if a user is logged in or not, and then it navigates the user to the login or chat home screen.

In the preceding code, the **replaceFragment()** is an extension function defined as follows:

```kotlin
fun AppCompatActivity.replaceFragment(
    @IdRes containerViewId: Int,
    fragment: Fragment,
    tag: String = fragment.javaClass.simpleName,
    allowStateLoss: Boolean = false
) {
    val transaction = supportFragmentManager
        .beginTransaction()
        .replace(containerViewId, fragment, tag)

    if (allowStateLoss) {
        transaction.commitAllowingStateLoss()
    } else {
        transaction.commit()
    }
}
```

MainActivity is implementing the **ChatAuthStateListener** interface, and the **onAuthStateChanged()** is the overridden method of **ChatAuthStateListener** to listen to login state change so if the login succeeds, we can show our chat home screen. While developing the Login screen, we will see how the Login screen will notify login success to **MainActivity** using this **ChatAuthStateListener**.

Let us write the interface **ChatAuthStateListener.kt** as well:

```kotlin
interface ChatAuthStateListener {
    fun onAuthStateChanged()
}
```

After developing **MainActivity**, let us develop our login screen as follows.

Developing login screen

To develop our login screen, we will be using **FirebaseUI**. We have already read about FirebaseUI in this chapter before. It provides us readymade UI for login with many different login methods. For the chat application, we will be using phone, email/password, and Gmail providers to perform login to our app. Let us see how these options on the Login screen will look like as in *figure 4.11*:

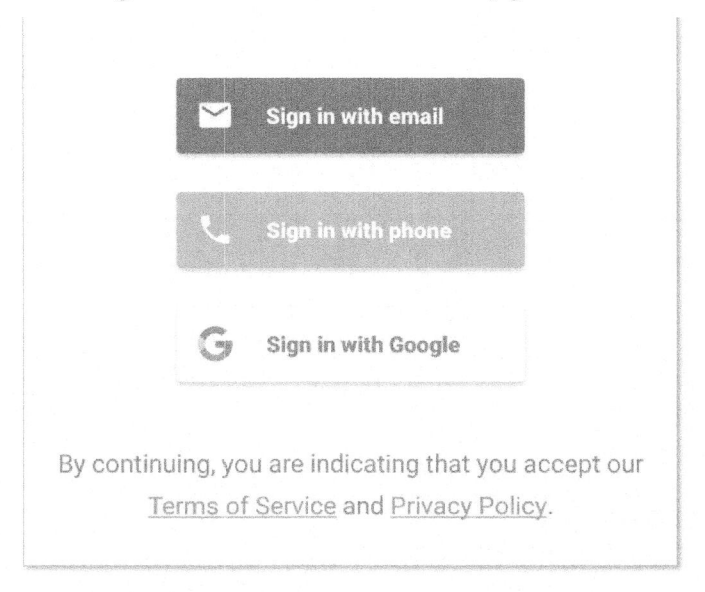

Figure 4.11: Login options from Firebase Auth UI

The preceding *figure 4.11* is of login options at **Login Screen**. Users can choose to login with an email, phone, or Google account, and screens for these options will be shown from Firebase UI.

When the user chooses any login option, the preceding screens for login are from the Firebase Auth UI library, so the best thing is that we are not going to write any layout for our login screens. Now let us write code to achieve these screens. First, we will write the basic code of **LoginFragment** as follows:

```
class LoginFragment : Fragment() {

    private var chatAuthStateListener: ChatAuthStateListener? = null

    override fun onAttach(context: Context) {
```

```
        super.onAttach(context)

        if (context is ChatAuthStateListener) {
            chatAuthStateListener = context
        }
    }

    override fun onCreate(savedInstanceState: Bundle?) {
        super.onCreate(savedInstanceState)

        doLogin()
    }
}
```

There are the following two things we are doing in the preceding code:

- In **onAttach()**, we are keeping a reference of **ChatAuthStateListener**, which is a type of **MainActivity**. Remember that our **MainActivity** is implementing this interface **ChatAuthStateListener**.
- In **onCreate()**, we are initiating login. We see what code we write inside the **doLogin()**.

To implement the **doLogin()** method, we first need to define the list of providers. Providers represent the type of login method that you want to add to the login screen. You can see how we have added login providers available in Firebase auth into an array list of providers and how we implemented the **doLogin()** in the following code:

```
class LoginFragment : Fragment() {
    ...
    // Choose authentication providers.
    Private val providers = arrayListOf(
        AuthUI.IdpConfig.EmailBuilder().build(),
        AuthUI.IdpConfig.PhoneBuilder().build(),
```

```kotlin
            AuthUI.IdpConfig.GoogleBuilder().build()
    )

    override fun onAttach(context: Context) { ... }

    override fun onCreate(savedInstanceState: Bundle?) { ... }

    private fun doLogin() {

        val signInIntent = AuthUI.getInstance()
            .createSignInIntentBuilder()
            .setAvailableProviders(providers)
            .setLogo(R.drawable.logo)
            .setTheme(R.style.ChatAppLogin)
            // Show account selection each time
            .setIsSmartLockEnabled(false)
            // Set privacy and terms url for login screen
            .setTosAndPrivacyPolicyUrls(
                "https://in.bpbonline.com/policies/terms-of-service",
                "https://in.bpbonline.com/pages/privacy-policy"
            )
            .build()
        signInLauncher.launch(signInIntent)
    }
}
```

In the preceding **doLogin()** code, **setAvailableProviders()** is being used to set providers, and other builder methods are optional, and **signInLauncher.launch(signInIntent)** is being used to show Auth screen of **FirebaseAuth** UI library.

NOTE: The sequence of providers added to the array list matters. The Firebase login screen will show login buttons in the same sequence as they are added to the array list.

Now, let us see the code for the `signInLauncher`:

```kotlin
class LoginFragment : Fragment() {

    ...

    private val signInLauncher = registerForActivityResult(
        FirebaseAuthUIActivityResultContract()
    ) { res ->
        this.onSignInResult(res)
    }

    override fun onAttach(context: Context) { ... }

    override fun onCreate(savedInstanceState: Bundle?) { ... }

    private fun doLogin() { ... }

    private fun onSignInResult(result: FirebaseAuthUIAuthenticationResult) {
        if (result.resultCode == AppCompatActivity.RESULT_OK) {
            // On success add this user to chat user firebase database
            FirebaseAuth.getInstance().currentUser?.also { user ->
                UserRepository().createOrUpdateUser(
                    mapFromFirebaseUser(user)
                )
                chatAuthStateListener?.onAuthStateChanged()
            } ?: showError(
                requireActivity(),
```

```
                "Something went wrong"
            )
        } else {
            // Sign in failed. If response is null the user canceled the
            // sign-in flow using the back button. Otherwise check
            // response.getError().getErrorCode() and handle the error.
            // ...
            if (result.idpResponse == null) {
                requireActivity().finish()
            } else {
                result.idpResponse?.error?.message?.let {
                    showError(requireActivity(), it)
                }
            }
        }
    }
}
```

NOTE: When a user does login, data will be added to the users section at Firebase console | Authentication | User tab. But Firebase does not allow to read all those users. But somehow, we need registered users to show as contacts. So, on login success, we will add/ update user info into Realtime Database. We have already read about Firebase Realtime Database in this chapter. In the preceding code UserRepository().createOrUpdateUser(mapFromFirebaseUser(user)) is being used to store user info at "users" path at Realtime Database.

Following is the code for **UserRepository().createOrUpdateUser()**:

```
fun createOrUpdateUser(user: ChatUser) {
    // Using firebase database KTX Lib
    val database = Firebase.database
    val userDbRef = database.getReference("users")
```

```
    val userNodeRef = userDbRef.child(user.uid)

    userNodeRef.setValue(user)

}
```

Where **ChatUser** is defined as follows:

```
@Parcelize

data class ChatUser(

    val uid: String = "",

    val displayName: String = "",

    val lastSeen: Long = System.currentTimeMillis(),

    var photoUrl: String? = ""

) : Parcelable
```

And at last, see the **showError()** method to error if the user gets any error while login:

```
class LoginFragment : Fragment() {

    // ...

    private fun showError(activity: Activity, errorMsg: String) {

        val builder = AlertDialog.Builder(activity)

        builder.apply {

            setPositiveButton(R.string.retry) { dialog, id ->

                doLogin()

            }

            setNegativeButton(R.string.exit) { dialog, id ->

                activity.finish()

            }

            setMessage(errorMsg)
```

       }
       // Create the AlertDialog
       builder.create().show()
    }
}

That is it, and we have developed our Login screen. Now, let us develop the chat home page.

Developing of chat home screen

In the preceding section *Introducing TabLayout and ViewPager*, we read about TabLayout and ViewPager. Using these two views, let us create our home page of the chat application. *Figure 4.12* is the output of the home page:

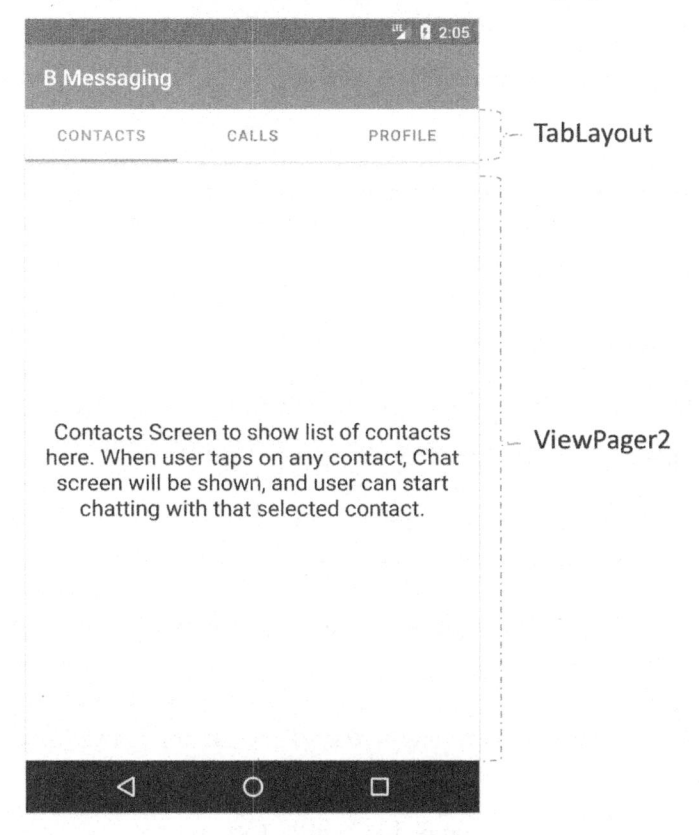

Figure 4.12: Home page

174 ■ *Building Android Projects with Kotlin*

To develop the preceding *figure 4.12*, let us first write code for the layout of the home page **fragment_chat_home.xml**, as follows:

```
<?xml version="1.0" encoding="utf-8"?>
<androidx.coordinatorlayout.widget.CoordinatorLayout
    xmlns:android="http://schemas.android.com/apk/res/android"
    xmlns:app="http://schemas.android.com/apk/res-auto"
    xmlns:tools="http://schemas.android.com/tools"
    android:layout_width="match_parent"
    android:layout_height="match_parent"
    tools:context=".MainActivity">

    <com.google.android.material.appbar.AppBarLayout
        android:layout_width="match_parent"
        android:layout_height="wrap_content"
        android:theme="@style/Theme.ChatApp.AppBarOverlay">

        <TextView
            android:id="@+id/title"
            android:layout_width="wrap_content"
            android:layout_height="wrap_content"
            android:gravity="center"
            android:minHeight="?actionBarSize"
            android:padding="@dimen/appbar_padding"
            android:text="@string/app_name"
            android:textAppearance="@style/ChatAppTitle" />

        <com.google.android.material.tabs.TabLayout
            android:id="@+id/tabLayout"
```

```
            android:layout_width="match_parent"
            android:layout_height="wrap_content" />
    </com.google.android.material.appbar.AppBarLayout>

    <androidx.viewpager2.widget.ViewPager2
        android:id="@+id/viewPager"
        android:layout_width="match_parent"
        android:layout_height="match_parent"
        android:layout_marginTop="@dimen/activity_horizontal_margin"
        app:layout_behavior="@string/appbar_scrolling_view_behavior" />

</androidx.coordinatorlayout.widget.CoordinatorLayout>
```

In the preceding code for **fragment_chat_home.xml**, you can see how we have added **TabLayout** and **ViewPager2**. To achieve our design, the TabLayout is the child of **AppBarLayout** and **ViewPager2** is in **CoordinatorLayout**. Note that you can add them in the same ViewGroup, too, like in LinearLayout or other layouts at the same level.

After designing the layout, let us create Fragment **ChatLandingFragment.kt** for the home page, as follows:

```
class ChatLandingFragment : Fragment(R.layout.fragment_chat_home) {

    override fun onViewCreated(view: View, savedInstanceState: Bundle?) {
        super.onViewCreated(view, savedInstanceState)

        viewPager.adapter = ChatViewPagerAdapter(this)
        TabLayoutMediator(tabLayout, viewPager) { tab, position ->
            tab.text = resources.getString(TAB_TITLES[position])
        }.attach()
    }
}
```

In the preceding code, see Lines 6–9. At line Number 6, we set an adapter to **ViewPager2** and from Line 7 to Line 9, and we are configuring **ViewPager2** and **TabLayout** to work together as per our requirement.

As you see, we set an adapter **ChatViewAdapter** to the **ViewPager2**; let us write code for the adapter as follows:

```kotlin
/**
 * A [FragmentStateAdapter] that returns a fragment corresponding to
 * one of the pages/ tabs. In our case tabs are Contacts, Calls and Profile
 */
class ChatViewPagerAdapter(fragment: Fragment) : FragmentStateAdapter(fragment) {

    /**
     * Return the fragment object for a specific position.
     */
    override fun createFragment(position: Int) = when (position) {
        0 -> {
            // Show contact list page
            ContactsFragment()
        }
        1 -> {
            // Show dummy fragment where you can add calls feature later.
            PlaceholderFragment()
        }
        2 -> {
            // Show user profile page
            UserProfileFragment()
        }
```

```
        else -> ContactsFragment()
    }

    override fun getItemCount() = TAB_TITLES.size
}
```

As you see, we have constant **TAB_TITLES** used in a few places. So this constant is as follow:

```
val TAB_TITLES = arrayOf(
    R.string.tab_text_1,
    R.string.tab_text_2,
    R.string.tab_text_3
)
```

Now, we are ready to write code for the contacts screen (**ContactsFragment**) and profile screen (**UserProfileFragment**). See **createFragment()** of **ChatViewPagerAdapter** to understand how we are calling these Fragments in Tab.

Developing contacts screen

On this screen, we will show a list of contacts. These contacts are not from our phonebook of the device but from Firebase Realtime Database. Remember that, on login success, we are saving user information to **users** data. We will read that data and show it in **RecyclerView**. So let us write the layout for **ContactsFragment** first, named as **fragment_contacts.xml**:

```
<?xml version="1.0" encoding="utf-8"?>
<androidx.recyclerview.widget.RecyclerView
    xmlns:android="http://schemas.android.com/apk/res/android"
    xmlns:tools="http://schemas.android.com/tools"
    android:id="@+id/contactRecyclerView"
    android:layout_width="match_parent"
    android:layout_height="match_parent"
    tools:listitem="@layout/item_view_contacts" />
```

In the preceding XML, we added one RecyclerView, which will be used to show contacts. Now let us write code for **ContactsFragment**:

```kotlin
class ContactsFragment : Fragment(R.layout.fragment_contacts) {

    private val userQuery =
    FirebaseDatabase.getInstance().getReference("users").limitToLast(50)

    private lateinit var adapter: ContactsAdapter

    override fun onViewCreated(view: View, savedInstanceState: Bundle?) {
        super.onViewCreated(view, savedInstanceState)

        prepareRecyclerView()
    }
}
```

In the preceding code, we defined **userQuery**, which will be used to read data from Firebase Realtime **users** data which we created and added user info before. We also create an object of **ContactsAdapter**, which will be used with **RecyclerView**, and we will see the code inside it right after writing this fragment code.

In **onViewCreated()**, we are calling where we will setup **RecyclerView**, adapter and configure **FirebaseRecyclerAdapter** as well. While writing code for the adapter, we will read about **FirebaseRecyclerAdapter**. As of now, let us write code for **prepareRecyclerView()** as follows:

```kotlin
private fun prepareRecyclerView() {
    // Config for FirebaseRecyclerAdapter
    val options = FirebaseRecyclerOptions.Builder<ChatUser>()
        .setLifecycleOwner(this)
        .setQuery(userQuery, ChatUser::class.java)
        .build()

    adapter = ContactsAdapter(options,
        object : ContactsAdapter.OnItemClickListener {
```

```kotlin
            override fun onItemClick(chatWith: ChatUser) {
                // Show ChatScreenFragment, where user can start chatting
                FirebaseAuth.getInstance().currentUser?.let { user ->
                    val currentUser = mapFromFirebaseUser(user)
                    ChatScreenFragment.getInstance(
                        currentUser,
                        chatWith
                    ).show(
                        childFragmentManager,
                        ChatScreenFragment::class.java.simpleName
                    )
                }
            }
        })

    // Common setup of RecyclerView
    val layoutManager = LinearLayoutManager(requireContext())
    contactRecyclerView.layoutManager = layoutManager
    contactRecyclerView.setHasFixedSize(true)
    contactRecyclerView.adapter = adapter
    contactRecyclerView.addItemDecoration(
        DividerItemDecoration(
            contactRecyclerView.context,
            layoutManager.orientation
        )
    )
}
```

In the preceding code, we have added a click listener to show a chat screen where the user can start chatting with the selected contact.

Let us write code for the adapter as follows:

```
class ContactsAdapter(
    private val options: FirebaseRecyclerOptions<ChatUser>,
    private val onItemClickListener: OnItemClickListener
) : FirebaseRecyclerAdapter<ChatUser, ContactsViewHolder>(options) {

    override fun onCreateViewHolder(
        parent: ViewGroup,
        viewType: Int
    ): ContactsViewHolder {
        val holder = ContactsViewHolder(
            LayoutInflater.from(parent.context).inflate(
                R.layout.item_view_contacts,
                parent,
                false
            )
        )

        holder.itemView.setOnClickListener {
            onItemClickListener.onItemClick(
                options.snapshots[holder.adapterPosition]
            )
        }

        return holder
    }
```

```kotlin
    override fun onBindViewHolder(
        holder: ContactsViewHolder,
        position: Int, chatUser: ChatUser
    ) {
        holder.bind(chatUser)
    }

    override fun onDataChanged() {
        // Can show empty view like
        // emptyContacts.isVisible = itemCount == 0
    }

    interface OnItemClickListener {
        fun onItemClick(chatWith: ChatUser)
    }
}
```

NOTE: FirebaseRecyclerAdapter is the class from FirebaseUI, which handles data source code as well as data change handling automatically for us.

In the preceding code, **ContactsViewHolder** is the ViewHolder that represents a single contact. The following is the code for it:

```kotlin
class ContactsViewHolder(
    itemView: View
) : RecyclerView.ViewHolder(itemView) {

    private val name: TextView = itemView.findViewById(R.id.contactTextView)
    private val pic: ImageView = itemView.findViewById(R.id.ivUserImage)

    fun bind(user: ChatUser) {
```

```kotlin
            name.text = user.displayName
            user.photoUrl?.let { _photoUrl ->
                if (_photoUrl.isNotEmpty()) {
                    Picasso.get().load(_photoUrl)
                        .placeholder(R.drawable.ic_anon_user_48dp)
                        .into(pic)
                }
            }
        }
    }
}
```

In the preceding code, we are using a **TextView** to show the name and an **ImageView** to show the contact's image. While creating an object of **ContactsViewHolder** into **ContactsAdapter**, we are inflating the view from **item_view_contacts.xml**. Let us write code for **item_view_contacts.xml** as follows:

```xml
<?xml version="1.0" encoding="utf-8"?>
<LinearLayout ... >

    <com.google.android.material.imageview.ShapeableImageView
        android:id="@+id/ivUserImage"
        android:layout_width="48dp"
        android:layout_height="48dp"
        android:scaleType="fitXY"
        android:src="@drawable/ic_anon_user_48dp"
        app:shapeAppearanceOverlay="@style/ShapeAppearanceOverlay.App.CircleShape" />

    <TextView
        android:id="@+id/contactTextView"
        android:layout_width="match_parent"
```

```
            android:layout_height="wrap_content"

            android:layout_marginStart="12dp"

            android:gravity="center_vertical"

            android:textColor="@color/primaryTextColor"

            android:textSize="20sp"

            tools:text="Contact" />
```
</LinearLayout>

That is it. We have done with writing our contacts screen. Now it is time to write code for the chat screen.

Developing chat screen

When a user selects any contact from the contacts screen, the user will be landed on to chat screen. *Figure 4.13* to understand the structure of views added for the chat screen layout. Note that full code is available on the GitHub repository:

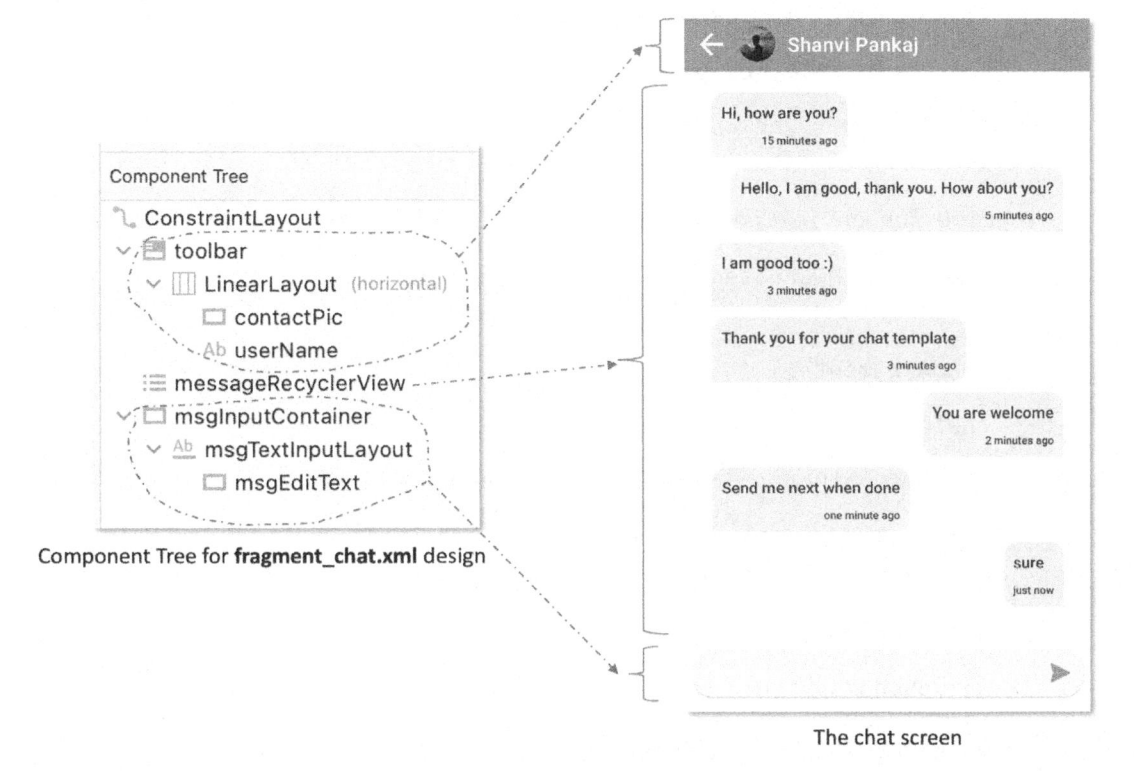

Figure 4.13: Component tree of Chat screen

To understand preceding *figure 4.13*, we will divide the screen into three parts:
1. **Top Section**: There will be a toolbar where we will show the image and name of the contact with whom a user is chatting.
2. **Bottom Section**: There will be a `CardView` with `TextInputLayout` and `TextInputEditText` to provide an input view to send messages.
3. **Middle Section**: We will use RecyclerView to show messages between contacts.

At first, we will write the initial code for `ChatScreenFragment` to understand the whole code. The following is the initial code:

```
class ChatScreenFragment : DialogFragment(R.layout.fragment_chat) {

    // Current user
    private lateinit var currentUser: ChatUser

    // User which will receive the chat
    private lateinit var chatWith: ChatUser

    val chatsHeadRef = FirebaseDatabase.getInstance()
        .reference.child("chats")

    private lateinit var chatQuery: Query

    override fun onViewCreated(view: View, savedInstanceState: Bundle?) {
        super.onViewCreated(view, savedInstanceState)

        readArguments()
        chatQuery = chatsHeadRef.child(
            getChatRoot(currentUser.uid, chatWith.uid)
        ).limitToLast(50)

        setupToolbar()
        setupSendMsgView()
        attachRecyclerViewAdapter()
```

```
    }

    private fun readArguments() {
        arguments?.let { args ->
            args.getParcelable<ChatUser>(EXTRA_CHAT_WITH)?.let {
            chatWith = it }
            args.getParcelable<ChatUser>(EXTRA_CURRENT_USER)?.let {
            currentUser = it }
        }
    }
    ...
}
```

In the preceding code, we are using **getChatRoot()**, which decides the child of **chats** by sorting the IDs of both users and adding them together. It would give us an easy way to store messages for two users, so either sender or receiver can see those messages easily. The following is the code:

```
fun getChatRoot(senderId: String, receiverId: String): String {
    return if (senderId.compareTo(receiverId) > 1) {
        "${senderId}_${receiverId}"
    } else {
        "${receiverId}_${senderId}"
    }
}
```

And our chat data will be created at **chats/senderId_receiverId** or **chats/receiverId_senderId** depending on preceding logic of **getChatRoot()**.

Now, let us write code for **setupToolbar()** as the following code to show the top section:

```
private fun setupToolbar() {
    toolbar.setNavigationOnClickListener { dismiss() }
```

```
        toolbar.text = chatWith.displayName

        if (!chatWith.photoUrl.isNullOrEmpty()) {

            Picasso.get().load(chatWith.photoUrl).placeholder(R.drawable.
            ic_anon_user_48dp)
                .into(contactPic)

        }

    }
```

In the preceding code, we are setting the name and contact's image in the toolbar. Now, let us write code to send a message. Following is the code for **setupSendMsgView()**:

```
    private fun setupSendMsgView() {

        ImeHelper.setImeOnDoneListener(msgEditText) { onSendMsgClick() }

        msgTextInputLayout.setEndIconOnClickListener { onSendMsgClick() }

    }


    private fun onSendMsgClick() {

        onAddMessage(

            ChatModel(

                senderUid = currentUser.uid,

                receiverUid = chatWith.uid,

                message = msgEditText.text.toString(),

                timestamp = System.currentTimeMillis()

            )

        )

        msgEditText.setText("")

    }

    private fun onAddMessage(chat: ChatModel) {

        chatQuery.ref.push().setValue(chat) { error, _ ->

            if (error != null) {
```

```
            Toast.makeText(
                requireContext(),
                "Failed to write message", Toast.LENGTH_SHORT
            ).show()
        }
    }
}
```

In the preceding code, **setupSendMsgView()** is the method which is used to setup the message input view. The **onSendMsgClick()** is being called when the user either clicks on send key from the keyboard or taps on send icon of the message input view. The **onSendMsgClick()** prepares an object of **ChatModel** and pass it to **onAddMessage()**. And **onAddMessage()** is the method which is adding message to Realtime Database at **chats/senderId_receiverId** or **chats/receiverId_senderId** data, using **getChatRoot()**.

And at last, we will write the following code for **attachRecyclerViewAdapter()** as the following to show the middle section:

```
private fun attachRecyclerViewAdapter() {
    val options: FirebaseRecyclerOptions<ChatModel> =
        FirebaseRecyclerOptions.Builder<ChatModel>()
            .setQuery(chatQuery, ChatModel::class.java)
            .setLifecycleOwner(this)
            .build()

    val adapter = ChatScreenAdapter(options, null)

    // Scroll to bottom on new messages
    adapter.registerAdapterDataObserver(object : AdapterDataObserver() {
        override fun onItemRangeInserted(positionStart: Int, itemCount: Int) {
            messageRecyclerView.smoothScrollToPosition(adapter.itemCount
```

```
        }

    })

    messageRecyclerView.adapter = adapter

}
```

Preceding code to show chats between contacts, and almost similar to the code of showing contacts in **RecyclerView**, which we developed for the **Contacts** screen. Here, we are also auto-scrolling **RecyclerView** on a new message. As we know that we need an adapter when you use **RecyclerView**, let us write code for **ViewHolder** and **Adapter**.

The following is the code for **ChatViewHolder**:

```
class ChatViewHolder(itemView: View) : RecyclerView.ViewHolder(itemView)
{

    private val name: TextView = itemView.findViewById(R.id.timeTv)

    private val msg: TextView = itemView.findViewById(R.id.messageTv)

    private val msgItemView: LinearLayout = itemView.findViewById(R.id.message)

    fun bind(chat: ChatModel) {
        name.text = chat.timestamp?.let {
            TimeAgo.using(it)
        } ?: run {
            TimeAgo.using(System.currentTimeMillis())
        }
        msg.text = chat.message
        val currentUser = FirebaseAuth.getInstance().currentUser
        setIsSender(currentUser != null && chat.senderUid == currentUser.uid)

    }

}
```

The **setIsSender()** is the method to do customizations on the message view, so the user can easily identify incoming and outgoing messages between the user and contact. Let us understand it in *figure 4.14*:

```
private fun setIsSender(isSender: Boolean) {
    (msgItemView.layoutParams as FrameLayout.LayoutParams).gravity =
        if (isSender) Gravity.END else Gravity.START

    msgItemView.background = ContextCompat.getDrawable(
        msgItemView.context,
        if (isSender)
            R.drawable.shape_outgoing_msg
        else
            R.drawable.shape_incoming_msg
    )
}
```

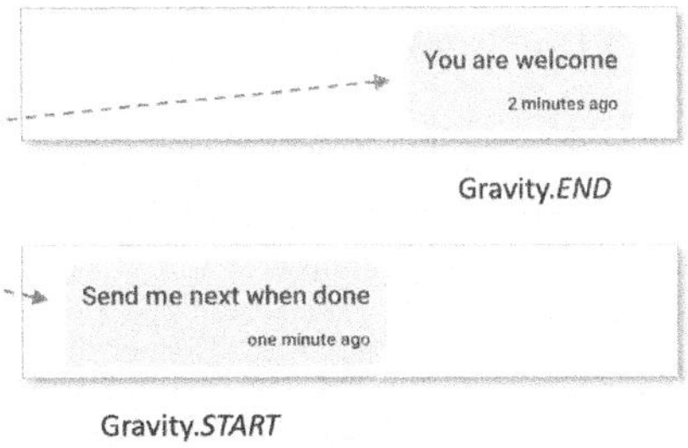

Figure 4.14: Aligning chat view for incoming/ outgoing messages

As you see in preceding *figure 4.14*, we change the gravity and background of the chat view to achieve differences between incoming and outgoing chats. You can achieve a similar implementation by using two view types for **RecyclerView**.

The layout **item_view_chat.xml** for **ChatViewHolder** is as the following (full code available at GitHub repository):

```
<FrameLayout android:id="@+id/message_container"...>

    <LinearLayout

    android:background="@drawable/shape_incoming_msg"

    android:id="@+id/message"...>

        <TextView android:id="@+id/messageTv"... />


        <TextView android:id="@+id/timeTv"... />

    </LinearLayout>


</FrameLayout>
```

In the preceding XML, we have two **TextViews** inside **LinearLayout** to show messages and time. And the **FrameLayout** is being used to handle left and right gravities for incoming and outgoing messages.

Now let us write code for **ChatScreenAdapter** as the following:

```
class ChatScreenAdapter(
    options: FirebaseRecyclerOptions<ChatModel>,
) : FirebaseRecyclerAdapter<ChatModel, ChatViewHolder>(options) {

    override fun onCreateViewHolder(parent: ViewGroup, viewType: Int): ChatViewHolder {

        return ChatViewHolder(
            LayoutInflater.from(parent.context).inflate(
                R.layout.item_view_chat,
                parent,
                false
            )
        )
    }

    override fun onBindViewHolder(holder: ChatViewHolder, position: Int, chat: ChatModel) {
        holder.bind(chat)
    }

    override fun onDataChanged() {
        // If there are no chat messages, show a empty msg view.
    }
}
```

The preceding code for the adapter is similar to the **ContactsAdapter** of the contacts screen. We are creating a view holder and binding it with **ChatModel** data:

```
data class ChatModel(
    val senderUid: String? = null,
    val receiverUid: String? = null,
    val message: String? = null,
    val timestamp: Long? = null
)
```

That is it. We have done with developing our chat screen too.

Developing profile screen

Let us write the code for the Profile screen. Here, we will write code to update the profile image, display name and email ID. We will also write code to perform the logout action. The following is the base code for the profile screen:

```
class UserProfileFragment : Fragment(R.layout.fragment_profile) {

    private lateinit var currentUser: ChatUser
    private lateinit var data: UserRepository
    private var profilePicUri: Uri? = null

    override fun onViewCreated(view: View, savedInstanceState: Bundle?) {

        fetchUserDetail()

        ivUserImage.setOnClickListener {
            chooseProfilePicture()
        }

        btnUpdateImage.setOnClickListener {
            FirebaseAuth.getInstance().currentUser?.uid?.let { userId ->
```

```kotlin
                    updateProfileImageOnStorage(userId)
                }
            }

            nameTextInputLayout.setEndIconOnClickListener {
                updateName()
            }

            emailTextInputLayout.setEndIconOnClickListener {
                updateEmail()
            }

            logout.setOnClickListener {
                AuthUI.getInstance().signOut(requireContext())
                startActivity(Intent(context, MainActivity::class.java))
                activity?.finish()
            }
        }
    }
```

In the preceding code, we are first loading information about the user using **fetchUserDetail()** to show current user info. There are some click events added to handle profile info updates. At the last of the code, we have added code to perform logout.

Now let us write code for methods that we are calling in the preceding code.

The following is the code to read user info from the real-time database.

```kotlin
private fun fetchUserDetail() {
    data = UserRepository()
    FirebaseAuth.getInstance().currentUser?.let { firebaseUser ->
        pageProgress.isVisible = true
```

```
        data.getCurrentUserByUid(firebaseUser, object :
        FetchChatUserListener {

            override fun onFetchUser(chatUser: ChatUser) {

                currentUser = chatUser

                showUserDetails(currentUser, firebaseUser)

            }

        })

    }

}
```

Where code for **getCurrentUserByUid()** is as following:

```
fun getCurrentUserByUid(firebaseUser: FirebaseUser, listener:
FetchChatUserListener) {

    // Using firebase database KTX Lib

    val userDbRef = Firebase.database.getReference("users")

    userDbRef.child(firebaseUser.uid).addListenerForSingleValueEvent(

        object : ValueEventListener {

            override fun onDataChange(dataSnapshot: DataSnapshot) {

                // Get user value

                val user = dataSnapshot.getValue<ChatUser>()

                listener.onFetchUser(user)

            }

            override fun onCancelled(databaseError: DatabaseError) {

                // Handle error

            }

        })

}
```

Note that the preceding code also shows you how you can read a single entry from the real-time database.

Now let us write code for the profile picture. This action includes a series of steps as follows:

1. Choose a profile picture.

    ```
    private fun chooseProfilePicture() {
        val intent = Intent()
        intent.type = "image/*"
        intent.action = Intent.ACTION_GET_CONTENT
        profilePicChooser.launch(intent)
    }
    ```

    Where **profilePicChooser** is defined as follows:

    ```
    private var profilePicChooser =
        registerForActivityResult(
            ActivityResultContracts.StartActivityForResult()
        ) { result ->
            if (result.resultCode == Activity.RESULT_OK) {
                result.data?.let { imageUri ->
                    ivUserImage.setImageURI(imageUri.data)
                    profilePicUri = imageUri.data
                }
            }
        }
    ```

    The preceding code is used to choose a picture from the device when the user taps on the updated image.

2. Upload image file on Cloud storage:

    ```
    private fun updateProfileImageOnStorage(userId: String) {
        pageProgress.isVisible = true
        val ref: StorageReference = FirebaseStorage.getInstance().reference
            .child("profile_pics/${userId}")
    ```

```
                profilePicUri?.let { profileUri ->
                    ref.putFile(profileUri)
                        .addOnSuccessListener {
                            // Picture has been updated to Database.
                            // Get uri of that picture and update
                            // it to user profile, so we can show
                            // new image on profile page from now.
                            ref.downloadUrl.addOnSuccessListener { uri ->
                                // After success uploading image at
                                // Cloud Storage, update image url
                                // at Realtime Storage for "Users"
                                // Data. So whenever you show user's
                                // info, latest image will be shown.
                                // And then hide progress.
                            }
                        }
                        .addOnFailureListener { e ->
                            // Error, Image not uploaded
                        }
                }
            }
```

The preceding code is to upload an image file on cloud storage.

3. Update **users** data for the user:
   ```
   fun createOrUpdateUser(user: ChatUser) {
       // Using firebase database KTX Lib
       val database = Firebase.database
       val userDbRef = database.getReference("users")
       val userNodeRef = userDbRef.child(user.uid)
       userNodeRef.setValue(user)
   }
   ```

In the preceding code, when you call the method, we pass an object of **ChatUser** which has the latest image, Uri, with other information such as name, email, and so on.

Now let us write code for updating the name as follows:

```kotlin
private fun updateName() {
    // Validations code removed for keep is shorter to explain

    // update the name here
    val nameUpdate = UserProfileChangeRequest.Builder()
        .setDisplayName(etName.text.toString())
        .build()

    FirebaseAuth.getInstance().currentUser?.updateProfile(nameUpdate)
        ?.addOnCompleteListener { task ->
            if (task.isSuccessful) {
                // Update name at our "users" data for this user
                updateUserAtRealtimeDatabase()
            }
        }
}
```

By using **UserProfileChangeRequest**, you can update the name and profile image of a user. Note that, in both cases, it updates info at users at Authentication, not on our own **users** data. So always remember to update user info at our **users** data as well.

Now let us write code for updating the email:

```kotlin
private fun updateEmail() {
    // Validations code removed for keep is shorter to explain
    FirebaseAuth.getInstance().currentUser?.updateEmail(
        etEmail.text.toString()
    )
}
```

NOTE: As you see in the preceding code, we are not updating email at our own "users" data, because we do not need the email of a user. Note that email-id and phone are a few examples of sensitive data of the user, so always avoid storing this info in your own database.

That is it, and we are done with our Chat application. We have added some nice features to it. We read about a few awesome libraries, and most importantly, we read about Firebase too.

Using of notifications

For any chat application, notifying the user is one of the most important features. If a user is not using the application and someone from his contacts sends him a message, the user will not get that message until he comes back to the chat application. So notifications are a solution for it.

There are a few ways to implement this feature, end to end. In our case, we can use a Firebase Cloud Function triggered by a real-time database trigger, which will notify all users or a specific **Topic**. Using **Topics** is preferable, as you send a notification to only a limited audience. Topics can be the user-id of the logged-in user.

To listen to these notifications, in the chat application, you can write your own **Service** class, which extends **FirebaseMessagingService**, and write your code to show notifications in overridden method, **onMessageReceived()**.

To show notifications, we use **NotificationCompat** in Android. The following code is a small example to understand how we show notifications:

```
var builder = NotificationCompat.Builder(this, CHANNEL_ID)
    .setSmallIcon(R.drawable.notification_icon)
    .setContentTitle(textTitle)
    .setContentText(textContent)
    .setPriority(NotificationCompat.PRIORITY_DEFAULT)
```

Finally, we build a real-time chat application using Firebase.

Conclusion

In this chapter, we developed a real-time chat application using Firebase, and during this development, we have learned about gathering a functional requirement, creating a user flow diagram, basics of server, BaaS, Firebase, and its services.

We learned about Android Jetpack, and we learned to use RecyclerView, TabLayout and ViewPager2.

We also learned about how to use the Firebase UI library and services such as real-time database, Cloud storage, and so on.

In the upcoming chapter, we will learn about each process during releasing an Android application.

Points to remember

- Security is the most important thing to consider while developing such an application. Chats of your application users must be secured. Email, phone number, and date of birth are a few sensitive information of a user, so avoid storing these. And if any of this information is required to store, make sure that you are using best practices to store such sensitive information.
- Using a dynamic module can be a good option when you are developing a messaging application with both free and paid features. The free feature can be part of the base module, and the paid feature can be provided by dynamic delivery.
- When you use BaaS, you do not have full control over the backend. You can do only those things which are allowed by the BaaS solution. So if in case you need features beyond BaaS solutions, you should develop your own backend for the application.
- Firebase UI makes our task so easy by providing many utilities. So whenever you use Firebase in your application, check if Firebase UI has some utility that can do your task so that you do not have to write code on your own.
- Firebase real-time database stores data in JSON format, so you can only store textual information in Realtime Database. If you want to store any file such as image, video, and so on, you can use Firebase cloud storage.

Multiple Choice Questions

1. Which service is provided by BaaS (Backend-as-a-service)

    A. Push notifications

    B. Cloud storage and database management

    C. Authentication

    D. All the above

2. How Firebase Auth UI arranges login options (such as login with the phone, Gmail account or Login with email buttons) at the login screen. The order of login options at the login screen depends on the order of authentication providers added into AuthUI.

   A. Login options are fixed in order

   B. Firebase decides the order itself

   C. It depends on the order of authentication providers added into AuthUI

   D. None of the above

3. ViewHolder in RecyclerView represents one single view inside RecyclerView

   A. True   B. False

4. Storing sensitive data into Firebase Realtime Database is recommended.

   A. True   B. False

5. RecyclerView uses a cached view pool to reuse views to show in the list?

   A. True   B. False

Answers

1. D
2. C
3. A
4. B
5. A

Questions

1. What is Firebase BoM?

2. What is the difference between Firebase Realtime Database and Firebase cloud storage?

3. What is FirebaseRecyclerAdapter and why it is better to use than writing own code to fetch chat messages and show them into RecyclerView?

4. Why do you need notifications in applications like chat applications?

Key Terms
- Functional requirement
- User flow diagrams
- Server
- BaaS
- Firebase
- Firebase configuration
- Firebase SDKs
- Firebase Authentication
- Firebase real-time database
- Firebase cloud storage
- FirebaseUI
- Android Jetpack
- RecyclerView
- TabLayout
- ViewPager
- Firebase BOM

CHAPTER 5
Publishing the Application

In the previous chapter, we created our Chat Application. Now, in this chapter, we will release our chat application. During this process, we will learn how to create different types of application versions from the same code and the importance of R8 or Proguard.

We will learn to create a release Keystore, create a release application, and pricing strategies/revenue model for the application, and we will prepare a checklist to release an application. We will also create a developer account, which is required to upload our application to the Google Play store, and we will learn the process to upload the release application. And at last, we will learn how to analyze the installation and uninstallation of the application and how to update the application on the Play Store.

Structure

In this chapter, we will learn the following topics:
- Introducing build variants
- Creating release key store
- Introducing R8 and Proguard

- Creating a app distributable file (release application)
- Creating a Google Play Store developer profile
- Pricing the application
- Getting screenshots for the application
- Preparing Android app release checklist
- Uploading application to Play Store
- Watching the number of installs
- Updating application at Play Store

Objectives

The objective of this chapter is to let you know about optimizing application size, creating different versions of the application from the same codebase, and the release process of the application. After completing this chapter, you will have a clear understanding of tools or libraries that help us in application file optimization and releasing applications at the Play Store. So, you can apply the same learning to release different applications too.

Introducing build variants

Android build system compiles app resources and source code and packages them into an APK (APKs) or .aab. To configure builds (APKs), we use Gradle, which we already read about in *Chapter 1: Creating Hello World Project*.

Gradle and Android plugins run independently on Android Studio. So, it gives us the flexibility to create Android builds using Android Studio or without using Android Studio (command-line tools or build automation tools).

The build system allows us to customize and automate multiple build configurations. Using these configurations, we can create a paid and free version of our application, lite and full version of the application, and so on. We can also include and exclude packages and resources while creating different types of builds.

Before reading about these configurations, let us first understand the build process in *figure 5.1*:

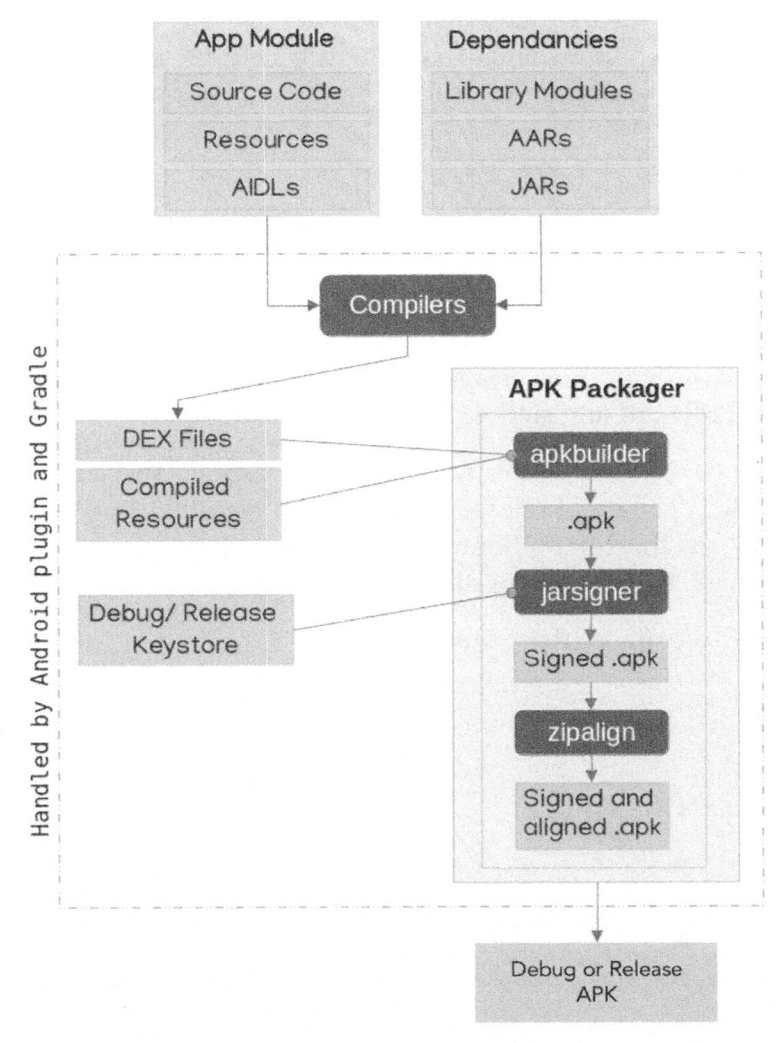

Figure 5.1: Android build process

In the preceding *figure 5.1*, you can see how the Android build system is used to create APK for any application. It shows how APK Manager takes **.dex** file and compiled resources and creates the **.aab** or the **.apk**, signs the **.apk** file, and then optimizes the APK using **zipalign**, and finally, we get an APK/AAB of debug, release, or another custom version.

Coming back to customizing and automating multiple build configurations topic, let us see how we use to customize build configurations.

Customizing build configurations

Build types, product flavors, and build variants are the main aspects that are provided by Android plugins and Gradle, which help us to customize our build configurations. Let us see these in detail.

Build types

Build type defines specific configurations that can be used by Gradle to build and package our APK. For example, debug and release are two default configurations that Android Studio adds while creating a new project. In debug build type configuration, it enables the debug option so that we can debug our APK, which is created by using debug build type configuration, and in release build type configuration, the default is to enable R8/Proguard and sign APK by release Keystore.

We can add more configurations to these build types. We can keep different application ids for debug and release the build, can handle debug and release API keys required by any third-party library, and many more. And we can also add more build types such as stagging, integration, and so on.

Let us see how we configure these build types:

```
android {

    ...

    defaultConfig {

        ...

        // You can change something in manifest for different
        // build configurations. There is a variable in manifest
        // like android:label="${hostName}". You can use such
        // variables for any attribute in manifest. See debug
        // and staging build types to understand how value of
        // hostName can be changed for a build.
        manifestPlaceholders += [
                hostName: "www.bpbonline.com"
        ]
```

```
    }

    signingConfigs {
        // This configuration is added to show you how you can
        // handle keystores for different build type easily.
        // In below config, assuming that we stored release
        // and debug keystore at ./config/
        release {
            storeFile file("${rootDir}/config/release.keystore")
            storePassword "STORE_PASSWORD"
            keyAlias "KEY_ALIAS"
            keyPassword "KEY_PASSWORD"
        }

        debug {
            storeFile file("${rootDir}/config/debug.keystore")
            storePassword "password"
            keyAlias "AndroidDebugKey"
            keyPassword "password"
        }
    }

    buildTypes {
        // Debug build type is optional, even if you do not
        // write it, Android Studio will create debug build
        // with default configurations.
        debug {
            applicationIdSuffix ".debug"
```

```
        manifestPlaceholders += [
                hostName: "www.integration.bpbonline.com"
        ]
        signingConfig signingConfigs.debug
    }

    release {
        minifyEnabled true
        zipAlignEnabled true
        shrinkResources true
        proguardFiles getDefaultProguardFile(
                'proguard-android-optimize.txt'
        ), 'proguard-rules.pro'
        signingConfig signingConfigs.release
    }

    staging {
        // The initWith property allows you to copy
        // configurations from other build types,
        // then configure only the settings you want
        // to change. Here we are copying everything of
        // debug build type, adding other configurations.

        initWith(buildTypes.debug)
        manifestPlaceholders += [
                hostName: "www.integration.bpbonline.com"
        ]
        applicationIdSuffix ".debugStaging"
```

```
            // Fallback to debug build type.
            matchingFallbacks = ['debug']
        }
    }
    ...
}
```

When we add the preceding code to the app/**build.gradle** file, we will be asked to sync the Gradle file. After successful sync, there will be three build types—**debug**, **staging**, and **release**, which will be shown in the **Build Variants** window, as in *figure 5.2*:

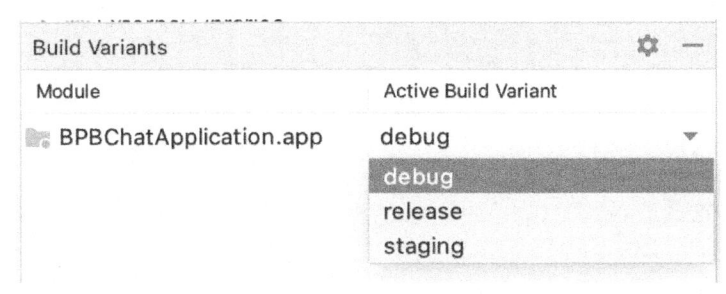

Figure 5.2: Build types

NOTE: **Android plugin automatically matches variants when consuming a library. It means that when you choose an application's debug variant, the Android plugin automatically consumes a library's debug variant and so on. And it throws a build error if the same build type does not exist in the library. So, when you define any build type other than debug and release, you must have to make sure that the new added build type is also defined in the library. But most of the time, it would not be possible as you would be using a third-party library, and you cannot change anything into the library's code/files. So matchingFallbacks is the solution for such cases when dependency does not include a build type. We can define more than one fallback where the plugin will select the first build type, which would be available in dependency. The matchingFallbacks can be written into the build Type config as follows:**

```
staging {
    ...
    matchingFallbacks = ['debug', 'release']
}
```

Product flavors

It allows us to configure the different versions of our application, where each version can have a different set of features, resources, and application id. Let us assume that we want to release two versions one is free, and another is paid for our application, and we use product flavors. In terms of product flavors, free and paid versions of the application are just an example; we can create any type of application version, like a country-specific application version.

Let us create free and pro (paid) versions; the code will be as follows:

```
android {
    ...
    buildTypes {
        debug { ... }
        release { ... }
        staging { ... }
    }

    // A flavorDimension is like a flavor category
    // where each combination of a flavor from
    // each dimension will produce a variant.
    // We can define more than one dimensions.
    flavorDimensions "version"
    productFlavors {
        free {
            // Each product flavor must be assigned to one
            // flavor dimensions.
            dimension "version"
            // Add .free at last of application id
            applicationIdSuffix ".free"
```

```
                versionCode 202100629
                versionName "1.0.0-free"
                // versionNameSuffix "-free"
                // resValue is to create string resource specific
                // to build. In below case
                // R.string.flavor_specific_string will be created
                // with value "Generated from free version".
                resValue "string",
                        "flavor_specific_string",
                        "Generated from free version"
            }
            pro {
                dimension "version"
                applicationIdSuffix ".full"
                versionCode 202100629
                versionName "1.0.0-full"
                // versionNameSuffix "-full"
                // R.string.flavor_specific_string will be created
                // with value "Generated from pro/full version"
                resValue "string",
                        "flavor_specific_string",
                        "Generated from pro/full version"
            }
        }
    ...
}
```

After adding product flavors, we need to sync Gradle, and after a successful build, we will see more options at **Build Variants**, as shown in *figure 5.3*:

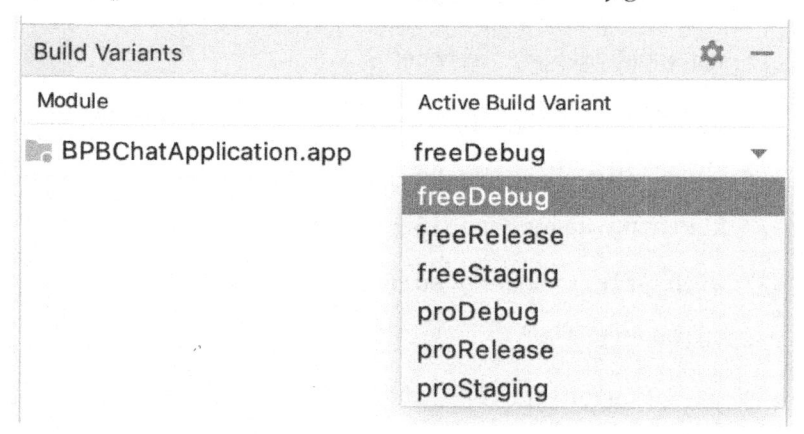

Build Variants	
Module	Active Build Variant
BPBChatApplication.app	freeDebug
	freeDebug
	freeRelease
	freeStaging
	proDebug
	proRelease
	proStaging

Figure 5.3: *Build types with product flavors*

In the preceding *figure 5.3*, you can see six options, which are the combination of [free, prod], [debug, staging, release]. These options are known as build variants.

Build variants

Build variants is an automatic configuration dependent on build types and product flavors. In our example, [debug, staging, release] are Build Types, and [free, prod] are product flavors.

When we configure product flavors, the Android plugin automatically creates build variants by combining build types and product flavors, as shown in preceding *figures 5.2* and *5.3*. Gradle uses this configuration to build our application.

To see build variants, click on **Build Variants** from the left side menu bar. In the preceding *figure 5.3*, **freeDebug** is selected, and other options are shown on drop-down options.

Now, we know how to configure different versions of our application. Let us create a release Keystore to sign our application.

Creating release Keystore

To run any version of APK or AAB, either debug or release, we need to sign the APK first. Even when you run the application from Android Studio, the APK used to be signed by debug Keystore provided by Android and installed on the device/emulator. But we cannot deploy our application on Play Store, which is signed by debug signing key. We need to create a release Keystore to sign our application.

Let us follow the following steps to create a release Keystore using Android Studio:

1. Go to the **Menu** bar and click on **Build | Generate Signed Bundle/APK...**
2. We will see **Generate Signed Bundle** or **APK** window. Select **Android App Bundle** or APK and click on **Next**.
3. Click on **Create new...**, and we will see the **New Key Store** window as shown in *figure 5.4*.
4. At this **New Key Store** window, we need to add information for Keystore and key.

   For Keystore, you need to add value to the following fields:
   - **Key store path**: Path/location at our machine for Keystore.
   - **Password and confirm**: Create a new password and confirm.

   And for key, we need to add value to the following fields:
   - **Alias**: Name for our key.
   - **Password**: Create a new password and confirm the key. We can keep the same password for Keystore and key, but the recommendation is to keep a different password for both.
   - **Validity (years)**: Validity of key in years. Normally the key should be valid at least for 25 years.
   - **Certificate**: In the Certificate section, we need to add some information about ourselves, such as First Name, Last Name, Organization Unit, Organization, City or Locality, State or province, and last Country Code(XX).

212 ■ *Building Android Projects with Kotlin*

After filling in all information, the New Key Store window will look like as shown in *figure 5.4*:

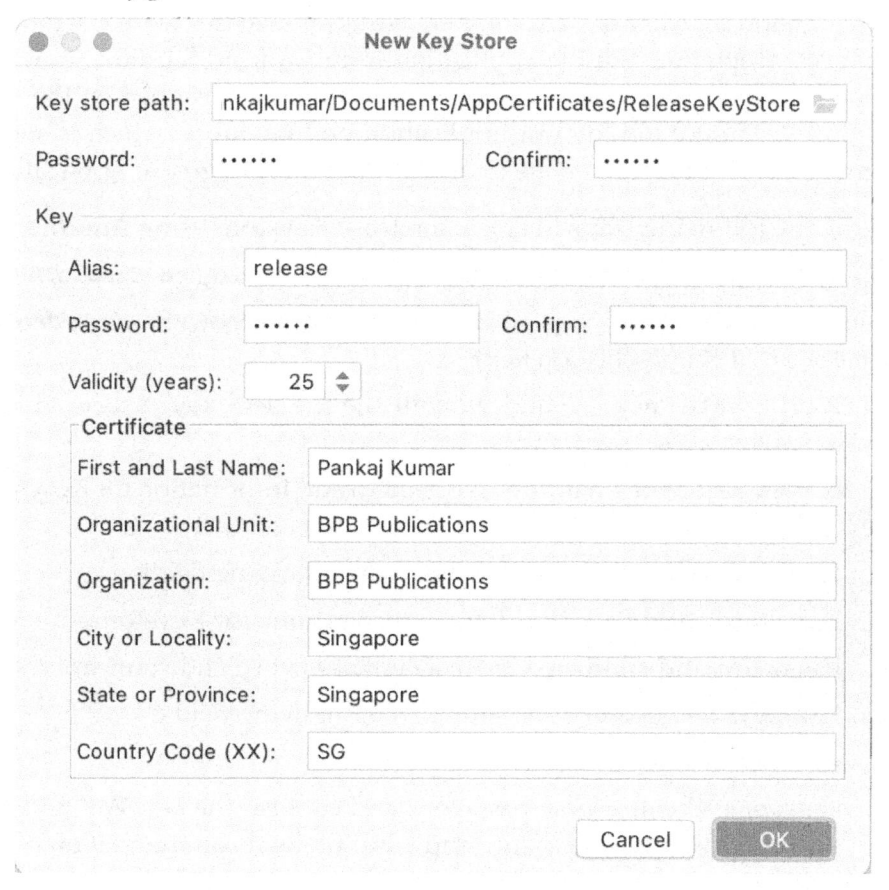

Figure 5.4: Creating a new release certificate

5. After filling in all the preceding information, click on **OK**.
6. Keystore file will be created and stored at the chosen path, and we will see `Generate Signed Bundle` or APK window as shown in *figure 5.5*. We can either continue to create a signed Bundle or APK or can cancel the build creation:

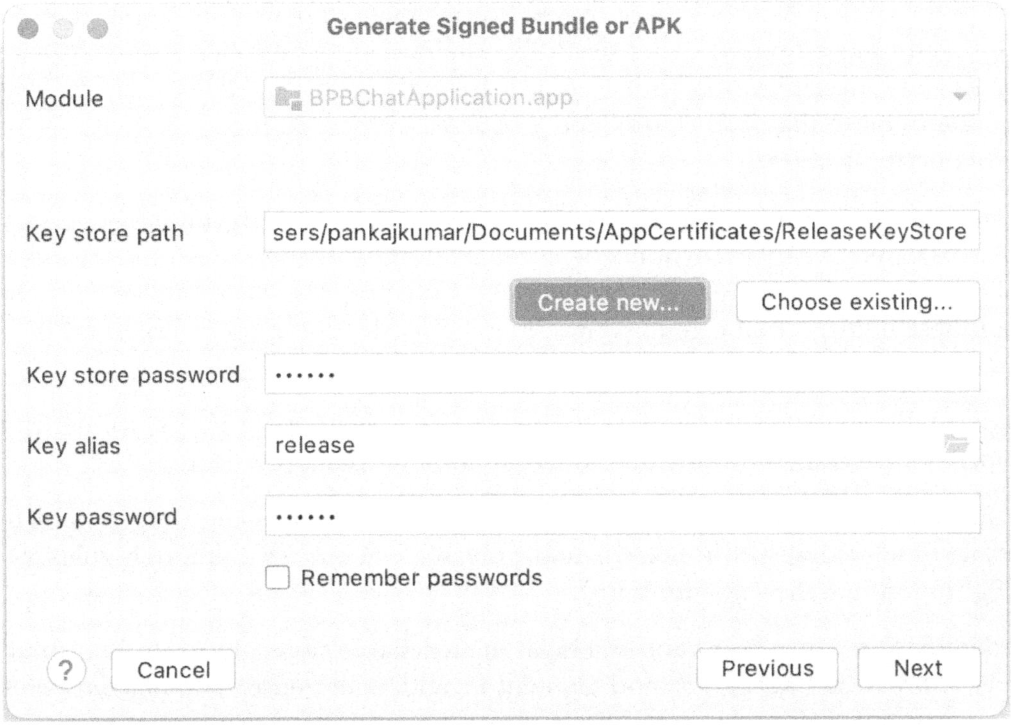

Figure 5.5: Adding password and alias to the newly created certificate

Now, we can use this Keystore file with **signingConfigs**, which we already learned while reading about build types in this chapter, or we can use this Keystore to create signed APKs manually using Android Studio.

NOTE: **Release Keystore file is a sensitive file that should not be exposed to everyone, and access to this file should be limited. Even you should think twice before adding this file to the code repository. And the most important thing is that we need to sign APK/aab of the next releases using this same Keystore/password. If you lost Keystore or password, you cannot update the App on the Play Store, so we need to store this file safely, and it should not be lost.**

Introducing R8 and Proguard

While developing our application, we use some libraries such as AndroidX, Jetpack libraries or Google play services, and so on, or maybe some other. Our application normally uses small code from libraries. For example, if we are using the material library to use material widgets in our application, typically, we use a very small part of the library (maybe just a few widgets), and this is the same case for each library that we use in our application.

Most of the code and resources of these libraries that we use in our application are unused, and those unused codes use to be retained in our application (apk file). It means even if an application with a single activity that shows a Hello world message can contain more than 100 classes and resources in the apk file. This increases the size of our application.

To make our applications smaller in size, we need to identify unused code and resources to remove them. In our code, we may identify unused code or resources by analyzing each file, and we can remove those unused codes or resources, but what about these libraries that cannot be modified by us? R8 compiler or Proguard is the answer to this problem.

Proguard: Before Android Gradle plugins 3.4.0, we were using Proguard, which is an open-source command-line tool for compile-time code optimization.

R8: Since Android Gradle plugins 3.4.0, the R8 compiler is the default tool for compile-time optimization. So, we will only read about R8 (although rules and configurations are the same for both).

R8 identifies the entry point and traces all the reachable codes. In Android Activity, Services, Broadcast Receivers, and Content Providers are entry points from where R8 can start tracing.

To optimize our build, R8 performs the following shrinking techniques:

- **Code shrinking**: This shrinking technique removes unused code and structure. It does static analysis of code, identifies unreachable code or uninstantiated type, and then removes those codes. It is also known as Tree shaking.
- **Resource shrinking**: This shrinking technique removes unused resources from the build of our application.
- **Optimization**: This shrinking technique uses the traditional compiler technique for optimizing the size, and to perform optimization, it does the following tasks:
    - **Dead code removal**: Detects and removes unreachable code blocks. For example, you have an if-else block that is always true; in this case else block is unreachable always and will be removed from the build. For example, refer to the following code:

        ```
        class R8ExampleClass {
            fun deadCodeExample() {
                val isDeadcode = true
        ```

```
            if (isDeadcode) {
                println("Dead code detected!!!")
            } else {
                println("No dead code detected!!!")
            }
        }
    }
```

This preceding code will be written as follows:

```
class R8ExampleClass {
    fun deadCodeExample() {
        val isDeadcode = true
        if (isDeadcode) {
            println("Dead code detected!!!")
        }
    }
}
```

o **Selective in-lining**: It can identify uses of the method, and if in-lining can be done, it does in-lining for the code block. For example, refer to the following code:

```
class R8ExampleClass {
    fun printMessage() {
        sayHello()
    }

    fun sayHello() {
        println("Hello, world!!!")
    }
}
```

This preceding code can be inlined as follows:

```
class R8ExampleClass {
    fun printMessage() {
        println("Hello, world!!!")
```

            }
        }

    o **Unused arguments removal**: Removes unused arguments from the method or class constructor.

    o **Class merging**: Merges supertypes with a single implementation into their single subtype. A common use-case for the class merge is to merge an interface into its single implementation. For example, let us see the following example code to understand it in a better way:

    ```
    public class Base {
        public void methodOne() { …}
    }

    public class Child extends Base {

        @Override
        public void methodOne() {
            super.methodOne();
            ...
        }
    }
    ```

    Class merging will merge class Base into class Child. Since class Child already has a method with the signature `void methodOn"()`, the method `Base.methodOne()` will be given a fresh name and moved to class Child. During this process, the method corresponding to `Base.methodOne()` will be made private such that it can be called via an invoke-direct instruction.

    o **Reduces debug information**: A shrinking technique to remove debug logs from the application. For example, like the following log, each debug log from the build will be removed:

    ```
    Log.d("BPBAppliation", "This is debug information")
    ```

Renaming identifiers

Even after removal of unused code or unused resources with applying all the preceding code shrinking, the remaining code can still be optimized for the size of the build (apk). R8 uses the renaming identifiers technique to shorten the name of classes, methods, and fields as well as squashes the package namespace down to the root. This technique is known as obfuscation. See *figure 5.6* to understand the obfuscation:

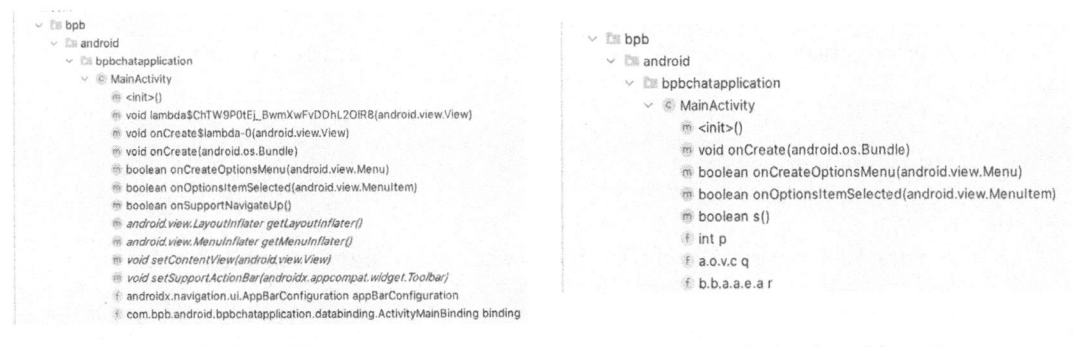

Code before obfuscation   Code after obfuscation

Figure 5.6: Code before and after obfuscation

You can see in the preceding *figure 5.6* how obfuscation has renamed methods of **MainActivity** class. Note that R8 or Proguard does not shorten Android components that you declare in the manifest; that is why the **MainActivity** word is not being obfuscated.

Till now, we read about how R8 helps us to remove unused code and unused resources and helps us to the removed size of an APK. Now, it is time to know about how we enable R8 for the application and how we can customize the rules.

Enabling of R8

To enable R8 for the build type, we need to add **minifyEnabled** true, and to shrink resources, we add **shrinkResources** true and Proguard configs as shown in the following code:

```
android {
    ...
    release {
        // Enables code shrinking, obfuscation, and optimization for
        // release build type. Can be added into any build type, like
        // debug but it take more time to build the apk than normal
        // debug build and for debug this optimization is not
        // necessary or useful too.
        minifyEnabled true

        // Enables resource shrinking, which is performed by the
        // Android Gradle plugin.
        shrinkResources true

        // Includes the default ProGuard rules files that are
        // packaged with the Android Gradle plugin.
        proguardFiles getDefaultProguardFile(
            'proguard-android-optimize.txt'),
        // We used to write additional ProGuard rules for
        // the given build type into proguard-rules.pro
        // By default, Android Studio creates and
        // includes an empty rules file for us.
        // (located at the root directory of each module).
            'proguard-rules.pro'
    }
    ...
}
```

Adding custom rules

Normally, we need not write custom rules, but there are a few cases where we need to force R8 to not optimize the specific class or method or the whole package. For example, any method from reflection cannot be traced, or JavaScript interface methods cannot be traced. In both cases, we know the code is being used and required, but R8 will treat it as an unreachable code block because R8 cannot find the entry point for those methods, so it will remove them. Sometimes, we reference **onClick()** of a view in XML and write a public method with the same name into Kotlin class. In this case too, R8 will treat that public method as unreachable, and that method will be removed or obfuscated.

In these cases, we need to add custom rules into proguard-rules.pro file to avoid this code from shrinking. See the following code for few rules:

```
# Force to not shrink a specific class
-keep public class com.bpb.android.ClassForRefletion


# Force to not shrink a package with all classes inside.
-keep class com.bpb.android.customviews.** { *; }


# Do not shrink all javascript interface with methods
-keepclassmembers class * {
    @android.webkit.JavascriptInterface <methods>;
}
```

In the preceding Proguard rules, we are forced to keep class **ClassForReflection**, all classes inside **com.bpb.android.customviews**, and methods of JavaScript interface. Similarly, we can do it for any other class or method too. There are few other rules, which you should explore if needed.

NOTE: **Alternatively, we can add the @Keep annotation to the code that we want to keep. Adding @Keep on a class keeps the entire class as is. Similarly, adding it to a method or field will keep the method/field (and its name) as well as the class name intact.**

Creating a distributable file (release application)

To create a `.aab` file, open the project in Android Studio. Go to the **Build** menu and choose `Generate Signed Bundle /APK...`. Choose `Android App Bundle` and click on **Next**. You will see a dialog to set the release key store and password, as shown in *figure 5.7*:

Figure 5.7: Creating release application

Set path of sing-in key and passwords and choose "**Next**". You will see the next window where you need to select the build variant to create the release app. As shown in *figure 5.8*, we are choosing `proRelease` to create a release application for the paid version:

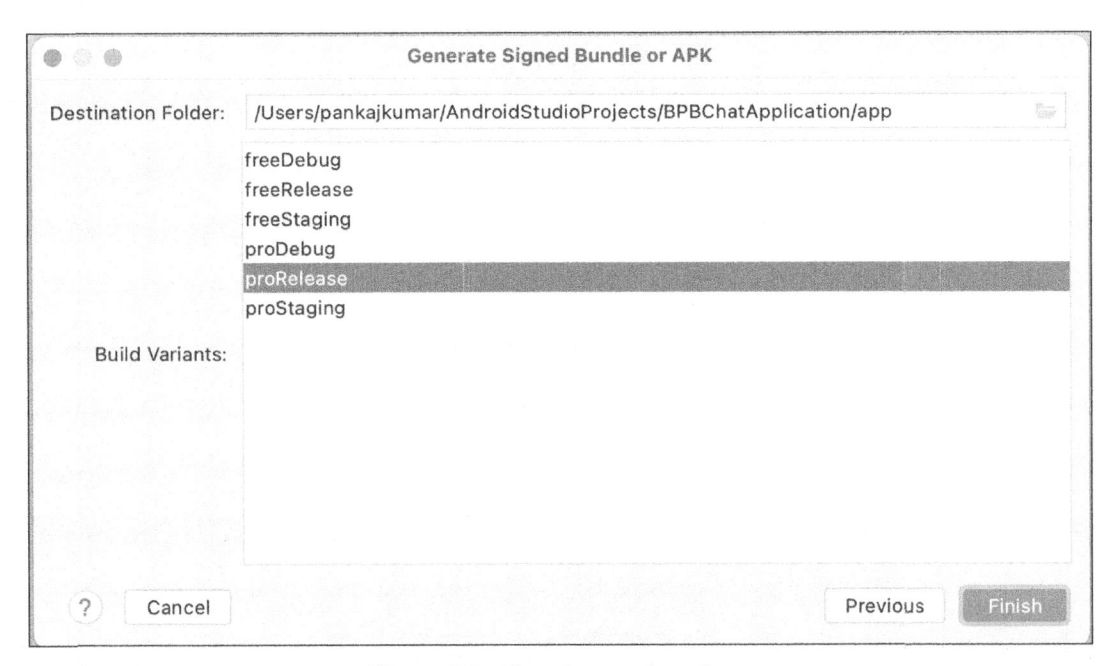

Figure 5.8: Choosing product flavor

After selecting the correct build variant, click on **Finish**. The `.aab` file will be created.

Creating a Google Play Store developer profile

To publish our application to the play store, we need a Google account and then a developer profile. To create a developer profile, you need to visit https://play.google.com/apps/publish/signup/, and this page asks you to create a Google account first or choose from existing logged-in email ids. After doing that, you will be navigated to a page like *figure 5.9*:

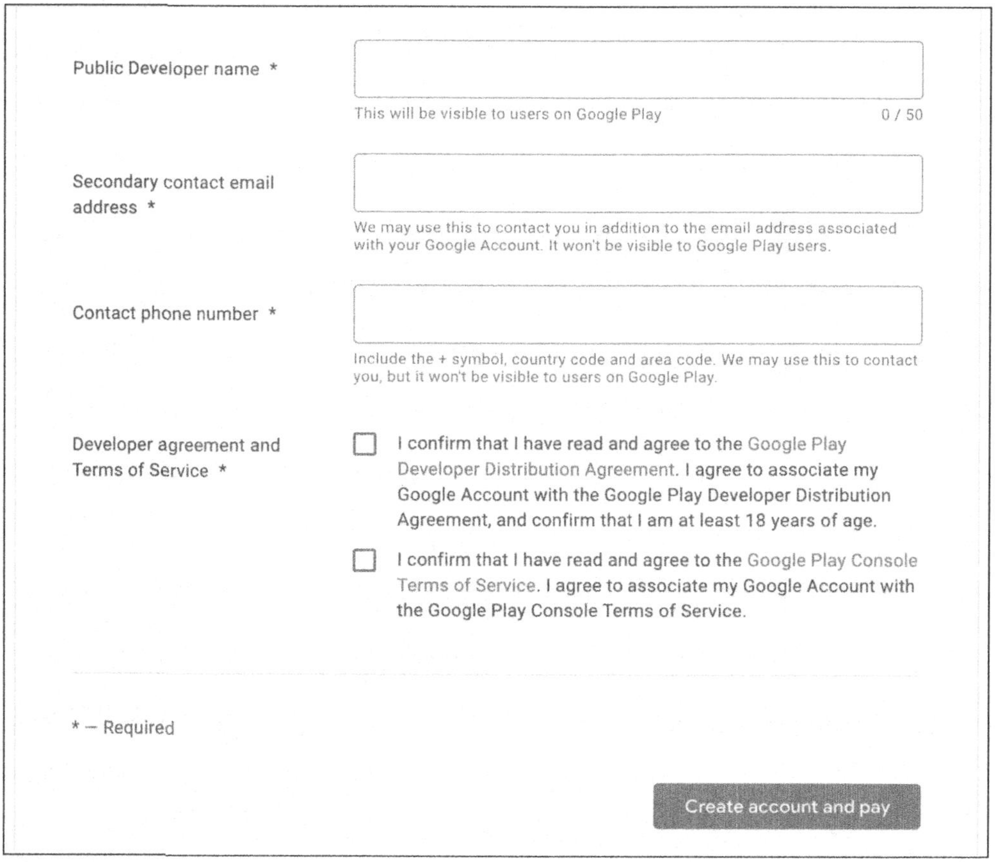

Figure 5.9: Play store signup

After providing these details and selecting **Create account and pay**, you will see the **Complete your purchase** dialog. At this dialog, you need to enter address details and then click on **Continue**. In the next dialog, you will be asked to pay $25 for the one-time registration fee, as shown in *figure 5.10*:

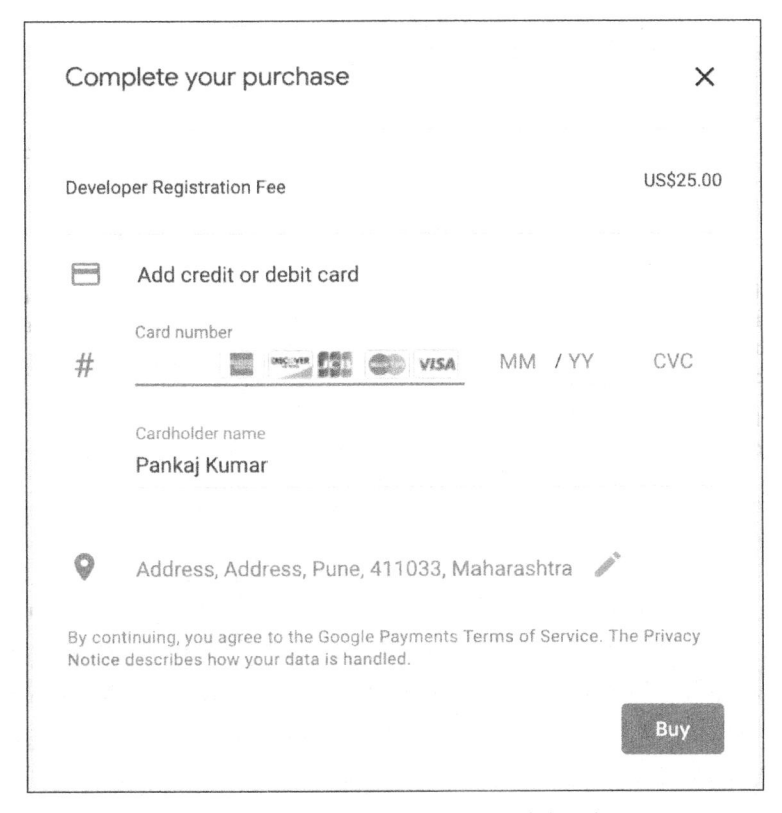

Figure 5.10: Adding credit card details

And after filling in all the information, click on **Buy**. After a successful transaction, your profile will be created, and you will be ready to upload your application to the Play Store.

Pricing the application

Deciding the price for your application is a very analytical task; it requires a lot of research to make a better price for your application. Until you have a good reputation for making high-quality applications, a high price can make users think twice before buying your application, and they can choose other similar applications at a cheaper price. And listing your app with low price than expected can attract more users, but you lose the chance to make more money.

Let us first look into some pricing strategies that open ways to make money, and then we will read about few major factors which we use to consider while pricing for an application.

Understanding pricing strategy

As a developer, we want to make money from our applications, and choosing the right price for the application is an important task. There are few strategies that can help you in deciding the pricing of the application. The following are commonly used strategies.

Free

Making your application free is the most effective way to attract the user. But as a developer or organization, we want to make money from our applications.

Commonly there are two pricing strategies you can choose even if the application is free:

- **Free Apps with Ads**: We can use Ads services and can show relevant ads to the application screen. There are many Ads services that you can integrate into the application; one of them and most popular is Google Ads.

  NOTE: **While integrating such Ads services in your application, follow best practices and do not overuse spaces for Ads. No one wants too much of Ads even in free applications. So better to be relevant and choose spaces wisely.**

- **Free Apps without Ads**: These applications use to provide services to the customers and can offer other paid services. The best examples are banking services applications, which provide free services to their customer, and those applications offer some paid services to the customer, and customers may opt for that service.

Freemium

In this pricing strategy, we ask the user to pay after using the application. There are few pricings strategy under Freemium:

- We can release an application with Ads and can ask the user to pay to remove Ads from the application. Some image/video editors usually add watermarks on edited images/videos and ask the user to pay to remove the watermark.

  In the case of gaming applications, we can provide few free levels and ask the user to pay to unlock more levels, power, or maybe a fee for the virtual tournament.

- We can offer a free application with limited features and can ask the user to pay if he/she wants to use the locked feature.
- We can offer users to *complete a task and get a reward*. In this strategy, users receive tasks such as watching ad videos, completing surveys, and so on. After completing the task, the user can be awarded some credits that can be used to purchase paid features.

Paid

It is a common application pricing strategy that needs a proper analysis to finalize the price of the application, and it is the least effective strategy.

In the case of paid apps, the user has no way to use our application before paying. So, we should have a well-written description at Play Store, strong marketing and support team, and obviously, a crash-free and clean UI that makes it easy to use the application. Note that no one likes an application that crashes or is not so user-friendly.

For paid applications, we can choose any strategy from the following:

- **Pay Once**: In this type of pricing strategy, we ask the user to pay only once before installing the application.
- **Pay For Features**: We can ask the user to pay for the feature which he/she may want to use. This strategy can be effective because the user will pay (pay less than the whole app pricing) only for the feature which the user requires. Similarly, in game applications, where we need to pay to unlock the level.
- **Trial application**: This strategy allows users to try our application before paying. There may be some user group that only uses applications till the trial period, and there is no way to force them to use them after the trial ends. We can also disable some features in the trial version and can ask the user to pay to enable those features.

Subscription plan

This strategy is becoming popular, and almost every OTT platform uses this pricing strategy, where they ask users to pay monthly or yearly for their services. We can choose this strategy for few other types of applications as well. Let us say you developed an application for an image editor or scanner, and you allow the user to save their modified or scanned documents to your remote datastore (cloud may be); you can ask the user to pay yearly for this service.

These were commonly used pricing strategies that you can choose. Now let us find out the most common factors which affect the price of our application, given as follows:

- Development cost
- Maintenance cost
- Market demand
- User group who will be using the application
- Cost of other similar applications

And before making any final decision, consider these points too:

- You cannot make a free application to paid, and Google Play will not allow you to do it. But you can play with pricing. You can set a higher price initially, and if you think you get fewer users or other competitors are selling their similar products at a lower price, you can decrease the price if the current price is less effective in attracting the user. Or you can set a lower price initially and can increase the price as per demand.
- Psychological pricing (left digit effect) is one of the most effective ways of pricing. According to a survey conducted by Schindler and Kibarian in 1996, there is a phycological impact when you price your product ending with 99, not 00. For example, 0.99USD can attract more users than 1.00USD. Similarly, other odd numbers are also impactful, like 1.75USD. That is why you see such odd prices on many products.

NOTE: **To make your application stable and consistent in the market, focus on trends, revise pricing strategy, and make sure that features of the application are still in demand. You should keep your eyes on research, analysis, and trends related to the category of your application. Also, you should join online communities, and these are good places to get the latest information.**

Getting screenshots for the application

To take screenshots of the application Android Studio gives us a tool. First of all, run your application and navigate to the screen to take the screenshot. Now to open the `Screen Capture` window, go to the **Logcat Window** and choose the device if you have attached more than one device to ADB. Click on the `Screen Capture` tool from the vertical toolbar at the Logcat Window. We have already read about this tool in section Logcat of *Chapter 1: Creating Hello World Project*.

After clicking on **Screen Capture**, you will see the **Screen Capture** window, as shown in *figure 5.11*. Wait for screen capture and click on **Save** to store the screenshot:

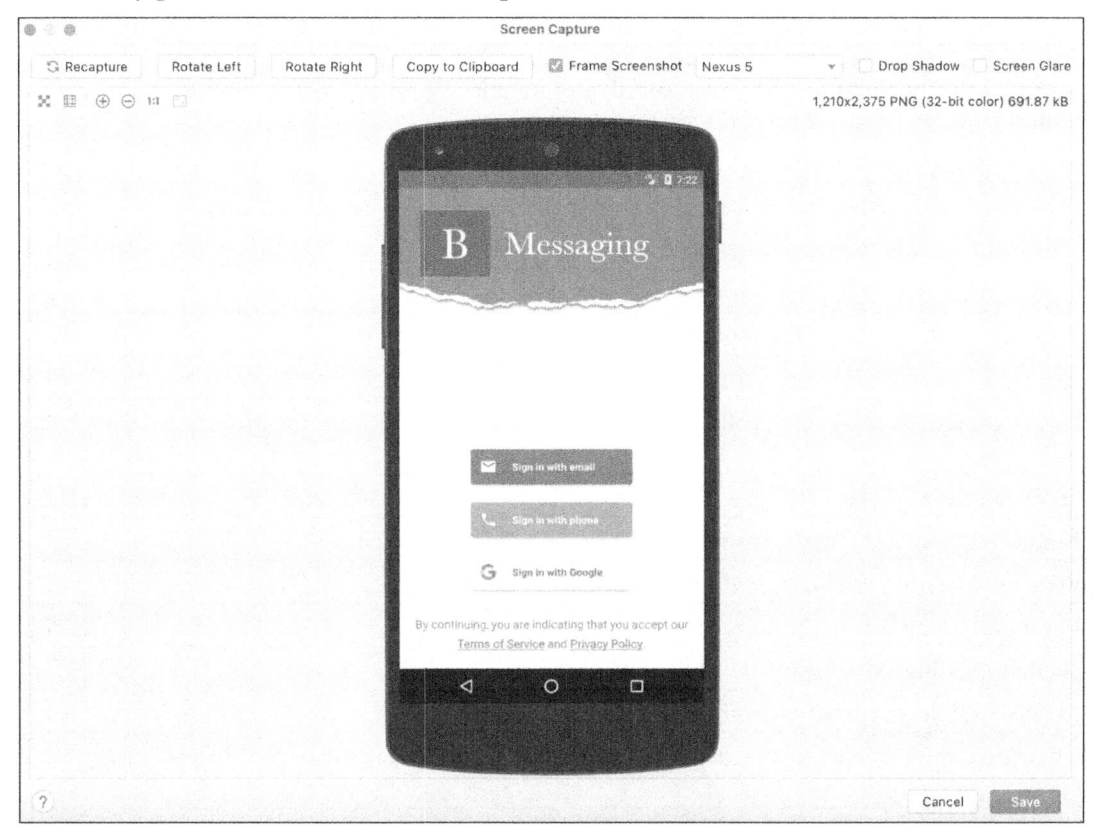

Figure 5.11: Capturing screenshots from Android Studio

In the preceding *figure 5.11*, there are some options available to recapture screenshots, rotate them, copy them to the clipboard and add frames in screenshots.

When you enable the **Frame Screenshot** option, you get a list of devices that can be used as the frame for the screenshot. In the preceding *figure 5.11*, we have used Nexus5. Drop shadow and Screen Glare options are to add some effects on your screenshots, as shown in *figure 5.11*, you see a shadow below the Nexus5 frame.

If you do not want to add a frame, uncheck **Frame Screenshot**, your screenshot will be taken without frame, and you can apply your styles to it using different tools.

The Play Store requires a minimum of two screenshots per-app listing, and the maximum, we can upload eight screenshots per supported device type (phone, tablets, Android TV, and Wearables). As of now, we developed our application for phones only, so we need two to eight screenshots to upload to Play Store.

Preparing Android app release checklist

Before going ahead, let us create a checklist that can help us to release the application:

Bumped up the version code (monotonically increasing integers) and version name (a descriptive string for this version).	☐
R8/Proguard is enabled	☐
Database migration schema added if any structural change into the database.	☐
Performance analysis has been performed	☐
Optimized the images/recourses (png/webp files)	☐
Fixed all Lint warnings (at least no major warning is remaining)	☐
Added localized texts into strings.xml	☐
New changes have been well tested on multiple devices and multiple Android versions	☐
Disabled debug logs	☐
Removed printstacktraces from code	☐
Removed hardcoded string/ literals	☐
No sensitive data is being logged	☐
Security testing performed	☐
Release API keys for any libraries have been added	☐
Checked expiry of certificates and updated if required (if certificate pinning is being used)	☐
APK is signed by release KeyStore	☐
Prepared changelog and what is new to add on Play Store	☐
Prepared Google Play Assets	☐

These checklists are not final and can differ a bit for each application. For example, if an application is related to a banking application, you may add more checklists related to security stuff; in the case of a game application, you may add more checklists specific to a game application.

Uploading application to the Play Store

We have created our release apk, prepared screenshots, and so on, and we are now ready to publish the application. Before publishing the application, we need to add few details to Google Play Console, as follows.

Settings for paid applications

If you want to upload paid apps, you will require a payment profile on the developer console. To create it, click on **Settings -> Developer account -> Payment settings -> Create payment profile**. Fill out the form and submit it.

Creating App at Google Play console

The first step to list your app in the Play Store is, Create App. Select **All Apps** at the google console menu, and click on the **Create App** button. You will see a page like *figure 5.12*:

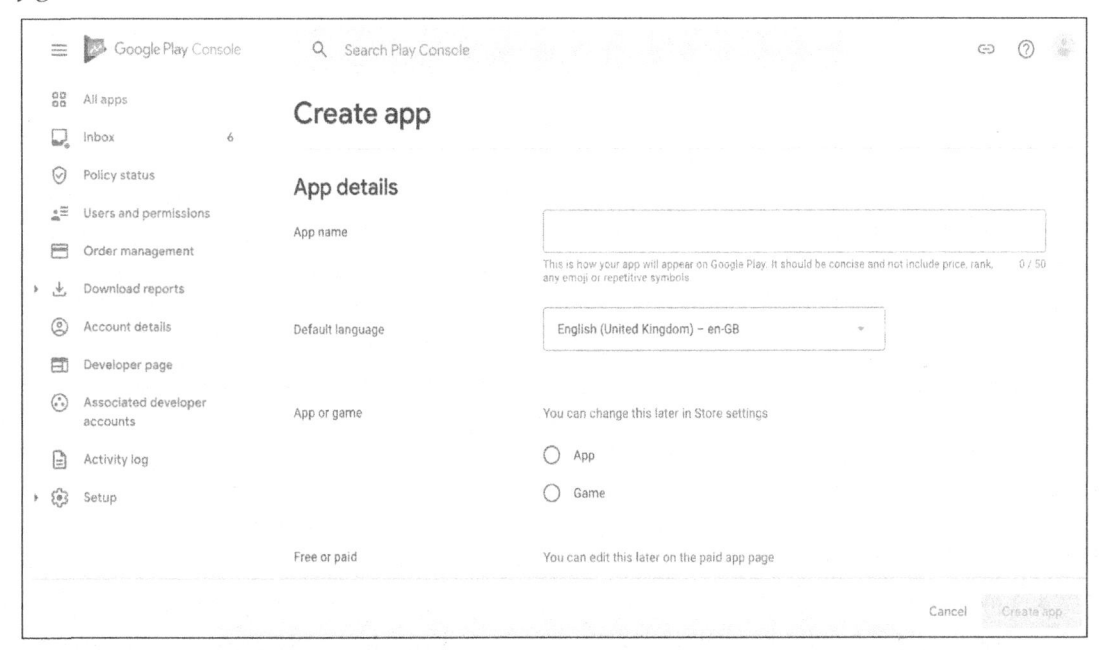

Figure 5.12: Creating an application on the Play console

Fill in the required data and click on the **Create app** button. After that, you will be taken to the app dashboard page. On this page, you see options like Internal testing of the app, open/close beta testing, and pre-registration for your application. In this chapter, we will look into the following most important things:

- Set up your app
- Publish your app on Google Play

Before setting up your application, there are few important things that you need to prepare first. The list is as follows:

- **Title**: This is the most important thing about your application. Keep a unique and creative title for your application. The best practice is to keep a combination of brand name and few most important keywords. The title of the application is related to App Store Optimization, and choosing the title wisely will improve the ranking of your application in Play Store.
- **Short Desc**: It should be more than enough to explain your application in short.
- **Full Desc**: A well-written description of your application.
- **App Screenshots**: Screenshots of applications from handset and tablet. Images should be two to eight in the count, and the allowed type is JPEG or 24-bit PNG without Alpha. Usually, screenshots taken from real devices work here.
- **App icon**: An application icon that should consist of 512 × 512 in dimension with alpha.
- **Feature Graphic**: This image will be placed at the top of your application page in Google Play Store. So, you should take this opportunity and create this image as much attractive and self-explanatory for features. Before creating this image, look for examples. The size of this asset must be 1,024W × 500h, and the type can be JPG or 24-bit PNG without alpha.
- **App Type**: Type of your application. For example, Application or Game.
- **Category**: Decide the category of your application. For example, Productivity, Shopping, Social, and so on.
- **Content Rating**: A questionnaire that needs to complete for content rating while creating an app on the Play store console.
- **Privacy Policy Url**: Prepare a privacy policy and be ready with the URL. You will be asked to add this URL. In some cases, this URL becomes optional, but the recommendation is to always add this URL.

NOTE: There are few websites and open-source tools that can help to get app icons, app screen, feature graphics, and privacy policy content.

Now let us set up the application at the Play store console.

Setting up your app

In this section, we will add information related to content rating, target audiences, and description of the application, as follow:

- **App Content**: Go to the left navigation menu, and under the **Policy** section, click on **App Content**. See *figure 5.13*:

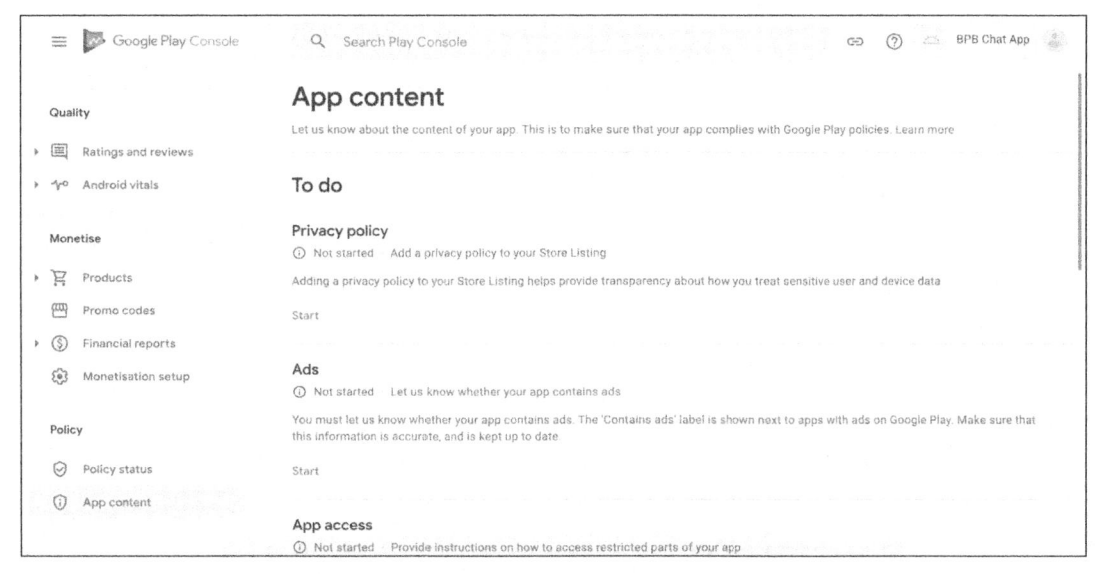

Figure 5.13: Adding information about the application

On this page, you need to set to **Content Ratings** and **Target audience** and content for the application. So users can decide that if the application is suitable for them based on the content rating. App Access and News apps are two more steps/configurations which you need to complete.

- **Main Store Listing**: Go to **Store presence** -> **Main store listing**. You will see a page as shown in *figure 5.14*:

Figure 5.14: Adding name, descriptions, and assets to show on the Play Store

Fill in all this information like **App Name** and **Short and Full description**. On the same page, you will be asked to upload image assets (App icon, Phone screenshots, Tablet screenshots, and feature graphic. These details will be shown on the Play Store for your application.

NOTE: **You can provide localized text for App Name, Short description and Full description, and localized texts on assets. By choosing "Manage translation" -> "Manage your own translation", you will see a fresh page like** *figure 5.14* **where you can add localized texts or assets.**

After adding all these details, click on **Save**.

Now, we are done with app creation and setting up the application. Now, we will read about how to release.

Publishing/releasing the application

Choose **Production** from the left navigation menu. You will see a page as shown in *figure 5.15*:

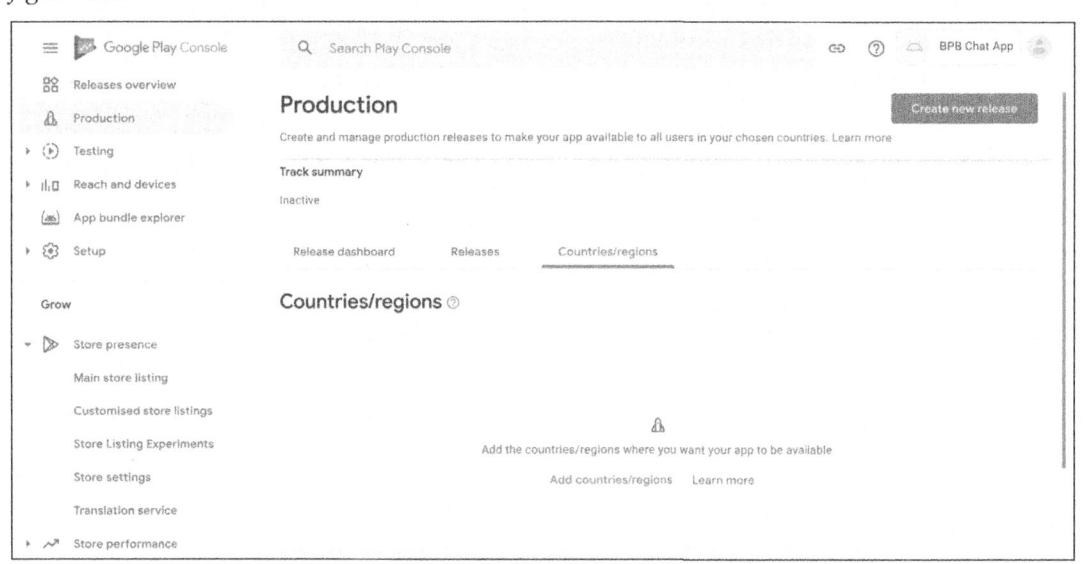

Figure 5.15: Creating a new release

On this page, you need to configure the following options:

- **Country/regions**: Select the **Country/regions** tab; here, you need to specify the list of countries where you want to release the App. Click on **Add countries/regions** and select countries from the list, and you can select All countries too. After selection, click on **Add countries/regions** -> **Add**.

- **Releases**: Select the `Releases` tab and click on `Create new release` to upload the app. Perform Play app signing steps, so Google can create and protect the signing key for the application and use it to sign each release.

  Under App bundle and APKs, select the file which we already created to upload. After uploading the file, the value for the release name will be added automatically (fetched from the application file). For Release notes, add text that gives an idea about a feature added or bug fixes to the application file, which you are uploading. It can be empty for the first release.

  After adding these values, click on `Save` -> `Review release`. Review and do changes by clicking on `Edit release` if you want to do. If everything is fine, then click on `Start roll-out to Production` -> `Rollout`.

NOTE: A staged rollout can be used to roll out an app update to the test and production environments. Few percent of app users receive the update with a phased rollout, and you can increase the percent as well to increase users for that release.

Remember that only app upgrades can employ staged rollouts; first-time app publishing is not permitted.

After rollout, the application goes to the verification/review phase, where your app will be verified, and if your app passes verification, it will be available at Google Play for those countries which you choose in the Production section (see country/regions tab in preceding *figure 5.15*). But if your application is found suspicious during verification or does not follow the Play store's guidelines, it can be rejected by Google.

There are following few best practices that you should follow:
- Be aligned with the developer policy written at https://play.google.com/about/developer-content-policy/. This is the kind of rule book that your app should follow. Else, most of the time, your application will be rejected.
- Read the Help Section of the Google play console.
- Keep eyes on app reviews and reply positively to the negative comment. Based on these, improve your app.

Watching the number of installs

On the Google Play console, the dashboard shows some statistics for your application. Note that this same dashboard shows you steps to prepare an app for release and release the application. And after release, it shows statistics of the app, as shown in *figure 5.16*:

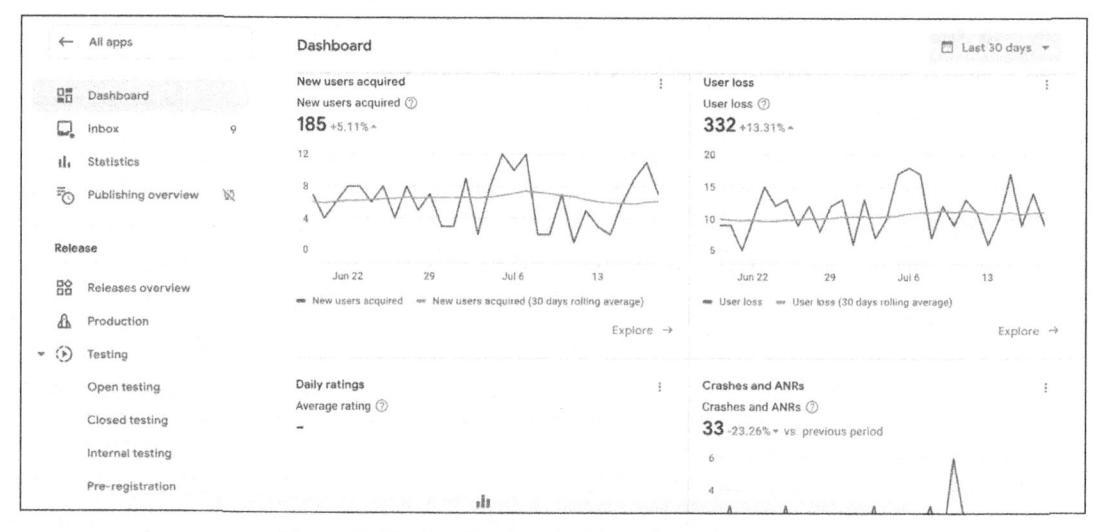

Figure 5.16: Application dashboard at Play console

On this page, you can see statistics for new users, users who uninstalled the application, daily ratings, crash or ANR details, and so on.

Updating application at Play Store

Before updating an application, there are few things that you need to handle:
- Make sure you are using the same singing key which was used for the previous version.
- Version code and version name should be updated.
- Backward compatible database schema changes. If anything changed in the database structure, you updated the database version and handled migration for an older version of the application.
- Prepare release notes and assets for updated application.
- Go through the checklist.

To update an application at Play Store, you need to follow similar steps which we did while releasing the first version of the app. Go to Play Store console -> Select **Application** -> Select **Production** from left navigation -> Click on **Create new release**. On this page, upload the latest application file and update release notes -> Click on **Save**. After this step, you can review the release or can roll it out to production. The steps are the same as in the new app release.

Conclusion

In this chapter, we have learned about build types, product flavors, and build variants, which help us to create different versions of the application from the same codebase. By using a combination of these, we can create Free and Paid applications from the same codebase.

We learned about R8 and Proguard to optimize the size of our application by removing unused code or unused resources and shrinking the name of classes and variables.

To release the application, we learned about creating release certificates, creating a developer account, and prepared some assets like app icons and screenshots. And at last, we learned how to release applications, how to update the application on Play Store, and looking at the dashboard to see the installations/uninstallations count of applications and crash trends.

In the upcoming chapter, we will develop our second application, which will be a Video Sharing application, and we will be learning to use the Exoplayer library and local data store.

Points to remember

- Before Android Gradle plugins 3.4.0, Proguard was the default tool to shrink code, but since Android Gradle plugins 3.4.0 R8 is the default tool. Proguard rules are still the same and are being used for R8.
- The release key store is the most important file to update your application. To update an application you need to sign the updated application file by the same key store which was used to sign the application file, which is already on Play Store.
- Configuration for build variants can exclude/include files or can be used different implementations for the same class, resource for each variant.
- Do not use many ads containers in the application. It may lead to a decrease interest of users in your application.
- If your application supports localization, do not forget to add localized app information and assets to Play Store.

Multiple Choice Questions

1. Which task can be done by R8 or Proguard?

   A. Code Shrinking   B. Resource Shrinking

   C. Optimization   D. All of the above

2. Build variant is:

   A. Same as build types

   B. Same as product flavors

   C. Combination of build types and product flavors

   D. None of the above

3. Any application which was free at the Play Store can be listed as Paid apps. True or False?

   A. True   B. False

Answers

1. D
2. C
3. B

Questions

1. How do you create different versions of the application from the same code base?
2. What are the benefits of code shrinking?
3. How does Tree shaking work?
4. What is the concept of dead code removal?

Key Terms

- Build types
- Product flavors
- Build variants
- Flavor dimensions
- MatchingFallbacks

- Release key store
- .aab
- .apk
- Zipalign
- Create release app
- Release checklist
- Releasing app
- Code shrinking
- Tree Shaking
- Resource shrinking
- Obfuscation
- Pricing strategy

CHAPTER 6
Developing Video Sharing Application

In the previous chapter, we learned about the process of releasing an application. Now, in this chapter, we will learn about developing video-sharing applications such as Tiktok or Facebook Watch. While developing this application, we will learn a few more Jetpack libraries and uses of the ExoPlayer library to play videos. There would be a few libraries that we have already used, such as View Pager and RecyclerView, in *Chapter 4: Developing Chat Application*.

We will also read about repository patterns to understand how you can separate the data layer from other layers of application code and how you can handle network calls and local database calls. After that, we will read about storing data at local, using Shared Preferences, SQLite (using Room), and Files. And we will learn to write CRUD operations for our video sharing application.

At the end of this chapter, we will learn about handling likes and sharing of videos and notifying users about new clips.

Structure

- Gathering functional requirement
- Creating user flow diagram
- Introducing material UI components
    - Introducing BottomNavigationView
- Introducing data storage in Android
    - Introducing files
        - Shared storage
        - App-specific storage
    - Storage Access Framework (SAF)
    - Preferences
    - Database
        - Room
- Creating CRUD for video sharing application
    - Creating database
- Introducing repository pattern
    - Introduction
    - Package structure for repository pattern
    - Implementing the repository pattern
- Introducing ExoPlayer
    - Introduction
    - Dependencies for ExoPlayer
- Understanding project structure
- Developing home screen
- Implementing the likes feature on clips
- Implementing the share feature for clips
- Implementing the comment feature on clips
- Developing add clips screen

Objectives

The objective of this chapter is to let you know about the basics of any video application and how you can develop such applications, repository patterns, and so on. After completing this chapter, you will have a clear understanding of separating the code at each layer, uses of ExoPlayer, local datastore options such as Files, Shared Preferences, and writing of create/read/update and delete operations using the local database for our video application. We already read about firebase in *Chapter 4: Developing Chat Application*, where we can use firebase services as the server. But to give you an idea about local storage, we will not be using any server, and we will use a repository so you can easily switch to network calls as well in the future with very minimal changes to code.

Note that, in our GitHub repository, you can find branches where you can see how you can use firebase for this application.

Gathering functional requirement

Similar to *Chapter 4, Developing Chat Application*, let us find out the functional requirement for the clip's application which are going to develop in this chapter:

- User can login or register. Basic login features should be there, like login by phone/email or Google, and so on.
- Show a list of clips to the user.
- User can create and add new clips.
- User can like and share the clips.
- User can see the profile page and can update it.

Note that the preceding requirements are not the complete list of requirements for any Video sharing application. There can be more features for the video-sharing application as follows:

- Any user can comment on clips or reply to any comment.
- Non-logged-in users can see clips.
- Users can have followers and can follow other users.

Creating user flow diagram

Let us see *figure 6.1*, which represents the user flow diagram for our clips application. It gives an idea about the overall clips application flow:

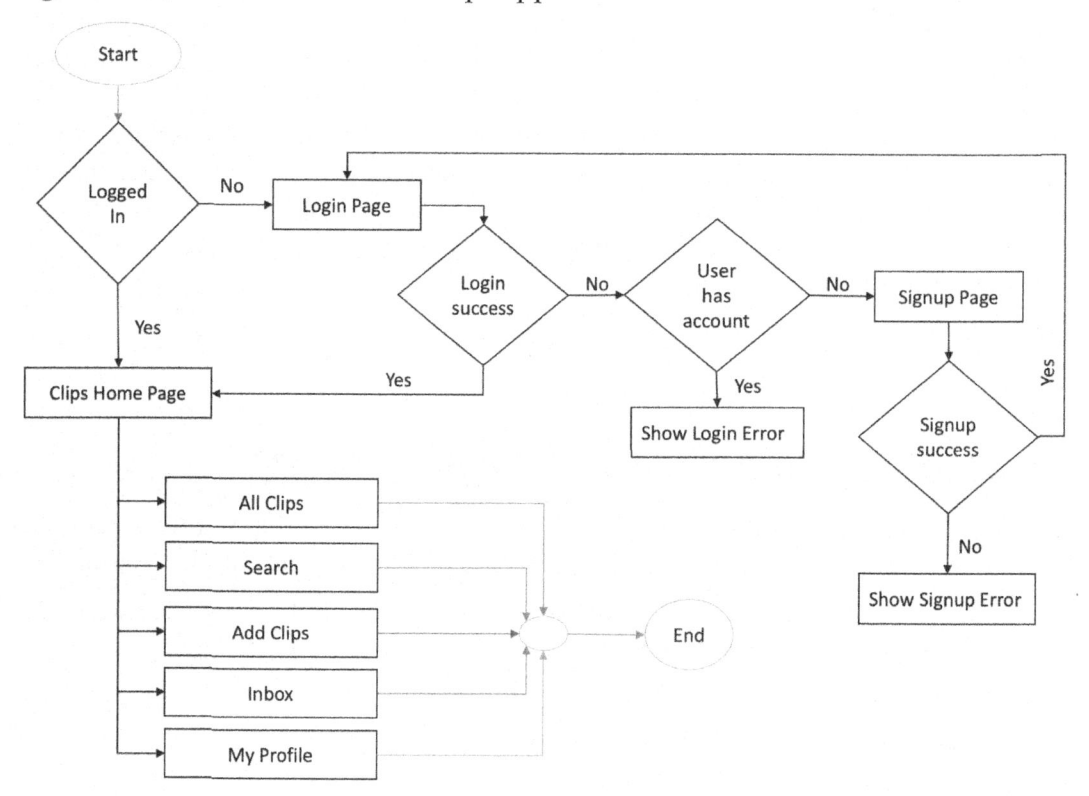

Figure 6.1: User flow diagram

In the preceding *figure 6.1*, the login flow is as same as our chat application, which we developed while reading *Chapter 4: Developing Chat Application*. Following is more information about screens added into flow in preceding *figure 6.1*:

- **Login Screen**: Uses FirebaseUI to allow the user to login into our application.
- **Clips Home Page**: After successful login, the user will land on this screen, where the user can navigate to any screen (Home, Search, Add Clips, Inbox, and Me) of the application.
- **All Clips (Home)**: This screen will be shown by default if the user is logged in. It shows all available clips to a user, where the user can swipe up/swipe down to navigate to the next/ previous clips. User can like, comment, and share the clips with anyone.

- **Search**: The user can search any specific clips created by the user or anyone.
- **Add Clips**: At this screen, the user can capture clips and upload them to the clips datastore.
- **Inbox**: This screen shows a list of messages sent or received by the user.
- **My Profile (Me)**: Profile screen, where the user can update profile picture, name, email, or password.

NOTE: "Login screen" and "My Profile screen" are as same pages that we developed in *Chapter 4: Developing Chat Application*, so we will not discuss these screens in this chapter again. And "Inbox" screen is almost the same as the chat feature, which we already developed, so you can follow the same for developing the "Inbox" screen.

The **Search** screen shows clips for a particular search term. Let us say the user search for the **car**; the **Search** screen page will show only those clips with the word **car** at any attribute, such as description, comment, or any other attribute of Clips object. It means we can reuse the same code of the **All Clips** screen for the **Search** screen as well, and the only difference will be in the login of the database, which will provide data after filtering clips for searched terms.

So, the pages we are going to develop in this chapter will look like as in *figure 6.2*:

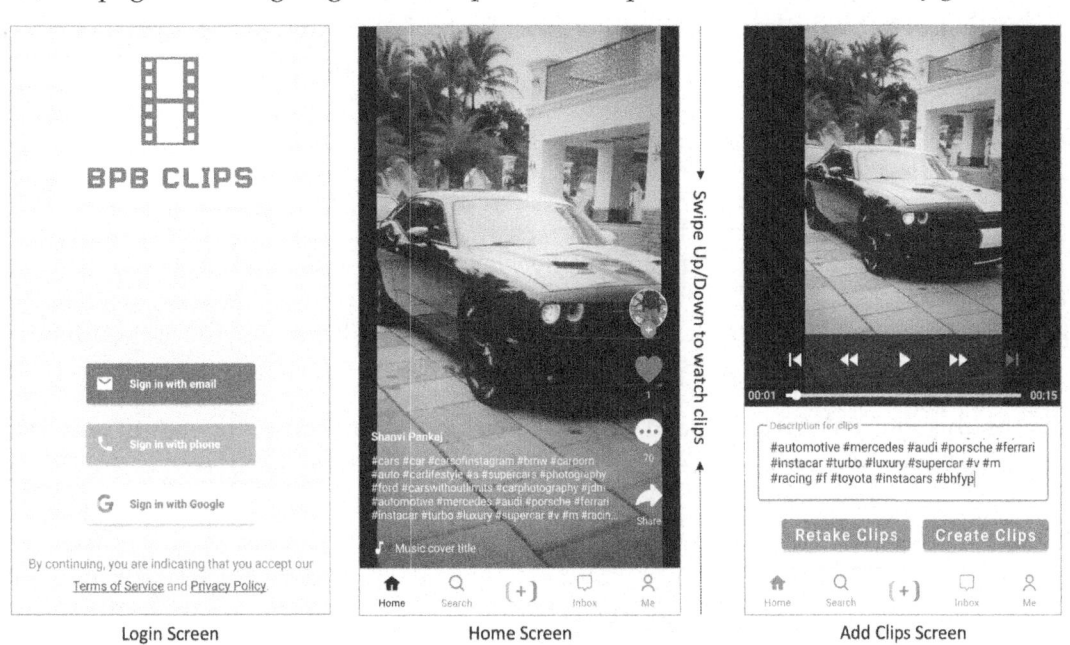

Figure 6.2: BpbClips screens

Introducing material UI components

In this section, we will focus on UI components that we are going to use in our Application. In our Clips Application, UI components that we will be using are ViewPager2, Video player, and **BottomNavigationView**. We read about ViewPager2 while developing a chat application in *Chapter 4: Developing Chat Application*. And for the video player, we will use ExoPlayer. We will read more about ExoPlayer in another section *Introducing ExoPlayer* in this chapter.

BottomNavigationView is the new component that we did not use or discussed yet. So, let us read more about this component and learn how we can use it.

Introducing BottomNavigationView

BottomNavigationView represents a standard bottom navigation bar for the application. It is an implementation of material design bottom navigation. It makes it easy for users to switch between top-level views with a single tap.

BottomNavigationView can be used when your application has three to five top-level destinations. Note that BottomNavigationView does not support more than five navigations.

Let us first see the bottom view, which will be added to the Home screen of this application. *Figure 6.3* represents the **BottomNavigationView**:

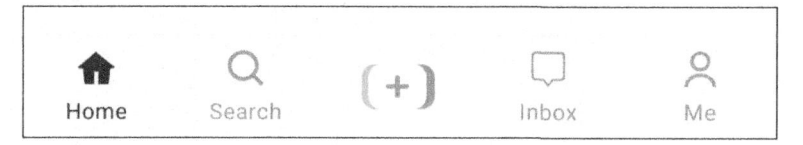

Figure 6.3: Bottom navigations

BottomNavigationView is part of the material design library, so the dependency added for material design will provide **BottomNavigationView** in our application.

Adding this view requires an XML, where we add each option to the menu, and the second is **BottomNavigationView**. Let us write code for the menu first:

res/menu/bottom_nav_menu.xml

```
<?xml version="1.0" encoding="utf-8"?>

<menu xmlns:android="http://schemas.android.com/apk/res/android">
```

```xml
<item
    android:id="@+id/navigation_home"
    android:icon="@drawable/ic_home_icon"
    android:title="@string/text_home" />

<item
    android:id="@+id/navigation_search_clips"
    android:icon="@drawable/ic_search_icon"
    android:title="@string/text_search" />

<item
    android:id="@+id/navigation_add"
    android:enabled="true"
    android:title="@null" />

<item
    android:id="@+id/navigation_inbox"
    android:icon="@drawable/ic_inbox_icon"
    android:title="@string/text_inbox" />

<item
    android:id="@+id/navigation_me"
    android:icon="@drawable/ic_person_icon"
    android:title="@string/text_me" />

</menu>
```

In the preceding XML, if you see code for menu **navigation_add**, we are not adding icons and text for the menu. There is a trick behind it. To show an icon for the **add clips**, we will be using an image view with the icon that you will see in the preceding image of the Bottom Navigation view.

Now let us write the code of **MainActivity**, where we will be adding BottomNavigationView and the **ImageView** to show the **Add Clips** option. The following is the layout code:

activity_main.xml

```xml
<?xml version="1.0" encoding="utf-8"?>
<androidx.constraintlayout.widget.ConstraintLayout ...>

    <com.google.android.material.bottomnavigation.BottomNavigationView
        android:id="@+id/navView"
        app:elevation="5dp"
        app:itemIconSize="20dp"
        app:labelVisibilityMode="labeled"
        ...
        app:menu="@menu/bottom_nav_menu" />

    <androidx.appcompat.widget.AppCompatImageView
        android:id="@+id/ivAddIcon"
        android:background="@android:color/transparent"
        android:elevation="6dp"
        ...
        app:srcCompat="@drawable/ic_add_icon_dark" />

    <fragment
        android:id="@+id/navHost"
        android:name="androidx.navigation.fragment.NavHostFragment"
        app:defaultNavHost="true"
        ...
        app:navGraph="@navigation/clips_navigation" />
```

```
</androidx.constraintlayout.widget.ConstraintLayout>
```

Here, you can see that we set **app:menu="@menu/bottom_nav_menu"** **BottomNavigationView**, and we are using the **ivAddIcon** image view, which acts as a placeholder for **Add clips**. And at last, we are using the **navHost** fragment to show Fragments for selected option/menu on **BottomNavigationView**.

Now let us write code to handle the selection of these menus and show the corresponding screen. To do that, we will write code in **MainActivity.kt** as follows:

```
private fun setBottomNavigation() {

    navView.setOnItemSelectedListener { menuItem ->

        var currentFragment =
            when (menuItem.itemId) {
                R.id.navigation_home -> HomeFragment()
                R.id.navigation_search_clips -> SearchClipsFragment()
                R.id.navigation_add -> AddClipsFragment()
                R.id.navigation_inbox -> InboxFragment()
                R.id.navigation_me -> ProfileFragment()
                else -> HomeFragment()
            }

        supportFragmentManager
            .beginTransaction()
            .replace(R.id.navHost, currentFragment)
            .commit()

        return@setOnItemSelectedListener true
    }
}
```

```
    // Show home screen as default
    navView.selectedItemId = R.id.navigation_home
}
```

In the preceding code, `navView` is the `BottomNavigationView`, and we are setting `setOnItemSelectedListener(…)` to this view to handle clicks and show different fragments.

That is it with `BottomNavigationView`.

Introducing data storage in Android

Storing data at the device is a usual task that you may do in any of your applications. There are more than one ways to store data, and you have to be attentive when choosing the right option to store your data on your device.

Android gives you the option to store data that would be accessible publicly or can be accessed by your application only which is data with private access. As we know, Android devices can be rooted, and the data with private access can be accessed by anyone on rooted devices. So choosing to store data at local or not is always a tricky thing to do in Android. The rule of thumb is, do not save any sensitive data, even with private access, and always look for other options like being dependent on the server for that sensitive data. You can think about any banking application, for example, where you cannot even store user information at local.

Although encryption is there to help you in some way, again, storing keys for encryption-decryption is another thing where you need to be an expert or do a lot of investigation as a newbie.

Let us see options available in Android to store the data:
- Files
    - Shared storage
    - App-specific storage
- Storage Access Framework (SAF)
- Preferences
- Database

Introducing files

We can write files of any type, such as text files, audio, video files, and so on; depending on the accessibility of these files, we categorize files into two types, files on shared storage and files on private storage:

- **Shared storage**: Files written at shared storage can be accessed by any other application too. Using **MediaStorage** we can write/read media files such as images, audio, or video files. If our application is running on API 28 or lower, we need **Manifest.permission.READ_EXTERNAL_STORAGE** to read files and Manifest.permission.WRITE_EXTERNAL_STORAGE to write files using **MediaStore** APIs. Note that from API 30, **Manifest.permission.READ_EXTERNAL_STORAGE** is needed only if you want to access files stored by another application. And from API 29 **Manifest.permission.WRITE_EXTERNAL_STORAGE** is needed only if you write something in another application's public storage.

- **App specific storage**: We can limit files to the application only, so other applications cannot access files written into app-specific storage. **Context.getFilesDir()** and **context.getCacheDir()** are two methods that can be used to write storage on internal storage and to write files on external storage, we can use **context.getExternalFilesDir()** and **context.getExternalCacheDir()**.

Storage Access Framework (SAF)

SAF allows us to browse, open or create documents, images, videos, or other files from the device. Following is an example code to open SAF to browse and select the image file on the device:

```
fun getImageFilePickerIntent(): Intent =
    Intent(Intent.ACTION_OPEN_DOCUMENT)
        .apply {
            addCategory(Intent.CATEGORY_OPENABLE)
            type = "image/*"
        }
```

You see a screen where you can choose an image file, similar to *figure 6.4*:

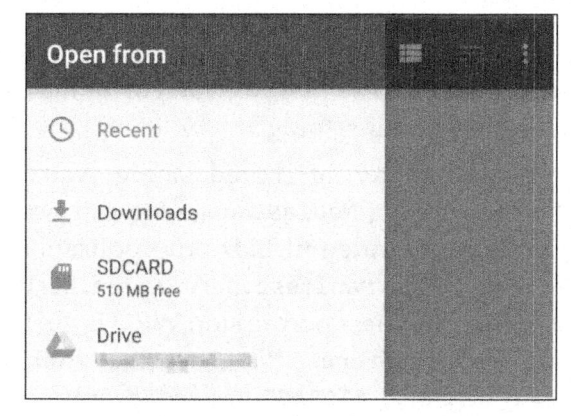

Figure 6.4: SAF UI from Android

And following is the example code to create files using SAF:

```
fun getTextFileCreateIntent(fileName: String): Intent =
    Intent(Intent.ACTION_CREATE_DOCUMENT)
        .apply {
            addCategory(Intent.CATEGORY_OPENABLE)
            type = "text/*"
            putExtra(Intent.EXTRA_TITLE, fileName)
        }
```

For the preceding code, we see a screen like as in *figure 6.5*:

Figure 6.5: Create a file using SAF

In the preceding *figure 6.5*, you see the navigation drawer indicator; by using that option, you can choose the location of the file.

NOTE: **The SAF is available since API 19.**

Preferences

Preferences are used to store key-value pairs in an XML file. These are usually faster than reading data from a File or Database. This type of storage can be used when you have less amount of data to save and not complex data. The most popular use of preferences is the settings screen of an application. Apart from it, you can store a flag to keep track of something, like you can show an intro screen to the user if the user visited your app for the first time and change the value of that flag to hide the intro screen for subsequent uses of your application.

There are three types of storage options available for Preferences, as follows:

(1) SharedPreferences

(2) Preferences Datastore

(3) Proto Datastore

SharedPreferences is deprecated now and Proto Datastore is almost the same as Preferences Datastore where Proto Datastore is type-safe, whereas Preferences Datastore is not type-safe. Let us see an example Preferences Datastore.

The following is the dependency for Preferences Datastore:

```
// Preferences DataStore. Prefer to use latest version
implementation "androidx.datastore:datastore-preferences:1.0.0"
```

We will store current user data, so that the same code we can use into our project. Let us first write data class for the user as follows:

```
data class UserInfo (val displayName : String, val profileImage: String)
```

Now let us write **DataStoreManager** class to handle read and write of data as follows:

```
class DataStoreManager(private val context: Context) {

    private val Context.dataStore: DataStore<Preferences>
            by preferencesDataStore(name = "user_datastore")

    companion object {
```

```kotlin
        val NAME = stringPreferencesKey("display_name")
        val PROFILE_IMAGE = stringPreferencesKey("profile_image")
    }

    suspend fun saveToDataStore(userInfo: UserInfo) {
        context.dataStore.edit {
            it[NAME] = userInfo.displayName
            it[PROFILE_IMAGE] = userInfo.profileImage
        }
    }

    suspend fun getFromDataStore() = context.dataStore.data.map {
        UserInfo(
            displayName = it[NAME] ?: "",
            profileImage = it[PROFILE_IMAGE] ?: ""
        )
    }
}
```

In the preceding class, **saveToDataStore()** is the method that can be used to write user data and **getFromDataStore()** will be used to read data. And as you see these methods are suspend functions, we can call these as follows:

```kotlin
lifecycleScope.launch(Dispatchers.IO) {
    dataStoreManager.saveToDataStore(
        userInfo = UserInfo(
            displayName = "Pankaj Kumar",
            profileImage = "url_of_profile_image"
        )
    )
}
```

Similarly, you can write calling code for **getFromDataStore()** as follows:

```
lifecycleScope.launch(Dispatchers.IO) {
    dataStoreManager.getFromDataStore().catch { e ->
        // Handle exception
    }.collect {
        withContext(Dispatchers.Main) {
            Log.d("Datastore", it.displayName)
            Log.d("Datastore", it.profileImage)
        }
    }
}
```

That is it. We learned how to use Preferences Datastore and how we can store logged-in user information of our video-sharing app.

Database

In Android, we can use the SQLite database to store structured data. The most common use case is to cache data, which can be used to serve the user when a device does not have an internet connection.

Room

We use Room from Jetpack, where Room is the persistence library that provides an abstraction layer over SQLite to allow fluent database access while harnessing the full power of SQLite. Room provides the following benefits:

- Annotations that minimize repetitive and error-prone boilerplate code.
- Compile-time verification of SQL queries.
- Streamlined database migration paths.
- Allows us to write less code

In our video sharing application, we will use Room to store data for videos. So let us first add the dependency for Room in our app module's **build.gradle** as follows:

```
implementation "androidx.room:room-runtime:2.3.0"
annotationProcessor "androidx.room:room-compiler:2.3.0"
```

The following are three primary components in Room:

(1) **Data access objects**: DAOs provides methods to do any type of operation in a database, such as query, update, insert, or delete.

(2) **Database class**: It defines the database and provides DAOs for that database. You can also write database migration into the database class. When you want to change anything in the database structure, you need to change the database version and write the code which defines how existing data at devices will be handled; this is known as database Migration.

(3) **Entities**: These data classes represent tables of our database.

Creating CRUD for video sharing application

Let us create the database for our video clips application using Room. As we read in the preceding topic about the Room, DAO, Entities, and Database class are three primary components. So we will create all these three components for our **Clips** database.

Creating database

Let us first define our entity data class, **Clips**, which will represent the video clip as follows:

```
@Entity(tableName = "clips")

data class Clips(

    @PrimaryKey(autoGenerate = true) val clipId: Long,

    @ColumnInfo(name = "url") var clipUrl: String? = null,

    @ColumnInfo(name = "thumbUrl") val thumbUrl: String? = null,

    @ColumnInfo(name = "desc") val description: String? = null,

    @ColumnInfo(name = "musicTitle") val coverTitle: String? = null,

    @ColumnInfo(name = "musicImageUrl") val coverImageLink: String? = null,

    @ColumnInfo(name = "userid") val userId: String? = null,

    @ColumnInfo(name = "profilePicUrl") val profilePicUrl: String? = null,
```

```
    @ColumnInfo(name = "userName") val userName: String? = null,

    @ColumnInfo(name = "likes") var likesCount: Long = 0,

    @ColumnInfo(name = "isLiked") var isLiked: Boolean = false,

    @ColumnInfo(name = "comments") var commentsCount: Long = 0,

    @ColumnInfo(name = "createdOn")
    var addedWhen: Long? = System.currentTimeMillis()
)
```

The preceding data class holds all attributes required to show on UI for a video clip.

@Entity defines data class as entity class to be used in Room. **@PrimaryKey** is used to mark the field as the primary key with the auto-increment attribute, and by using **@ColumnInfo** you can define the column name in the table for that field of the data class. For example, the field **addedWhen** will be created as **createdOn** column in table clips.

NOTE: **Considering the clips as a table, the clips table is not normalized. To normalize the clips table, we should extract user info into a different table and keep comments in a different table. So the possible normalized tables for our application would be as follows:**

- `Clips (clipId, userId, clipUrl, thumbUrl, description, coverTitle, coverImageLink, likesCount, comments, addedWhen)`
- `User (userId, profilePicUrl, userName)`
- `Comments (commentId, commentThreadId, parentCommentId, userId, commentText, commentedWhen)`
- `CommentThreads (commentThreadId, threadName, startedWhen)`

To keep our chapter simple and easy to understand, we will be using a single table "Clips".

Now let us write DAO class **ClipsDao**. In the **Data access object** (**DAO**), we specify SQL queries and associate them with method calls. The compiler checks the SQL and generates queries from convenience annotations for common queries, such as **@Insert**, **@Query** or **@Update**. The Room uses the DAO to create a clean API for our code. So, the code for **ClipsDao** would be as follows:

```
@Dao
interface ClipsDao {
```

```kotlin
    @Insert(onConflict = OnConflictStrategy.IGNORE)
    suspend fun insertClips(vararg clips: Clips)

    @Query("SELECT * FROM clips")
    fun getAllClips(): List<Clips>

    @Query("UPDATE clips SET likes = likes + 1, isLiked = 1 " +
            "WHERE clipId = :clipId")
    suspend fun incrementLikes(clipId: Long)

    @Query("UPDATE clips SET likes = likes - 1,  isLiked = 0 " +
            "WHERE clipId = :clipId")
    suspend fun decrementLikes(clipId: Long)

    @Update
    suspend fun updateComments(clips: Clips)

    @Delete
    suspend fun delete(clip: Clips)
}
```

NOTE: **The DAO must be an interface or abstract class.**

In DAO class, we wrote methods for each operation such as adding clips, updating likes and comments, or getting all clips from the database. So, if you plan to write network calls, you can think each method in the DAO can be an API and you must write network and data parsing for those methods.

And now, let us write the database **ClipsDatabase**. The database class should be an abstract class that extends **RoomDatabase** and **@Database** annotation with the list of each entity that is being used in the database. The **version** defines the current version of the database, which helps you to manage versions for the database and migration between versions. The code for **ClipsDatabase** will be similar to the following code:

```
@Database(entities = [Clips::class], version = 1)
abstract class ClipsDatabase : RoomDatabase() {

    abstract fun clipsDao(): ClipsDao

    companion object {

        @Volatile
        private var INSTANCE: ClipsDatabase? = null

        fun getDatabase(
            context: Context, scope: CoroutineScope
        ): ClipsDatabase {
            // If INSTANCE is null, then create the database
            // else return INSTANCE
            return INSTANCE ?: synchronized(this) {
                val instance = Room.databaseBuilder(
                    context.applicationContext,
                    ClipsDatabase::class.java,
                    "bpb_clips_db"
                ).fallbackToDestructiveMigration().build()
                INSTANCE = instance
                // return instance
                instance
            }
        }
    }
}
```

We only need one instance of a **Room** database for the whole app. So in the preceding code, by using **getDatabase(…)**, we are also making sure that we are not creating more than one instance for the class **ClipsDatabase** and only one database opened at the same time.

In other words, **ClipsDatabase** is implemented as a singleton class.

We have read each type of storage in Android, and we have implemented the data layer for the video sharing app. Now, we will read one more interesting topic that helps us write clean code.

Introducing repository pattern

In *Chapter 3: Architecture Patterns*, we read a little bit about the repository while reading about the MVP/MVVM architectural pattern. In this chapter, we will read it in detail.

Introduction

The repository pattern makes our task easy to de-couple the data layer and the business logic of our application. It helps us to hide the details of how we retrieve data from the datastore or store data in the datastore. The datastore can be a database at the device or can be on the server.

In other words, the repository pattern implements separation of concern by abstracting the data logic in our application.

Apart from abstracting the data layer of our application, another benefit of the repository pattern is that we can easily swap with a different type of datastore without changing the API or without changing the code of the other layer of our application. For example, we can show data from the local database/cache if a device does not have an internet connection and can show data from the network if a device has an internet connection.

Before writing classes, lets first look at *figure 6.6* for the repository in MVVM and repository's class hierarchy to understand it in a better way:

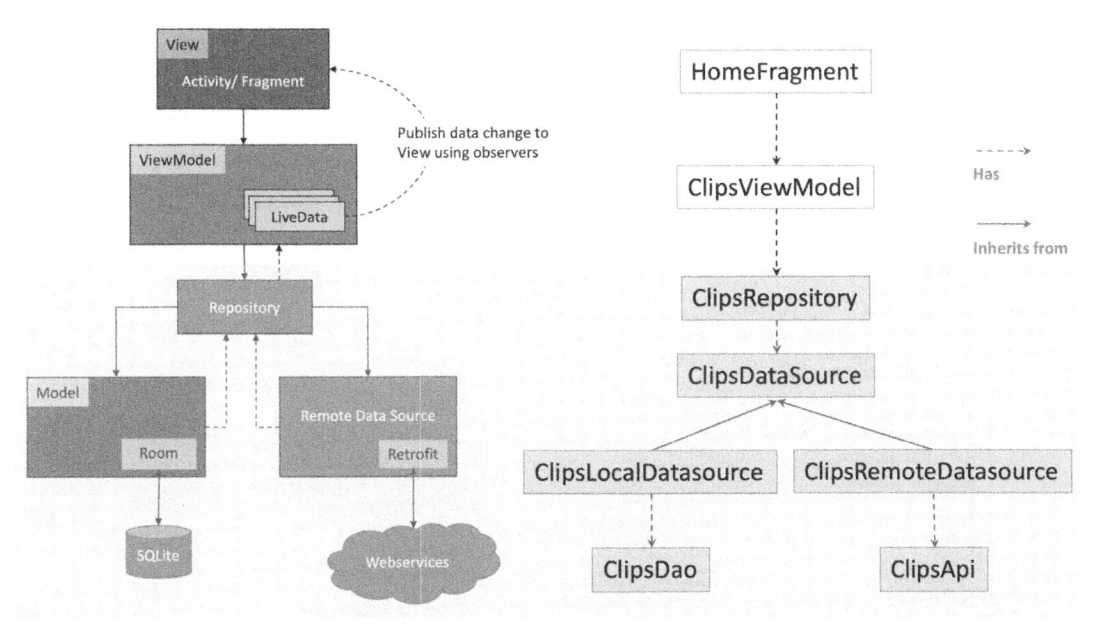

Figure 6.6: Repository classes hierarchy

In the preceding *figure 6.6*, at the left, you see the repository in MVVM, which we already saw while reading *Chapter 3: Architecture Patterns*. On the right, you see the class hierarchy for the home page screen, which shows clips. The class hierarchy shows how we create classes to implement repository patterns.

In the class hierarchy:

- **ClipsRepository** is the class which encapsulates the logic required to access data sources.
- **ClipsDataSource** is an interface and must be implemented by **ClipsLocalDataSource** and **ClipsRemoteDataSource**.
- **ClipsLocalDataSource** is a class containing code to read clip data from the local database via **ClipsDao**. While reading about the database, we already read about **ClipsDao**.
- **ClipsRemoteDataSource** is the class that will provide data from the network by using **ClipsApi**. **ClipsApi** will be an interface for configuring API calls for each type of data request.

Package structure for repository pattern

Before writing code, let us understand how you can organise classes in a repository pattern. *Figure 6.7* shows classes for clips:

```
repository
  data
    clips
   ① model
        Clips
   ② source
        local
          ClipsLocalDataSource
        remote
          ClipsRemoteDataSource
        ClipsDataSource
        ClipsRepository
    login
      Result
    database        ③
      ClipsDao
      ClipsDatabase
    ext
    network         ④
      api
        ClipsApi
      ApiResponse
```

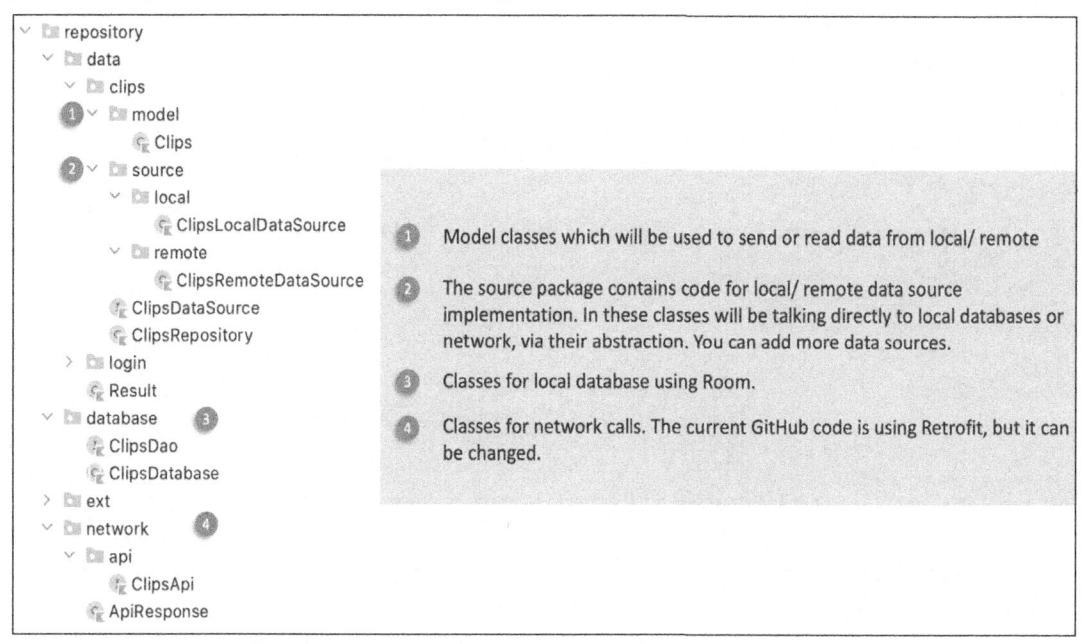

① Model classes which will be used to send or read data from local/ remote

② The source package contains code for local/ remote data source implementation. In these classes will be talking directly to local databases or network, via their abstraction. You can add more data sources.

③ Classes for local database using Room.

④ Classes for network calls. The current GitHub code is using Retrofit, but it can be changed.

Figure 6.7: Package structure in repository pattern

Implementing the repository pattern

Now, let us write code for the repository.

ClipsDataSource.kt:

The **ClipsDataSource** interface provides a contract for different data sources. This interface will be implemented by a class that can provide data from local or remote:

```
interface ClipsDataSource {

    suspend fun getClips(): List<Clips>

    suspend fun insertClips(vararg clips: Clips)

    suspend fun incrementLikes(clipId: Long)

    suspend fun decrementLikes(clipId: Long)

}
```

ClipsLocalDataSource.kt:

ClipsLocalDataSource is the class which implements **ClipsDataSource** and provides data from the local database via **ClipsDao**. The following is the code:

```
class ClipsLocalDataSource(
    private val clipsDao: ClipsDao
) : ClipsDataSource {

    override suspend fun getClips(): List<Clips> {
        return clipsDao.getAllClips()
    }

    override suspend fun insertClips(vararg clips: Clips) {
        return clipsDao.insertClips(*clips)
    }

    override suspend fun incrementLikes(clipId: Long) {
        return clipsDao.incrementLikes(clipId)
    }

    override suspend fun decrementLikes(clipId: Long) {
        return clipsDao.decrementLikes(clipId)
    }
}
```

ClipsRemoteDataSource.kt:

ClipsRemoteDataSource is the class which implements **ClipsDataSource** and provides data from the network/server via **ClipsApi**. Where **ClipsApi** is an interface which provides a way to define HTTP calls and methods to read/write data on the server. For our project, we do not have data on the network/server, so we will not investigate the code of **ClipsApi** and Retrofit setup. But you can check the GitHub repository to learn more about retrofit setup and Remote Data Sources. As of now, you can assume that **ClipsApi** is a helper class that will provide data from the network somehow.

The following is the code for **ClipsRemoteDataSource**:

```kotlin
class ClipsRemoteDataSource(
    private val api: ClipsApi
) : ClipsDataSource {
    override suspend fun getClips(): List<Clips> {

        return when (val result = api.getClipsAsync().getResult()) {
            is Result.Success -> result.data
            else -> listOf()
        }
    }

    override suspend fun insertClips(vararg clips: Clips) {
        api.insertClips(*clips)
    }

    override suspend fun incrementLikes(clipId: Long) {
        api.incrementLikes(clipId)
    }

    override suspend fun decrementLikes(clipId: Long) {
        api.decrementLikes(clipId)
    }
}
```

NOTE: **Remember that your data sources should follow Liskov substitution of SOLID principles.**

ClipsRepository.kt:

The repository class, where you can write code to decide the data source. It means here you can decide to read data from local or get it from the network or some other data source if you have:

```
class ClipsRepository(
    private val dataSource: ClipsDataSource
) {

    suspend fun getClips() = dataSource.getClips()

    suspend fun insertClips(vararg clips: Clips) {
        dataSource.insertClips(*clips)
    }

    suspend fun incrementLikes(clipId: Long) {
        dataSource.incrementLikes(clipId)
    }

    suspend fun decrementLikes(clipId: Long) {
        dataSource.decrementLikes(clipId)
    }

}
```

In the preceding code of **ClipsRepository**, we are providing one argument as **ClipsDataSource**. Remember that **ClipsRemoteDataSource** and **ClipsLocalDataSource**, both classes are the type of **ClipsDataSource**, as these classes implement **ClipsDataSource**. It means you can pass an object of either **ClipsRemoteDataSource** or **ClipsLocalDataSource** to the **ClipsRepository**. This is how you get the flexibility to switch between local or remote data, depending on your need. In our **BpbClips** application, we will read data from the local database, so we will pass an object of **ClipsLocalDataSource** to the **ClipsRepository**.

NOTE: **Sometimes, we require to implement caching. For example, if you want to show data from the local database when a user does not have an internet connection and show data from remote if the user does have internet. There would be other use cases as well to decide on local or remote data sources.**

In such cases, ClipsRepository can take two ClipsDataSource arguments. One for local and another for remote so that we can decide which data source should be used in a specific condition.

Sometimes developers define a repository class that implements ClipsDataSource. This is not a good practice so avoid doing that.

That is it. Now, we know about the repository pattern and the benefits of using it.

Introducing ExoPlayer

ExoPlayer is a library for video players by Google. It is built on top of low-level media APIs in Android, so it supports almost all video file formats supported by low-level media API and additional formats like DASH and SmoothStreaming. ExoPlayer is more customizable and flexible than the media APIs (VideoView and MediaPlayer).

It is an open-source project and is being used by many Google applications, like YouTube.

In our video sharing application, we will be using ExoPlayer. So, let us see the basic configurations and code required to use ExoPlayer.

Dependencies for ExoPlayer

Let us write the dependency of ExoPlayer into the **app/build.gradle** file as follow:

```
implementation 'com.google.android.exoplayer:exoplayer:2.10.4'
```

The preceding dependency is for the full library, which includes the core library, content supports (DASH, HLS, RTSP), UI components and more. If you want to add these dependencies individually, you need to add dependencies as follows:

```
implementation 'com.google.android.exoplayer:exoplayer-core:2.10.4'
implementation 'com.google.android.exoplayer:exoplayer-dash:2.10.4'
implementation 'com.google.android.exoplayer:exoplayer-ui:2.10.4'
```

Now let us write code to play video clips. The following are steps that are required to complete the setup.

First, let us add **PlayerView** into the layout XML file (**clips_view.xml** for our project) as follows:

```
<com.google.android.exoplayer2.ui.PlayerView

    android:id="@+id/playerView"

    android:layout_width="match_parent"

    android:layout_height="match_parent"

    app:use_controller="false" />
```

Preceding code is just a basic configuration; the ExoPlayer library provides many customization attributes. We are using **use_controller** to hide controllers from the player view. These play/pause or other controllers are not required in our project. But in case you need these controllers, either you can set it true or can remove **app:use_controller="false"**, the default is **true**.

Now, let us initialize and set videos to play. We will divide code into methods to understand each step during preparing media and playing the video using the ExoPlayer, as follows:

```
private lateinit var simplePlayer: SimpleExoPlayer

private lateinit var cacheDataSourceFactory: CacheDataSourceFactory


private fun getPlayer(): SimpleExoPlayer {

    // Initialise it, if not done already

    if (!::simplePlayer.isInitialized) {

        initPlayer()

    }

    return simplePlayer

}
```

The preceding code is simple where we are initializing **simplePlayer** in not initialised already, and then we are returning the initialized object. Let us write code for **initPlayer()** as follows:

```
private fun initPlayer() {

    simplePlayer = ExoPlayerFactory.newSimpleInstance(context)
```

```
        cacheDataSourceFactory = CacheDataSourceFactory(
            simpleCache, // Cache to provide better experience to user.
            DefaultHttpDataSourceFactory(
                Util.getUserAgent(
                    context,
                    "BPB Clips"
                )
            )
        )
}
```

In the preceding code of **initPlayer()**, **simplePlayer** is being initialized, and the object of **CacheDataSourceFactory** is being created.

NOTE: ExoPlayer can download chunks and show the video. So, on slow networks, the user might see a lag while watching clips. To provide a better user experience, one solution can be that you can pre-download videos by using a caching mechanism. So, whenever the user accesses a particular clip, it can be shown without delay. But keep in mind that, by this approach, we have the cache memory limitation.

So, the initialisation and configuration code for **simpleCache** will be written as follows:

```
val lruCacheEvictor = LeastRecentlyUsedCacheEvictor(90 * 1024 * 1024)
val databaseProvider: DatabaseProvider = ExoDatabaseProvider(this)

if (simpleCache == null) {
    simpleCache = SimpleCache(cacheDir, lruCacheEvictor, databaseProvider)
}
```

The preceding code will be written into the **Application** class to configure it globally. See our GitHub repository for more details.

Coming back to ExoPlayer configuration and initialization:

```
private fun prepareMediaAndPlay(videoUrl: String) {
```

```
val uri = Uri.parse(videoUrl)

val mediaSource = ProgressiveMediaSource.Factory(
    cacheDataSourceFactory
).createMediaSource(uri)

simplePlayer.prepare(mediaSource, true, true)
simplePlayer.repeatMode = Player.REPEAT_MODE_ONE
simplePlayer.playWhenReady = true
}
```

We are done with configurations. Let us see how we can use these methods in our clip's application. So, we can write the following code to play clips in ExoPlayer:

```
private fun playClips(videoUrl: String) {
    val simplePlayer = getPlayer()
    // playerView is defined in XML at first step.
    playerView.player = simplePlayer
    prepareMediaAndPlay(videoUrl)
}
```

The preceding code will be used on the screen where we will show a list of clips, and the user can swipe and play the clip.

Apart from these basic configurations, you need to make sure that you are acquiring and releasing player instances correctly. To do that, we need to handle the lifecycle of a Fragment or an Activity. For example, the following code can be written to handle it:

```
override fun onPause() {
    pauseVideo()
    super.onPause()
}
```

```kotlin
override fun onResume() {

    restartVideo()

    super.onResume()

}

override fun onDestroy() {

    releasePlayer()

    super.onDestroy()

}

private fun restartVideo() {

    if (::simplePlayer.isInitialized) {

        simplePlayer.seekToDefaultPosition()

        simplePlayer.playWhenReady = true

    }

}

private fun pauseVideo() {

    simplePlayer.playWhenReady = false

}

private fun releasePlayer() {

    simplePlayer.stop(true)

    simplePlayer.release()

}
```

NOTE: For a better user experience and to deliver videos with lower latency, we can define ExoPlayer buffering strategy. ExoPlayer provides a class **DefaultLoadControl**, the customizable implementation of the LoadControl interface. The class DefaultLoadControl covers most of the use cases and fits in our requirements. And this approach can be better than caching approach, as it allows you to deliver the video faster without using device memory for pre-caching videos.

That is it from configurations of ExoPlayer and how we will use it in our clips sharing application.

Understanding project structure

Figure 6.8 represents the project files structure of the Clips application:

```
v com
  v bpb
    v android
      v clips
        > repository          (1)
        v ui
          v addclips          (2)
              AddClipsFragment
              AddClipsViewModel
          v home              (3)
              ClipFragment
              ClipsPagerAdapter
              HomeFragment.kt
              HomeViewModel.kt
      (4)> inbox
          > login             (5)
      (6)v main
              MainActivity
      (7)> profile
          v search            (8)
              SearchClipsFragment
              SearchClipsViewModel
          > utils
          BpbClipsApp
      (9) BpbClipsBaseActivity
          BpbClipsBaseFragment
```

(1) The repository package introduced while reading repository pattern.

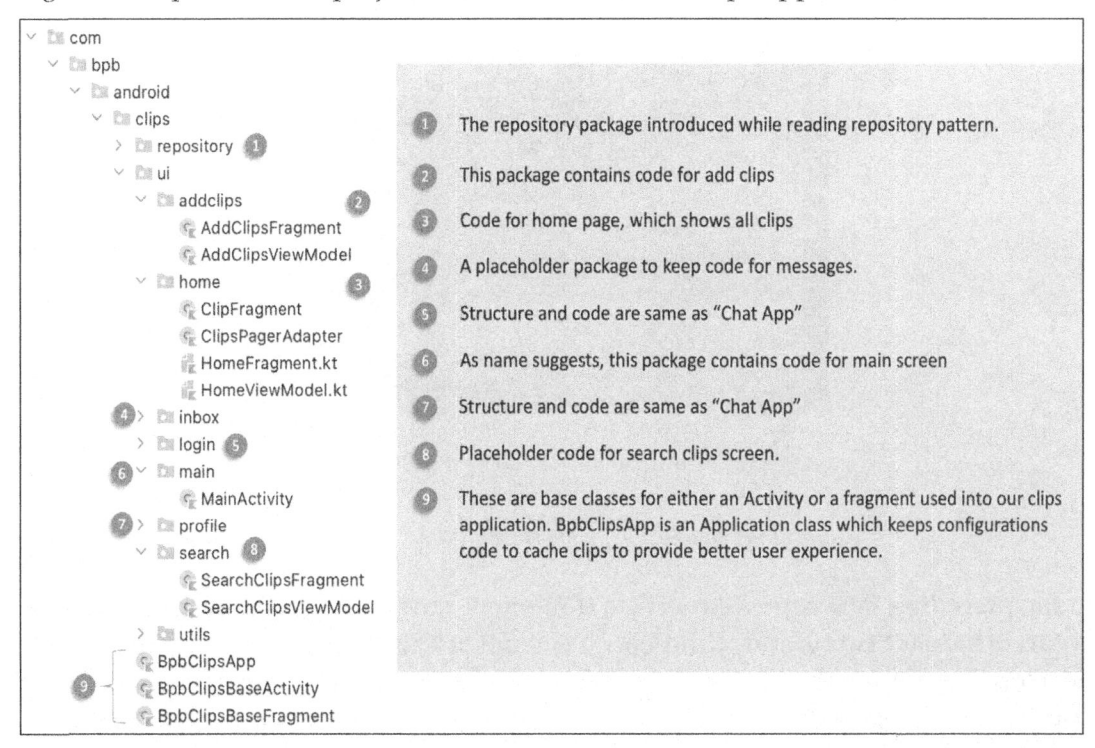

(2) This package contains code for add clips

(3) Code for home page, which shows all clips

(4) A placeholder package to keep code for messages.

(5) Structure and code are same as "Chat App"

(6) As name suggests, this package contains code for main screen

(7) Structure and code are same as "Chat App"

(8) Placeholder code for search clips screen.

(9) These are base classes for either an Activity or a fragment used into our clips application. BpbClipsApp is an Application class which keeps configurations code to cache clips to provide better user experience.

Figure 6.8: Project structure

The preceding package structure is the same as how we structured our chat application. Only the repository package is new, and that has already been discussed in the repository section.

Developing home screen

The home screen will show a list of clips where users can like and share clips as well. This page will be shown first by default when the user does login or already logged-in launches the application. *Figure 6.9* represents the home page:

Figure 6.9: *The home screen/list of clips*

In the preceding figure, the red section (Fragment host and **BottomNavigationView**) is part of **MainActivity**, and while learning about **BottomNavigationView** we already developed code for this red section. When the user taps on **Home** or launches the application, the **Home** option will be the default selection on **BottomNavigationView**, and **HomeFragment** will be attached at fragment host (fragment host can be **FrameLayout** or **FragmentContainerView**). It means the green section (area marked for **ViewPager2**) is the place where our **HomeFragment** will be added and shown to the user.

As you see in the preceding figure, **HomeFragment** will have **ViewPager2**, which will show another fragment by using the adapter. The fragment handled by the adapter will represent a Clips (the UI for clips which you see in the preceding figure).

Let us write code for **HomeFragment** first:

fragment_home.xml:

Following is the layout code for **HomeFragment**, whether we only need a **ViewPager2**:

```xml
<?xml version="1.0" encoding="utf-8"?>
<androidx.viewpager2.widget.ViewPager2
    xmlns:android="http://schemas.android.com/apk/res/android"
    xmlns:tools="http://schemas.android.com/tools"
    android:id="@+id/vpClips"
    android:layout_width="match_parent"
    android:layout_height="match_parent"
    android:orientation="vertical" />
```

HomeFragment.kt:

Let us write code for **HomeFragment**, where we will fetch clips data and set it to the adapter:

```kotlin
class HomeFragment : BpbClipsBaseFragment(R.layout.fragment_home),
    OnClipsListener {

    private val clipsViewModel by activityViewModels<ClipsViewModel> {
        ClipsViewModelFactory((activity?.application as BpbClipsApp)
            .repository)
    }

    private lateinit var clipsPagerAdapter: ClipsPagerAdapter

    override fun onViewCreated(view: View, savedInstanceState: Bundle?) {
        super.onViewCreated(view, savedInstanceState)
        // Create adapter with empty data set
        clipsPagerAdapter = ClipsPagerAdapter(this, arrayListOf())
        vpClips.adapter = clipsPagerAdapter
```

```kotlin
        // Fetch clips
        clipsViewModel.getClips()
        // Observe for clips data. Update adapter to show
        // newly fetched clips
        clipsViewModel.clipsLiveData.observe(
            viewLifecycleOwner
        ) { clips ->
            val size = clipsPagerAdapter.dataList.size
            clipsPagerAdapter.dataList.addAll(clips)
            clipsPagerAdapter.notifyItemRangeInserted(size, clips.size)
        }
    }

    override fun onLikeClicked(position: Int, liked: Boolean, clips: Clips) {
        // We will see the code for this method while
        // writing code for like clips
    }

    override fun onCommentsClicked(position: Int, clips: Clips) {
        // Open comment screen, where user can add comment or reply
    }
}
```

NOTE: **In the preceding code, we are setting up an adapter for ViewPager2. In *Chapter 4: Developing Chat Application*, we have used ViewPager2. The only difference in both places is the orientation. In our chat application, ViewPager2 allows users to swipe from left to right or vice-versa, and in the Clips application, ViewPager2 allows user to swipe from top to bottom or vice-versa. That is handled by android:orientation attribute in ViewPager2. Other configuration/ code is almost the same.**

The **HomeFragment** implements **OnClipsListener**, which code will be as follows:

```
interface OnClipsListener {
    fun onLikeClicked(position: Int, liked: Boolean, clips: Clips)
    fun onCommentsClicked(position: Int, clips: Clips)
}
```

It provides call-backs if the user clicks on the like or the comment icon. Similarly, you can add one more method in the preceding interface for handling call-back for share clips. While writing code for **ClipFragment**, we will understand how **HomeFragment** will be notified.

The **HomeFragment** uses **ClipsViewModel** to interact with the data source. We are passing the repository for a local data source to this ViewModel so that it will use the local database. Similarly, we can use a remote data source. To keep a single instance of the repository, we are preparing the object into Application class **BpbClipsApp**, so this repository object will be available throughout the life of the Clips application. Following is the repository initialisation code in **BpbClipsApp** class:

```
private val coroutineScope = CoroutineScope(SupervisorJob())

val database by lazy { ClipsDatabase.getDatabase(this, coroutineScope) }

private val datasource: ClipsDataSource by lazy {
    ClipsLocalDataSource(database.clipsDao()) }

val repository: ClipsRepository by lazy { ClipsRepository(datasource) }
```

NOTE: **The preceding code for creating an object of the repository can be done via any dependency injection solution, and we would not be writing such long code to initialise or provide instances to the class which needs it. We will read about dependency injection solutions in** *Chapter 10: Important Tools/Libs,* **which you must Try.**

Coming back to **ClipsViewModel**, the following is the code that talks to the repository via a given data source (in our current implementation, it is a local data source) and notifies **HomeFragment** via LiveData after fetching new clips:

```
class ClipsViewModel(
    private val repository: ClipsRepository
) : ViewModel() {
```

```kotlin
    private val _clipsLiveData = MutableLiveData<List<Clips>>()
    val clipsLiveData: LiveData<List<Clips>> = _clipsLiveData

    fun getClips() = viewModelScope.launch(Dispatchers.IO) {
        val clips = repository.getClips()
        _clipsLiveData.postValue(clips)
    }
}
```

ClipsPagerAdapter.kt:

Let us write code for **ClipsPagerAdapter**, which is an adapter for **ViewPager2** used at the **HomeFragment** screen:

```kotlin
class ClipsPagerAdapter(
    val fragment: HomeFragment,
    val dataList: ArrayList<Clips> = arrayListOf()
) : FragmentStateAdapter(fragment) {

    override fun getItemCount(): Int {
        return dataList.size
    }

    override fun createFragment(position: Int): Fragment {
        val clipsFragment = ClipFragment.newInstance(
            position, dataList[position]
        )
        clipsFragment.listener = fragment
        return clipsFragment
    }
```

```
    fun updateClipsAt(index: Int, clips: Clips) {
        if (index < 0 || index >= dataList.size) return
        dataList[index] = clips
    }
}
```

NOTE: Similar to the chat application, this adapter for ViewPager2 uses createFragment() to create new fragments and provide data set for the position where this newly created fragment will be shown. In the chat application, ViewPager2 was being used to show tabs, and we had a completely different screen design for each page of the tab, so we were creating a different fragment. But in the case of Clips, each page in ViewPager2 has the same design with different clips data. That is why we are creating an object of the same fragment ClipFragment and setting different data depending on the current position of this new fragment in the adapter. Now you understand the use cases and can make better decisions while writing code for ViewPager2.

That is it for **HomeFragment**. Now, we need to design and create **ClipFragment**, which represents the clip at the home screen and is being created from **ClipsPagerAdapter**.

Before looking into the code for **ClipFragment**, note that the following code only shows important code which can explain functions in the **ClipFragment**. The full source code of **ClipFragment** and **clips_view.xml** are available at our GitHub repository:

```
class ClipFragment : Fragment(R.layout.fragment_clips_view) {
    private var clipsData: Clips? = null
    private var positionInAdapter = 0
    ...

    override fun onViewCreated(view: View, savedInstanceState: Bundle?) {
        super.onViewCreated(view, savedInstanceState)

        arguments?.let { args ->
            clipsData = args.getParcelable(EXTRA_CLIPS)
            positionInAdapter = args.getInt(EXTRA_POS, 0)
```

```kotlin
        }
        clipsData?.let { it ->
            setClipData(it)
            setListeners(it)
            showLikes(it)
            it.clipUrl?.let { _clipUrl ->
                playClips(_clipUrl)
            }
        }
    }

    private fun setClipData(clips: Clips) {
        tvAccountHandle.text = clips.userName
        tvVideoDescription.text = clips.description
        tvMusicTitle.text = clips.coverTitle
        tvCommentTitle.text =
            clips.commentsCount.formatNumberAsReadableFormat()

        // Loading image using Glide. loadUsingGlide is an
        // extension which used Glide config inside.
        ivProfilePic?.loadUsingGlide(clips.profilePicUrl)
        ...
    }

    private fun setListeners(clips: Clips) {
        ivLikeClips.setOnClickListener {
            // Implementation will be added in the section
            // "Implementing likes feature on clips"
```

```
        }

        ivShare.setOnClickListener {
            // Implementation of this method will be written in
            // the "Implementing share feature for clips."
            shareClips(clips)
        }
    }
   ....
}
```

In the preceding code, `Line 13-20` is the most important to understand. Here, we are calling a few methods to bind clips data and play clips. Following is details of these methods:

- **setClipData(…)**: This method is being used to bind clips data to view.
- **setListeners(…)**: This method is being used to handle user actions, for example, clicking on like, comment, or share icon. We pass call-backs via **OnClipsListener** to **HomeFragment**. You can write code to handle likes/clips/share in ClipFragment as well, but keeping data access only till **HomeFragment** and making **ClipFragment** as dumb as possible can be a good way.
- **showLikes(…)**: Code of this method can be merged into **setClipData()** as well. In this method, we check if the current user liked the clip or not and depending on the state, we change the like icon with the following code:

```
private fun showLikes(clips: Clips) {
    ivLikeClips.setImageResource(
        if (clips.isLiked) R.drawable.ic_heart_select_icon
        else R.drawable.ic_heart_icon
    )

    tvLikeClipsTitle?.text =
        clips.likesCount.formatNumberAsReadableFormat()
}
```

- **playClips(…)**: This method does configurations for ExoPlayer and play the video automatically. While reading about ExoPlayer, we wrote code for this method with other configurations of ExoPlayer. For more details, refer to the section *Introducing ExoPlayer*.

In summary, we are writing similar code as **ViewHolder** into **ClipFragment**. Like **ViewHolder**, we get a model class to bind with UI components, and we add listeners to handle user actions.

NOTE: **We will see the code for the likes feature in** *Implementing likes feature on clips* **and the share feature in the "Implementing share feature on clips" section in this chapter.**

Congratulations, we have developed our home screen, where users can now see a list of clips. Now, let us write code to allow the user to record and create clips.

Implementing the likes feature on clips

To implement likes feature on clips, we need to understand the structure for data to handle likes and dislikes at the server. There would be different ways to handle it, and one of them can be like, keeping two attributes of clips as arrays, likes and dislikes. These two arrays will keep the ids of each user who liked or disliked the clips as follows:

```
data class Clips(
    val usersWhoLiked: List<Int> = listOf(),
    val usersWhoDisliked: List<Int> = listOf(),
    ...
)
```

But if you think in terms of a specific user, we need not require these two attributes at the client (which is our Android application). We just need the count of total likes and a flag that says whether the current user has liked the video or not. It means, on an actual network call, you send an identifier for the user, and the server will send you clips data in terms of that user only, without the list of users who liked or disliked the clip.

As we are not writing network calls for our app, we will implement the behavior just for the client, and we will write code for likes-count and the current user liked the clips. If you look at our entity class, **Clips**, we have the following attributes to handle likes:

```kotlin
data class Clips(
    var likesCount: Long = 0,
    var isLiked: Boolean = false,
    ...
)
```

Figure 6.10 explains each state of like:

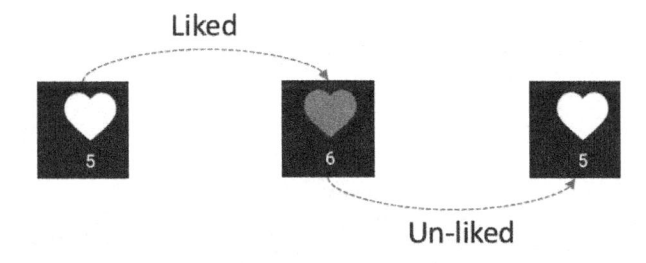

Figure 6.10: Like clips state

To implement this feature, first, we need to handle the click on the like button and then update the database and then update the UI.

Let us first write code in **ClipFragment** to be executed by clicking on the **like** icon as follows:

```kotlin
ivLikeClips.setOnClickListener {
    // 1. Update clips object
    updateLikes(clips)
    // 2. Notify HomeFragment to update database
    listener?.onLikeClicked(positionInAdapter, clips.isLiked, clips)
    // 3. Update UI
    showLikes(clips)
}
```

We are just updating the value of likes and **isLiked** in **updateLikes()** as follows:

```kotlin
private fun updateLikes(clips: Clips) {
    clips.isLiked = !clips.isLiked
```

```
        if (clips.isLiked) clips.likesCount++ else clips.likesCount--
}
```

To update the database, we notify **HomeFragment** by **listener?.onLikeClicked(…)**, and then **HomeFragment** uses **ViewModel**, which talks with the local repository to update clips. As following code of **onLikeClicked(…)** in **HomeFragment**:

```
override fun onLikeClicked(position: Int, liked: Boolean, clips: Clips) {

    // Update clips in database

    if (liked) {

        clipsViewModel.incrementLikes(clips.clipId)

    } else {

        clipsViewModel.decrementLikes(clips.clipId)

    }


    // Update clips in adapter. Note that we will not notify adapter

    // for this change. Notifying adapter will reloads the fragment

    // again and cause video to load and play again.

    clipsPagerAdapter.updateClipsAt(position, clips)

}
```

In the preceding code, we are using **clipsViewModel** to update likes.

NOTE: **We are also using clipsPagerAdapter.updateClipsAt(), which updates data in dataset of adapter. Updating data in the adapter is required, so if the user scrolls to other clips on the device and comes back again to that previous clip, the adapter will bind data again, so updated data will be picked to be shown. Usually, we used to notify the adapter about any change in the dataset, but in our case, if we do, the video will be reloaded, so for better UX, we are just updating data in the adapter without notifying the adapter.**

And the code inside **ClipsViewModel** for updating likes is as follows:

```
class ClipsViewModel(private val repository: ClipsRepository) : ViewModel()
{

    ...
```

```kotlin
fun incrementLikes(clipsId: Long) = viewModelScope.launch {
    repository.incrementLikes(clipsId)
}

fun decrementLikes(clipsId: Long) = viewModelScope.launch {
    repository.decrementLikes(clipsId)
}
}
```

And the rest is handled by the repository, which we already saw while reading about the repository pattern. That is it, we have implemented the like feature on clips.

TIP: When you implement API for handling likes, we need not do modifications to the object of the clips model. We can just send clipsId and isLiked to the API and after a successful response from the server, we can update the UI and data set of the adapter.

Implementing the share feature for clips

We can share clips with anyone in the world via other applications. Android provides an Intent action **Intent.ACTION_SEND**, which can be used to share the clips. So, when the user clicks on the **share** icon on the clips screen, we will write code as follows to share clips:

```kotlin
private fun shareClips(clips: Clips) {
    val text = "I am sharing you this amazing clip ${clips.clipUrl} " +
        "to watch. You can find many amazing clips at " +
        "https://play.google.com/store/apps/details?id=com.bpb.android.clips"

    val sendIntent: Intent = Intent().apply {
        action = Intent.ACTION_SEND
        putExtra(Intent.EXTRA_SUBJECT, "Have you seen this Clip?")
        putExtra(Intent.EXTRA_TEXT, text)
```

```
        type = "text/plain"
    }
    val shareIntent = Intent.createChooser(sendIntent, "Share this clip 
    via")
    startActivity(shareIntent)
}
```

In the preceding code, we set subject and text as extra to autofill fields on chosen application.

NOTE: You can use the share feature for the promotion of your application as well. If you see in the variable text in the preceding code, the first sentence contains the information about the clips that the user wanted to share. But the sentence "You can find many amazing clips at https://play.google.com/store/apps/details?id=com.bpb.android.clips" is a promotional message which says that the receiver can install our application to see such interesting clips.

Figure 6.11 will explain the flow of sharing the Clips via another application and let you know how text used in the preceding method will be used by the Android system:

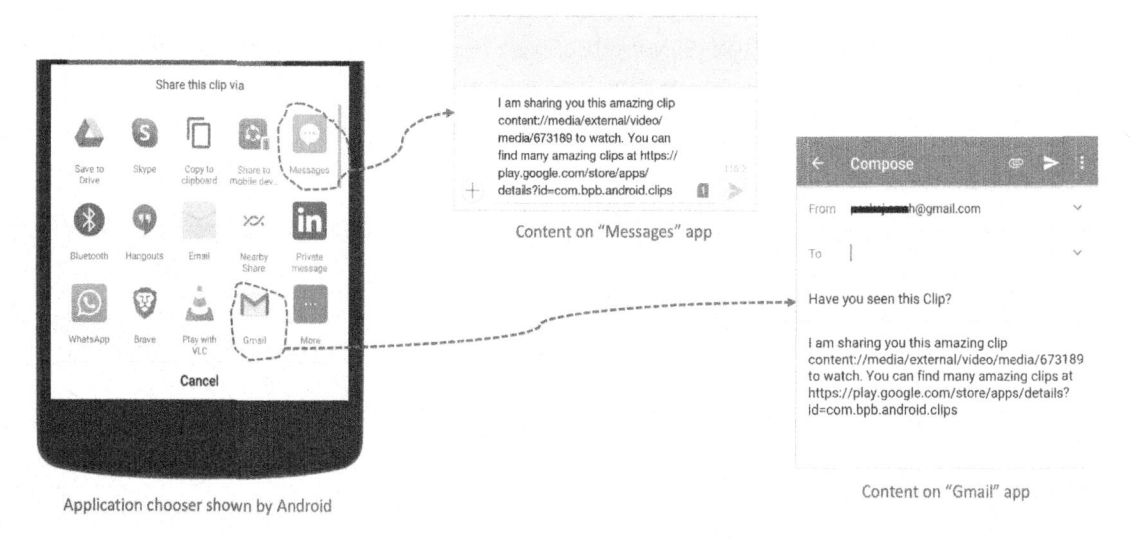

Figure 6.11: Sharing the Clips flow

That is how we can implement the share feature for any other application too.

Implementing the comment feature on clips

While creating table *clips*, we 8discussed normalized tables, and we talked about comments as well. Following structure, we discussed tables for comments can be as follows:

- `Comments(commentId, commentThreadId, parentCommentId, userId, commentText, commentedWhen)`
- `CommentThreads(commentThreadId, threadName, startedWhen)`

This structure can be on the backend, and the server can handle it for us. There can be an API to give us comments for the video clip. *Figure 6.12* is the example JSON and UI design for the comment list:

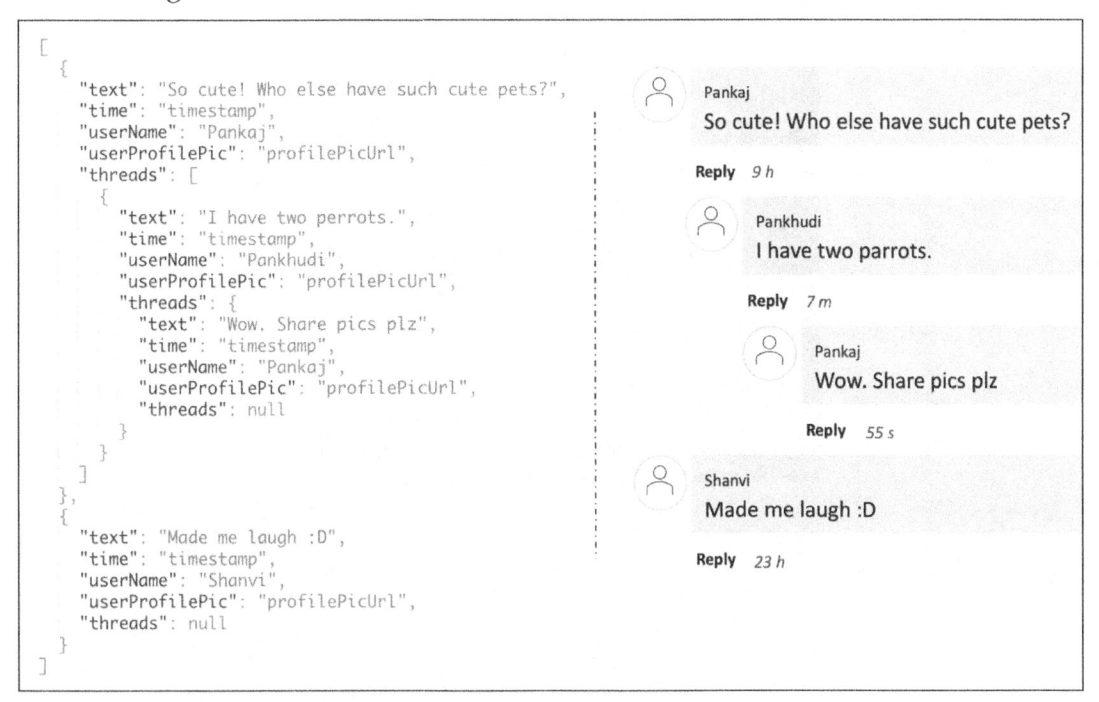

```
[
  {
    "text": "So cute! Who else have such cute pets?",
    "time": "timestamp",
    "userName": "Pankaj",
    "userProfilePic": "profilePicUrl",
    "threads": [
      {
        "text": "I have two perrots.",
        "time": "timestamp",
        "userName": "Pankhudi",
        "userProfilePic": "profilePicUrl",
        "threads": {
          "text": "Wow. Share pics plz",
          "time": "timestamp",
          "userName": "Pankaj",
          "userProfilePic": "profilePicUrl",
          "threads": null
        }
      }
    ]
  },
  {
    "text": "Made me laugh :D",
    "time": "timestamp",
    "userName": "Shanvi",
    "userProfilePic": "profilePicUrl",
    "threads": null
  }
]
```

Figure 6.12: Comments feature payload and UI

For the comment screen, you can use `RecyclerView`, which we already discussed.

That is it with the idea of developing a comments screen for clips.

Developing add clips screen

In this screen, we will write code to allow the user to record the video and create the Clips. To avoid discussing the same code again, we will skip discussing ExoPlayer-specific code. We will learn about how we can create video from our Clips app via the existing camera application on the device and write code to add clips data into the database.

Note that the code for **fragment_add_clips.xml** is available on our GitHub repository.

At first, let us investigate the screen design. *Figure 6.13* also explains which UI component is being used at add clips screen:

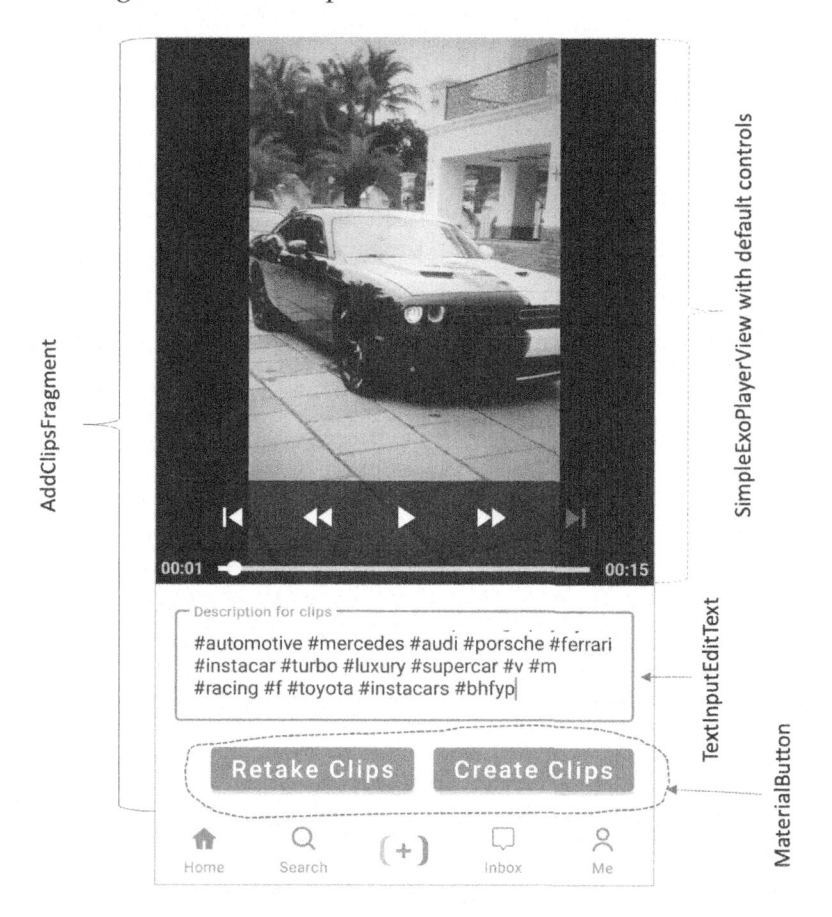

Figure 6.13: The Add clips screen

Before we create a clip, a user needs to record the video first. Android provides an Intent to access camera app and record video (or Image as well) via **MediaStore.ACTION_VIDEO_CAPTURE** intent, so instead of writing code for a camera application, we will be using existing camera apps and getting recorded video info to proceed with the creation of Clips.

Following is the code written inside **AddClipsFragment** where we sent an Intent to the system, and the system shows the camera application (or app chooser in case of multiple camera apps):

```
private fun captureVideo() {
    Intent(MediaStore.ACTION_VIDEO_CAPTURE).also { takeVideoIntent ->
        takeVideoIntent.resolveActivity(requireActivity().packageManager)
            ?.also {
                takeVideoIntent.putExtra(MediaStore.EXTRA_DURATION_
                LIMIT, 15)
                takeVideoIntent.putExtra(
                    MediaStore.EXTRA_VIDEO_QUALITY,
                    1 // ZERO is for low quality
                )
                captureVideoIntentLaunch.launch(takeVideoIntent)
            }
    }
}
```

In **AddClipsFragment**, the preceding code will be called automatically as soon as the user taps on the **Add Clips +** option at the bottom to navigate the user directly to the camera app to record a video. The preceding code will also be called when the user taps on **Retake Clips** button.

As we are setting a time limit in the preceding code via **MediaStore.EXTRA_DURATION_ LIMIT**, so the default camera application can record a video of 15 seconds long.

After recording the video via the camera application, the user will be navigated back to **AddClipsFragment** with a recorded video **uri**. We will capture the **uri** of that video on activity result by writing the following code:

```
private var captureVideoIntentLaunch = registerForActivityResult(
    ActivityResultContracts.StartActivityForResult()
```

```
) { result ->
    if (result.resultCode == Activity.RESULT_OK) {
        result?.data?.data?.let {
            currentLocalUri = it
            playVideo(it)
        }
    } else {
        requireContext().showToast("Something went wrong")
        redirectToHomeScreen()
    }
}
```

In the preceding code, **captureVideoIntentLaunch** is the **ActivityResultLauncher**, which is being used to launch the camera intent and listen to the result. After getting a successful result, we are caching **uri** into **currentLocalUri** and starting playing **Clips**.

NOTE: **Similar to captureVideoIntentLaunch, we can write code to open other applications from our application and listen to the result. Previous to this way, startActivityForResult() and onActivityResults() were being used for same purpose. Now, these methods are deprecated.**

Now, let us write code for **AddClipsFragment** as follows:

```
class AddClipsFragment : BpbClipsBaseFragment(
    R.layout.fragment_add_clips
) {

    private val viewModel by activityViewModels<AddClipsViewModel> {
        ClipsViewModelFactory((activity?.application as BpbClipsApp).
        repository)
    }

    private val user = FirebaseAuth.getInstance().currentUser
    private var currentLocalUri: Uri? = null
```

```
    private var captureVideoIntentLaunch = ...

    override fun onViewCreated(view: View, savedInstanceState: Bundle?) {
        super.onViewCreated(view, savedInstanceState)

        initializePlayer()

        captureVideo()

        initListeners()
    }
    ...
}
```

In the preceding code, there are three important methods. First is **initializePlayer()**, which configures ExoPlayer, and the code is the same as what we used on HomeFragment or what we learned while reading about ExoPlayer. The second is **captureVideo()**, which redirects the user to the camera app, where we get the result back to **captureVideoIntentLaunch**. And we already saw the code for the third method **captureVideo()**.

Now, let us write code for **initListeners()** as follows:

```
private fun initListeners() {
    retakeVideo.setOnClickListener { captureVideo() }
    uploadClips.setOnClickListener {
        currentLocalUri?.let {
            viewModel.createClips(prepareClips(it))
        }
    }
    viewModel.progressState.observe(viewLifecycleOwner) { state ->
        pageProgress.isVisible = state == AddClipsViewModel.State.IN_PROGRESS

        when (state) {
```

```
            AddClipsViewModel.State.SUCCESS -> {
                redirectToHomeScreen()
            }
            AddClipsViewModel.State.ERROR -> {
                requireContext().showToast("Something went wrong. Please
                try again")
            }
        }
    }
}
```

In the preceding code, we are calling **captureVideo()** on click of **Retake Video** button. And on click of **Create Clips**, we are creating clips object and passing it to **createClips()** of **ViewModel**, where **ViewModel** will store the clips data into the database via repository. The **prepareClips(…)** for creating clips objects can be written as follows:

```
private fun prepareClips(uri: Uri): Clips {
    return Clips(
        clipId = System.currentTimeMillis(),
        clipUrl = uri.toString(),
        thumbUrl = "",
        description = clipsDesc.text.toString(),
        coverTitle = "Music cover title",
        coverImageLink = "",
        userId = user.uid,
        profilePicUrl = user.photoUrl?.toString(),
        userName = user.displayName,
        likesCount = 0,
        commentsCount = 0,
```

```
        addedWhen = System.currentTimeMillis()
    )
}
```

In the preceding code, we are adding a few default or hardcoded values. Instead of hardcoding, we can add more input views to the **AddClipsFragment** and can take input from the user for these fields, similar to the description field. For example, we can have the field where user can choose a song track for the clips, which can be used for the cover title and cover image link.

Now, let us write code for the **AddClipsViewModel** to insert clips data into the database:

```
class AddClipsViewModel(
    private val repository: ClipsRepository
) : ViewModel() {

    enum class State { IN_PROGRESS, ERROR, SUCCESS }

    private val _progressState = MutableLiveData<State>()
    val progressState: LiveData<State> = _progressState

    fun createClips(clips: Clips) = viewModelScope.launch(Dispatchers.IO) {
        progressState.postValue(State.IN_PROGRESS)
        repository.insertClips(clips)
        progressState.postValue(State.SUCCESS)
    }
}
```

Remember that, when you do actual network calls for adding clips, a better way is to wait till the **createClips api** gives a successful response with newly created clips data.

NOTE: While using local storage, we did not consider uploading the video somewhere, as we already have that newly recorded video on the local device where our application is running. We are just using the file's local uri for that video to access and play on player view.

But, this will not be the same when you will work with the remote data source, where you will have a server. In that scenario, the clip's path at your local will not work for users other than you, as the recorded video is on your phone only. To make this clip available to other users, you have to upload the newly created video first at the remote. After successful upload, you will get an url for that Clips, so you can put other detail of Clips with the clips-url into an object of Clips and can do one more API call to store clips information at the server.

Coming back to the code of `initListeners()`, we are adding the observer to listen to changes and depending on the success or failure of the `insertClips()`, we can navigate the user back to the home screen or can show an error message. The `redirectToHomeScreen()` is being used to redirect to the home screen after success; the code for this method is as follows:

```
private fun redirectToHomeScreen() {
    if (activity is MainActivity) {
        (activity as MainActivity).getNavigationView().selectedItemId =
            R.id.navigation_home
    }
}
```

In the preceding code, we get the reference of `BottomNavigationView` and reset the selected option to home to show the clips (home) screen.

TIP: Server architecture and implementation play a big role in applications like TikTok. Defiant security and high scalability are a few of the most important things for video apps, but how fast you serve videos to the user is the most important thing for such applications. You should read about how applications like TikTok stores videos and make these videos available anywhere in the world with minimum latency. On a large level, you should also read about Netflix's architecture and how they used to serve such large videos to viewers.

We have now developed **Add clips** screen, and we have developed our video sharing application **Bpb Clips**. Remember that the full source code is available at our code repository with documentation for your reference.

Conclusion

In this chapter, we developed a video sharing application named BpbClips. While developing this application, we learned about functional requirements for video sharing applications and user flow and limited our feature to be developed for BpbClips to understand it easily. We also learned about BottomNavigationView and its uses.

We learned about data storage options in Android; now, we can easily choose the best-fit storage option for any requirement in future. We learned about the Room library and created CRUD for our BpbClips application.

We also learned about repository patterns, and now we know how we can separate the data layer from other layers of the application, we also know about switching local and remote data in a better way.

We learned about ExoPlayer and explored it in terms of our BpbClips application. And at last, we developed the Home (list of clips) screen and Add Clips screen. While developing these pages, we also discussed how particular things can be done when you would have a server instead of the local database. We also developed a feature for like and share the clips and read about how we can implement the comments feature.

In the upcoming chapter, we will learn about game development in Android.

Points to remember

- For any video application, one of the most important features would be how fast you provide video to the user without any lag. Most of the things used to be handled by server implementation, but improving buffering logic of the player app is also an important thing.
- Data sources in the repository pattern should be aligned with the Liskov substitution principle.
- Use preferences if fewer data to be stored.
- You can implement caching to provide data faster to the user if the data size is not huge.

Multiple Choice Questions

1. BottomNavigationView is part of the material library.

   A. True   B. False

2. Intent.ACTION_OPEN_DOCUMENT is required to access the Storage Access Framework.

   A. True   B. False

3. Which library can be used to store data in the database?

   A. Proto Datastore   B. Storage Access Framework
   C. Room   D. Preferences Datastore

4. Which annotation can be used to define the primary key in Room?

   A. @PrimaryKey   B. @Entity
   C. @ColumnInfo   D. None of the above

5. DefaultLoadControl class of ExoPlayer can be used to define buffering strategy.

   A. True   B. False

Answers

1. A
2. A
3. C
4. A
5. A

Questions

1. What is the repository pattern, and why should we use it?
2. Can you define the data structure for the comments feature of the video application?
3. What permissions are required to access public storage?
4. How to launch a camera app to record a video and get Uri of the recorded video?

Key Terms

- BottomNavigationView
- Shared preferences
- Proto Datastore
- Storage Access Framework
- Room
- Repository pattern
- MediaStorage
- Cache
- ViewPager
- ExoPlayer
- DefaultLoadControl
- Like
- Comment
- Share
- Create video clip
- Record video
- Uri
- Local datastore
- Remote datastore

Chapter 7
Introduction to Game Development

Introduction

In the previous chapter, we developed our first video-sharing application. In this chapter, we will introduce you to game development in Android. We will also learn about some of the most used game engines. Furthermore, we will learn about Unity, and we will learn to install UnityHub and UnityEditor. We will also create a "Hello Unity" project and learn about the project workspace. We will learn how to apply texture to the unity object and how to add a C# script to the game.

At the end of the chapter, we will learn about building a build for Android using the Android build system.

Structure

In this chapter, we will discuss the following topics:
- Introducing game engine
    - Unity
    - Unreal engine
    - Buildbox

- o Solar2D
- o GameMaker Studio 2
- Introducing Unity
  - o Installing Unity
  - o Creating Hello Unity project
  - o Introduction to Unity workspace
  - o Adding game objects to the project
  - o Adding texture to objects
  - o Adding Cube to the Scene
  - o Adding bricks image file
  - o Adding material object
  - o Applying bricks image to material object
  - o Applying bricks material object to the Cube
  - o Introducing important terms in Unity
- Introducing C# script
- Creating an Android build

Objectives

The objective of this chapter is to let you know about the basics of game development. You will learn to choose a game engine for your awesome game. You will also learn about the basics of Unity, where we will learn to create a Unity project using the template. You will also learn to add unity objects to the Scene and apply texture to the object. You will learn about creating Android builds. After completing this chapter, you will have a clear understanding of game engines, the basics of Unity, scripting, and applying texture to the unity object, and you can create an Android build for your awesome game.

Introducing game engine

There are many game engines available for game development. Depending on our requirements specific to the game or expertise, the budget also plays an important role when choosing to choose a better game engine.

A game engine is a framework for the development of the game. The game engine includes collection libraries and tools for developing games. Any game engine typically provides features such as 2D/3D graphics renderer, physics engine, collision detection, scripting, AI, sound, animation, networking, memory management, threading, localization, and many more.

Sometimes we call game engines middleware because these engines provide a reusable software platform that provides all the core functionality needed for game development, which reduces cost and time to market. For example, if you are developing a game where a character is flying, you do not need to implement physics by yourself for the movement of that character. The game engine does it for you. Similarly, while developing our game in the upcoming chapter, "Chapter 8: Development of the first game", we are not going to write the code that defines how our ball will move, what would be the speed, or how it will collide with other objects and even we not going to write code to make a bouncing effect for the ball. We just need to configure the required components, and the game engine will do everything for us.

As of now, there are many game engines on the market. So, our first question will be, *which game engine is best?*

To answer this question, we need to consider a few things like the platform supported by the game, whether the game is 2D or 3D, and if that is supported by the game engine, community support, and most importantly, the pricing.

To evaluate game engines, let us know more about these game engines.

Unity

Unity supports 2D and 3D game development. Using Unity, you can create interactive simulations for games and animations. It is popular among indie developers and very easy to use, so any beginner can start developing the game using Unity.

There are many famous games developed in Unity, for example, Call of Duty: Mobile, Pokémon Go, Monument Valley, Cuphead, and many more.

Unity has very good community support, so you can easily find materials and models.

Platforms supported: iOS, Android, Windows, Mac, Linux, Consoles, and VR platforms.

Pricing: Free for personal use and student with college email id. Paid for plus, pro, or enterprise editions.

NOTE: **There are different roles while developing the game. One can design characters, one can work on storylines, one can work on sound design, and so on. The indie developer is someone who develops the whole game alone. That means indie developers work on each part of the game individually.**

Unreal engine

Unreal is famous for 3D games and mostly being used in film industries to create virtual sets and animated movies. The main advantage of using this game engine is that you do not require any programming skills to develop the game.

Games like The Matrix Awakens and Fortnite were developed in *Unreal Engine*.

Platform supported: iOS, Android, Windows, Mac, Linux, Consoles and VR platforms, Stadia.

Pricing: Free with publishing and creator's license. Paid for custom license and enterprise edition.

Buildbox

Buildbox is one of the famous game engines for developing games for Android and iOS. It is easy to use for beginners with no coding experience or scripting knowledge.

You can create 2D and 3D games in a short time by just doing the drag-drop feature. It also has very good community support.

Games like Color Switch, Ball Jump, and Blue Edge was developed using the Buildbox game engine.

Platform supported: iOS, Android

Pricing: Free with some limited features. Plus and pro are two paid subscriptions.

Solar2D

Solar2D is a Lua-based game engine focusing on ease of iterations and usage.

There was a game engine known as Corona SDK, which was a 2D game engine, and it was completely free; now, commercial support has been stopped. The Solar2D is forked from Corona SDK, and it is fully open-source.

Games like Flappy Bird were developed using Solar2D.

Platform supported: iOS, Android, Kindle, Windows, Linux, macOS, and TV.

Pricing: Free

GameMaker Studio 2

GameMaker is another easy game engine to use. It provides a drag-drop programming language known as Game Maker Language. Initially, this game engine was developed for beginners, but it can be used for advanced game development as well.

Games like Undertale, Forager, and Hyper Light Drifter were developed using the GameMaker.

Platform supported: iOS, Android, Windows, macOS, Ubuntu, PlayStation, Xbox, HTML5, and more.

Pricing: Free. And there are three different types of yearly paid subscriptions *Creator, Indie,* and *Enterprise.*

These are just a few mostly used game engines. There are many more game engines. Before you start developing a game, you should analyze the requirement and game engines available in the market. It will help you decide how to choose the best-fit game engine.

As Unity supports multiple platforms and it is Free for Students as well, we will be reading about the Unity engine in this book, and in the next *Chapter 8: Development of the First Game,* we will develop our game using Unity.

NOTE: **Android introduced the Android Game Development Kit (AGDK), which is a full range of tools and libraries to help you develop, optimize, launch, and iterate on high-quality Android games. AGDK brings together new and existing libraries,tools, and functionality.**

You can use the Android Game Development Extension for Visual Studio to add Android as a target platform in your existing Visual C++ game projects. This allows you to develop multiplatform games in C or C++ on Windows using Microsoft Visual Studio and then deploy them to Android.

AGDK has introduced a year before writing this book, but even with this small-time, it gained a lot of interest from the community because of its awesome features. So, when you develop a game for Android, the recommendation is to explore AGDK and use it for your game.

Introducing Unity

Unity is a cross-platform game engine that is developed by Unity technology. It can be used to create 2D and 3D games and interactive simulations. Besides video gaming, the Unity game engine is used in films, engineering, automotive, and many more. Now, let us install Unity.

Installing Unity

To install Unity, go to https://unity.com/download. Download and install UnityHub. UnityHub allows us to install more than one Unity Editor. We can create a new project and access our project using UnityHub.

After installing UnityHub, open it. You will see UnityHub as shown in *figure 7.1*:

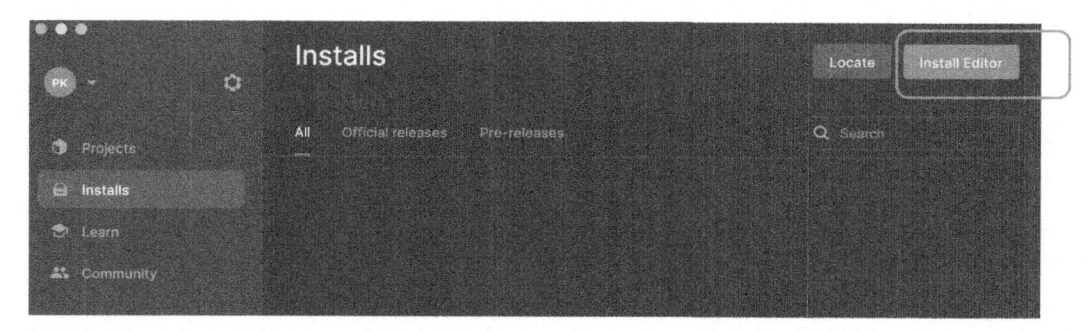

Figure 7.1: Installing Editor

Click on **Install Editor** as shown in preceding *figure 7.1*. After clicking on **Install Editor**, you will see the **Install Unity Editor** window with the list of unity editors, as shown in *figure 7.2*.

Choose the version which you want to install. It is better to install recommended version suggested by UnityHub. As you can see in *figure 7.2* it is showing one recommended version:

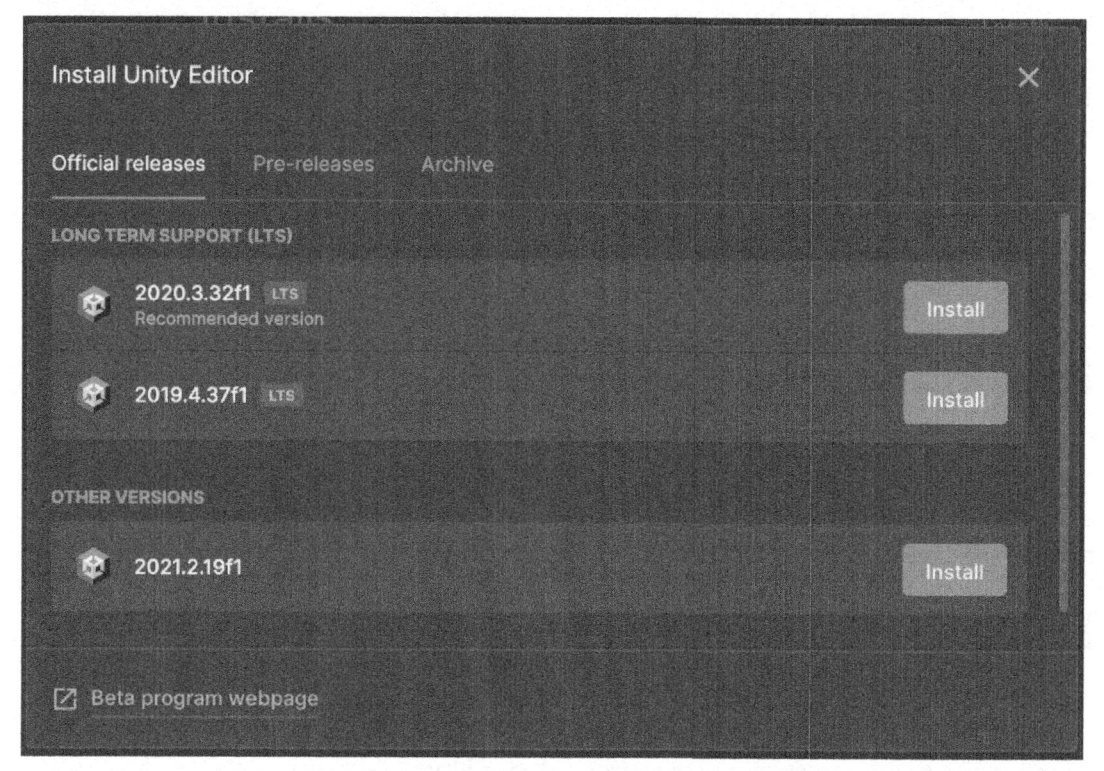

Figure 7.2: Choosing the version for UnityEditor

As shown in preceding *figure 7.2*, choose the version which you want to install and click on the **Install** button. Note that choosing recommended version is a better choice if you are going to use Unity the first time.

NOTE: **There are options like "Learn" and "Community" available on UnityHub's first page, as shown in preceding *figure 7.1*. The "Learn" tab provides you with many basic tutorials which can help you to develop a game. And the "Community" tab provides you links where you can connect to the developer community or get help from the community. It provides likes such as Unity Blogs, Forums, Answers, and so on.**

After installing it, Unity will ask you to install some modules, as shown in *figure 7.3*:

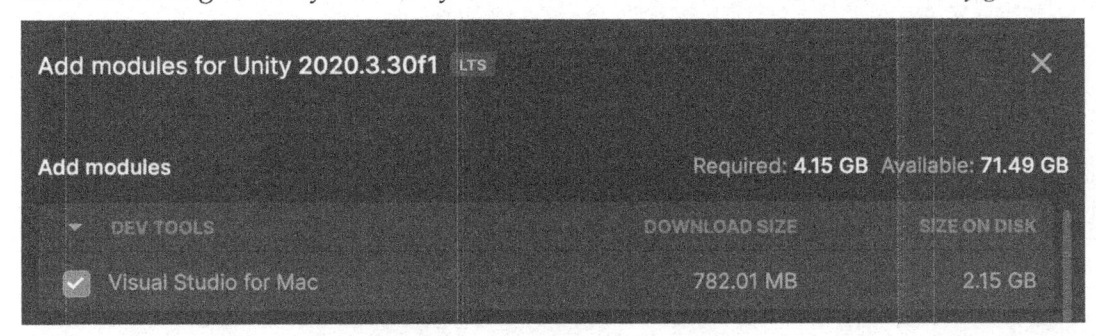

Figure 7.3: Installing Visual Studio

Check **Visual Studio** and install it. Note that you can install Visual Studio later as well, and you can skip installing modules. You can install build supports from here as well, but as of now, we will not install any build support. We will install the build system while learning about creating of android build in the section *Creating an Android build* of this chapter.

Now, we are done with the installation of UnityHub and UnityEditor. Let us create a project using Unity templates.

Creating Hello Unity project

Open Unity Hub and click on the **New Project** button as shown in the following *Figure 7.4*. Note that you can choose the **Open** button to locate and open an existing Unity project.

Figure 7.4: Creating a new project

After that, you will see the **New Project** window. At this window, you can see multiple templates where you can select **2D Mobile** or **3D Mobile**. In the Project name field, let us write **Hello Unity**, and in the location field, you can set the location where you want to store the project. You can keep the default location as well. *Figure 7.5* shows the **New project** window:

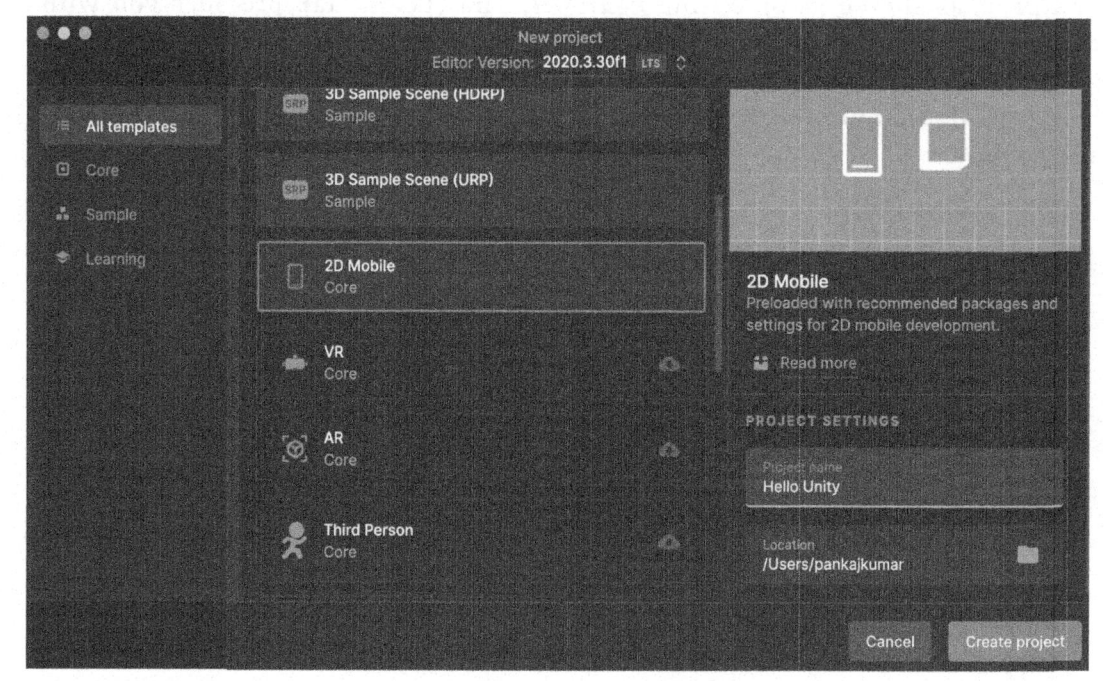

Figure 7.5: Selecting the template

Now tap on the **Create project** button. Unity will be launched with the newly created project.

Before moving ahead, we need to know the Unity workspace.

Introduction to Unity workspace

First off, let us understand the views available at the workspace. *Figure 7.6* shows the workspace for our Hello Unity project:

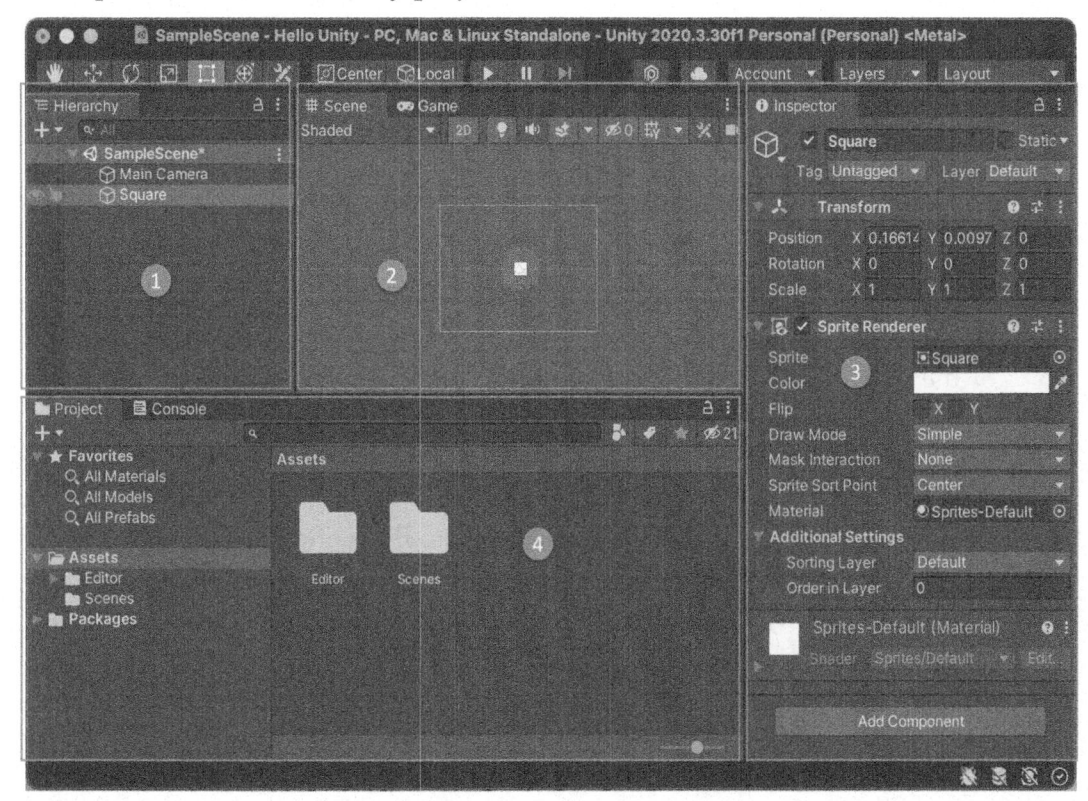

Figure 7.6: Unity workspace

The preceding *figure 7.6* shows all available default views in the Unity workspace. Let us know more about them.

- **Hierarchy View**: The hierarchy view represents each game object added to the Scene. It reveals the structure of how game objects attach to each other.

  You can add a new game object by "right-click on the empty area at the hierarchy view" | `2D Object` | `Sprites` | `Square`. Similarly, you can create many types of game objects.

  We select the game object in the hierarchy view and do the modification via the `Inspection view` for the selected game object.

- **Scene View and Game View**: The scene view shows all added game objects. The game object can be of any type, like 2D or 3D. The scene view allows us to navigate and modify the Scene as follows:
  o Use drag-drop game object to the place where you want to place that.
  o You can increase/decrease the size of the game object by using by selecting the view and using circle handles.
  o You can use the scroll wheel to zoom in or zoom out.

  And many more.

  On the right side of the Scene view, you see the **Game** tab. This tab shows each object added to a scene like the exact output of the game. When you click on Play to run the game, the game will run in the **Game** view.

- **Inspector View**: Inspector view allows us to view and edit all the properties of the currently selected game object. You can select the game object from other views like the Hierarchy view, Scene view, or Project view. Depending on the type of game object, you see a different set of attributes in the Inspector view.

  We can add additional components as well to the game object by clicking on the **Add Component** button and searching for the required component.

- **Project View**: The project view displays assets and packages which are added to our project. In other words, it displays the different types of files and directories either added by default to the project or by us. We add objects like prefabs, scripts, or textures in the Assets directory, and all installed packages for the project can be found in the **Packages** directory.

We will use these views/windows extensively while developing our first game in the next chapter, *Chapter 8: Development of the First Game*.

Adding game objects to the project

To add game objects, right-click on an empty area of the Hierarchy view. Select your desired object from the popup window. *Figure 7.7* shows most of the 3D objects which can be used in any game; similarly, you can choose a 2D object or any View inside UI:

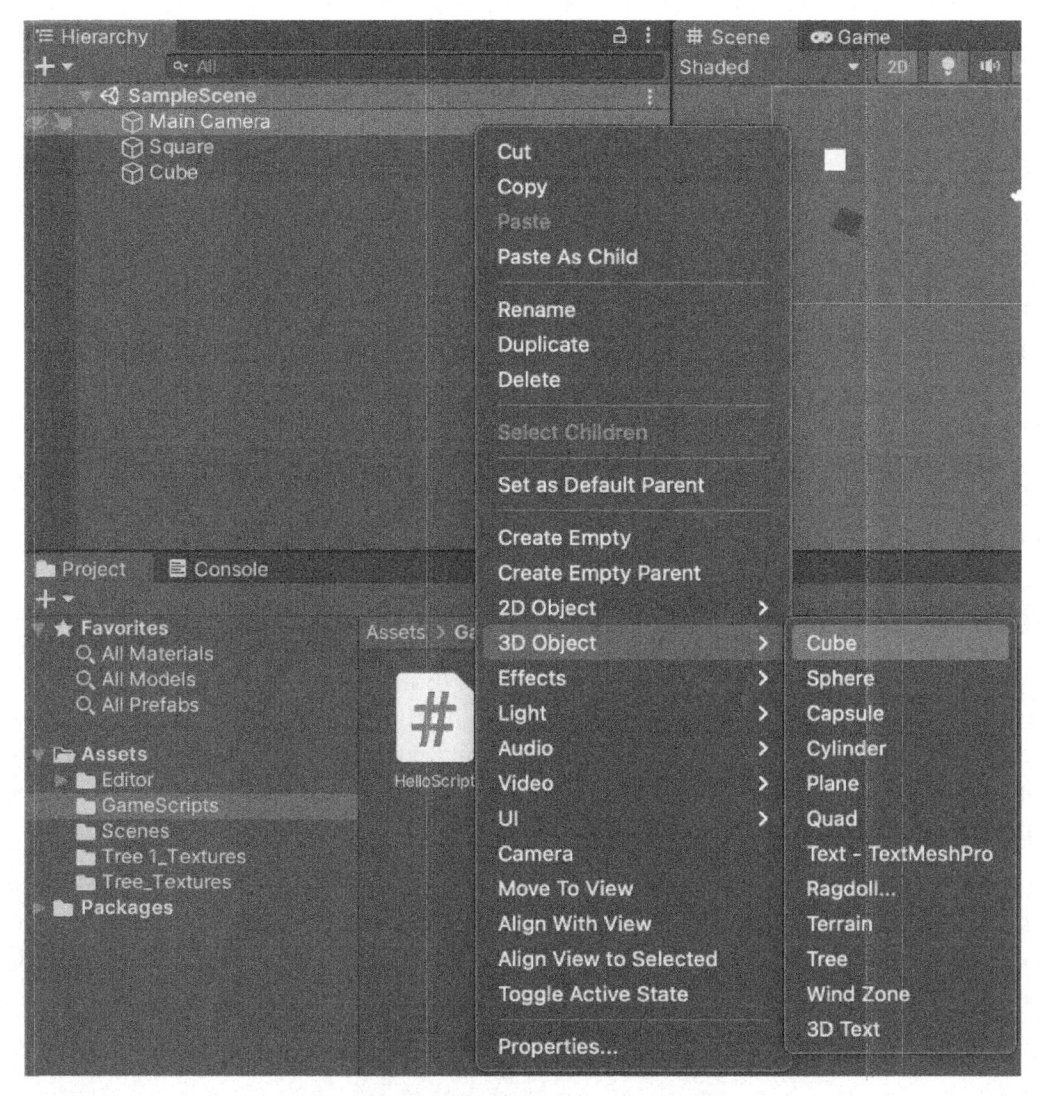

Figure 7.7: 3D Objects available in Unity

Adding texture to objects

In this section, we will add bricks texture to the Cube object. Let us do it.

Adding Cube to the Scene

First, let us add a 3D object to the Scene; by following right-click on the empty area at **Hierarchy View | 3D Object | Cube,** we will add a cube to the Scene. After adding the **Cube** object, do the scaling as shown in *figure 7.8*:

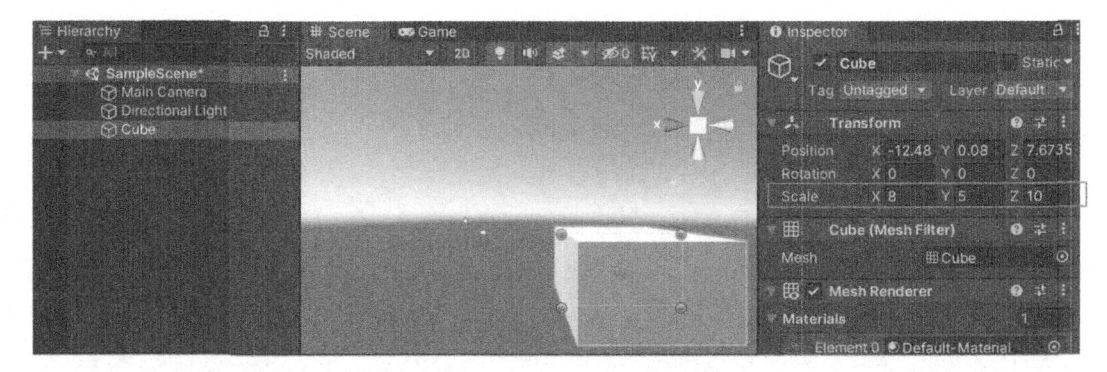

Figure 7.8: Adding Cube to the Scene

And place this **Cube** object at the Scene such that three sides are visible to you, as shown in the preceding *figure 7.8*, so when we add texture, we can easily understand how the texture is being added to this Cube.

Adding bricks image file

Now, we need an image that shows bricks. Note that while looking for such images, you need to look for such images which support tiling. This is not only for bricks but for any image, which you want to apply as texture. When you use any image as a texture, that image may be used for repeating, so if the image does not support tiling, the texture applied in any GameObject will not look good.

You can search for such images at https://assetstore.unity.com/ or on Google. For this example, we are going to use the image of a brick wall that supports tiling, as shown in *figure 7.9* [note that the image is copied from the internet, and the whole credit goes to the designer of this image]:

Figure 7.9: Bricks image which supports tiling

Copy this file in the **Assets** directory and rename it to **bricks_tile**, as shown in *figure 7.10*:

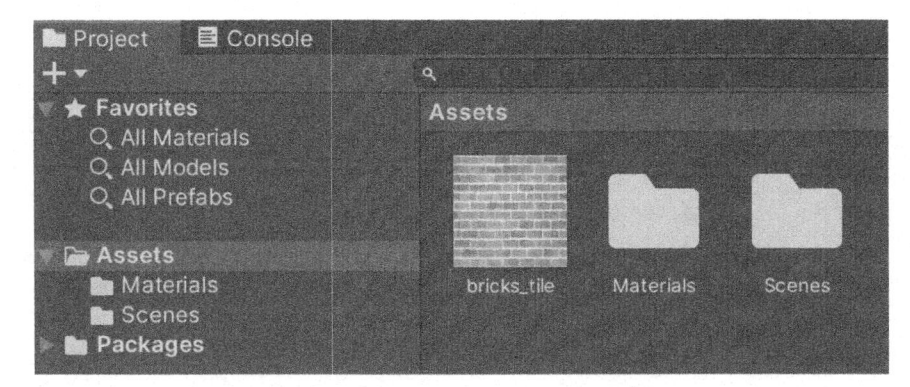

Figure 7.10: Adding bricks image to assets

Adding material object

We need a material object where we will apply the brick wall image. To do that, right-click on the empty area of **Assets** | **Create** | **material**. One object will be added to the Assets directory, as shown in *figure 7.11*. Rename it to **Bricks Texture**:

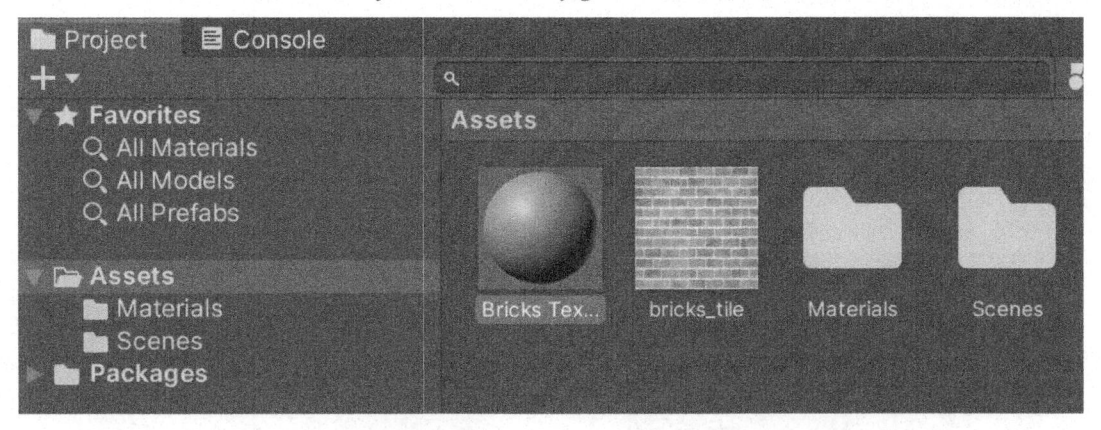

Figure 7.11: Creating material object

Applying bricks image to material object

First, we need to change the shader for the material object. To do that, select **material** and go to **Inspector view** | Tap on **Shader** drop-down (in *figure 7.12*, you can see, **Standard** is set by default) | Choose **Legacy Shaders** | Choose **Diffuse**, as shown in *figure 7.12*:

308 ■ *Building Android Projects with Kotlin*

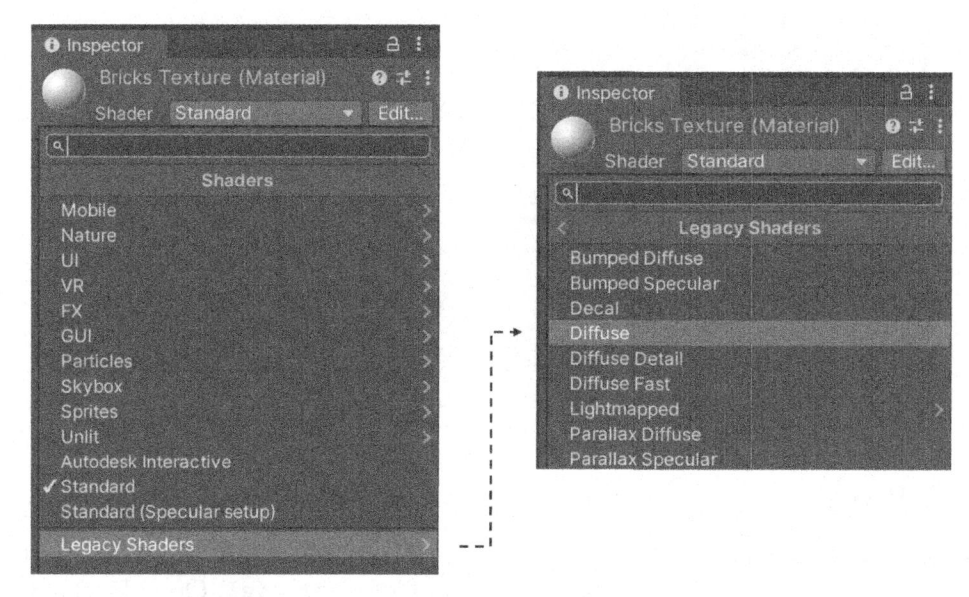

Figure 7.12: Changing Shaders of Material object

After applying the Diffuse shader to the material, we will get the option to add a brick wall image to the material.

From the **Inspector view**, click on **Select**. A **Select Texture** window will appear. In this window, you can see our **bricks tile** image file. Select it, as shown in *figure 7.13*:

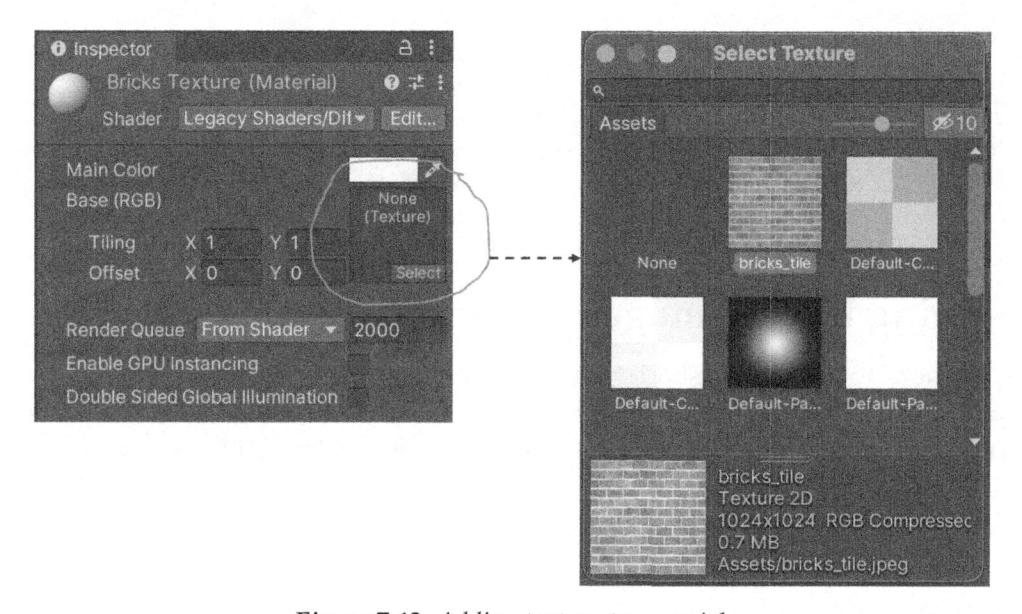

Figure 7.13: Adding texture to material

After applying the `bricks_tile` image to the material, the material will look like *figure 7.14*:

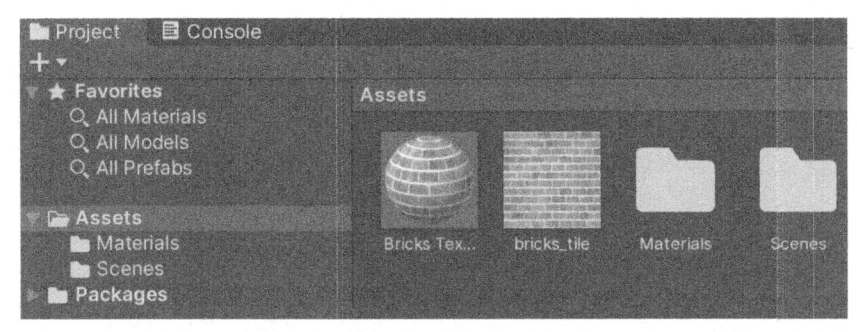

Figure 7.14: Material object with bricks texture

Now, we are ready with a fully configured material, which can be applied to Cube 3D object.

Applying bricks material object to the Cube

Adding material to the Cube is just a drag-drop. To apply bricks material to the Cube, select material `Brick Texture` and drag-drop on the `Cube` object in the `Scene` view, as shown in *figure 7.15*:

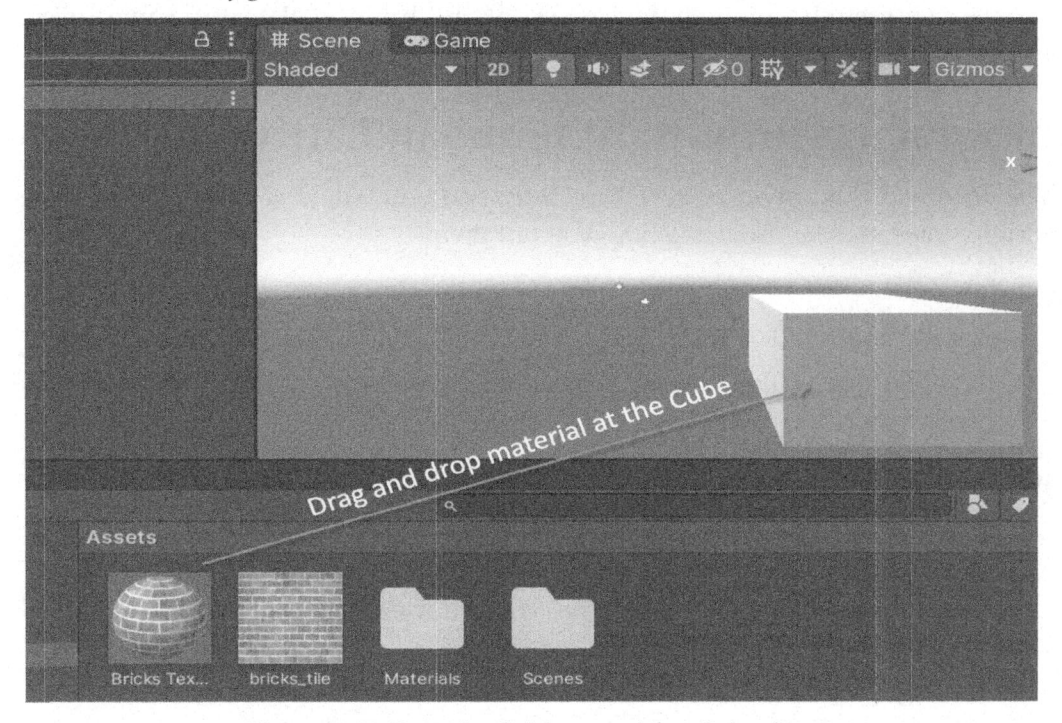

Figure 7.15: Dragging bricks material to Cube object

After applying the material, the cube object will now look like a real bricks wall, as shown in *figure 7.16*:

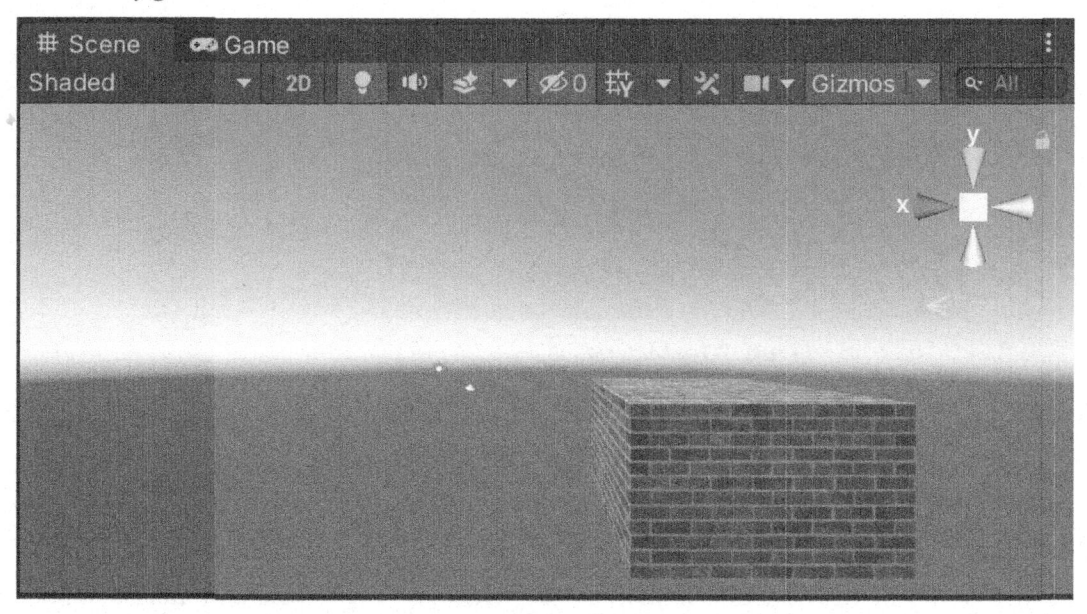

Figure 7.16: Cube object after applying texture

We have successfully applied the texture of the brick wall to the Cube object. Similarly, we can apply any texture to any Unity 3D object.

Introducing important terms in Unity

There are few commonly used terms in Unity, and you will hear these words/terms multiple times in a day. So, let us know about them.

Material:
- Unity material defines the appearance of the surface.
- In other words, the material is a way to define how a GameObject should be rendered. It can be a flat color, texture, and so on.

Packages:
- Packages are similar to libraries in Android. Packages are a collection of Assets, Scripts, and Resources.
- We will be using a few packages while developing the game in *Chapter 8: Development of the First Game*.

GameObject:
- Any object that represents characters, properties, and scenery is known as GameObject.
- In general, each GameObject uses to have a component that defines its behavior or allows to set attributes.

Component:
- A component is a set of properties and behavior. These properties and behavior can be assigned to GameObject.
- It defines behavior or provides attributes for GameObject, so a GameObject can become a 2D shape, 3D shapes, a UI button, a camera, and so on.

Scene:
- In very simple words, the level of the game is a scene. A multi-level game or larger games are developed with multiple scenes. Like any layout in Android where you add Views/ViewGroups, in the Scene, you can add GameObjects.
- You can add/ modify a scene from Scene View or Game View, as shown in preceding *figure 7.16*.

Renderer:
- As the name suggests, it helps GameObject to appear on the screen.
- The Renderer can be used to hide or show the GameObject. When you disable Renderer for an object, that object will be hidden.

Collider:
- Colliders define the shape of a GameObject for physical collisions.
- It provides collision detection using various *Bounding Boxes*. These boundaries boxes are Box, Sphere, Capsule, and Mesh.
- There are Box Collider, Sphere Collider, Capsule Collider for 3D GameObjects, and Box Collider 2D and Circle Collider 2D for 2D GameObjects.

RigidBody:
- The RigidBody allows the object to receive forces and to be influenced by gravity. It means that by using RigidBody, our GameObject can be enabled to react to physics.

Script:
- The script is a Component that allows us to add behavior or properties to a GameObject.

- We use C# to write scripts. Each class written in C# must inherit **MonoBehaviour** class.

Prefab:
- Prefab is a GameObject that has a predefined set of behavior and attributes, and you can reuse them in a scene or in the different levels of the game multiple times, either statically or adding dynamically.
- Prefab is similar to the template. We will create and use Prefab in our game in *Chapter 8: Development of the First Game*.

Asset:
- An Asset represents any item that can be used in any game.
- It can be any type of file such as a 3D model, audio file, image files or texture, audio mixer, and so on.

Screen Space and World Space:
- Screen space is the position in terms of pixels on your screen.
- World space is the position of an object in the overall space of Unity (game world).
- We will also use these two terms while developing our first game in *Chapter 8: Development of the First Game*.

Transform:
- Each object placed in a scene has a Transform component. It is used to store and modify the position, rotation, and scale of the GameObject.

SerializeField:
- SerializeField is used to adjust variables in the inspector view.
- Normally, Unity serializes public fields while serializing the script. But if you want to force Unity to serialize private fields as well, SerializeField can be used. We will use SerializeField as well while writing the script for the game in *Chapter 8: Development of the First Game*.

These are a few important terms used in Unity. Now, let us learn about scripting.

Introducing C# script

Scripting helps us define the behavior of a GameObject. We can add GameObjects and change the behavior of GameObject dynamically via script. In Unity, we use C# language to write scripts. We can use editors like Visual Studio and Sublime text to write scripts.

Let us first understand how to create a script.

To add a Script in Unity, click on **Assets** | **Create** | **C# Script** as shown in *figure 7.17*:

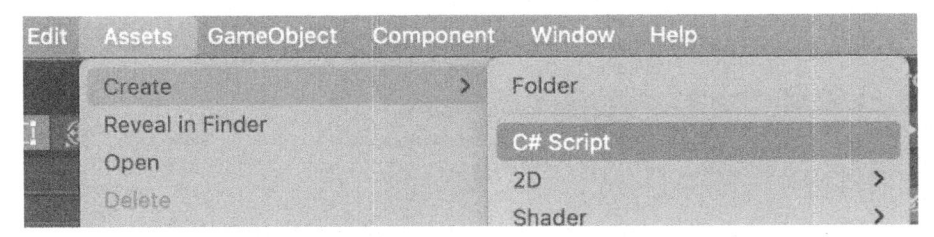

Figure 7.17: Creating C# script

Or right-click on **Assets** or empty area in **Assets** directory | **Create** | **C# Script**. A file will be added to the **Assets** directory. If you organize all your assets, you can create directories specific to their type and can move all assets into those directories. Similarly, for this newly created script file, you can create a folder like **GameScripts** and move this new file into the directory, as shown in *figure 7.18*:

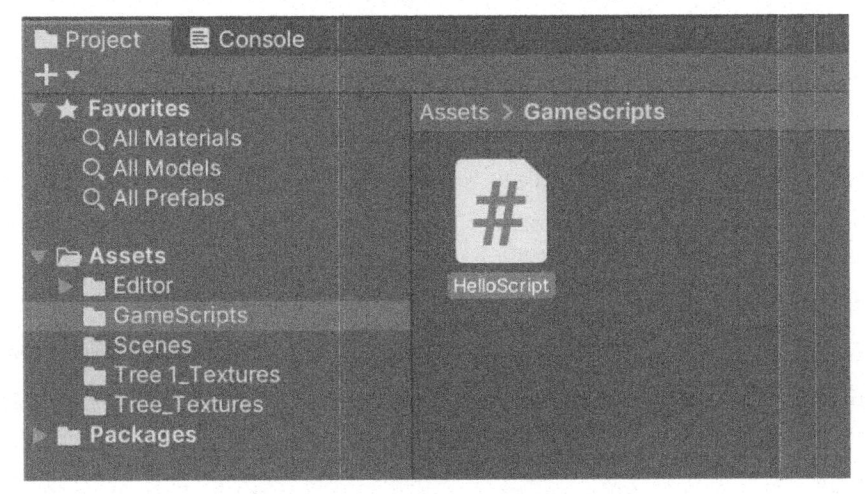

Figure 7.18: Newly created C# script

Now, let us open this file into any of your favorite editor which supports C# and see the code inside it.

A default class looks like the following code:

```
using System.Collections;

using System.Collections.Generic;

using UnityEngine;
```

```
public class HelloScript : MonoBehaviour
{
    // Start is called before the first frame update
    void Start()
    {

    }

    // Update is called once per frame
    void Update()
    {

    }
}
```

In the preceding code, you see the class **HelloScript** extends **MonoBehaviour**. The class **MonoBehaviour** is the base class of any script class in Unity. And as the code comments say, the method **Start()** is called before the first frame update, and the method **Update()** is called once per frame.

Writing code in C# is similar to other programming languages; of course, there will be a change in code syntax or other features as well, but to keep our chapter simpler, we will not deep dive. Here in scripts you write a class, can write multiple functions inside the class, and can declare variables.

Note that there are a few methods that run automatically inside the script. To understand it better, you can relate these methods of lifecycle methods of any Activity, View, and so on in Android. Following are those methods:

- **Awake()**
- **Start()**
- **Update()**
- **FixedUpdate()**
- **LateUpdate()**

- **Awake()**: This method is called only once when GameObject is instantiated. You can use this method to initialize all the variables. Note that this method will not be called if GameObject is inactive. And if GameObject is active, this method will be called even if the component is disabled.
- **Start()**: Similar to **Awake()**, this method will be called if a GameObject is active. **Awake()** can be called even if the component is disabled, but **Start()** will be called only if the component is enabled. This is one of the differences between **Awake()** and **Start()**.
- **Update()**: As we see in the preceding code as well, this method is called once per frame. In this method, we write code that runs continuously, such as animations or updating the state of GameObject state continuously, and so on.
- **FixedUpdate()**: Similar to **Update()** but this method gets called after fixed time interval, whereas **Update()** call interval is dynamic. The code which affects a rigid body (physics object) should be written in **FixedUpdate()**, not in **Update()**.
- **LateUpdate()**: This method is the same as Update(), but it will be called only at the end of the frame.

So, a script file can look like the following code after a few modifications:

```
using System.Collections;
using System.Collections.Generic;
using UnityEngine;

public class HelloScript: MonoBehaviour
{
    // Variables for example. DO NOT WRITE such names in your
    // actual code, these names are only to explain to you easily.
    // It is not a good practice to write such names for
    // variable, methods etc.
    public int publicVariable;
    private int privateVariable;
    [SerializeField]
```

```
private int privateSerializableVariable;

// Initialize all variables
void Awake()
{
    FunctionToBeCalledInsideAwake();
}

// Start is called before the first frame update
void Start()
{
    FunctionToBeCalledInsideStart();
}

// Update is called once per frame
void Update()
{
    FunctionToBeCalledInsideUpdate();
}

private void FunctionToBeCalledInsideAwake()
{

}

private void FunctionToBeCalledInsideStart()
{

}
```

```
    private void FunctionToBeCalledInsideUpdate()
    {

    }
}
```

Note that the variable and method name does not follow better naming conventions. Do not make such practice in your real code.

We will learn a bit more about script while developing our game in *Chapter 8: Development of the First Game*. The recommendation is to learn the basics of C#, which will help you to write better code for your game.

Creating an Android build

To release your game to the market, you need to publish it. For that, you need to create application files like `.apk` for Android and `.ipa` for iOS devices. Let us create an application file for Android.

First of all, we need to install the Android module. To do that, open **Unity Hub** | Select **Installs** tab | and click on the settings icon, as shown in *figure 7.19*:

Figure 7.19: Settings options in UnityHub

On older Unity hub versions, you may see the three dots menu icon instead of the settings icon. After you click on the settings icon, you will see a popup window, as shown in *figure 7.20*:

318 ■ Building Android Projects with Kotlin

Figure 7.20: Choosing add modules from settings

Click on **Add modules** shown in the preceding *figure 7.20*. You will see a list of modules like Android build support, iOS build support, and so on, as shown in *figure 7.21*:

Figure 7.21: Choosing Android build support

As of now, we are building for Android; let us select **Android Build Support**, and click on the **Continue** button | **Accept privacy and terms** | click on the **Install** button.

Note that you need to follow these same steps to add **iOS Build Support** for iOS or to add other modules to create builds for the specific platform.

After installation of this module, move to the Unity project and click on **File | Build Settings...**. The build settings window will appear. Select **Android** platform and click on **Switch Platform** as shown in *figure 7.22*:

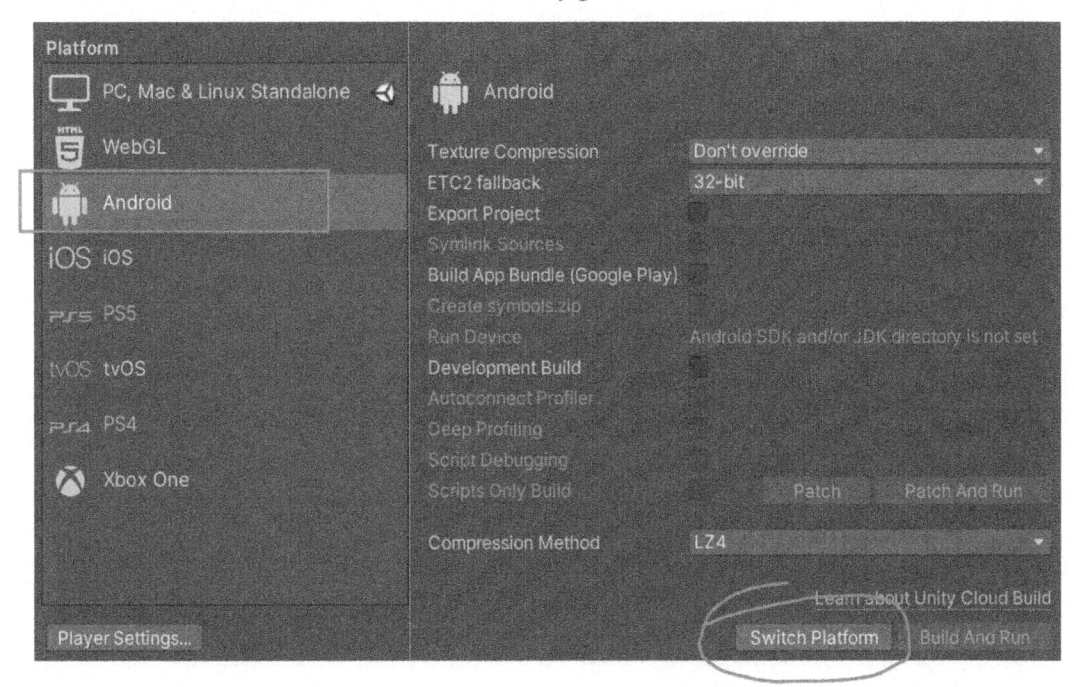

Figure 7.22: Switching platform to Android

After switching the platform to Android, the **Switch Platform** button will be changed to Build, and the **Build And Run** button is shown in the preceding *figure 7.22* will be enabled.

Now click on the **Player Settings...** button, which is shown at the bottom left of the preceding *figure 7.22*.

After clicking on this button, you will see the project settings window like *figure 7.23*, where you see settings for the project. Here at this window, you can configure services such as Ads, Clouds, Analytics, or in-app purchasing. But as of now, we will focus on the **Settings** for Android under **Player** settings:

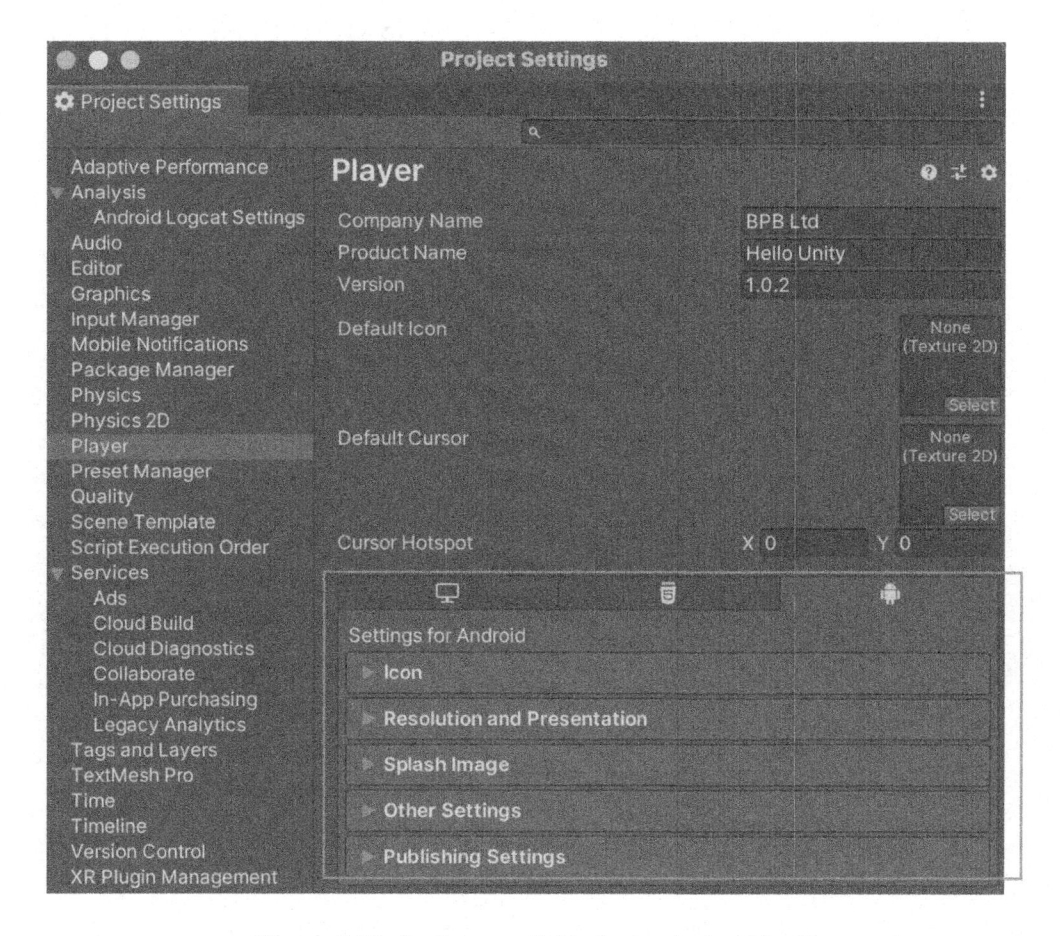

Figure 7.23: Settings available for an Android build

There are configurations as follows:
- Icon
- Resolution and presentation
- Splash image
- Other settings
- Publishing settings

Let us know about these settings.
- **Icon**: You can add resolution-specific icons by using this setting.
- **Resolution and Presentation**: In these settings, you can do configurations like screen resolutions, orientation, and so on. As shown in *figure 7.24*:

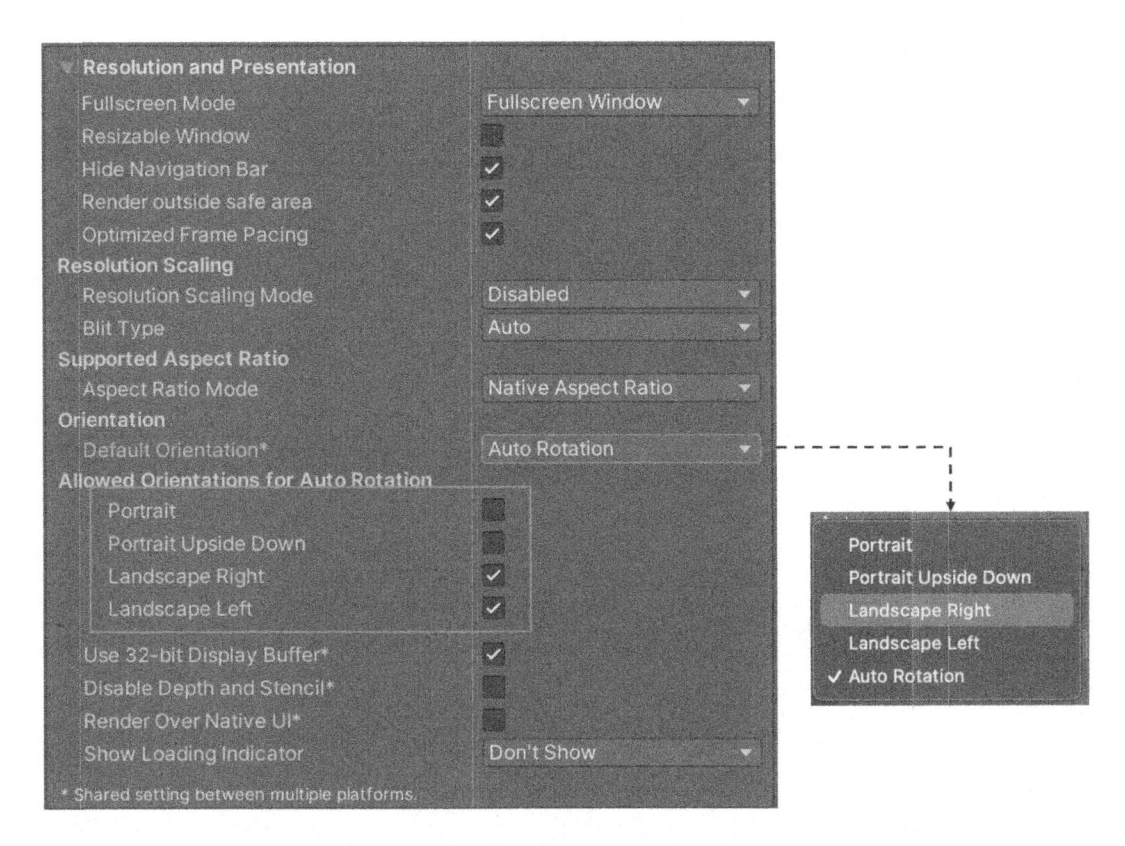

Figure 7.24: Configuring orientation for the game

In the preceding *figure 7.24*, orientation is the most important setting for the game. Most of the games we design to run on landscape mode, and such types of games cannot provide a good user experience in portrait mode. So we need to lock device orientation into landscape mode. To do that, either you can select **Landscape Right** or **Landscape Left** from **Auto Rotation** mode, or you can select **Landscape Right** or **Landscape Left** from the orientation drop-down menu.

- **Splash Image**: Set an image for the Splash screen. When you launch any application, you see some nice animation or static image or something else about the application before you see the home page of the application; this screen is known as the Splash screen.
- **Other Settings**: It provides many miscellaneous settings, such as graphics, Vulkan, and so on.

- **Publishing Settings**: As we know, to create a release build for Android, we need to sign the application file with the release certificate. In Unity, this publishing setting will help you to set a release certificate. Configuring this setting is almost the same as Android studio, which we saw earlier in this book.

After configuring these settings, Let us connect the Android device to the laptop.

The assumption is that you already know how to enable Android phones in developer mode, and you know how to run an Android application on the phone (real device) from Android Studio.

So let us connect our device to a laptop/pc and click on the **Build And Run** button, which is shown in *figure 7.22*. After that, you will see a window, as shown in *figure 7.25*:

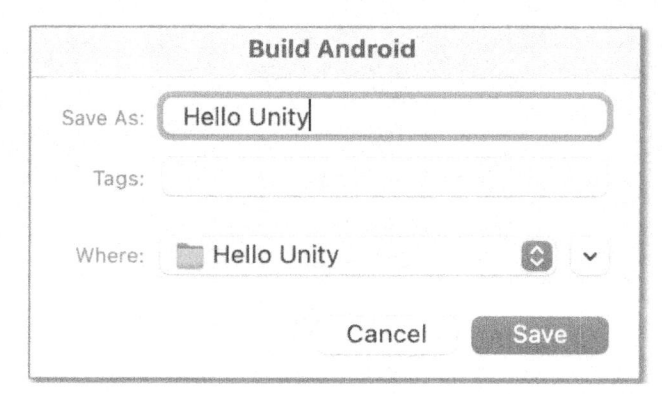

Figure 7.25: Adding name and location for Android build

In the window, as shown in the preceding *figure 7.25*, you need to add the file name in the **Save As** and the location of that file in the **Where** input field. After setting these two, click on **Save**. Unity will take some time to build and run the game on your connected device. And you can find the **.apk** file at the same location set as **Where** in the preceding *figure 7.25*.

That is it from this chapter. In the upcoming chapter, we will learn to develop our first awesome game and use the learning from this chapter.

Conclusion

In this chapter, we learned about game engines. We read about the basics of Unity and a few commonly used Unity terms. We also learned about adding game objects to the Scene and applying texture to those objects. We also added a C# script to the Hello Unity project. We learned about creating Android build Android build system.

In the upcoming chapter, we will develop our first Unity game, where we will try to create a game similar to Angry Birds.

Points to remember

- While starting the development of any game, do proper research about available game engines.
- You need to install the iOS build system to create an iOS build (.ipa).
- Colliders define the shape of a GameObject for physical collisions. We need to add colliders when the added object is going to collide with another object.
- AGDK is a full range of tools and libraries to help you develop, optimize, launch, and iterate on high-quality Android games.

Multiple Choice Questions

1. The hierarchy view represents each game object added to the Scene.

   A. True   B. False

2. Inspector view allows us to view and edit all the properties of the currently selected game object.

   A. True   B. False

3. We should choose only those images which support tiling to apply texture to the object.

   A. True   B. False

4. .... defines the appearance of the surface.

   A. Material   B. Scene   C. Renderer   D. Collider

5. Which of the following provides a collection of assets, scripts, and resources?

   A. GameObject   B. Component   C. Packages   D. Renderer

Answers

1. A
2. A
3. A
4. A
5. C

Questions

1. What is Collider?
2. What is RigidBody?
3. What is Prefab?
4. What is the difference between screen space and world space?
5. What is the benefit of declaring a variable as SerializeField?

Key Terms

- Game Engine
- Indie
- 2D games
- 3D games
- Unity
- Unreal Engine
- Buildbox
- Solar2D
- GameMaker Studio 2
- Android Game Development Kit (AGDK)
- UnityHub
- UnityEditor
- Visual Studio
- Templates
- 2D Mobile Template
- 3D Mobile Template
- Hierarchy View
- Scene View and Game View
- Inspector View
- Project View
- GameObject
- Texture
- Material
- Package

- Component
- Scene
- Renderer
- Collider
- RigidBody
- Script
- Prefab
- Asset
- Screen Space
- World Space
- Transform
- SerializeField
- C#
- Create Android Build

CHAPTER 8
Development of the First Game

In the previous chapter, we learned about some game engines and the basics of Unity.

In this chapter, we will develop our first game using Unity. We will develop a game similar to Angry Birds. There will be one level of the game, and instead of birds, we will use a circle object (to treat as a ball) to shoot the target.

We will also learn about developing the game for different screen resolutions or different Android devices.

Structure

- Introducing the project requirement
- Creating the project
    - Adding game objects
    - Adding floor
    - Adding target objects
        - Adding blocks
        - Adding diamond
    - Adding the ball
    - Adding the bouncing effect to the ball

- o Adding ball pin object
- Adding C# script
- Adding ball to the game dynamically
  - o Creating Prefab for ball
  - o Modifying script to use ball prefab
- Adding support for multiple screens

Objectives

This chapter aims to let you know how we can develop a game for Android using Unity. You will learn about developing a game, and while developing, we will learn about components that will be used while developing the game.

You will also know about handling different Android devices with different resolutions.

Introducing the project requirement

We will develop a game similar to one of the popular games, Angry Birds. In our game, we will have one level, and instead of Angry Birds, we will use the ball. *Figure 8.1* shows the final output of the game:

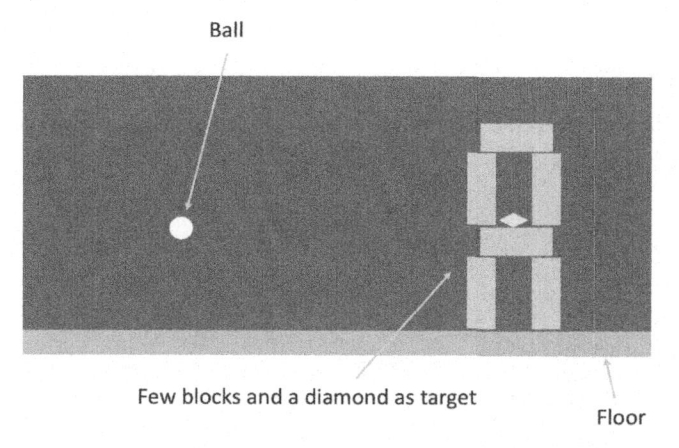

Figure 8.1: The final output of the game

As you see in the preceding *figure 8.1*, our game will have a target with a diamond, one ball to hit the target, and there would be a floor.

NOTE: **While developing a game, you need to think about how you can increase the interest of users in your game. Adding surprises is one of the ways to do so. In** the preceding *figure 8.1*, you see a diamond; similarly, you can do it in your game. If your game has limited lifelines for users, you can add lives for users if they perform or achieve something while playing the level. Or you can award them with extra points if your game handles the scoring.

Creating the project

Let us create a project in Unity to proceed.

Open Unity Hub, select the **Projects** tab, and click on **New project** or go to **File | New Project...**, as shown in *figure 8.2*:

Figure 8.2: Creating new project

After clicking on **New project**, you will be navigated to the **New project** window, where you need to select the project template and then you need to add the name. Let us select the **2D** template and enter **BPB Angry Balls** and click on **Create project**, as shown in *figure 8.3*:

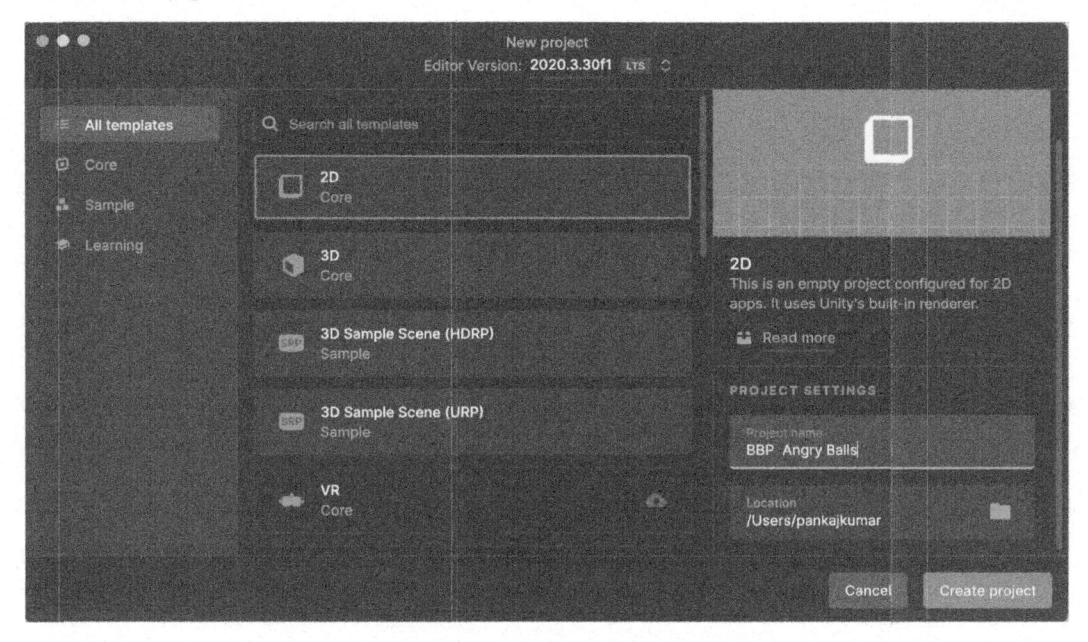

Figure 8.3: Selecting a template

Now, the new project will be created, and you will be navigated to Unity with the new project.

NOTE: **For mobile games, the best-suited template is "2D Mobile" or "3D Mobile". But these templates will require many packages, which are not required as of now for our game. So, a better option is to choose a "2D" template.**

Adding game objects

As we saw in the preceding *figure 8.1*, we will have a few Unity objects which will be used in our game. Let us first know which type of Unity objects we will use. See *figure 8.4*:

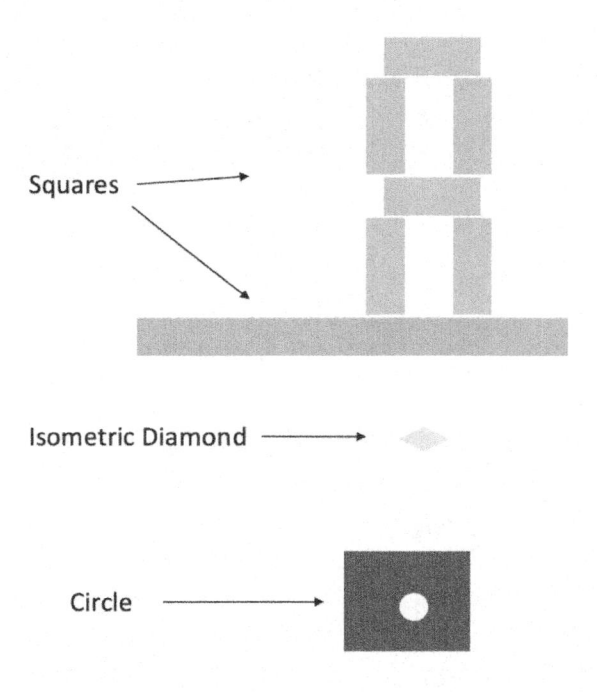

Figure 8.4: Introduction of each game object

As you see in the preceding *figure 8.4*, we need seven Squares, one Isometric Diamond, and one Circle. Note that we will need one more Circle object, which we will discuss later in this chapter.

Let us first create/add components to the scene view.

Adding floor

The floor will be the type of Square object. We will scale it to achieve the expected shape. To add it, follow these steps

Right-click on empty space at **Hierarchy view** | **2D Object** | **Sprites** | **Square**.

You will see a Square object on the Scene view. You can see this object while being in the Game or Simulator view as well, but doing modification is easy in the Scene view so remember to move to the Scene view if you are on another view.

Now, we need to scale it to the width of the screen and move it to the bottom. *Figure 8.5* shows how to do these:

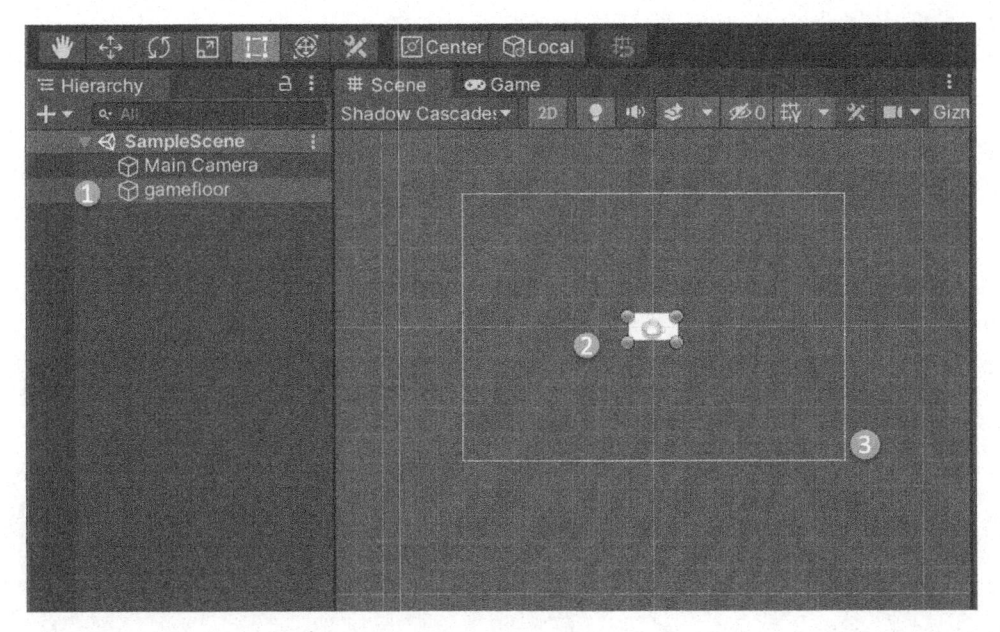

① Select **gamefloor** object. In the scene view this object will be selected and you see four circular handles which can be used to scale this object.

② Using left or right handles of **gamefloor,** scale it's width so it can fit with the maximum width of screen. And then drag it to bottom.

③ And at last, we need to move **gamefloor** at bottom. Press mouse on this object, drag it to the bottom of Scene

Figure 8.5: Adding floor

Note that you can scale or move objects from the **Game** view as well by playing with **Scale** and **Position** in the **Inspector** view, as shown in *figure 8.6*:

332 ■ *Building Android Projects with Kotlin*

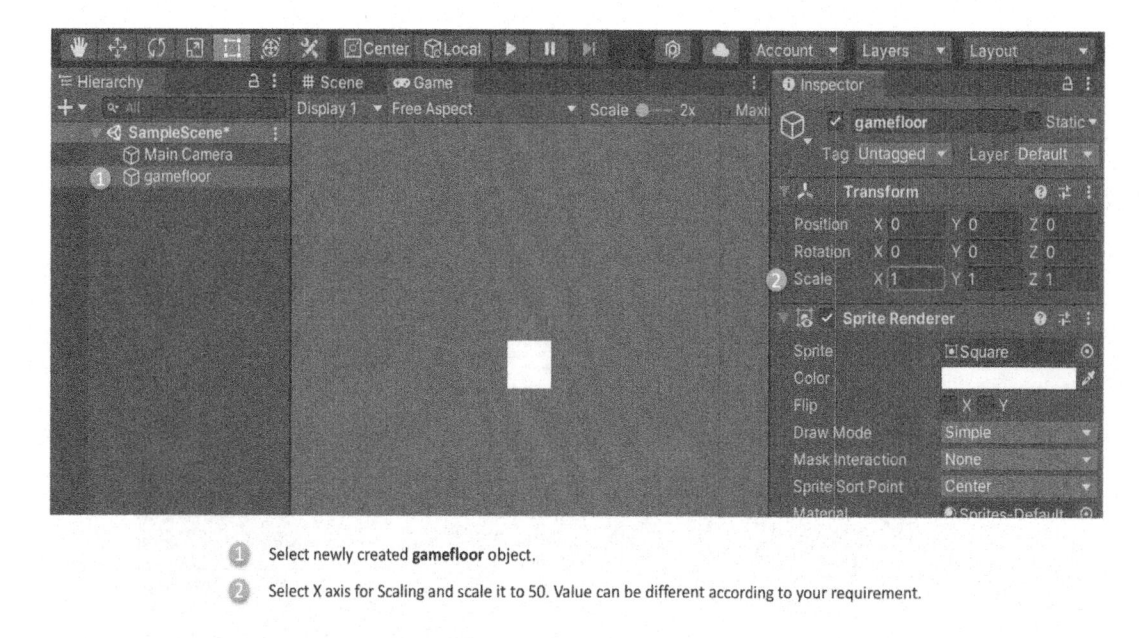

① Select newly created **gamefloor** object.

② Select X axis for Scaling and scale it to 50. Value can be different according to your requirement.

Figure 8.6: *Floor from game view*

After scaling and positioning this object, the **Scene** view should look like as shown in *figure 8.7*:

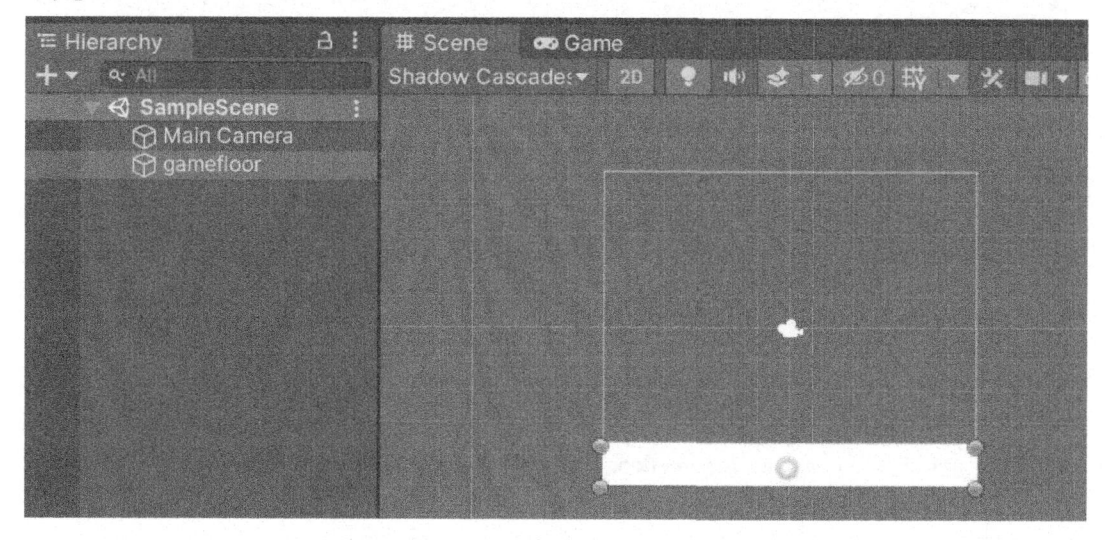

Figure 8.7: *Scaling* floor from Scene view

In real life, anything which falls from height collides with the earth. Similarly, in our game as well, anything (either ball or target objects) that falls from height should collide with the floor object.

To collide with other objects, we need to add **Box Collider 2D**. To do that, select the **gamefloor** object | go to **Inspector window** | Click on **Add Component** | Search for **Box Collider 2D** and select it, as shown in *figure 8.8*:

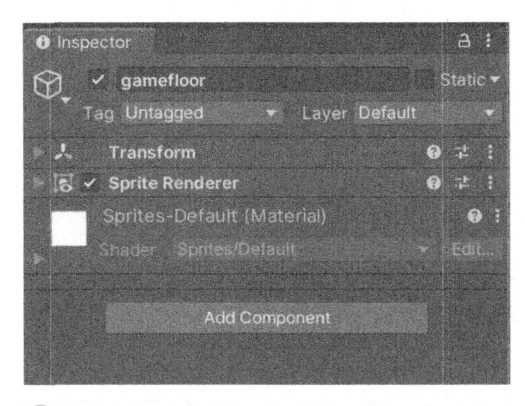

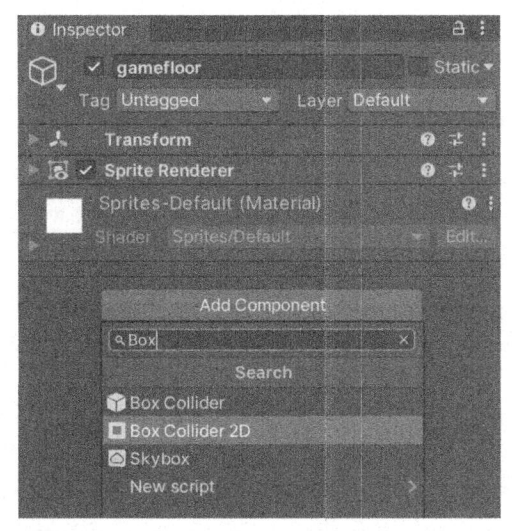

Figure 8.8: Adding collider

Now, **gamefloor** is ready to collide with other objects.

We can change the color of **gamefloor** or apply texture similar to any other unity object. Let us apply color (#ADB0AD) to it by clicking on the color picker as the arrow shown in *figure 8.9*:

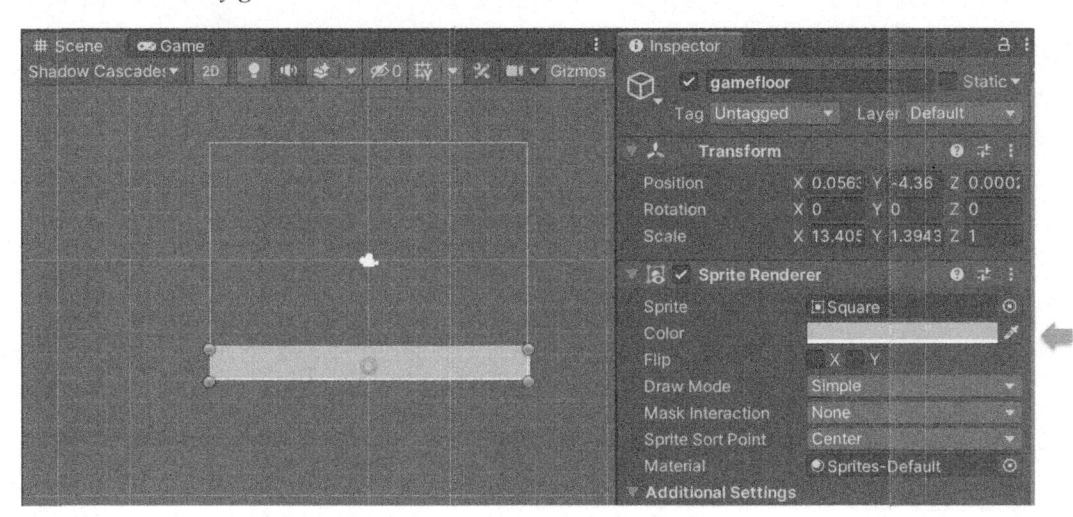

Figure 8.9: Changing color of floor object

Now, we have done almost all the settings required for the floor object.

Adding target objects

Target objects in our game are six boxes and one diamond. Let us place blocks first.

Adding blocks

Right-click on empty space at `Hierarchy view` | `2D Object` | `Sprites` | `Square`. One square box will appear on the scene view. Configure the following for this box:
- Name it `block_1`.
- Change the color of the box to #D7BA89 so it looks like a wooden block.
- Scale it to 1:2.5 (X:Y) ratio.
- Change position of this block above of floor. So visually, it would feel like a box placed on the floor.

Now, we need to configure it with two different components:
- **Box Collider 2D**: This box will collide with the ball and floor, so we need to add this component to `block_1`.

    To add it, Select `block_1` object | go to `Inspector window` | Click on `Add Component` | Search for `Box Collider 2D` and select it. The step is similar to the `gamefloor` object shown in *figure 8.8*.

- **Rigidbody 2D**: These boxes will not only collide with the ball or floor, but they will fly in the air or jump a bit on the floor as well after hitting by the ball. As we know, RigidBody allows the object to receive forces and to be affected by gravity, so we need to add it to `block_1`.

To add it, Select `block_1` object | go to `Inspector window` | Click on `Add Component` | Search for `Rigidbody 2D` and select it.

We have configured the first block. It should look like as shown in *figure 8.10*:

Figure 8.10: Adding game targets

We need five more blocks. So, repeat the same steps five times, or if you feel that repeating steps will take time, let us do it quickly.

In Hierarchy viewer, right-click on **block_1** | click on **Duplicate**. Perform this step until six boxes get added to the game. After adding these boxes, rename them as **block_1**, **block_2**, and so on till **block_6**. So, the scene view will look like as shown in *figure 8.11*:

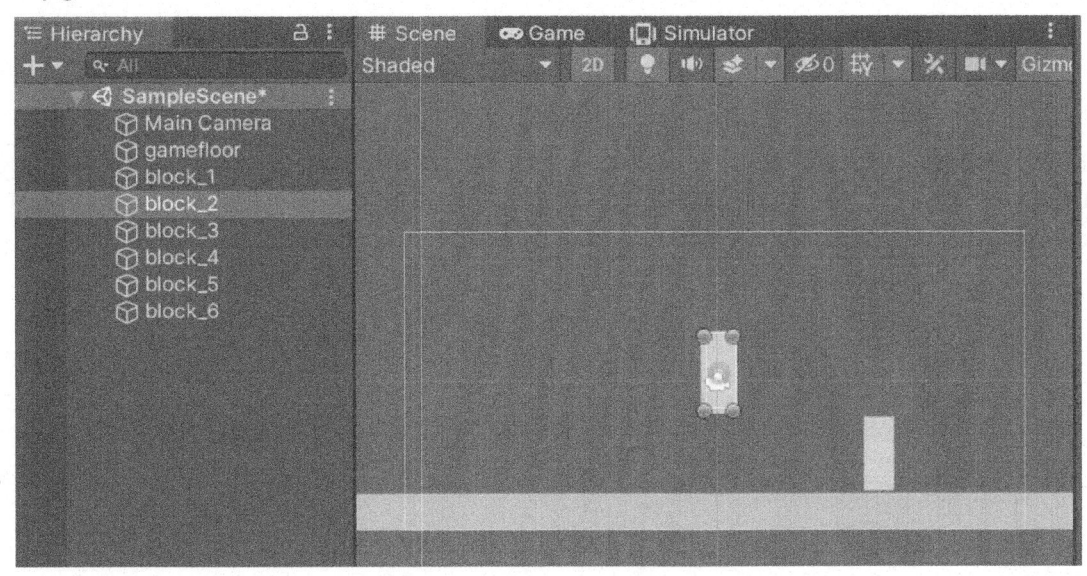

Figure 8.11: Creating duplicate blocks

Note that all configuration of **block_1** is already applied to these newly created boxes. So, no need to configure these boxes again. Now, let us arrange these blocks as shown in *figure 8.1*. After arranging these boxes, they should look like as shown in *figure 8.12*:

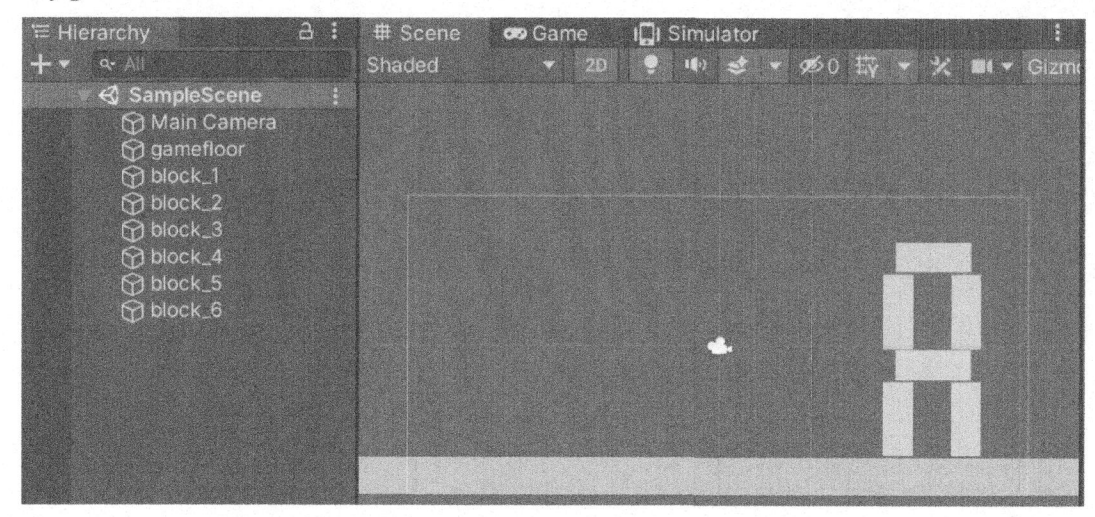

Figure 8.12: Arranging blocks as required target

Note that, for the two vertical blocks in the preceding *figure 8.12*, the ratio of scaling would be 2.5:1 (X: Y).

Adding diamond

Now, let us add a diamond by following these steps:

Right-click on empty space at **Hierarchy view** | **2D Object** | **Sprites** | **Isometric Diamond**. One diamond 2D shape would appear on scene view. Do the following configurations to this object?

- Name it "diamond".
- Change the color of the object to #FFD700.
- Change the position of this object, as shown in *figure 8.1*.
- And at last, add Box Collider 2D and RigidBody 2D, similar to blocks.

Now, the target in the game will look like as shown in *figure 8.13*:

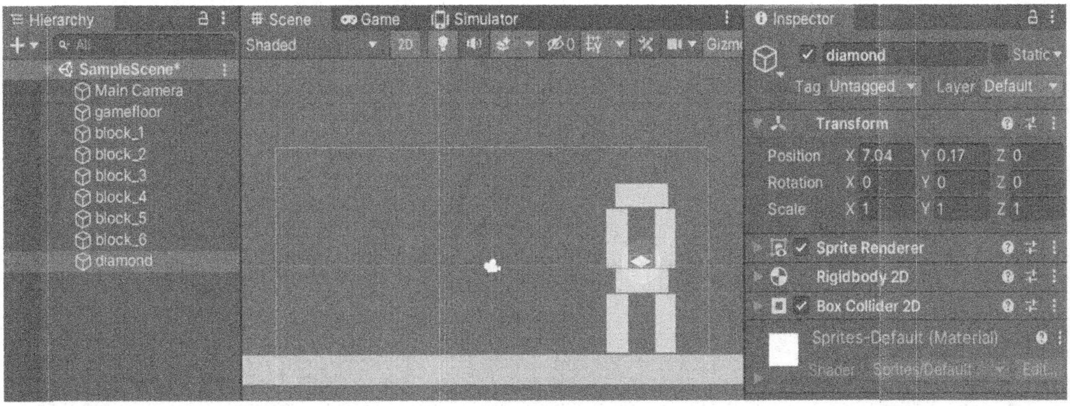

Figure 8.13: Adding diamond as target

Now, we are ready with the game floor and target. We just need a ball to hit the target.

Adding the ball

It is time to create the ball. The ball is going to be affected by gravity and will hit objects like the target and the floor. So, the ball object will be a little bit different from targets or floor objects.

We need a dynamic Physics object for the ball. So, let us create it with the following steps:

Right-click on empty space at **Hierarchy view | 2D Object | Physics | Dynamic Sprite**. One circle object will appear on scene view. Do the following configurations to this object:

- Rename it to **ball**.
- Change the color of the object to #FFFFFF.
- Change the position of the ball, as shown in *figure 8.1*.

After adding the ball and components to the ball, it should look like as shown in *figure 8.14*:

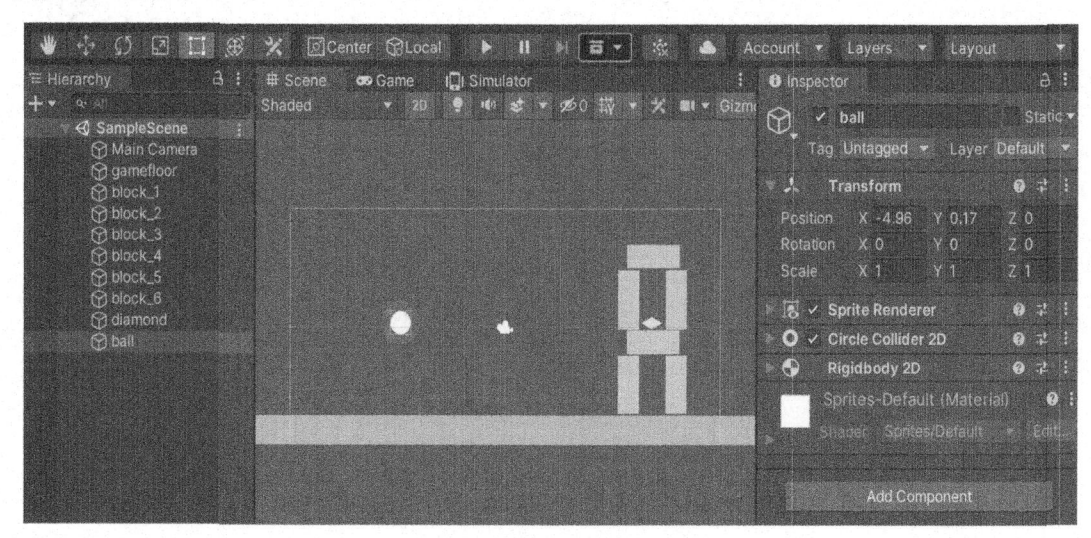

Figure 8.14: Adding circle for ball at Scene

If you see the **Inspector** view in the preceding *figure 8.14* carefully, there are two components, `Circle Collider 2D` and `Rigidbody 2D`, which are already added to this ball object. Note that when you add a dynamic physics object, these two components will be added by default to it.

If you tap on the play icon (▶), the ball will drop to the floor and will stay there without bouncing. So now, let us add a bouncing effect to the ball.

Adding the bouncing effect to the ball

To add a bouncing effect to the ball, we need to create a Physics material 2D by following the steps.

Right-click on **Assets** or empty area on Assets | `Create` | `2D` | `Physics Material 2D`, as shown in *figure 8.15*:

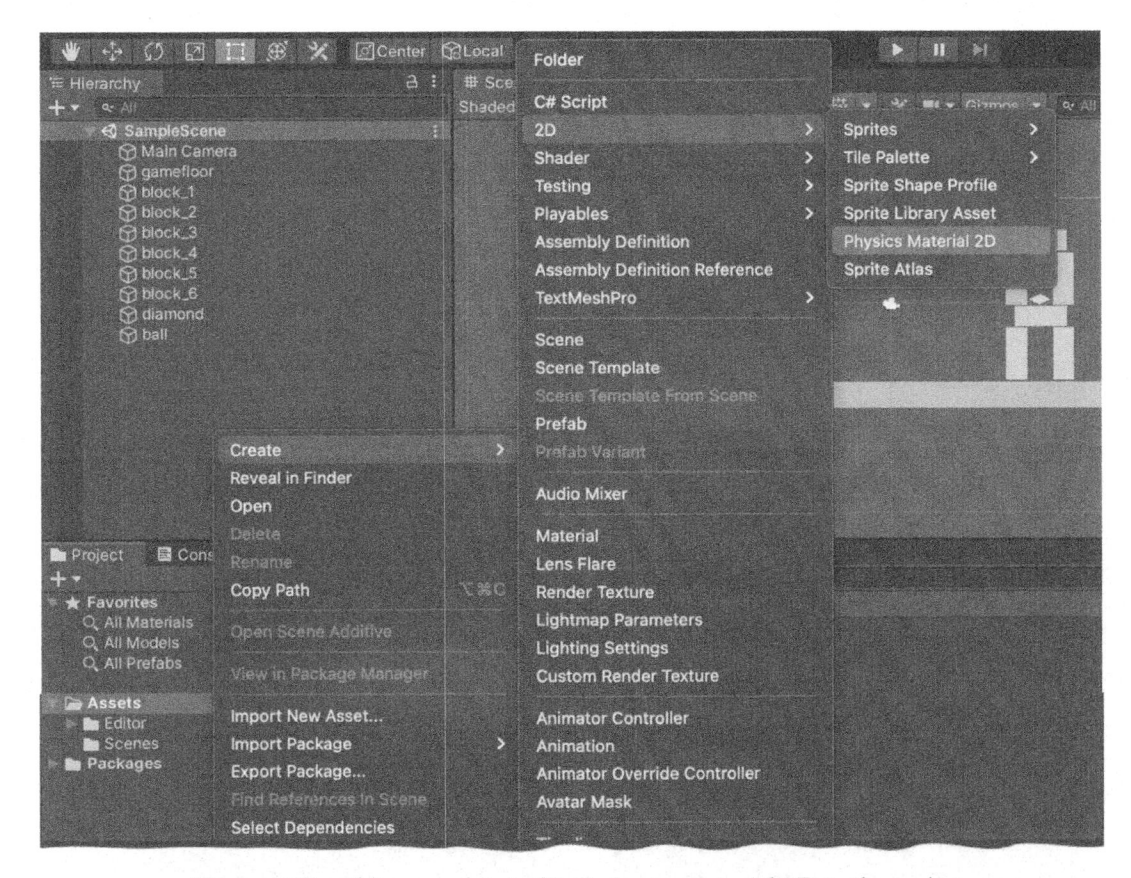

Development of the First Game ■ 339

Figure 8.15: Adding an object of Ball physics material 2D to the project

An object will be added. Rename it to `Ball Physics Material 2D`.

NOTE: **To organize assets, you can create a dedicated directory where all physics materials can be placed. While creating big games, such approaches help you to organize the project in a good way. So for our game, let us create a directory "CustomMaterials" and put this "Ball Physics Material 2D" into it.**

The newly created `Ball Physics Material 2D` will look like as shown in *figure 8.16*:

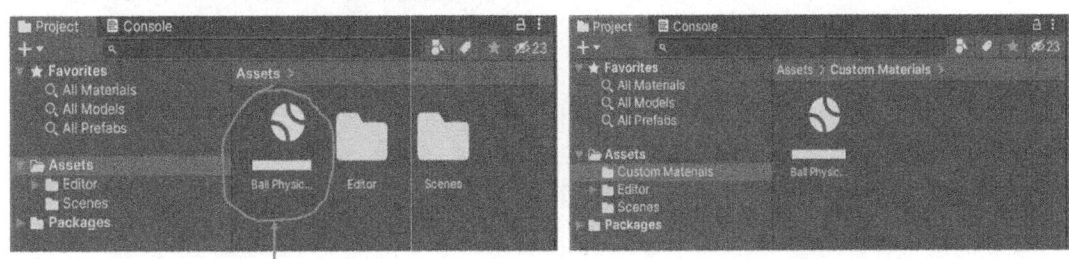

A newly created "Ball Physics Material 2D"   "Ball Physics Material 2D" moved into "Custom Materials"

Figure 8.16: Arranging Ball physics material 2D object

Now select the **Ball Physics Material 2D** and go to the **Inspector** view. Change the value of **Bounciness** to 0.5 as shown in *figure 8.17*:

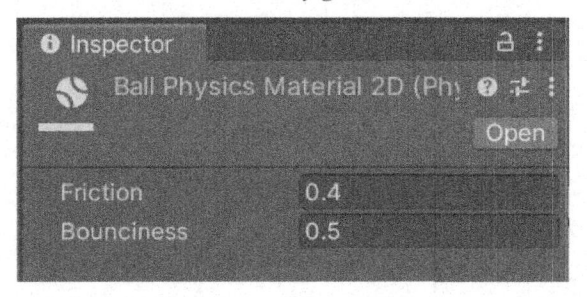

Figure 8.17: Changing the value of bounciness

Note that the value 0.5 is not fixed; you can change the value of it by playing with the ball and observing bouncing behavior.

Now, we need to add **Ball Physics Material 2D** to the ball.

To do that, select the ball object and drag **Ball Physics Material 2D** to the Material of Circle Collider 2D and RigidBody 2D of the ball, as shown in *figure 8.18*:

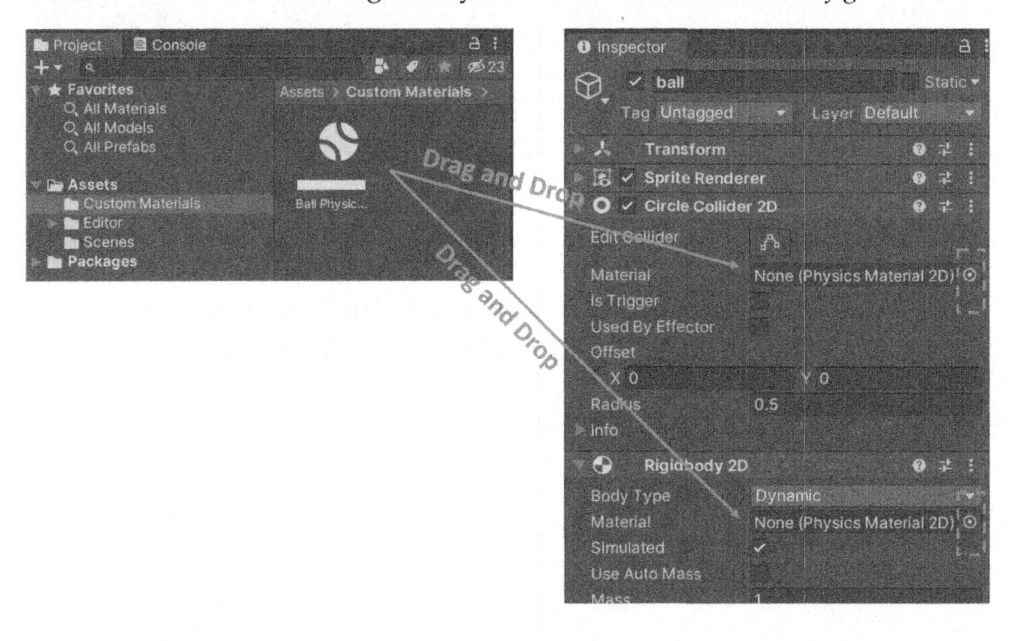

You can apply physics material by drag-drop or by clicking on the right most icon of Material.

Figure 8.18: Adding Ball Physics Material 2D to the ball object

Now, you can see the ball bouncing on the floor if you run the game.

Creating ball pin object

As of now, our ball can only fall down to the floor and bounce. Now, it is time to add a physics system to the ball, so it can swing to the target and break it.

To do this, we need to add one Static Sprite Physics object and relate it with the ball via the Spring Joint component. Remember that our ball is Dynamic Sprite Physics because the ball is movable.

NOTE: **As we know, the Spring works like an elastic that tries to pull two anchor points together to the exact same position. The Spring joint ties two rigid bodies together. The Spring attempts to maintain the distance it had when it started out.**

Let us proceed.

Right-click on empty space at **Hierarchy view** | **2D Object** | **Physics** | **Static Sprite**. One circle object will appear on scene view. Do the following configurations to this object:

- Rename it to **ball pin**.
- Remove the **Box Collider 2D** object from the Inspector view for this **ball pin**. The steps are, right-click on **Box Collider 2D** | **Remove Component**.
- Change its shape to a circle by changing Sprite from Sprite Renderer in Inspector.
- Change the color of the object to #000000.
- Change the position of the ball pin as same as the ball as shown in *figure 8.19*, which also shows all changes applied to the ball pin. Note that this positioning is temporary; we will reposition it soon in this chapter.

342 ■ *Building Android Projects with Kotlin*

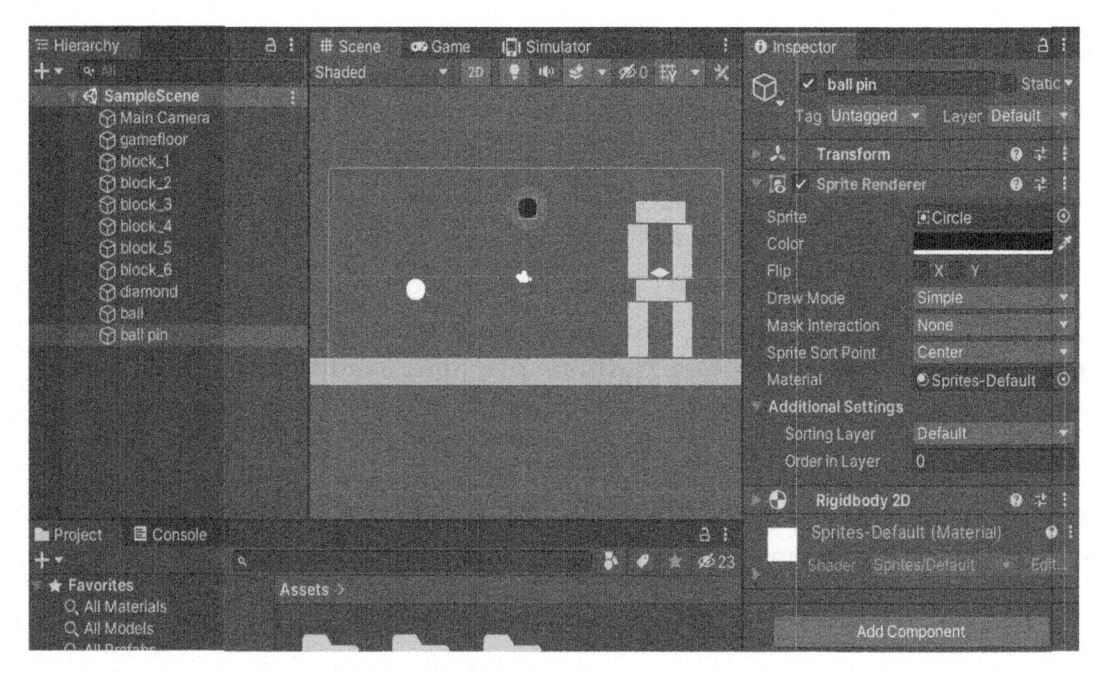

Figure 8.19: Adding Ball Pin to the Scene

Now, we need to attach the ball to the ball-pin via Spring Joint via the following steps.

Select the ball | Click on **Add Component** | Add **Spring Joint 2D**. When the **Spring Joint 2D** component is added, drag the ball-pin to the **Connected Rigid Body** to connect the ball with the ball-pin object. *Figure 8.20* shows the configuration of **Spring Joint 2D** for the ball:

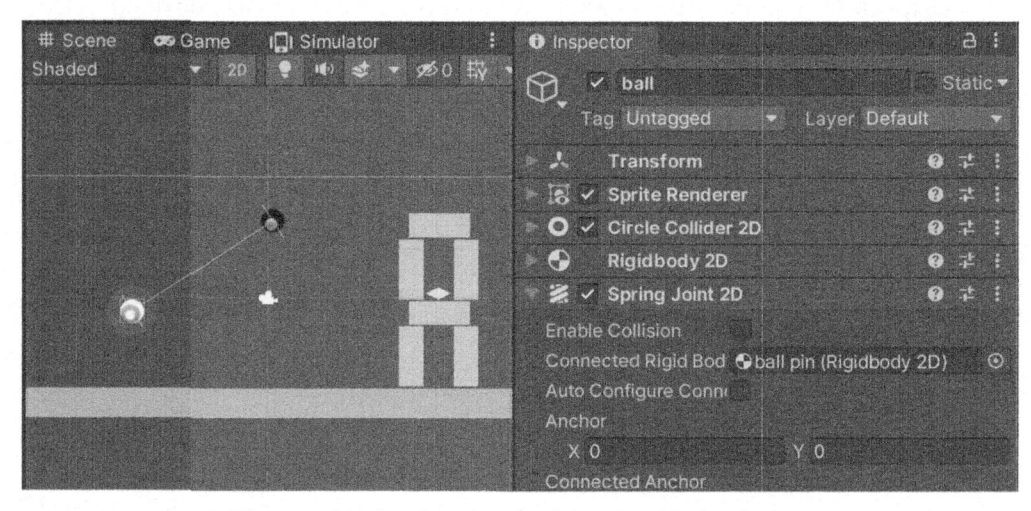

Figure 8.20: Configuring Spring Joint 2D for the ball

If you see the Scene view in the preceding *figure 8.20*, you will realize that now the ball may work as same as the pendulum. If you forget about the pendulum, the pendulum works as shown in *figure 8.21*:

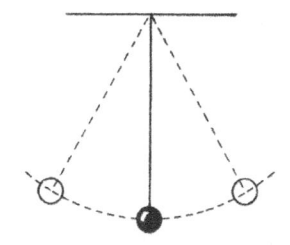

Figure 8.21: *Working of Pendulum*

Yes, you are right; when you run the game, you will see the ball moving like a pendulum where the ball pin will be like something to which the pendulum is attached with.

Till now, the ball is moving without user action (touch event), and the current movement of the ball is also not as required for the game. So, to handle user actions, we need a C# script.

But before doing that, let us make a few changes to the ball and the ball-pin objects. Let us move these two objects at some points at the left of the screen. So, the user can pull and release the ball similar to Angry Birds. Let us first move the ball-pin at the left of the screen like the red circled position as shown in *figure 8.22* and remember the position:

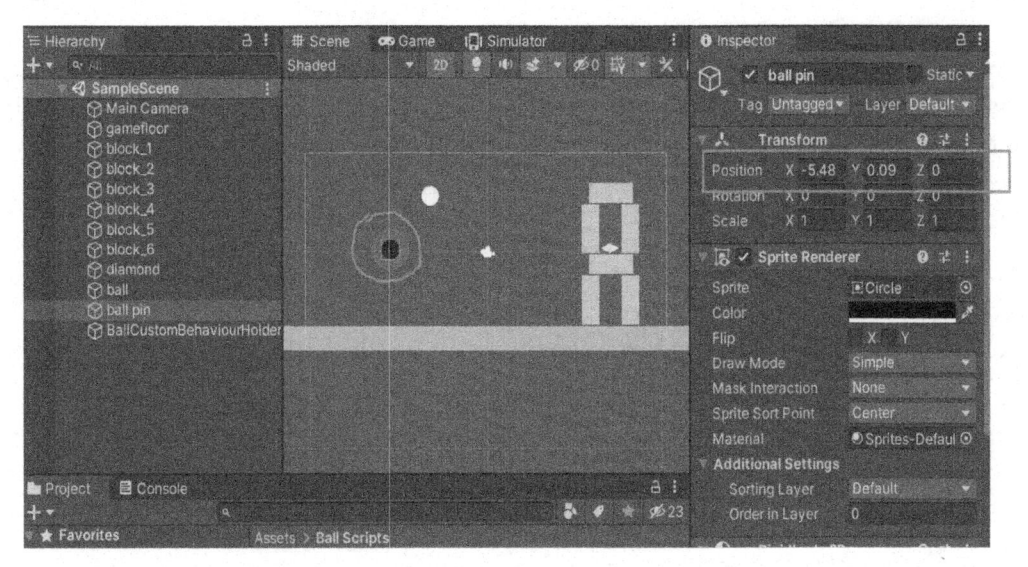

Figure 8.22: *Moving ball-pin to the final position*

NOTE: **As the ball-pin is just an anchor for the ball and can be used to produce potential and kinetic energy for the ball, you can set the background of this ball-pin as transparent to make it invisible, but as we already discussed to keep this ball-pin visible in our example, we will not set the transparent background, at least in this chapter.**

Now, let us move the ball and keep the position [−5.48, 0.09] as same as the ball-pin, as shown in the preceding *figure 8.22* and the following *figure 8.23*:

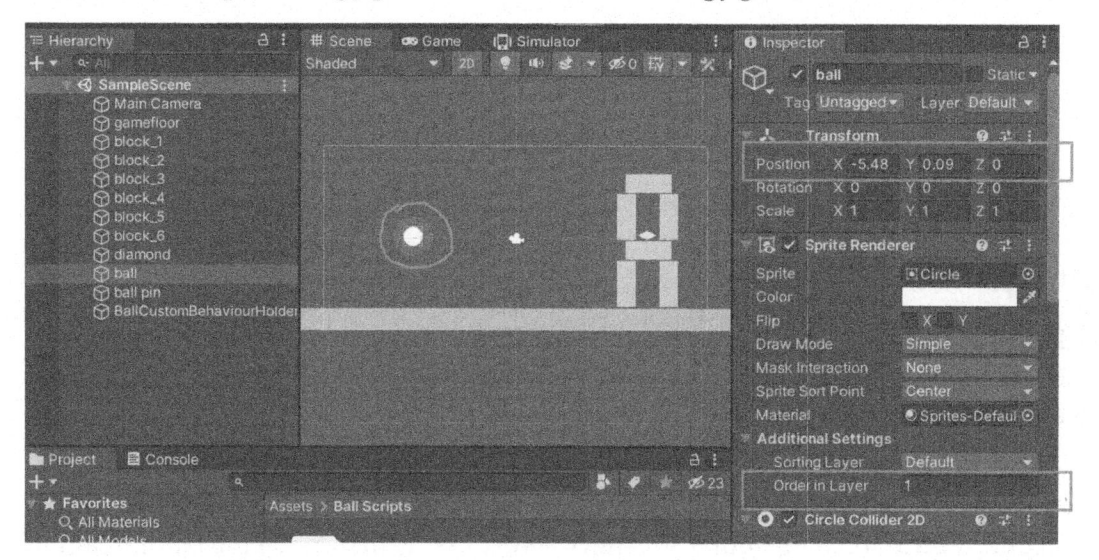

Figure 8.23: *Moving* ball at the same position as ball-pin

In the preceding *figure 8.23*, there is one more change, that is, `Order in Layer`. When you move the ball-pin and ball at the same position, the ball-pin might appear on top of the ball. So, to show the ball is always on the top of the ball-pin, set the value of `Order in Layer` to higher than the value of `Order in Layer` for the ball-pin. In our project value of `Order in Layer` in the ball-pin is zero, so we can set the value for `Order in Layer` to one in the ball.

Now, let us correct the anchor for the ball. Set `Anchor` and `Connected Anchor` values to zero into the `Spring Joint 2D` component, as shown in *figure 8.24*. So, the ball will stick to the ball pin and can only move when you touch it and move it:

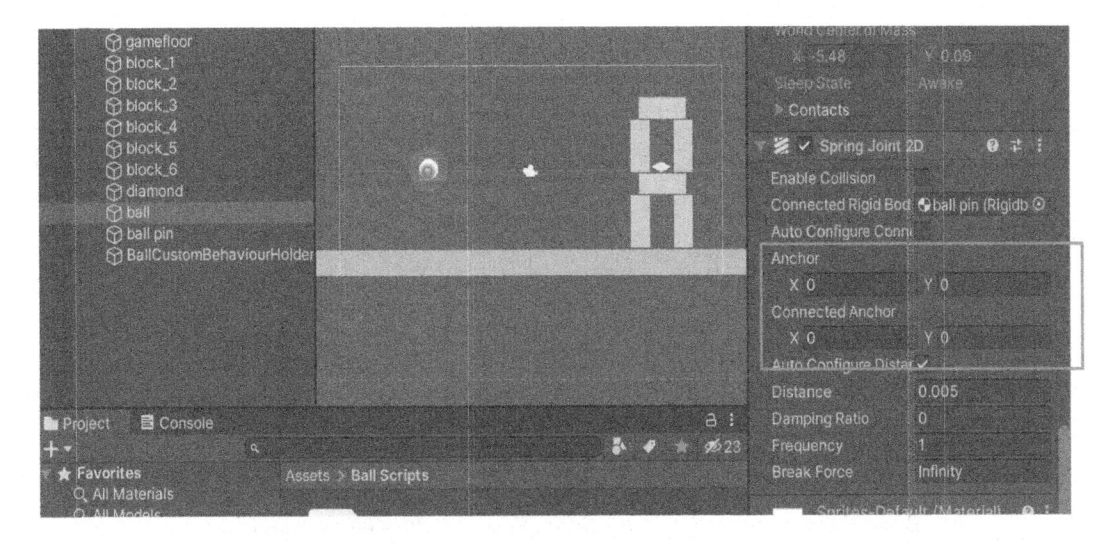

Figure 8.24: Correcting anchor of the ball

You can see a little blue circle above the ball in the preceding *figure 8.24*, and it shows the anchor place. While following these steps, make sure that the anchor position shows at the ball and ball-pin and not outside of the ball or ball-pin. If you set anchor far from the ball, the ball will again move like a pendulum.

So, the configuration is done with ball and ball-pin; now, it is time to write the C# script.

Adding C# script

Let us add the script to enable the touch event and move the ball with the touch event to break the target. At first, we need to add a script file by the following steps:

1. Right-click on **Assets** or empty area on Assets | **Create** | **Folder** and rename it to **Ball Scripts**.

2. And now go to the **Game Scripts** directory, right-click on the empty area | **Create** | **C# Script**, and rename it to **BallCustomBehaviour**.

Now create an empty game object to hold the script. So, to do that, Right-click on the empty area at **Hierarchy** view | **Empty Object** and rename it to **BallCustomBehaviourHolder**.

Then, we need to attach the script **BallCustomBehaviour** to this game object **BallCustomBehaviourHolder**. To do that, select **BallCustomBehaviourHolder** and drag-drop **BallCustomBehaviour** script to the component area of **BallCustomBehaviourHolder** in the Inspector view, as shown in *figure 8.25*:

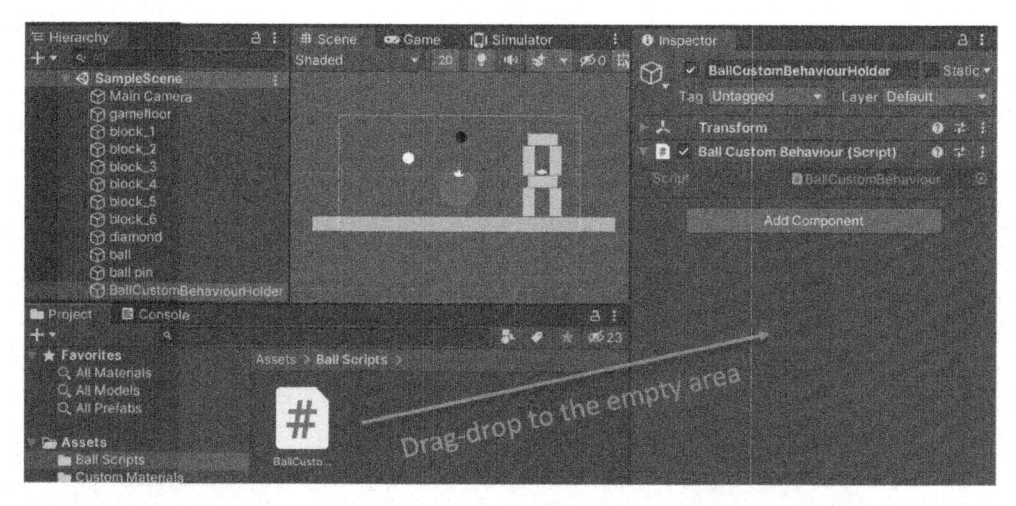

Figure 8.25: Adding the script to the BallCustomBehaviourHolder

We have added a script to the **BallCustomBehaviourHolder**. Now open the **BallCustomBehaviour** into Visual Studio. Note that if you click on the BallCustomBehaviour script file, it will open in the Visual Studio editor.

In the script file, let us add the following code:

```
using System.Collections;

using System.Collections.Generic;

using UnityEngine;

using UnityEngine.InputSystem;


public class BallCustomBehaviour : MonoBehaviour {

    // Note that when you add something with Serializedfield

    // that will be available in inspector view.

    [SerializeField] private Rigidbody2D ballRigidbody;

    [SerializeField] private SpringJoint2D ballSpringJoint;

    [SerializeField] private float ballRemoveDelay;


    private Camera camera;

    private bool isDragging;
```

```
// Start is called before the first frame update
void Start() {
    camera = Camera.main;
}

// Update is called once per frame
void Update() {
    if (ballRigidbody == null) return;

    if (Touchscreen.current.primaryTouch.press.isPressed) {
        // When user is touching (and moving on) the screen.
        dragBall();
    } else {
        // User not touching the screen now
        if (isDragging) {
            releaseBall();
        }
        isDragging = false;
    }
}

private void dragBall() { ... }

private void releaseBall() { ... }

private void removeTheBall() { ... }
}
```

Now, let us write code for empty methods **dragBall()**, **releaseBall()**, and **removeTheBall()**. The following code shows you how we will drag the ball by using world position:

```
private void dragBall() {

    isDragging = true;

    ballRigidbody.isKinematic = true;

    // Reading the touch position, in terms of Screen Space

    Vector2 touchPosition = Touchscreen.current.primaryTouch.position.ReadValue();


    // Coverting touch position to World Space position

    Vector3 worldPosition = camera.ScreenToWorldPoint(touchPosition);


    // Set ball position to current world position

    ballRigidbody.position = worldPosition;

}
```

The following code to handle the release of the ball. The method will be called after the user touches the ball:

```
private void releaseBall() {

    ballRigidbody.isKinematic = false;

    ballRigidbody = null;


    Invoke(nameof(removeTheBall), ballRemoveDelay);

}
```

And this last code **removeTheBall()** handles the removal of the spring joint from the ball:

```
private void removeTheBall() {

    ballSpringJoint.enabled = false;

    ballSpringJoint = null;
```

}

And when you run the game, you will be able to pull the ball and release the ball. You see, the ball will break the target if they collide, as shown in *figure 8.26*:

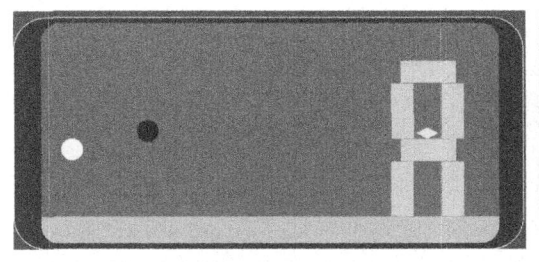

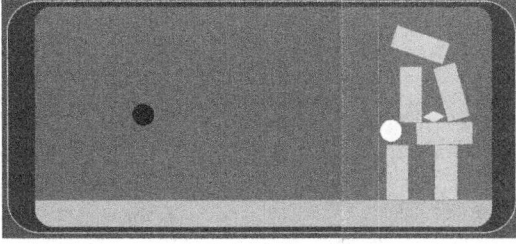

1. Pull the ball and release   2. Boom!!! Ball reaches to the target and break it

Figure 8.26: Output after modifying the script

But there would be a limitation as of now. When you release the ball, the ball never comes back to the pin, and it means you have only one ball to shoot the target. And having only one chance to break the target is not so interesting. So, let us add more balls to the game.

Adding ball to the game dynamically

Adding new balls to the game is similar to awarding users with more lives when they achieve some level in our game. When you develop any game, consider adding such surprises or awards.

Now, let us come back to Unity and prepare configs to create many balls.

Creating Prefab for ball

Prefab in Unity is like a template. The prefab system allows us to create, configure and store a GameObject with property values and components. So, it can be reused.

Most of the time, you need similar objects in your game, either in a scene or in multiple scenes (different levels) of the game. For example, if you are making a racing game, you want to add buildings and streetlights to the Scene. In this case, you can make a prefab for buildings and streetlights and place them in the Scene at any level of your game.

So in our game as well, we will utilize the benefits of Prefab. We will make our game object a prefab and add it dynamically to the Scene when needed. Let us first make a prefab.

350 ■ *Building Android Projects with Kotlin*

To do that, let us drag-drop the ball to the empty area in the **Assets** directory. Or we can make a directory for prefabs and keep all prefabs in that directory. *Figure 8.27* shows both options. We will create **Ball Prefabs** in our project and drag-drop the ball into the **Ball Prefabs** directory:

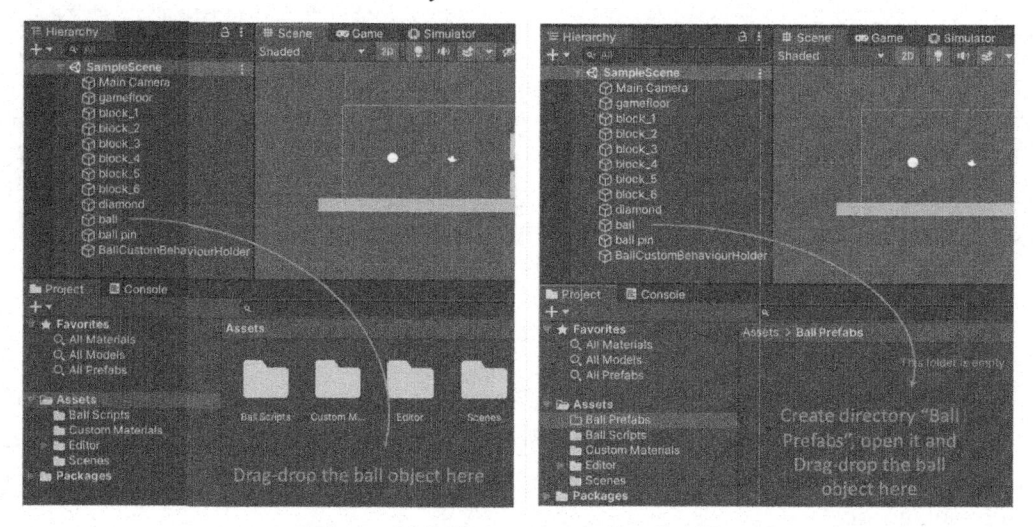

Figure 8.27: Converting ball to Prefab

After drag-drop **ball** object into **Ball Prefabs**, you will see the ball prefabs created in the place where you dragged-dropped the ball object, as same as *figure 8.28*:

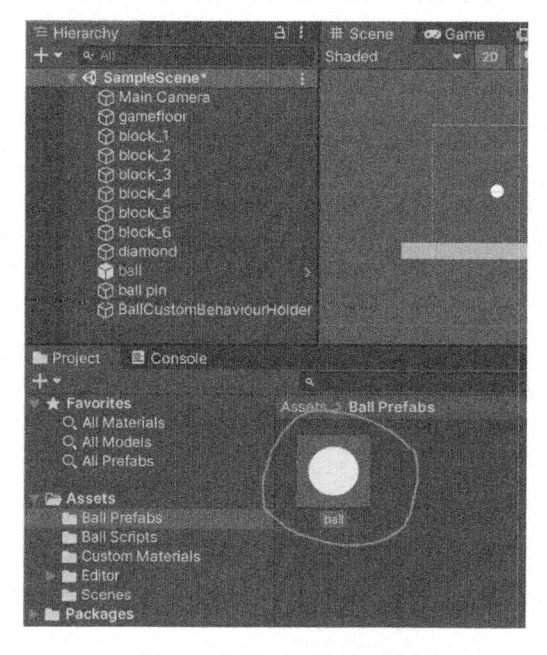

Figure 8.28: Ball Prefab

Now, we have created a ball prefab, which means we can add this Prefab to anywhere in the Scene in our game, with all configurations that we have done till now for the game object. You can verify it by dragging it from assets to the hierarchy view, and the ball should appear as same as the previous ball, and configurations would also be the same.

As we planned, we are going to add this ball dynamically, then let us remove the current ball from the Scene and let us modify our script, where we will add the ball when the user starts the game or releases the current ball from the pin. It means we need to follow these three steps to achieve this:

- Remove the ball from the Scene by doing Right-click on the **ball** | **Delete**, as shown in *figure 8.29*:

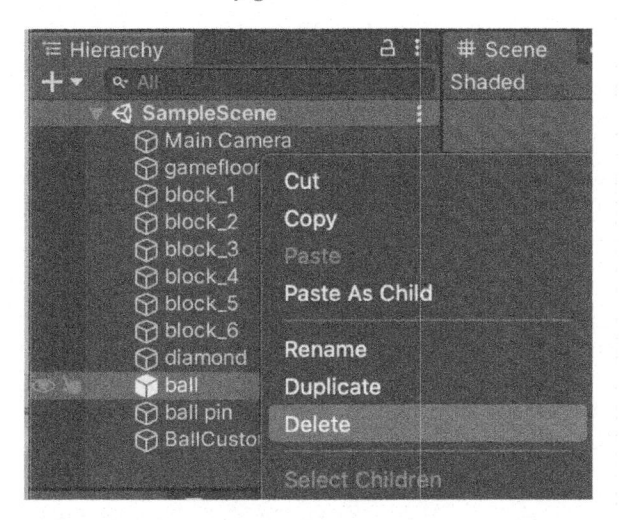

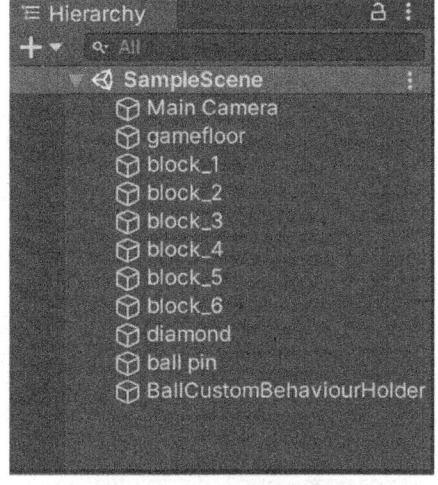

Before deleting the ball   After deleting the ball

Figure 8.29: Deleting ball object from Hierarchy

- Add the ball dynamically when the game starts. So, we will add code for adding the ball in **Start() {}** method.
- Add a new ball dynamically after a few milliseconds of releasing the current ball. So, we will add a code for adding the ball in **removeTheBall() {}**.

Modifying script to use ball prefab

As we removed the ball from the Scene, configurations done into the script will not work, and we have to get the reference of the ball via code. So, let us first modify our code to get references of ball-prefab and ball-pin as follows:

```
public class BallCustomBehaviour : MonoBehaviour {
    // Get delay to respawn the ball
    [SerializeField] private float ballRespawnDelay;
    // The time delay which may take to hit the target,
    // so we can remove the ball
    [SerializeField] private float ballRemoveDelay;
    // Get the Ball Prefab
    [SerializeField] private GameObject ballPrefab;
    // Get the Ball Pin
    [SerializeField] private Rigidbody2D ballPin;

    // As the Ball is removed from Scene, ballRigidbody and
    // ballSpringJoint has no meaning to be added as
    // SerializeField.
    private Rigidbody2D ballRigidbody;
    private SpringJoint2D ballSpringJoint;
    private Camera camera;
    private bool isDragging;

    // ...
}
```

In the preceding code, we have removed **SerializeField** from **ballRigidbody** and **ballSpringJoint** and added **SerializeField** to **ballPrefab**, **ballPin**, and **ballRespawnDelay**. The **ballRemoveDelay** was already declared as **SerializeField**.

The reference **ballPrefab** will be used to get the ball object, whereas **ballPin** will be used to set the position of the ball.

After modifying the above code, let us come back to Unity and do some configurations to set references for each **SerializeField** object in our code.

Select **BallCustomBehaviourHolder** and see the **Inspector** view. Each `SerializeField` field will be added as shown in *figure 8.30*, and we can set values for each:

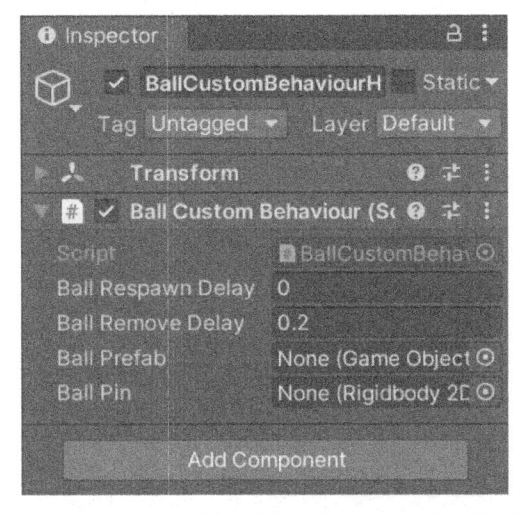

Figure 8.30: The view after adding new SerializeField objects

So, let us set the ball prefab reference to `Ball Prefab`, ball-pin reference to `Ball Pin`, and set delay values for `Ball Respawn Delay` to 2 and `Ball Remove Delay` to 0.2, as shown in *figure 8.31*:

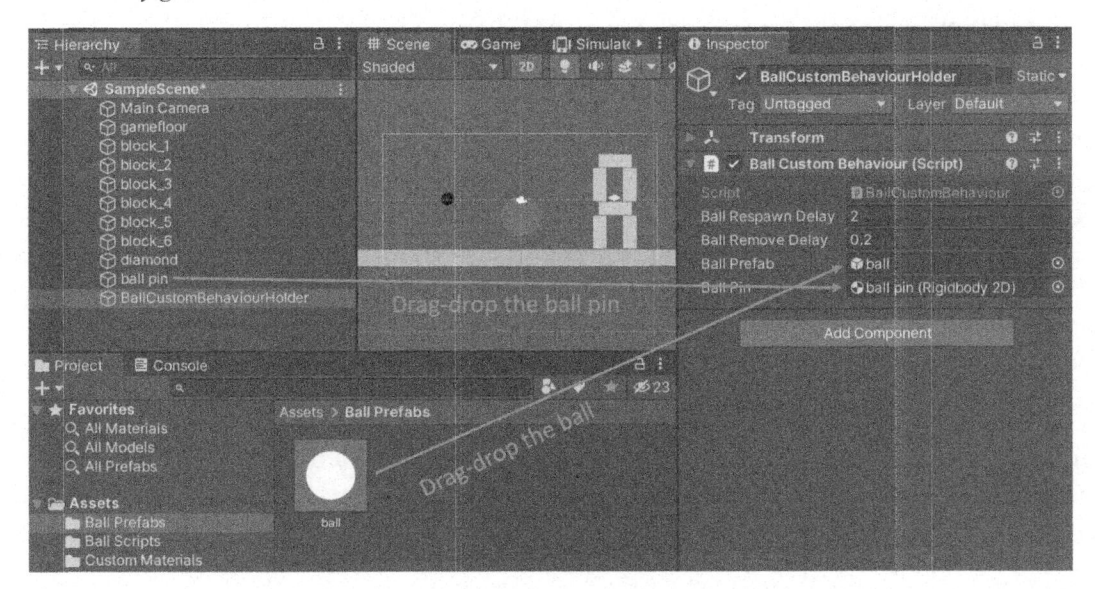

Figure 8.31: Adding ball-pin and ball prefab to the script

Now, let us write code to read these references and create a new ball:

```
private void respawnTheBall() {
    // Create an instance of the Ball prefab, set it to
    // the same position of Ball pin and set the default
    // rotation as rotation does not matter as of now.
    GameObject ball = Instantiate(
        ballPrefab,
        ballPin.position,
        Quaternion.identity);

    // Set Rigidbody and SpringJoint
    ballRigidbody = ball.GetComponent<Rigidbody2D>();
    ballSpringJoint = ball.GetComponent<SpringJoint2D>();
    // Attach the ball to ball-pin
    ballSpringJoint.connectedBody = ballPin;
}
```

In the preceding code, in Line 5, we are creating a ball object from **ballPrefab** and proving its position as the same as the **ballPin**. Lines 11 and 12 are being used to set values for **ballRigidbody** and **ballSpringJoint** using the ball object. If you remember, we were setting values for these two from the Inspector view; see *figures 8.18* and *8.20*. Now by using **respawnTheBall()**, we can create new balls as many as we want. If you run the code, as of now, you will not see any ball on the game because we have removed the pre-added ball object, and we did not add a ball dynamically yet to the game.

To show the ball object, let us call the **respawnTheBall()** method from **Start()** and **removeTheBall()** methods, as shown in the following code:

```
public class BallCustomBehaviour : MonoBehaviour {
    ...
    void Start() {
        camera = Camera.main;
```

```
        // Make the first ball available
        respawnTheBall();
    }
    ...
    private void removeTheBall() {
        ballSpringJoint.enabled = false;
        ballSpringJoint = null;

        // Respawn the ball after delay
        Invoke(nameof(respawnTheBall), ballRespawnDelay);
    }
    ...
}
```

Now, go to Unity, let the script compile, and run the code. You will see the ball on the launch of the game, and when you release the ball, you see another ball after a delay to the Scene, as shown in *figure 8.32*:

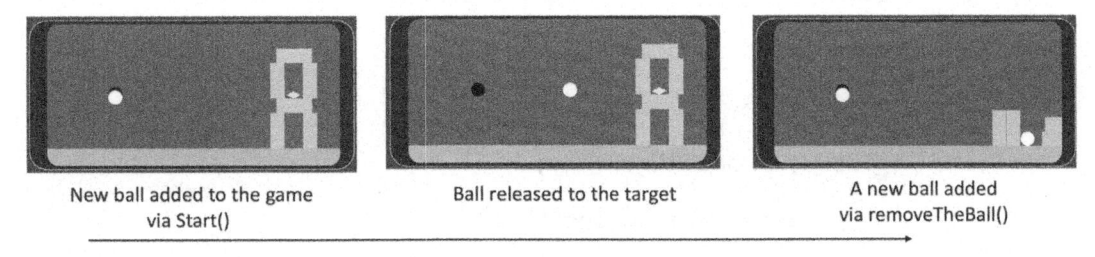

Figure 8.32: Output after adding code for adding new ball dynamically

The following is the full source code for our script file:

```
using System.Collections;
using System.Collections.Generic;
using UnityEngine;
using UnityEngine.InputSystem;
```

```
public class BallCustomBehaviour : MonoBehaviour {
    // Note that when you add something with Serializedfield
    // that will be available in inspector view. So we can
    // set value/ reference to these fields from inspector view.

    // Get delay to respawn the ball
    [SerializeField] private float ballRespawnDelay;
    // The time delay which may take to hit the target,
    // so we can remove the ball
    [SerializeField] private float ballRemoveDelay;
    // Get the Ball Prefab
    [SerializeField] private GameObject ballPrefab;
    // Get the Ball Pin
    [SerializeField] private Rigidbody2D ballPin;

    // As the Ball is removed from Scene, ballRigidbody and
    // ballSpringJoint has no meaning to be added as
    // SerializeField.
    private Rigidbody2D ballRigidbody;
    private SpringJoint2D ballSpringJoint;
    private Camera camera;
    private bool isDragging;

    // Start is called before the first frame update
    void Start() {
        camera = Camera.main;
```

```csharp
        // Make the first ball available
        respawnTheBall();
    }

    // Update is called once per frame
    void Update() {
        if (ballRigidbody == null) return;

        if (Touchscreen.current.primaryTouch.press.isPressed) {
            // When user is touching (and moving on) the screen.
            dragBall();
        } else {
            // User not touching the screen now
            if (isDragging) {
                releaseBall();
            }
            isDragging = false;
        }
    }

    private void dragBall() {
        isDragging = true;
        ballRigidbody.isKinematic = true;
        // Reading the touch position, in terms of Screen Space
        Vector2 touchPosition =
            Touchscreen.current.primaryTouch.position.ReadValue();

        // Coverting touch position to World Space position
```

```
        Vector3 worldPosition = camera.ScreenToWorldPoint(touchPosition);

        // Set ball position to current world position
        ballRigidbody.position = worldPosition;
    }

    private void releaseBall() {
        ballRigidbody.isKinematic = false;
        ballRigidbody = null;

        Invoke(nameof(removeTheBall), ballRemoveDelay);
    }

    private void removeTheBall() {
        ballSpringJoint.enabled = false;
        ballSpringJoint = null;

        // Respawn the ball after delay
        Invoke(nameof(respawnTheBall), ballRespawnDelay);
    }

    private void respawnTheBall() {
        // Create an instance of the Ball prefab, set it to
        // the same position of Ball pin and set the default
        // rotation as rotation does not matter as of now.
        GameObject ball = Instantiate(
            ballPrefab,
            ballPin.position,
            Quaternion.identity);
```

```
    // Set Rigidbody and SpringJoint
    ballRigidbody = ball.GetComponent<Rigidbody2D>();
    ballSpringJoint = ball.GetComponent<SpringJoint2D>();
    // Attach the ball to ball-pin
    ballSpringJoint.connectedBody = ballPin;
    }
}
```

We already discussed each code snippet of the preceding script file. Now run the code and enjoy your first game.

Adding support for multiple screens

As there are different types of mobile devices in the world with different resolutions and screen sizes, it is very important to run your game on different devices to verify that your game provides the same user experience on each device.

When you run our game on different devices, our game will not look as per expectation on a few devices. *Figure 8.33* shows our game on **Apple iPad mini** and **Apple iPad Pro**:

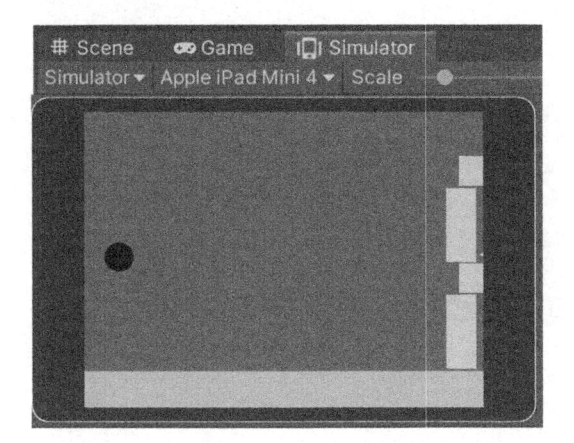

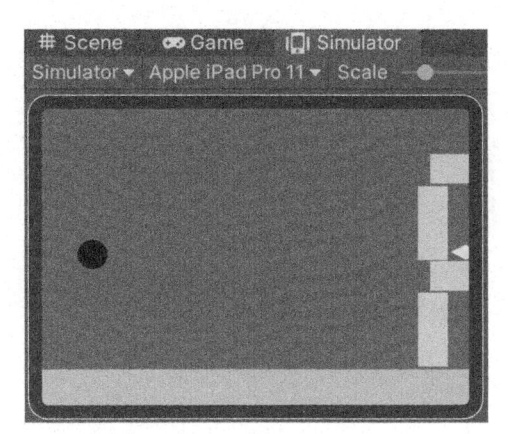

Figure 8.33: UX issue on a few tablets

As the preceding *figure 8.33* shows, we cannot see the target completely. Let us fix it.

360 ■ *Building Android Projects with Kotlin*

Let us add two game objects, left and right, to the Scene. The idea is to place these two objects at the location, which should always be visible on the left and right sides of the screen. To add these two objects, right-click in the `Hierarchy` view | `Create Empty`. Rename these two empty objects as *left* and *right*, and place them on the left and right sides of the screen, as shown in *figure 8.34*:

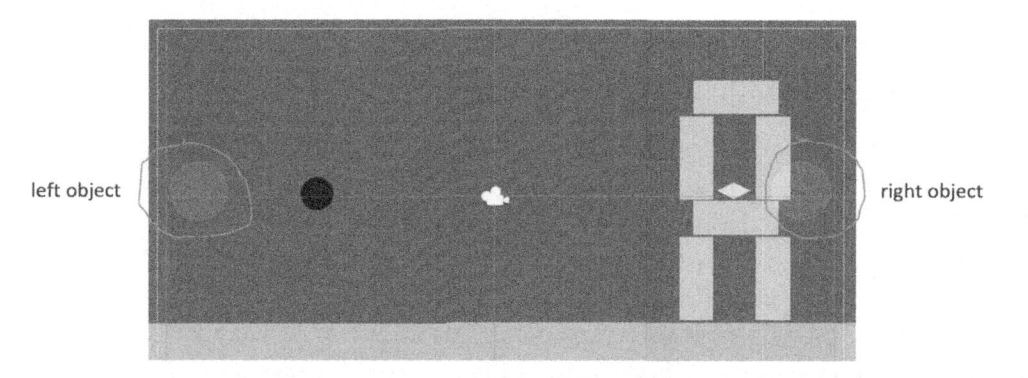

Figure 8.34: Adding two objects at the left and right of the Scene

Now, we need a package `Cinemachine`. To add that, click on `Window` | `Package Manager` | `Cinemachine` and click on `Install`, as shown in *figure 8.35*:

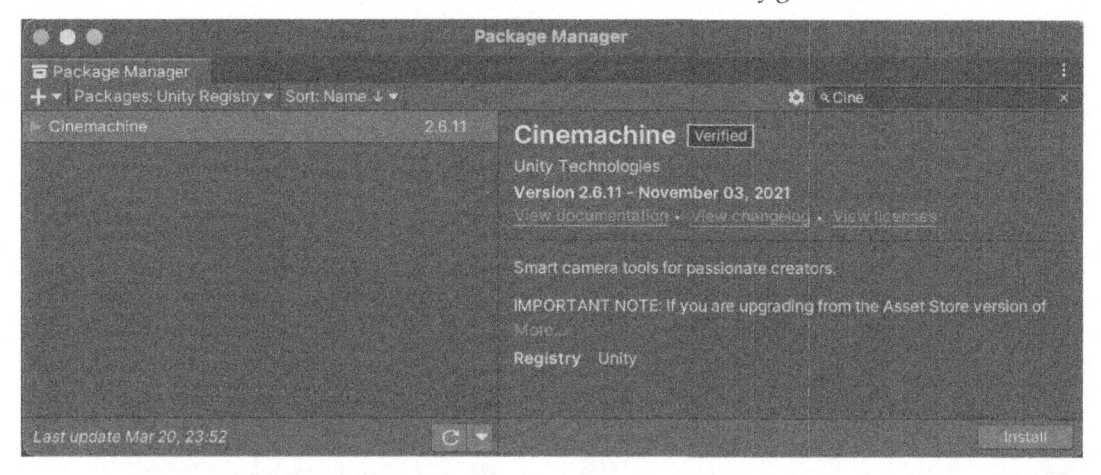

Figure 8.35: Adding Cinemachine package to the project

After installing this package, go to Toolbar and click on **Cinemachine | Create Target Group Camera**, as shown in *figure 8.36*:

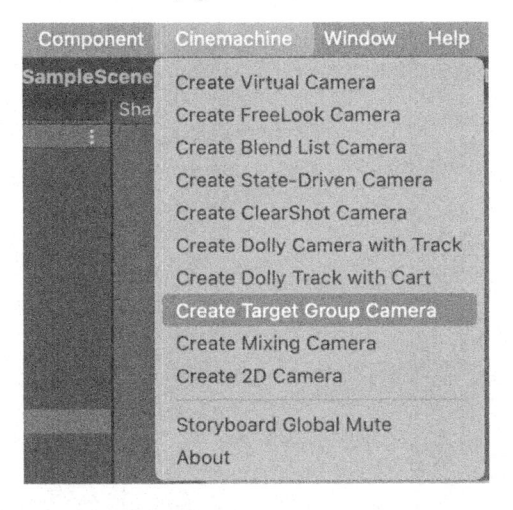

Figure 8.36: Creating target group camera

Two objects, **CM vcam1** and **TargetGroup1,** will be added, as shown at the left of *figure 8.37*. Now, select **TargetGroup1** and go to the Inspector view. And to add two targets *left* and *right*, click on the + icon two times, as shown in *figure 8.37*:

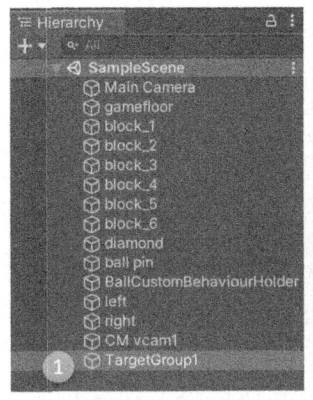

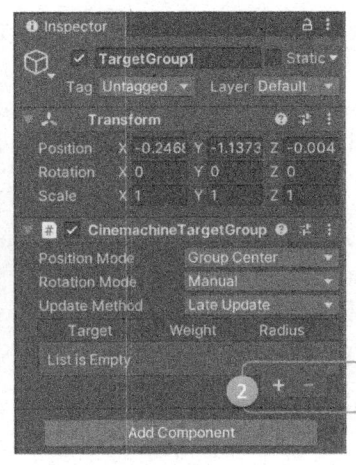

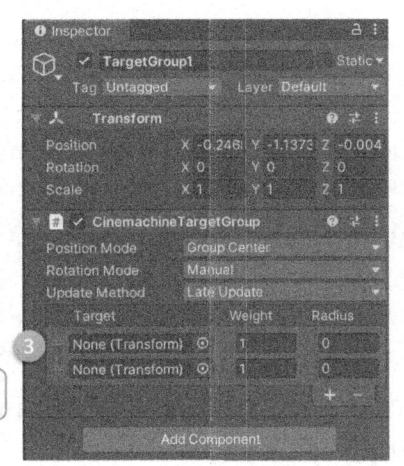

① Select "TargetGroup1" and go to Inspector view

② Click on "+" icon two times to add two targets

③ After step 2, there would be two targets added in inspector view

Figure 8.37: Adding two empty targets to the target group object

Now drag-drop the *left* and the *right* objects to these two targets, as shown in *figure 8.38*:

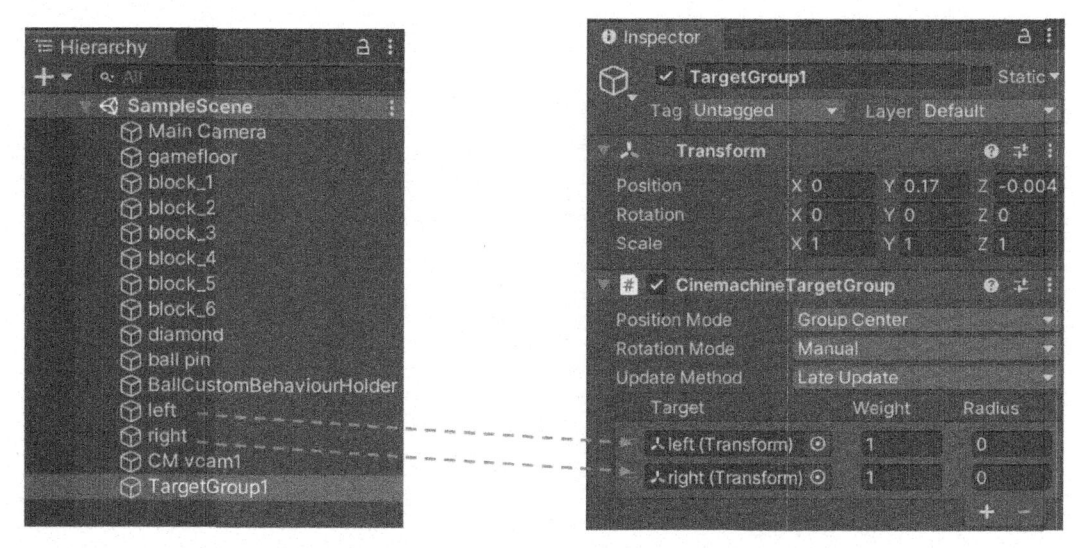

Figure 8.38: Adding left and right to the target group object

Save the project and run the game. Now our game will look identical on different devices and different resolutions.

Congratulations, we have developed our first Unity game, and now we know how you can develop other games in Unity for Android. Try to convert this game into 3D mobile and apply some nice textures to objects like creating a nice-looking ball, better-looking target objects, and the floor. We already know how to add texture, so use that knowledge and explore Unity.

We also learned about creating Android builds in previous *Chapter 7: Introduction to Game Development*, so create a build for your game and deploy it to Play Store. Deployment of the game at the Play Store is the same as deploying an application, and we already know how to deploy an application.

That is it from this chapter. In the upcoming chapter, we will learn about adding support for multi Screens.

Conclusion

In this chapter, we learned about how to develop games using Unity. We have created a small game that is similar to the Angry Birds game. We learned how to add animations, touch events, and objects dynamically to the game scene. We also learned to support different devices with different resolutions.

In the upcoming chapter, we will learn about supporting multiple screens and regions in Android applications.

Points to remember

- While working with touch events, always work with the world position instead of the touch position.
- Prefab is similar to the template, and by using Prefab, you to make reusable game objects.
- Remember to support different devices with different screen resolutions.

Multiple Choice Questions

1. We should convert touch location to world location for a better location position for a game object.

    A. True　　　　　　　　　　　　B. False

2. Ball Physics Material 2D can be used to add a bouncing effect to the game object.

    A. True　　　　　　　　　　　　B. False

3. When to sue the Cinemachine package?

    A. To support different devices with different resolutions

    B. Convert touch location to world location

    C. Add animations to the unity object

    D. None of the object

Answers

1. A
2. A
3. A

Questions

1. What is the difference between touch location and world location?
2. How to add a Spring object?
3. What is Prefab?
4. What is SerializeField?
5. What is Spring Joint Component?

Key Terms

- 2D Template
- 2D Mobile Template
- 2D Object
- Sprites
- Box Collider 2D
- Rigidbody 2D
- Square
- Circle
- Isometric Diamond
- Ball Physics Material 2D
- Spring Joint Component
- Prefab
- Reusable game objects
- SerializeField
- Multiscreen
- Cinemachine

CHAPTER 9
Adding Support for Big Screens

In the previous chapter, we developed our first Android game.

In this chapter, we will learn about Android resources and different qualifiers and get an idea about how we can add resources for the applications that we developed while reading this book. We will also learn how to use dimensions to handle different screen sizes, especially for tablets.

We will also learn about optimizing layout for tablets and prepare a checklist for the application to release for tablets.

At the end of this chapter, we will learn about the basic development of an application for wearables and TV.

Structure

- Introducing resources in Android
  - Understanding resources
  - Introducing different qualifiers
    - Qualifiers for drawables
    - Qualifiers for layouts
    - Qualifiers for values

- o   Working with resources
- Choosing the optimized image resource type
- Designing and developing the app for Tablets
  - o   Introducing tablet-specific dimensions and layout qualifiers
  - o   Optimizing layouts for tablets
  - o   Preparing checklist for tablet app quality
- Developing apps for wearables and TV
  - o   Creating project for wearables
    - Creating an AVD for wearables
  - o   Creating project for TV
    - Declaring leanback support
    - Declaring touchscreen not required
    - Creating an AVD for TV application

Objectives

The objective of this chapter is to let you know about Android resources, different qualifiers for resources, and handling of resources to provide a better user experience, such as how you can provide localization, handling of drawable, and so on. You will also learn about tablet app development and you will learn about the handling of dimensions and optimizing layout for tablets. After completing this chapter, you will have a clear understanding of handling multiple screens for an Android application, and you will know the basics of wearable and TV app development.

Introducing resources in Android

While developing an Android application, you may need to support localizations, different screen sizes, and so on. Android provides different resources to handle these use cases. You can show localized text in your application, and you can show different UI or different sized icons for different sizes of screens. In this section, we will read about resources and the handling of these resources.

Before reading more about resources, let us understand the following *figure 9.1*:

Output on Phone

Output on Tablet

Figure 9.1: Comparing views on handset and tablet

In the preceding *figure 9.1*, we see the output of six buttons on a phone and a tablet. On the phone, you see only four buttons visible completely, and on the tablet, you see all six. So, the question is how you can make all six buttons visible on the phone. You can handle it via code, or you can use a different layout that supports horizontal scroll. But handling it with resources is the easiest and most recommended way. Also, using resources with best practices helps us to implement the responsive UI. Now, let us understand resources in detail.

Understanding resources

Android uses appropriate resources based on the current configuration of the device. At runtime, it uses to filter out the best suitable resource for the current configuration. Here, the configuration can be anything like device orientation or locale.

We should always externalize application resources like images, icons, and strings from the code and maintain them independently. We should also provide resources for specific device configurations by grouping them with resource directories, where these resource directories will have a special name. *Figure 9.2* shows the summarized structure of the resource directory:

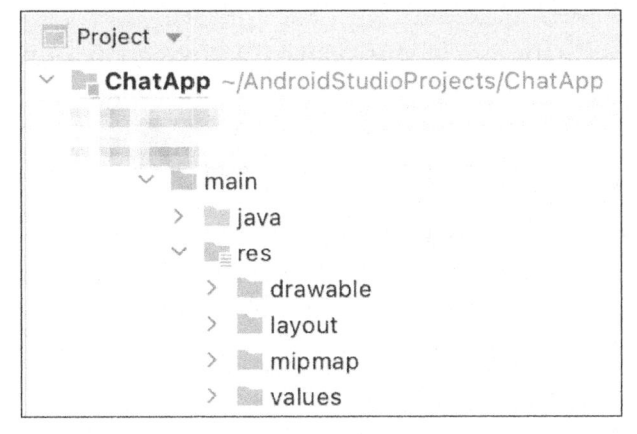

Figure 9.2: Resource directory in the application

In the preceding *figure 9.2*, you see a **res** directory; in Android, we put each resource in this directory. There are subdirectories under the **res** directory with a few other directories inside it. Let us know more about these directories:

- **drawable/**: A drawable is a graphic that can be drawn to the screen. You can use these drawable in XML layout files with **Android:drawable**, **Android:icon**, or via code using **getDrawable(R.drawable.name_of_drawable)**. There are different types of drawable we can use in Android:
    - Bitmap file png, WebP, Gif, Jpeg, 9 patch, vectors, shapes, and so on.
- **layout/**: This directory keeps layout files for User Interface.
- **mipmap/**: This directory is dedicated to launcher icons. You can also put your application icons in the drawable directory, but it is best practice to place your app icons in mipmap- folders because they are used at resolutions different from the device's current density. For example, an **xxxhdpi** app icon can be used on the launcher for an **xxhdpi** device.
- **values/**: This directory contains values such as strings, integers, colors, XML, raw, animator, and so on, for the following purposes:
    - **arrays.xml** for resource arrays
    - **colors.xml** for colors values
    - **dimens.xml** for dimension sizes
    - **strings.xml** for localization strings values
    - **styles.xml** for styles of views
- **color/**: state-list color definitions in XML files.
- **anim/**: XML files for tween animation.
- **font/**: font files such as **.ttf**, **.otf**, or **.ttc**, or XML file that includes **<font-family>** element.
- **menu/**: XML files for app menus such as Option menu, Context menu, or Sub menu.

Introducing different qualifiers

Resource qualifiers are used to provide the best matching resource at runtime, depending on the current configurations of the device. Qualifiers help us to provide different resources for screen size (width and height), languages, orientations, and OS version.

Qualifiers for drawables

When we put bitmaps in **/drawable** directory, Android uses to scale bitmaps to the available size for the container of that bitmap (such as ImageView, the background of any View, and so on), and it may result in a blurry image on the screen. To avoid this, sometimes developers put drawables of high resolution in the drawable directory. It may solve the blur issue but create a performance issue. The devices with low density which do not need such drawable with high resolution will spend more time to draw that drawable of high resolution. So remember that it is bad practice to place a high-resolution image in the drawable directory.

Let us find out a recommended way to handle images for devices with different resolutions. We add more drawable directories with qualifiers **-ldpi**, **-mdpi**, **-hdpi**, **-xhdpi**, **-xxhdpi**, and **-xxxhdpi** and place images with the same name in each directory as shown in *figure 9.3*:

```
res/
    drawable-xxxhdpi/
        icon.png            192x192 px
        background.png
    drawable-xxhdpi/
        icon.png            144x144 px
        background.png
    drawable-xhdpi/
        icon.png            96x96 px
        background.png
    drawable-hdpi/
        icon.png            72x72 px
        background.png
    drawable-mdpi/
        icon.png            48x48 px
        background.png
    drawable-ldpi/
        icon.png            36x36 px
        background.png
```

Scaling ratio 3:4:6:8:12:16

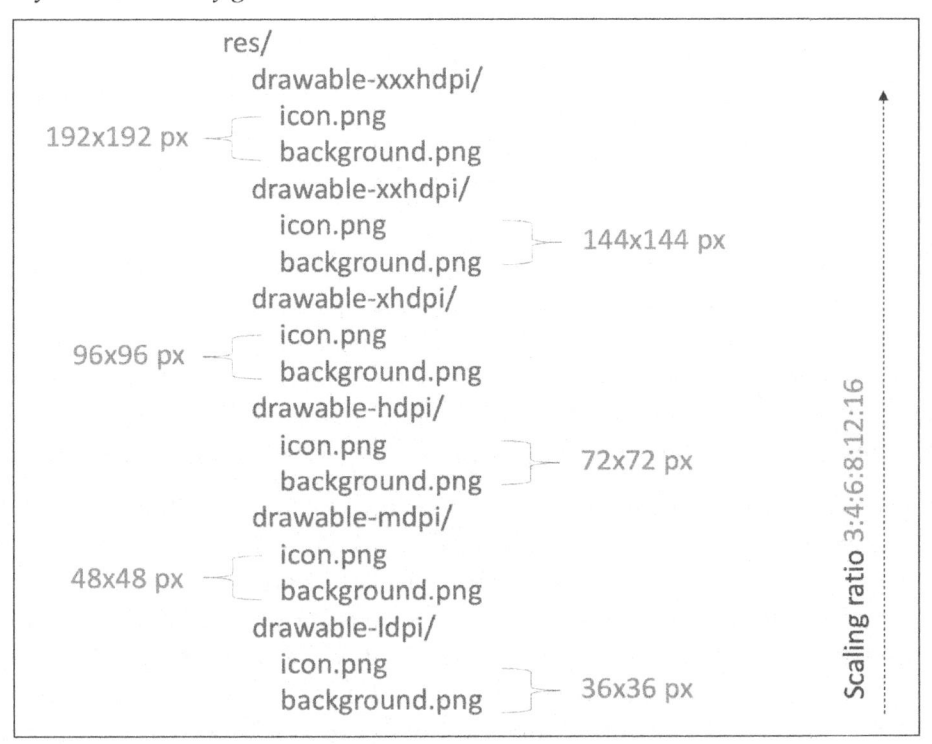

Figure 9.3: Drawables for different densities

As you see in preceding *figure 9.3*, Android guides us by scaling ratio, which should be followed while creating bitmap drawables for different densities. The scaling ratio which we need to follow is **[ldpi:mdpi:hdpi:xhdpi:xxhdpi:xxxhdpi]** => **[3:4:6:8:12:16]**.

Let us understand the preceding image by example. Assume that you have a bitmap drawable of 48×48 pixels for `mdpi` (medium-density screens). Then, after following the 3:4:6:8:12:16 scaling ratio, the drawable for each density bucket will be as shown in *Table 9.1*, which also explains about scaling factor for each density bucket:

Density	Density bucket	Scaling factor	Scaling ratio	Bitmap size in px
ldpi	~120dpi	0.75×	3	36×36
mdpi	~160dpi	1.0×	4	48×48
hdpi	~240dpi	1.5×	6	72×72
xhdpi	~320dpi	2.0×	8	96×96
xxhdpi	~480dpi	3.0×	12	144×144
xxxhdpi	~640dpi	4.0×	16	192×192

Table 9.1: Density buckets with scaling rules

After creating images by following the preceding rule, we need to place these image files in the appropriate subdirectory under `res/` and use drawable like `R.drawable.icon` in code and `@drawable/icon` in XML, and the Android system will pick the correct image automatically based on the pixel density of the device your app is running on.

NOTE: **As you read, we provide the same image with different sizes in multiple directories to handle scaling so that the image appears on the device without losing quality. There is one major drawback to this approach. You add the same image with at least four sizes, and these files used to be part of the application file. It means if the device density is HDPI, the same image added into other drawable folders is useless for that device and increases the size of the application file.**

Vector drawables are the solution for it. You can use only one file for any density without losing the quality of the image. So instead of adding multiple files for the same image, you add only one vector file. It has limitations as well. You should not use any image as Vector drawable if the size is larger than 200×200, as it can take more time to render on UI than the png file for the same image. And Text on Image effects such as drop shadows blurs, and the color matrix is not supported. Read more about it in the topic "Choosing the optimized image resource type" in this chapter.

In some cases, we use 9-Patch images as well, which can be scalable horizontally or vertically.

Qualifiers for layouts

We can use width, height, or orientation qualifiers for layouts as follows.

Width and height qualifiers

We use these qualifiers when we want to change the layout based on how much width or height is available. For example, if we want to show all six buttons in preceding *figure 9.1* aligned horizontally only when the screen provides at least 600dp of width, we can add a layout like **res/layout-w600dp/main_activity.xml**, and in normal cases, we can keep all six buttons aligned vertically and can add layout like **res/layout/main_activity.xml** as follows:

res/layout/main_activity.xml

res/layout-w600dp/main_activity.xml

To add qualifiers for height, for example, if we want to use a different layout if the available height is more than 600dp, we can use layout-h600dp instead of layout-w600dp as follows:

res/layout-h600dp/main_activity.xml

Orientation qualifiers

Sometimes we want to use a different layout for landscape and portrait. We can use **-land** qualifiers for adding layouts for landscape mode, as follows:

res/layout/main_activity.xml

res/layout-land/main_activity.xml

res/layout-sw600dp/main_activity.xml

res/layout-sw600dp-land/main_activity.xml

In the preceding example, **res/layout/main_activity.xml** and **res/layout-sw600dp/main_activity.xml** are layouts for portrait mode, and **res/layout-land/main_activity.xml** and **res/layout-sw600dp-land/main_activity.xml** are layouts for landscape orientation.

We will use **R.layout.activity_main**, and depending on current configurations Android system will find out the best matching layout files named **main_activity.xml** and show them on UI.

372 ■ *Building Android Projects with Kotlin*

NOTE: To be compatible with as many devices as possible, you should test your apps for as many of these screen ratios as you can. While testing your application on multiple devices, you can ensure that your UI scales correctly.

Qualifiers for values

Qualifiers for values help us to provide strings, dimensions, styles, and so on for different locales, device configurations such as portrait and landscape, or API levels. *Figure 9.4* is the example of qualifiers for values:

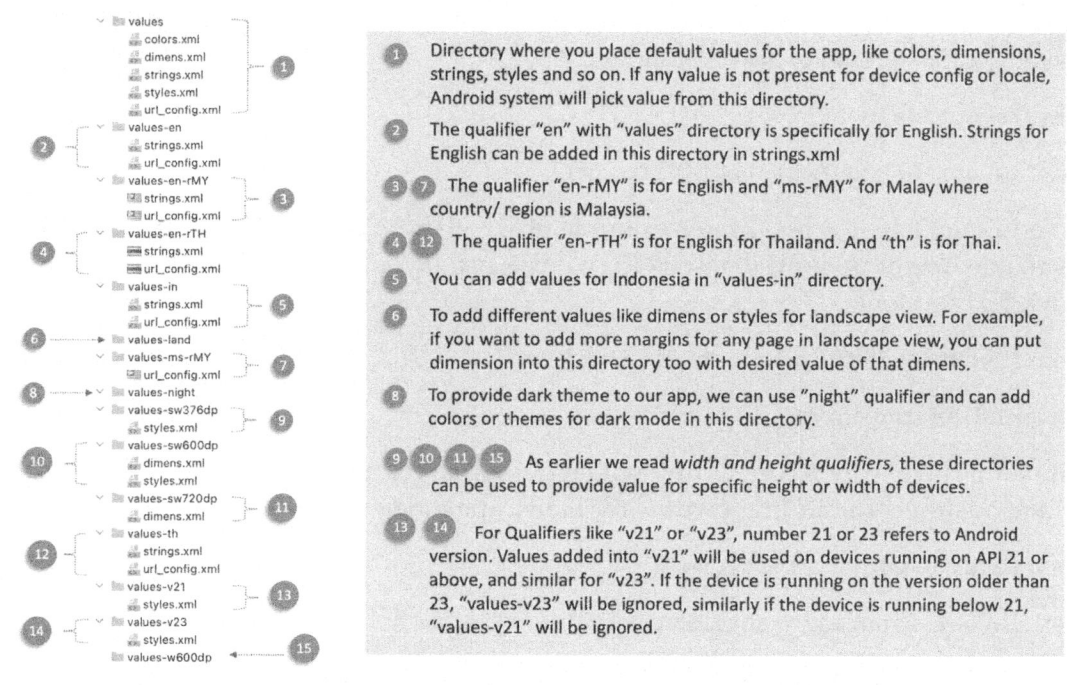

Figure 9.4: Resource qualifiers

Figure 9.4 shows different qualifiers for values that can be used in any project. *Figure 9.5* shows all available qualifiers in Android:

Available qualifiers:
- Country Code
- Network Code
- Locale
- Layout Direction
- Smallest Screen Width
- Screen Width
- Screen Height
- Size
- Ratio
- Orientation
- UI Mode
- Night Mode
- Density
- Touch Screen
- Keyboard
- Text Input
- Navigation State
- Navigation Method
- Dimension
- Version

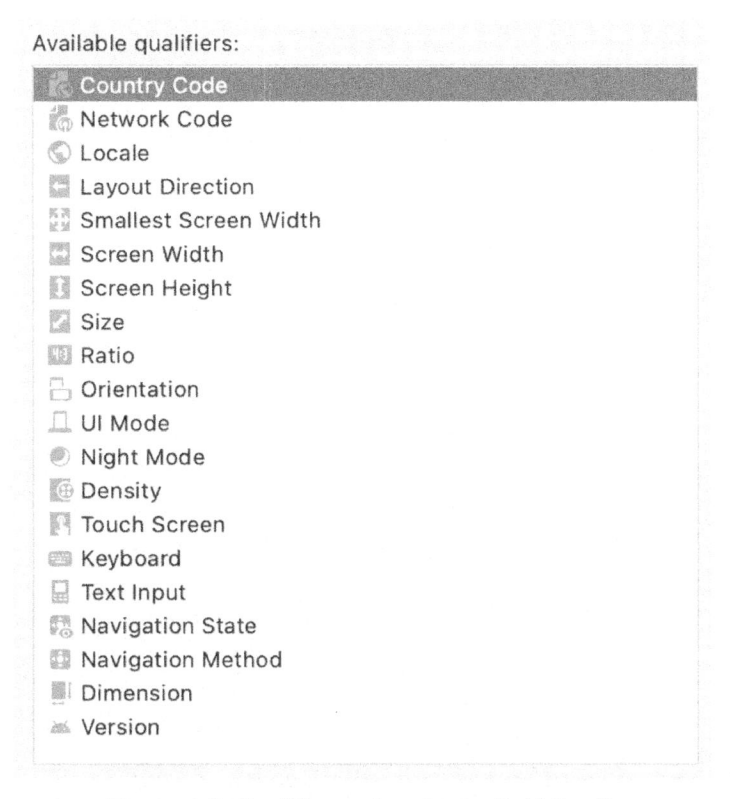

Figure 9.5: Qualifier options in Android Studio

Let us see how we can add these resources using Android Studio tools in the next section.

Working with resources

To create any resource, we can create a folder manually and add the file of the resource type, or we can use the resource creation wizard of Android Studio to create resources and directories. Let us see it via Android Studio.

In Android Studio, select a module and click on **File | New | Android Resource File** or right-click on the module **New | Android Resource File**; a resource creation screen will be shown, as shown in *figure 9.6*:

374 ■ *Building Android Projects with Kotlin*

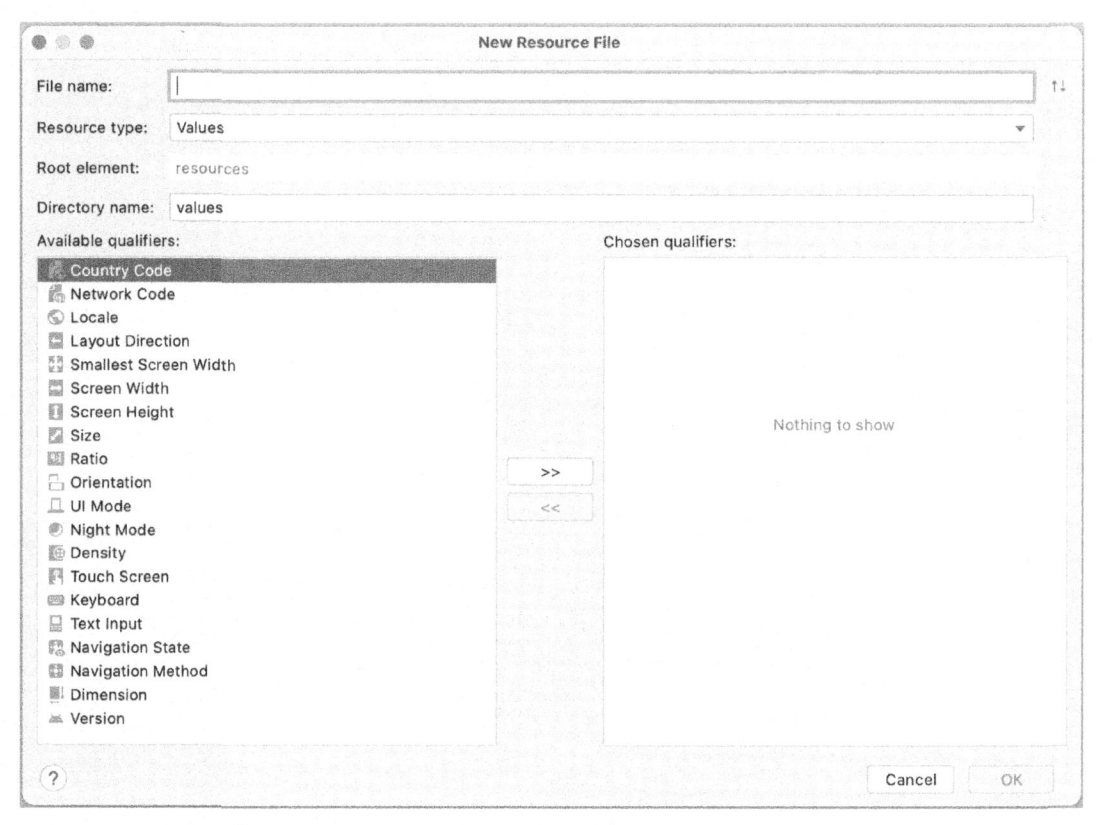

Figure 9.6: Creating resources

In preceding *figure 9.6*, the file name can be anything, but to be consistent and to follow Android coding practices, we should name it as strings.xml if we are going to add strings to this application. Button **>>** will be used to add selected qualifiers. For example, we want to add qualifiers for locales, so the preceding *figure 9.6* will look as shown in *figure 9.7*:

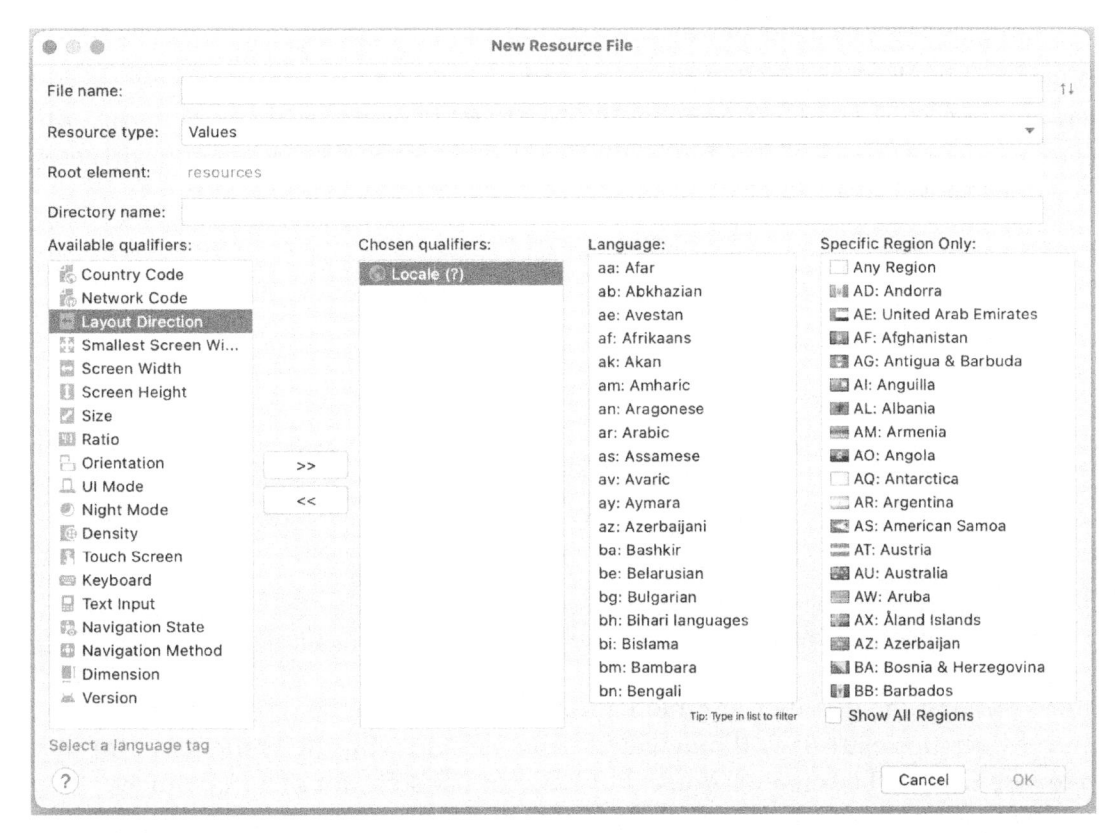

Figure 9.7: Creating values

For example, let us assume that we want to add strings for **bh: Bihari language**. So, after selecting **bh: Bihari language**, the screen will look like as shown in *figure 9.8*:

Figure 9.8: Adding values directory for language for any reason

As per the preceding *figure 9.8*, we see regions to select after selecting **bh: Bihari languages**. Look at the field **Directory name**, which shows **values-bh** when **Any Region** is selected, similar to **values-in** or **values-th** in the qualifier example; see *figure 9.9*. When we select **IN: India**, the directory name will be changed to **values-bh-rIN** as shown in *figure 9.9*:

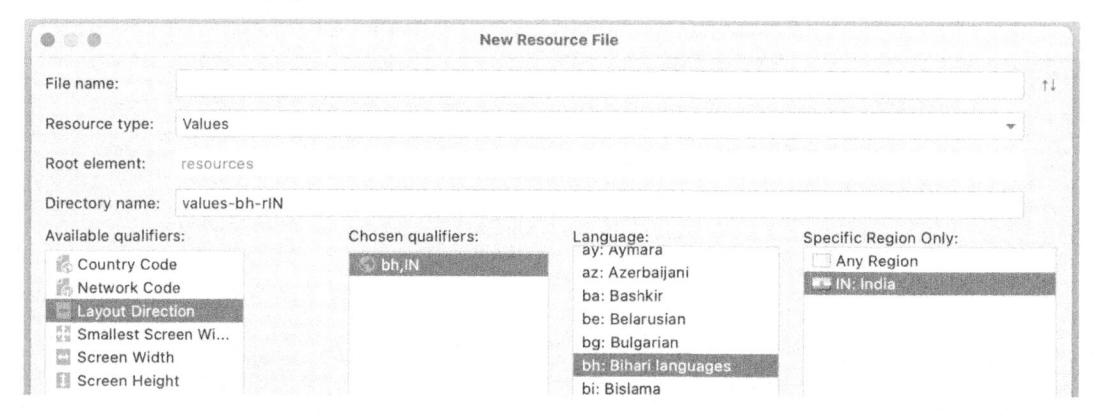

Figure 9.9: Adding values directory for language and specific region

After selecting the qualifier and file name, press on **OK** button. If directory values-bh-rIN does not exist, it will be created. And the file with the name given in the **Filename** field will be created. You can follow similar steps for other qualifiers.

Note that, for any application, providing localized text makes a better impression on the user, and the user connects to the app easily because the application shows each info in the user's locale or user's native language. To develop an application for multiple countries, we need to support internationalization. It means the same view can show text in English for users in the US or other locals (if the qualifier does not match with any values), and in Thailand, it may show the text in Thai. For example, **help_support** is the string resource and has translations for English and Thai. Like the following example:

../res/values-th/strings.xml

```
<?xml version="1.0" encoding="utf-8"?>

<resources>

    <string name="help_support">ช่วยเหลือและสนับสนุน</string>

</resources>
```

../res/values-en/strings.xml

```xml
<?xml version="1.0" encoding="utf-8"?>
<resources>
    <string name="help_support">Help &amp; Support</string>
</resources>
```

When we set this `help_support` string to `TextView`, the same code will be able to show `help_support` in different languages, depending on the device config.

NOTE: While developing an Android application, do not hardcode any string; instead of it, declare each string as a resource in the strings.xml file. It will be easy to maintain all strings in the same place, and the most important thing is that it makes it easy to localize. It gives us the flexibility to add any number of translated string.xml files without making any change in Kotlin/ Java code. Remember to move each hardcoded string into strings.xml, which we used in our chat application or video-sharing application.

Now, we know about Android resources and qualifiers as well.

Choosing the optimized image resource type

Choosing a good file type for an image or an icon in Android helps you to develop an application that is smaller in size and faster in showing the page to the user. Note that the smaller file will take lesser time to render on UI than the bigger file, and if we achieve that without losing image quality, what can be better than this? Is it not? Let us read how we can choose a better file type for the image/icon by looking into the following options available on Android.

There are two categories of digital images, Raster and Vector. Let us understand these two categories and file types that can be used in Android.

Raster Image

Images in this category are best for complex images like photographs. PNG, WebP, and JPG are a few commonly used raster graphics images that can be used in Android. Remember that raster images cannot be scaled without losing image quality. Let us read about PNG and WebP.

PNG

In the past, PNG was the most frequently used type in Android for any size of images or icons. Following are a few reasons why Android chose PNG over JPG:

- PNG beats JPG on transparency and quality.
- It is crisp yet remains lightweight and fast to display.
- Bitmap files may be automatically optimized with lossless image compression by the AAPT/ AAPT2 tool during the build process. For example, a true color PNG.

But it has some limitations or drawbacks too:

- PNGs cannot be stretched without losing quality, so we must use more than one PNG file of different sizes. For example, we use 5+ difference sizes for the same icon in `/drawable-mdpi`, `/drawable-hdpi`, `/drawable-xhdpi`, `/drawable-xxhdpi`, and `/drawable-xxxhdpi` directories. You need different sizes of tablets as well for better UI.
- There is no Right to Left (RTL) support for PNGs.

Note that you can use some tools such as **TinyPNG**, **pngquant**, or **Pngcrush** to optimize PNGs if no other file type suits your requirement.

WebP

WebP is an image format that is developed by Google and focuses mainly on optimization and quality. The following are benefits of using WebP:

- WebP supports lossy and lossless modes, making it an ideal replacement for both PNG and JPG.
- WebP files are 26% smaller than PNGs and 25%–34% smaller than JPGs on average.
- You can convert existing PNG files into WebP by following steps in Android Studio without any code change.

1. Right-click on an image file or a folder containing a few image files, and then click `Convert to WebP`.
2. The `Converting Images to WebP` dialog will open.
3. Select encoding and quality, and click on **OK**.
4. Android Studio will show you the difference between the old file (the PNG) and the new file (the WebP).
5. Click on `Accept All`.

6. The existing PNG will be replaced by a new WebP image. In case you choose the directory of more than a file, Android Studio will replace all images with WebP files.

You can read more about WebP at https://developer.android.com/studio/write/convert-webp.

Vector image

Vector graphics are digital images produced by computers using a series of instructions or mathematical formulas that position lines and shapes in a two- or three-dimensional space.

Vector files are the best choice when you need an image that can be scaled/resized without losing image quality and can retain crisp details. Vectors used to be small comparing Raster images.

Image file types SVG, EMF, EPS, and VectorDrawable are the types of Vectors. Note that we only use VectorDrawable in Android. Let us explore VectorDrawable.

Vector drawables

A Vector drawable is defined in the XML file, and it is a set of points, lines, and curves with color information. The following are benefits of using Vector drawable:

- Vector drawables are stretchable/scalable. It means that a single file can be used, and you can resize the same file for different screen densities without losing image quality.
- Compared with PNG or WebP, you just need to place one file of Vector Drawable in **/drawable** directory.
- Vector drawable supports RTL.
- We can create animated graphics also using vector files.

We can create Vector drawables by using the following steps in Android Studio:
1. Right-click on **drawable** directory | **New** | **Vector Asset**, or select **drawable** directory | Click on **File** from toolbar | **New** | **Vector Asset**.
2. You will see a dialog **Asset Studio**, where you can choose Clip Art or Local SVG/PSD file. Add the name of the file. If required, you can set opacity and RTL settings.
3. Then click on **Next** | **Finish**. A Vector drawable will be added in the **/drawable** directory.

Each good thing has a few drawbacks so as Vector drawables. Following are a few drawbacks/limitations of Vector drawables:
- Images with text cannot be used as Vector drawables.
- Images having gradient backgrounds cannot be used as Vector drawables.
- The initial loading of the Vector Drawable can take more CPU cycles than the PNG or WebP images. So, Android recommends that the maximum size of Vector drawable should be 200X200.
- Considering the preceding drawback, we can say that Vector drawables are ideal for icons.

You can read more about Vector drawables at https://developer.android.com/guide/topics/graphics/vector-drawable-resources.

You have read all popular image types that can be used in Android, and we also know about the benefits and limitations of each. You can now decide which image type can be the best fit in your case. Also, *figure 9.10* can be used for decision-making:

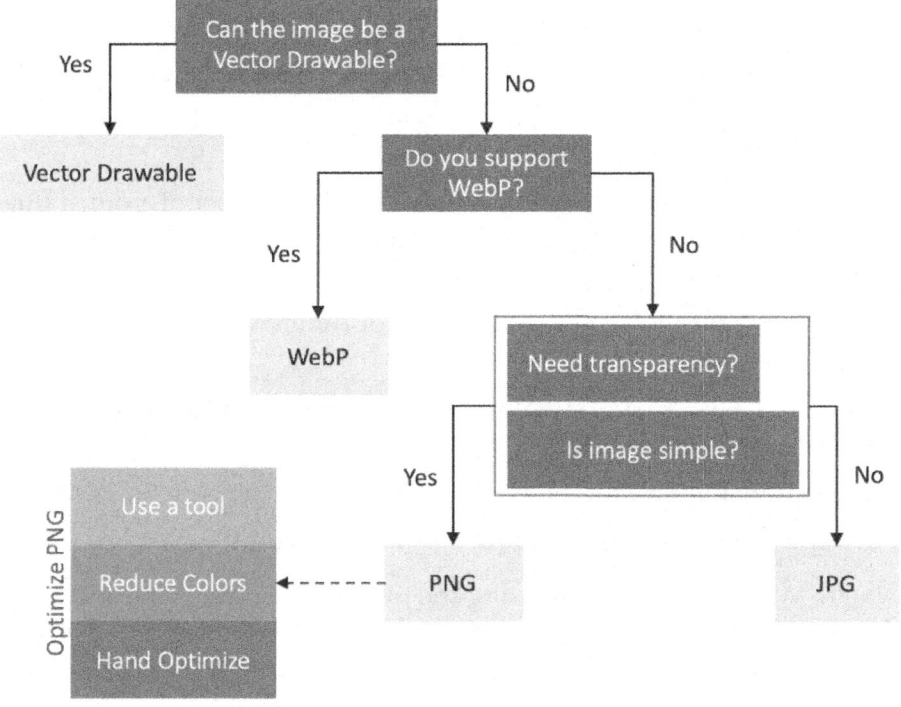

Figure 9.10: *Choosing an optimized image for your application*

Designing and developing an app for Tablets

Most of the time, we use to develop Android application that supports Android tablets as well. To provide a better user experience on Tablets, we should have a better understanding of how to use tablet screens in a better way, and we should have a better understanding of design guidelines for Tablet devices. Let us understand the important points to develop an app for tablets.

Introducing tablet-specific dimensions and layout qualifiers

Let us understand qualifiers and dimensions for handset and tablet first, and then we will understand how we can develop a responsive screen:

Mobile device type	Smallest width (dp)	Margin (dp)	Layout qualifiers	Value qualifiers
Handset	Default	16	layout	values
Tablet (small)	600	24	layout-sw600dp	values-sw600dp
Tablet (large)	720	24	layout-sw720dp	values-sw720dp

Table 9.2: Tablet-specific dimensions mapping

Preceding *Table 9.2* explains qualifiers and margin for the screen. As per the material design, page margins in the handset should be 16dp, and in the tablets, it can be a minimum of 24dp. For a better user experience, you should follow material design guidelines, which help you to design/develop UI for multiple screen sizes.

Developing the user interface with different margins according to the device screen size helps us to develop a flexible layout. Most of the time, it works well, and our application can provide a good user experience. Sometimes layout for the application on the handset can lead to a bad user experience, and we need optimization of layouts to user spaces in a better way. Let us understand how optimization of layout can increase user experience.

Optimizing layouts for tablets

For any application, a flexible layout is very important, but you should also design different layouts that optimize the user experience for the available space on different screen sizes. As we know about layout qualifiers and saw in the preceding table, by

382 ■ *Building Android Projects with Kotlin*

using layout qualifiers, we can provide an alternative layout file that the system applies at runtime based on the screen size of the current device. *Figures 9.11* and *9.12* shows how the layout of the handset can be optimized to be used in the tablet:

Figure 9.11: *Handset and Tablet screen design*

As in the preceding *figure 9.11*, the handset can show left navigation and a grid layout, where the tablet is showing both together.

And *figure 9.12* is taken from the Plants app developed and explained by Ivy knight for Android codelabs:

Figure 9.12: *Handset and Tablet screen design in Plants app*

These two examples show how we can use spaces on a larger screen to provide a better user experience. You should always look for some existing applications, follow design communities and do some analysis while designing UI for tablets.

Now, let us prepare a checklist that can be used to evaluate our application for a tablet before release.

Preparing checklist for Tablet app quality

While developing an application for tablets, we need to evaluate our application to make sure that the application is compatible with tablets. *Table 9.3* shows the checklist which you can use to evaluate your application. You can add more points to the checklist as you get experience in tablet application development:

Category	Checklist
UI and graphics	Make sure that the app supports both orientations (landscape and portrait). Until it is not required, do not force your app to run in either portrait or landscape only.
	Make sure that the application uses the whole screen in both orientations and does not do major changes in the information, and shows the same features and actions in both orientations.
	If you support both orientations, make sure that the application handles transition without rendering issues or losing state.
Multi-window and multi-resume support	Make sure that the application supports Multi-Window mode.
	Make sure that the application can update the UI even if the application is not focused. For example, the application must continue downloading files, continue playing videos, notify for messages, and so on.
Configuration changes	The app must handle configuration changes and retain or restore the state as the device goes through configuration changes such as folding/unfolding, window resizing, or rotation. The application must retain and restore the state during config changes.
	Make sure that the application can handle combinations of configuration changes as well, like resizing window followed by orientation change or orientation change followed by folding/unfolding.
App UX for Tablet	Make sure that the application shows appropriate layouts for the larger screens. Secondary screens like modals and options menus are designed/formatted well for all screen types and states.
Touch target	Make sure that the application follows best practices for accessibility. For example, touch targets should be at least 48dp.

Category	Checklist
Input Support	The application's user flows should support keyboard navigation, including arrow keys and tab navigation.
	Make sure that the application supports keyboard shortcuts for text selection, cut/copy/paste, and undo/redo.
	For applications like media players, the application plays/pauses video when the spacebar key is pressed.
	Apps should support basic mouse/trackpad support, including scrolling and right-click handling.
Drag and drop functionality	If an application has a drag-drop feature, make sure that you have implemented natural drag and drop for views.
Foldables	Make sure that the applications are usable while in tent mode, tabletop mode, or book mode for foldable devices, and if applicable, the application provides a user experience optimized for the device state for foldable devices.
	If the application is a camera app, make sure that it supports a dual display (front and back screen) preview.
Stylus support	If the application handles free-form user input, make sure that it handles stylus input devices, including different tool types and palm rejection.
	If applicable, the application handles advanced stylus input events, including pressure sensitivity and tilt detection

Table 9.3: Checklist for Tablet applications

Developing apps for wearables and TV

Let us get the basic idea about how to develop an application for wearables or Android TV.

Creating project for wearables

As we read in *Chapter 1: Creating Hello World Project*, Android Studio provides templates for projects. We will use one of those templates for wearables by following steps:

1. Click on **File | New | New Project…**:

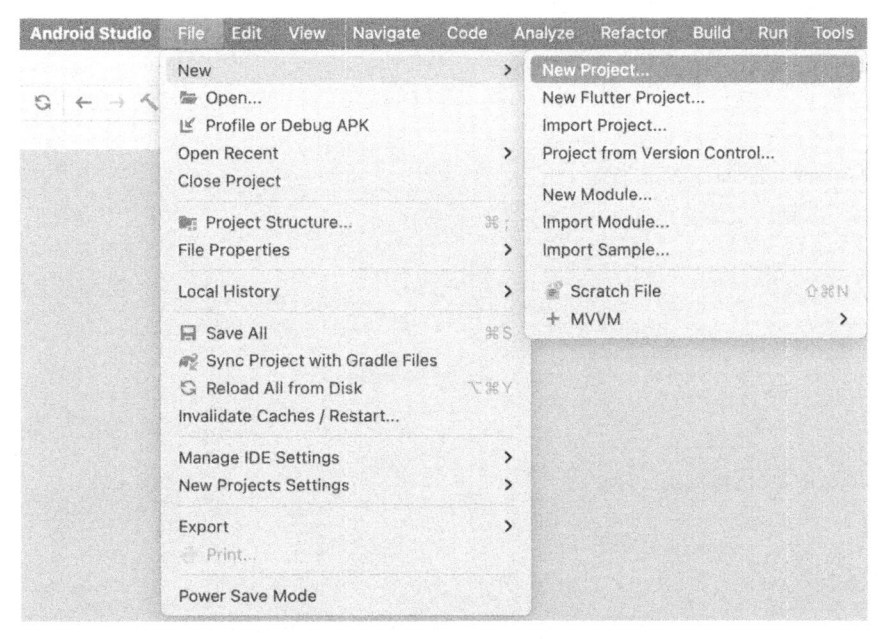

Figure 9.13: Creating a wearable application

2. In the **New Project** window, click the **Wear OS** tab, select **Blank Activity**, and click the **Next** button:

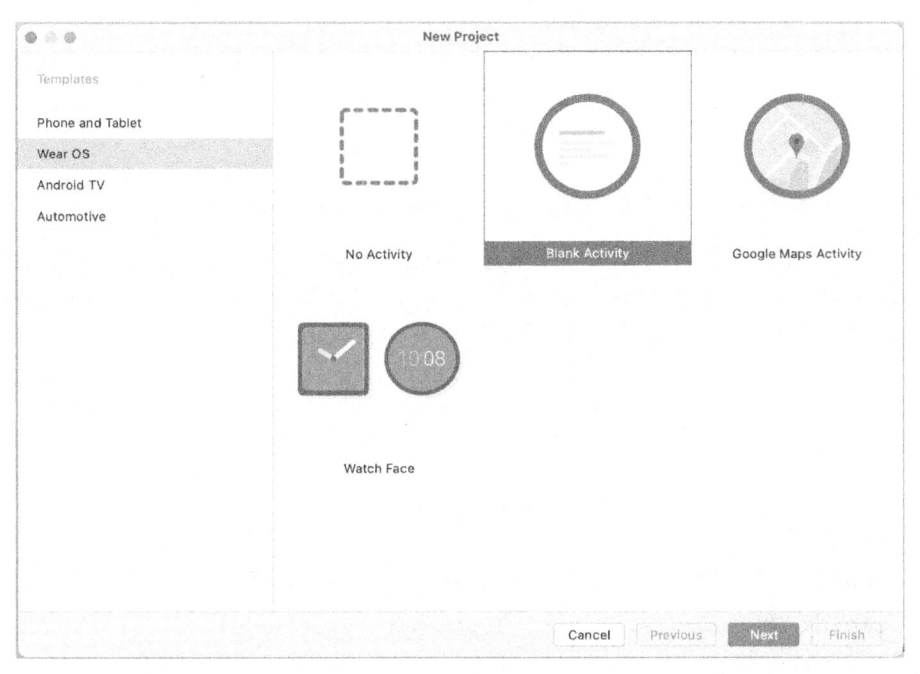

Figure 9.14: Creating a wearable application

3. In the **New Project** window, name your project, fill out the standard project information, and click **Finish**:

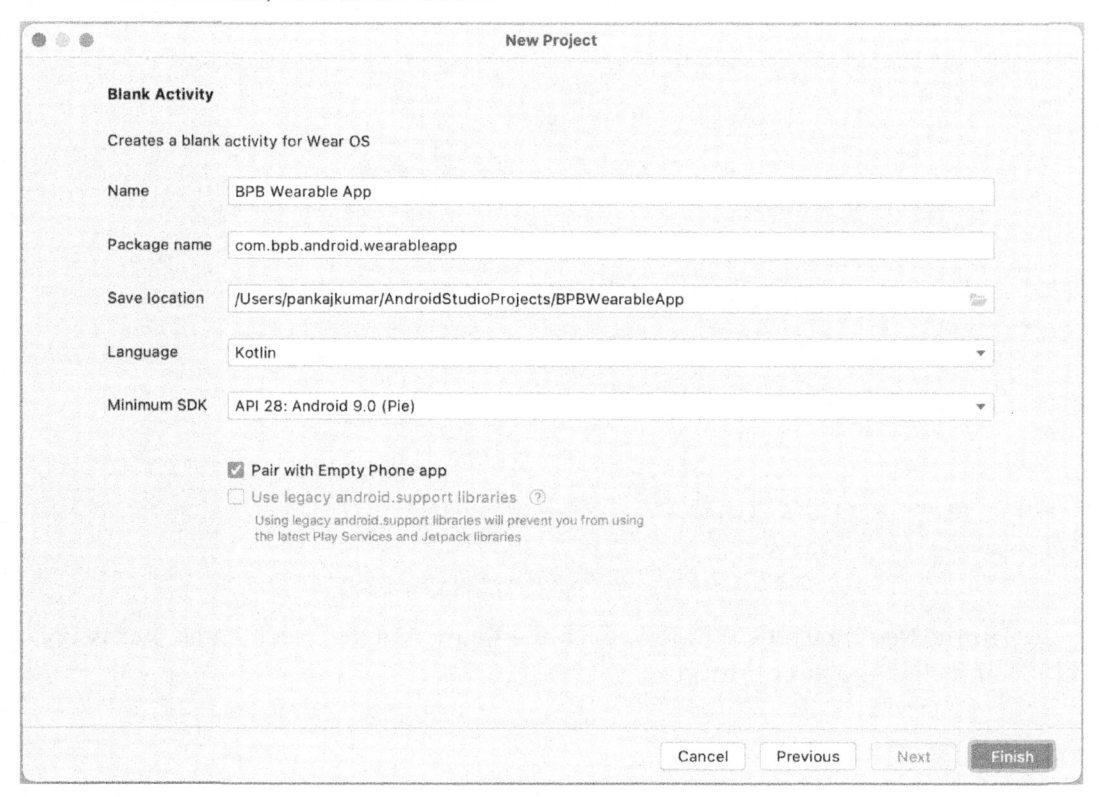

Figure 9.15: Creating a wearable application

Clicking on **Finish**, Android Studio will create a wearable project.

After creating the project, open the **app/build.gradle** and make sure you have set **compileSdk** and **targetSdk** set to 30, and dependencies for Wearable Support Library have been added, similar to the following code:

```
android {

    compileSdk 30

    defaultConfig {
        applicationId "com.bpb.android.wearableapp"
        minSdk 28
        targetSdk 30
        versionCode 1
```

```
        versionName "1.0"

    }
    ...
}

dependencies {
    implementation 'androidx.wear:wear:1.2.0'
    // The support library dependencies below are mainly needed for
    // the production watch face library.
    // There are Jetpack libraries specific to wearables as well,
    // so check list of latest libraries and use them when you need.
    implementation 'com.google.android.support:wearable:2.8.1'
    compileOnly 'com.google.android.wearable:wearable:2.8.1'
    // ... OTHER DEPENDENCIES BELOW
}
```

NOTE: While defining the target SDK version or compiling the SDK version, make sure that the version you are specifying is supported for wearables. Not all Android APIs are applicable for wearables like handsets or tablets. For example, API 28 and 30 are supported for wearables, but API 29 is not supported for wearables.

After verifying **build.gradle** file, let us look into the manifest file and make sure that **<uses-feature android:name="android.hardware.type.watch" />** and **<uses-library android:name="com.google.android.wearable" android:required="true" />** has been added, as similar to following manifest file. Note that the preceding file does not contain the whole code, but it shows only important code for wearables applications:

```
<manifest xmlns:android="http://schemas.android.com/apk/res/android"
    package="com.bpb.android.wearableapp">

    <uses-permission android:name="android.permission.WAKE_LOCK" />

    <uses-feature android:name="android.hardware.type.watch" />

    <application
```

```
            android:allowBackup="false"
            android:icon="@mipmap/ic_launcher"
            android:label="@string/app_name"
            android:supportsRtl="true"
            android:theme="@android:style/Theme.DeviceDefault">
        <uses-library
            android:name="com.google.android.wearable"
            android:required="true" />

        <!--
            Set to true if your app is Standalone, that is,
            it does not require the handheld app to run.
        -|
        <meta-data
            android:name="com.google.android.wearable.standalone"
            android:value="true" />

        // OTHER COMPONENTS SETTINGS
    </application>

</manifest>
```

Now, we are ready with the basic setup of wearable projects.

NOTE: **Values qualifiers for wearables are a little bit different from handset and tablet. The default "values" directory is used for square wearables, and the "-round" qualifiers to added to "values" for round wearables, as shown in** *figure 9.16*:

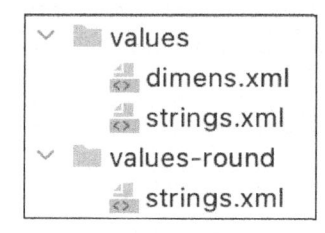

Figure 9.16: Value qualifiers for wearables

Creating an AVD for wearables

Creating AVD for wearables is the same as creating AVD for Android Phones. Let us see these steps:

1. In Android Studio, open the Android Virtual Device Manager by selecting **Tools | AVD Manager**.
2. Click **Create Virtual Device...**
3. In the **Category** section, select **Wear OS** and choose one of the hardware profiles from **Square**, **Round Chin**, and **Round**. And then click on **Next**.
4. Select a system image to download. You can choose any API level which is either equal or greater to the min SDK defined in Gradle or equal to or less than the target SDK defined. After selecting the system image, click on Finish

After that, you can select the newly created AVD and run the wearable application.

Creating project for TV

Creating a project for TV is the same as a handset/tablet or wearables. Let us create the project first using the template as follows:

1. Click on **File | New | New Project...**:

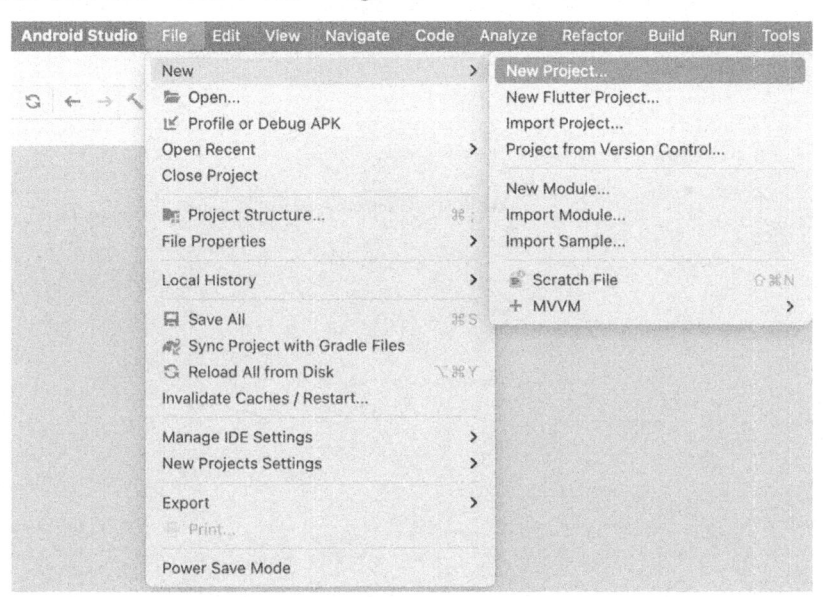

Figure 9.17: Creating an application for TV

2. In the **New Project** window, click the **Android TV** tab, select **Blank Activity**, and click on the **Next** button:

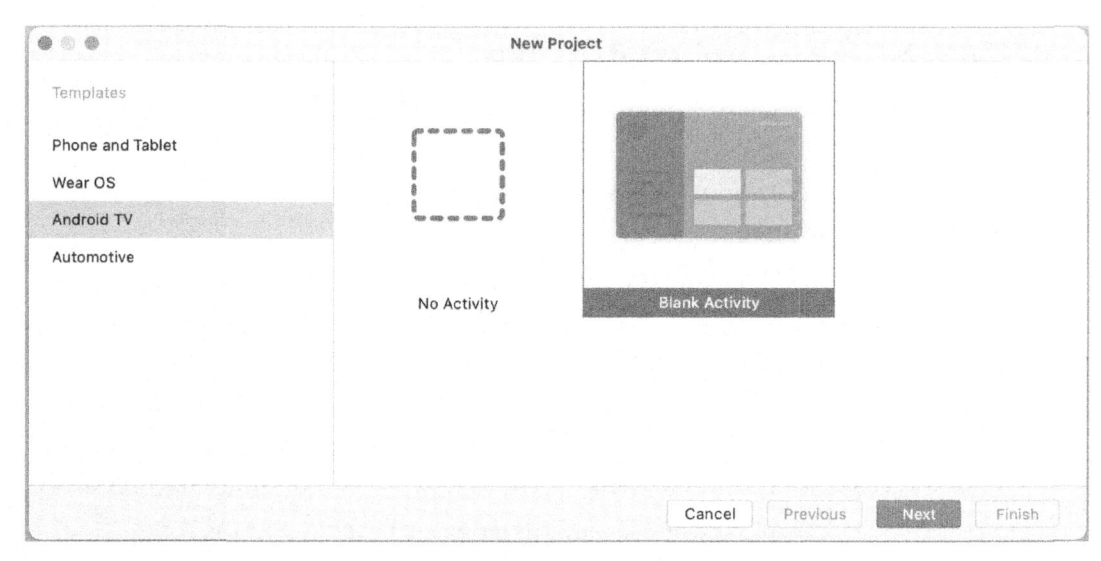

Figure 9.18: Creating an application for TV

3. In the **New Project** window, name your project, fill out the standard project information, and click **Finish**:

Figure 9.19: Creating an application for TV

4. Clicking on **Finish**, Android Studio will create a project for TV, and the project will look like as shown in *figure 9.20*:

Figure 9.20: Project structure for TV

In the preceding *figure 9.20*, you see two modules: mobile and TV. As the name suggests, the mobile module is for phone and tablet devices, and the TV module is for TV. We already know about phone and tablet development, so let us explore into tv module and learn about TV app development.

First of all, we need to create an Activity specifically for TV in the application. If you create a project using the template, Android Studio will create and configure this Activity automatically. This Activity must be defined with category **android.intent.category.LEANBACK_LAUNCHER** as follows:

```
<activity
    android:name=".MainActivity"
    ...
    android:screenOrientation="landscape">
    <intent-filter>
        <action android:name="android.intent.action.MAIN" />
```

```xml
        <category android:name="android.intent.category.LEANBACK_LAUNCHER"/>
    </intent-filter>
</activity>
```

If you are adding TV support into the existing application in the same module (like in the app module), the Activity for handset/tablet and the Activity for TV will be declared as follows:

```xml
<activity
    android:name="com.bpb.android.bpbapp.MainActivity"
    android:label="@string/app_name">

    <intent-filter>
        <action android:name="android.intent.action.MAIN" />
        <category android:name="android.intent.category.LAUNCHER" />
    </intent-filter>
</activity>


<activity
    android:name="com.bpb.android.bpbapp.TvActivity"
    ...
    android:screenOrientation="landscape">

    <intent-filter>
        <action android:name="android.intent.action.MAIN" />
        <category android:name="android.intent.category.LEANBACK_LAUNCHER"/>
    </intent-filter>

</activity>
```

NOTE: **If you are adding support for TV into the existing application, remember to declare different Activities and layouts for TV devices.**

android.intent.category.LEANBACK_LAUNCHER is used by the Google Play store as well to identify that the application is supported by TV devices. Make sure that you specify this category for the Activity, which is for TV; else, your application will not be visible on Google Play on TV devices.

Declaring Leanback support

Declaring Leanback support is required for TV applications. Value can be **true** or **false** depending on the application type. If your application runs on phones or tablets and Android TV, then you need to set this attribute to false, so devices that do not support Leanback can also install your application. When you set the attribute value to true, your application will run only on devices that use the Leanback UI. Following is an example:

```
<manifest xmlns:android="http://schemas.android.com/apk/res/android"

    package="com.bpb.android.bpbtvapp">

    <uses-feature

        android:name="android.software.leanback"

        android:required="true" />

</manifest>
```

Declaring touchscreen not required

Applications for TV devices do not depend on the touch screen for input. The TV application must declare in manifest that the feature **android.hardware.touchscreen** is not required. Google Play also uses this attribute to identify applications for TV:

```
<manifest xmlns:android="http://schemas.android.com/apk/res/android"

    package="com.bpb.android.bpbtvapp">

    <uses-feature

        android:name="android.hardware.touchscreen"

        android:required="false" />

</manifest>
```

Make sure that you declare that the touch screen is not required; else, your TV application will not appear in Google Play on TV devices.

Creating an AVD for TV application

Like other device types, creating AVD for TV is almost the same. Let us follow the following steps:

1. In Android Studio, open the **Android Virtual Device Manager** by selecting **Tools | AVD Manager**.
2. Click **Create Virtual Device…**
3. In the Category section, select TV and choose one of the hardware profiles, such as Android TV (720p) or Android TV (1,080p). And then click on **Next**.
4. Select a system image to download (or select if already downloaded). Select ×86 system image and enable **Use Host GPU** for best performance. After selecting the system image, click on **Finish**.

After that, you can select the newly created AVD and run the TV application.

While developing a TV application, make sure that you follow design principles from the material for the TV application.

Conclusion

In this chapter, we learned about how to provide a better user experience using resource qualifiers. We read about why we need qualifiers and learned about the uses of qualifiers for drawable, layouts, and values.

We also learned about developing/supporting an application for tablet devices. We learned about qualifiers specific to tablets and optimization of layouts for tablets. We also prepared a checklist to evaluate the quality of tablet applications.

We learned about creating applications and basic setups for wearables or TV devices. We did not discuss a few large topics in this chapter, like developing an application for Auto (https://developer.android.com/cars) or IoT (https://developer.android.com/things); you should explore them as well.

In the upcoming chapter, we will learn about a few important libraries which can be used in our Android application development.

Points to remember

- Use qualifiers for strings to provide localization.
- Use qualifiers for drawable to provide a better-sized image for the device with a specific density.
- Do some research on tablet screen design before implementing designs. Follow best practices and use large screens in a better way.
- Check if an image can be used as a vector drawable in the application.

Multiple Choice Questions

1. Qualifiers for resources help us to provide a better user experience.
   A. True   B. False

2. The touchscreen feature is required to develop TV apps.
   A. True   B. False

3. If an application supports handsets, tablets, and TV as well, then the value for Android.software.leanback feature should be false.
   A. True   B. False

4. To add support for the Thai language in an Android application, which qualifier should be used for the values directory?
   A. values-bh   B. values-in
   C. values-th   D. None of the above

Answers

1. A
2. B
3. A
4. C

Questions

1. What are qualifiers, and why should we use them?
2. How to add a different layout for tablet devices?
3. What is Vector drawable, and why should it be used?
4. What is the basic requirement for a project which supports a TV application?

Key Terms

- Android resources
- Drawables
- Layouts
- Multiscreen support
- Localization
- Strings
- Qualifiers
- SVG
- JPG
- PNG
- 9-Patch
- Raster Image
- Vector Image
- Vector Drawables
- Tablet support
- Checklist for tablet app
- Wearables
- TV
- Leanback

CHAPTER 10
Introducing Important Tools/Libs for Android

In the previous chapter, we learned about Adding support for big Screens, where we learned to develop an application for tablets or other screens.

In this final chapter of the book, we will learn about tools and libraries that can help you in the development of a good application. These tools will help you to debug the application and optimizing the application.

We will also learn about some libraries which are most important to know for Android development, such as App bundles, SafetyNet, and Hilt. We will also learn to write local tests or UI tests.

We will also read about designing UI for the application without XML layouts.

At the end of this chapter, we will learn about best practices and a few third-party libraries, which can be used in our daily Android app development.

Structure

In this chapter, we will cover the following topics:
- Introducing Jetpack compose
    - Introducing Row

- - Introducing Column
  - Introducing Box
  - Introducing ConstraintLayout
- Introducing App Bundles
  - Understanding benefits of App bundles
- Introducing SafetyNet
- Introducing Hilt
  - Exploring dependency injection
  - Understanding benefits of dependency injection solutions
  - Adding dependency for Hilt
  - Introducing annotations in Hilt
- Writing test cases with JUnit/Robolectric
  - Introducing Test cases
  - Writing good test cases
  - Writing local test cases using JUnit
  - Introducing Espresso
  - Introducing Robolectric
- Best practices to follow
- Third party libraries you should know

Objectives

The objective of this chapter is to let you know about some important libraries by explaining "why you require them in your project", and let you know about best practices and a few important libraries that make our task easy while developing an Android application.

For a well-structured application, dependency injection tools matter, and Hilt is going to help us in that. We need secure communication or secure our data of the application, so we will read about SafetyNet, Jetpack secure, and other security libs. We will learn about Junit, Espresso, and Robolectric. And you will know about how you can modularize your application and what benefits you can get from it.

Introducing Jetpack compose

Compose provides different layouts that help us to develop different types of UI, which we have been developing using XML till now.

Introducing Important Tools/Libs for Android ■ 399

To create Compose project steps are the same as creating other Android projects. But while selecting a project, we need to select **Empty Compose Activity** and do **Next**, and so on, as shown in *figure 10.1*:

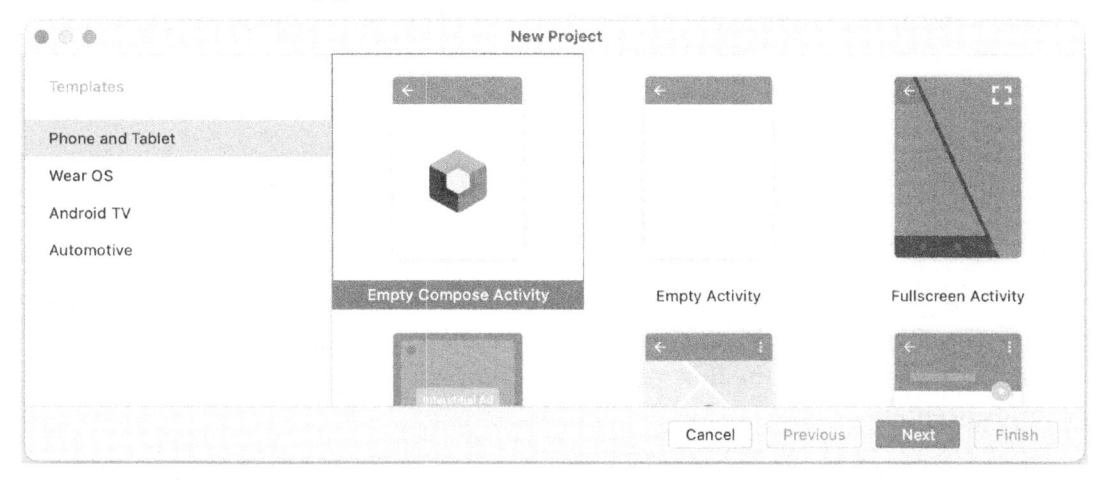

***Figure 10.1**: Creating Compose project using the Android Studio Template*

Figure 10.2 shows the code to show one image and text using compose:

```
class MainActivity : ComponentActivity() {
    override fun onCreate(savedInstanceState: Bundle?) {
        super.onCreate(savedInstanceState)
        setContent {
            BpbComposeAppTheme {
                BpbCard()
            }
        }
    }
}

@Composable
fun BpbCard() {
    Column(
        modifier = Modifier.fillMaxSize(),
        verticalArrangement = Arrangement.Center,
        horizontalAlignment = Alignment.CenterHorizontally
    ) { this: ColumnScope
        BpbCardView()
    }
}
```

```
@Composable
fun BpbCardView() {
    Card(
        modifier = Modifier.padding(8.dp).fillMaxWidth(),
        elevation = 4.dp,
        shape = RoundedCornerShape(4.dp)
    ) {
        var expanded by remember { mutableStateOf( value: false) }
        Column(
            Modifier.clickable { expanded = !expanded },
            verticalArrangement = Arrangement.Center,
            horizontalAlignment = Alignment.CenterHorizontally
        ) { this: ColumnScope
            Image(
                painter = painterResource(id = R.drawable.bpb_logo),
                contentDescription = "BPB Logo",
                modifier = Modifier.size(300.dp, 150.dp).padding(8.dp)
            )
            Text(
                text = "Hello, Jetpack Compose",
                style = MaterialTheme.typography.body1,
                modifier = Modifier.padding(all = 4.dp)
            )
        }
    }
}
```

Output at center of device screen

***Figure 10.2**: Compose sample to show Image and Text*

In the code shown in the preceding *figure 10.2*, you can see @composable annotation for functions that creates views. There are some view elements and layouts as well, such as Column, Card, Image, Text, and so on. Similar to XML layouts, Compose provides some layouts which can be used to design our UI. The following are layouts in Compose:

- Row
- Column
- Box
- ConstraintLayout

NOTE: **There might be some new layouts as well when you read this book because the Compose is in the early stage of its development and just a week before Android released the first version of Compose after more than two years of its announcement.**

Let us look a little bit more at these layouts.

Introducing Row

The Row is used to show Views horizontally on the screen. It is like LinearLayout with horizontal orientation and weight attributes. See *figure 10.3*, which shows code, output, and how the Row layout works:

```
@Composable
@Preview
fun BpbRowExample() {
    Row(
        modifier = Modifier
            .fillMaxWidth()
            .background(Color.White),
    ) { this: RowScope
        Text(
            text = "This is",
            style = MaterialTheme.typography.h6,
            modifier = Modifier
                .background(Color.Gray)
                .padding(16.dp)
        )
        Text(
            text = "Row example",
            style = MaterialTheme.typography.h6,
            modifier = Modifier
                .background(Color.LightGray)
                .padding(16.dp)
        )
    }
}
```

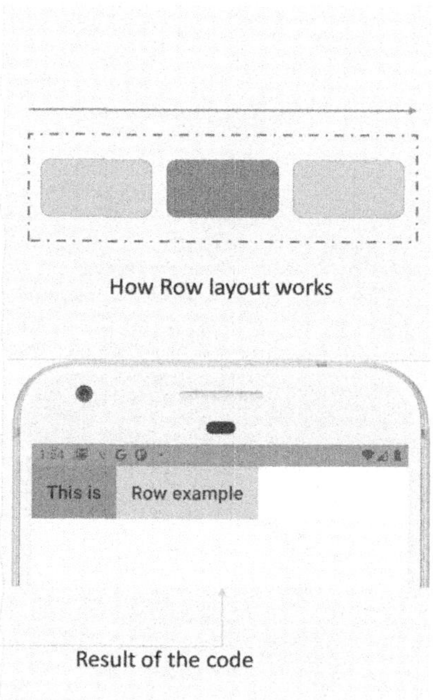

Figure 10.3: Row layout example

Introducing Column

The column is used to show the view vertically on the screen. It is like LinearLayout with vertical orientation and weight attributes. See *figure 10.4*, which shows code, output, and how the Column layout works:

```
@Composable
@Preview
fun BpbColumnExample() {
    Column(
        modifier = Modifier
            .fillMaxWidth()
            .background(Color.White),
    ) { this: ColumnScope

        Text(
            text = "This is",
            style = MaterialTheme.typography.h5,
            modifier = Modifier
                .padding(start = 16.dp, top = 16.dp)
                .background(Color.Gray)
        )

        Text(
            text = "Column example",
            style = MaterialTheme.typography.h6,
            modifier = Modifier
                .padding(start = 16.dp, bottom = 16.dp)
                .background(Color.LightGray)
        )
    }
}
```

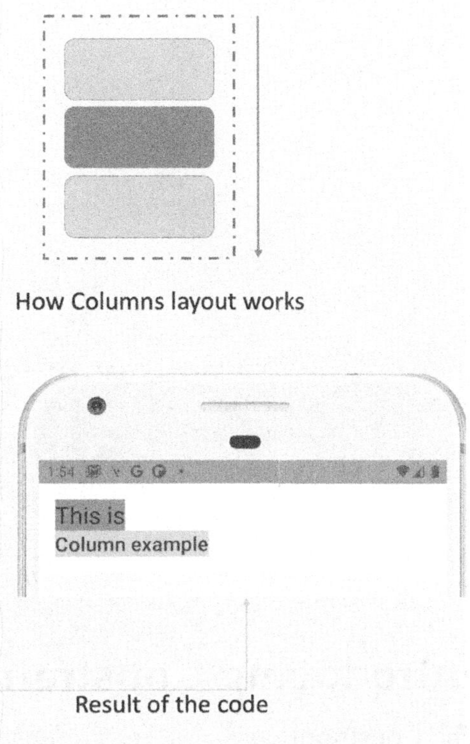

Figure 10.4: Column layout example

Introducing Box

The Box is like **FrameLayout** or the **RelativeLayout** with no relation given between children. Children inside Box are used to stack over each other. There is an alignment modifier to align children inside the Box layout. See *figure 10.5*, which shows code, output, and how the Box layout works:

```kotlin
@Composable
@Preview
fun BpbBoxExample() {
    Box(
        modifier = Modifier
            .fillMaxWidth()
            .background(Color.White),
    ) { this: BoxScope
        Text(
            text = "This is",
            style = MaterialTheme.typography.h4,
            modifier = Modifier.padding(16.dp),
            color = Color.Red
        )

        Text(
            text = "Box example",
            style = MaterialTheme.typography.h5,
            modifier = Modifier.padding(16.dp),
            color = Color.Blue
        )
    }
}
```

Figure 10.5: Box layout example

Introducing ConstraintLayout

The ConstraintLayout is used to design complex UI with a flat hierarchy, the same as the traditional ConstraintLayout which we were using in XML. While using this layout, you need to remember three attributes:

- **createRefs**: It creates references for each composable in ConstraintLayout.
- **constrainAs**: By using **constrainAs**, we define constraints for a composable.
- **linkTo**: It is used to define constraints.

Creating a layout with **ConstraintLayout** in Compose is interesting and easy same as the traditional XML layout. For a quick look, let us design the UI as shown in *figure 10.6* in **ConstraintLayout**:

Figure 10.6: Designing layout using ConstraintLayout

Following is the code using **ConstraintLayout** in Compose for the preceding UI:

```
@Composable
@Preview(showBackground = true)
fun BpbConstraintLayoutExample() {

    Card(...) {
        ConstraintLayout(
            modifier = Modifier.fillMaxWidth().padding(16.dp)
        ) {

            val (titleLayout, amountLayout) = createRefs()

            /* Column to display "Total price" & "You saved on this order" */
            Column(modifier = Modifier.constrainAs(titleLayout) {
                start.linkTo(parent.start)
                top.linkTo(parent.top)
                bottom.linkTo(parent.bottom)
            }) {

                Text(...)
                Spacer(Modifier.height(4.dp))
                Text(...)

            }

            /* Column to display amounts */
            Column(modifier = Modifier.constrainAs(amountLayout) {
                end.linkTo(parent.end)
                top.linkTo(parent.top)
```

```
        }) {

            Text(...)

            Spacer(Modifier.height(4.dp))

            Text(...)

        }

      }

   }

}
```

Note that the full source code is available at the BPB GitHub repository.

In the preceding code at Line number 10, we are creating references using `createRefs` for two Columns which we are using as children of `ConstraintLayout`. On Lines number 13 and 25, we are using `constrainAs` to define constraints for both Columns. And at Lines 1.

In Lines 4–16, 26, and 27, we are using `linkTo` to define constraints between composable (that is, Column in our example).

In the preceding code, on Lines 26 and 27, we can define constraints using `linkTo` as `titleLayout.end` and `titleLayout.top`, or other available constraints, and that is how we create constraints between each composable inside `ConstraintLayout`.

That is it from Composable. The recommendation is to keep an eye on new updates and explore Composable more.

Introducing App Bundles

While reading *Chapter 1: Creating Hello World Project*, we read a little bit about modularization and Android app bundle (`.aab`). In this section, we will explore a bit more about app bundles and modularization.

Understanding benefits of App bundles

When you create an APK file, Android includes each directory for resources and the whole source code. Assume that there are two different sets of users for your application. One group uses HDPI devices and the second set of users use XHDPI devices. So in the case of APK, you publish a single file for both user groups, but you know that for the first user group, each resource is useless and does not fall in the HDPI bucket and the same for the second user group where each resource is useless other than who belongs to XHDPI bucket. In other words, even though resources are not being used now or in the future, a device configuration is always part of APK and taking memory.

Think about a feature where you can create APK depending on device configuration or custom configuration, and you can share an APK excluding all unnecessary resources for your user group, which falls in the HDPI density bucket, and another APK excluding all unnecessary resources for those users who fall in XHDPI density bucket. Interesting, right? App bundle is the feature that does the same.

Let us see *figure 10.7* to understand how it works:

① We create .aab file

② We upload .aab file on Play Store

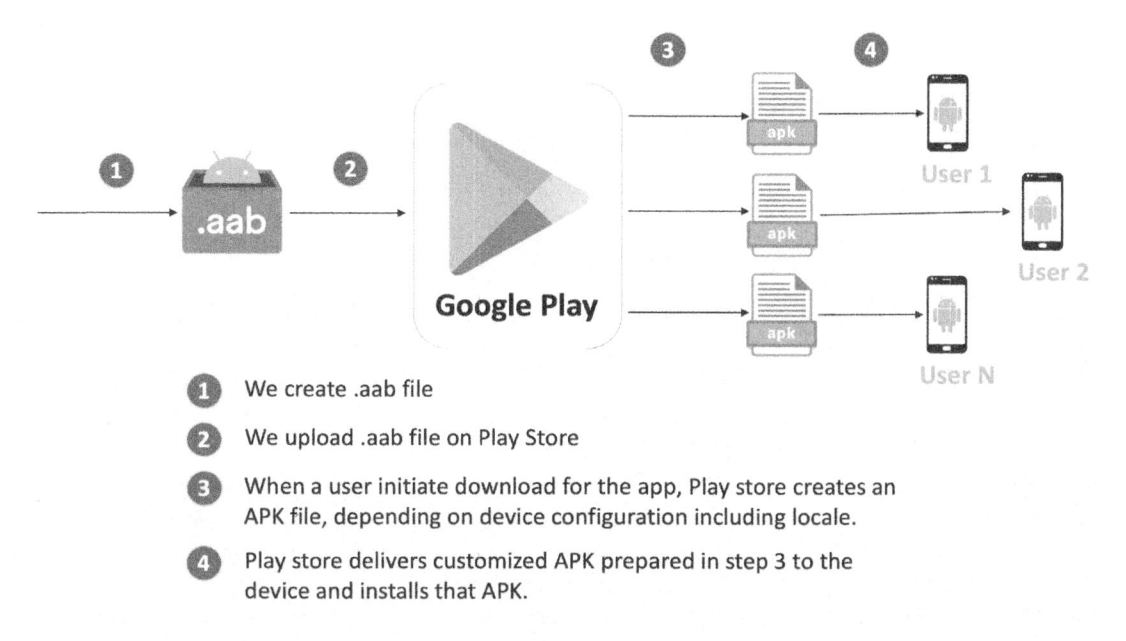

③ When a user initiate download for the app, Play store creates an APK file, depending on device configuration including locale.

④ Play store delivers customized APK prepared in step 3 to the device and installs that APK.

Figure 10.7: How Google play delivers .aab as optimized APK

As you see in the preceding *figure 10.7*, Play Store uses an app bundle to generate and serve optimized APKs for each user's device configuration, so users can download only the code and resources they need to run your app on the user's device. Thus, users can get smaller and more optimized downloads. Let us understand the APK optimization with *figures 10.8 and 10.9*:

Let us assume *figure 10.8* represents one APK without optimization by Play Store:

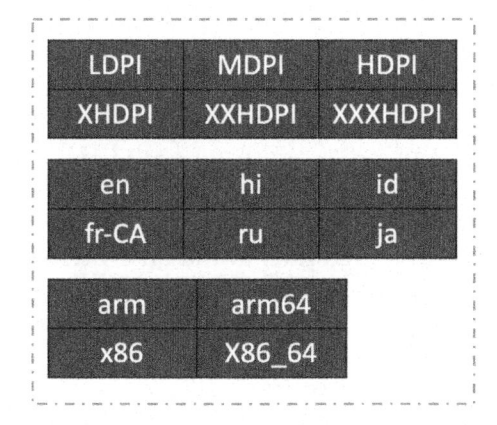

Figure 10.8: APK without optimization contains each directory

When we create `.aab` for the preceding *figure 10.8*, Play Store will split APK (optimize APK depending on device configuration) and deliver it to the device, as shown in *figure 10.9*:

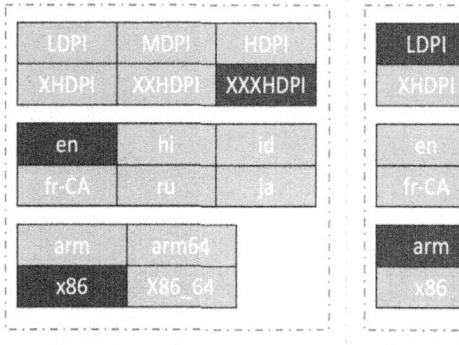

According to device configuration **XXXHDPI**, **en** and **X86** added to the APK.

According to device configuration **LDPI**, **hi** and **arm** added to the APK.

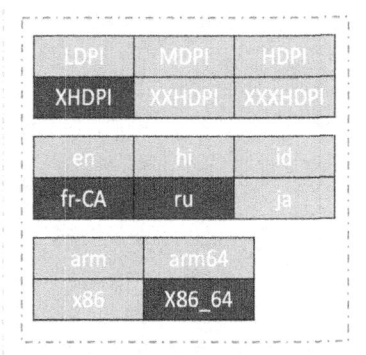

According to device configuration **XHDPI**, **fr-CA** and **X86_64** added to the APK. And if user changes device locale for example Russia, then Play Store will download "**ru**" as well and add it to existing app.

Figure 10.9: Optimized APK depending on device configuration

App bundle provides us with the flexibility to modularize our application and deploy these modules as a module at Play Store, and users can access that module on demand. For example, you are developing a chat application. There are two main features, chat and video call, in that application. You want to make the `video call` feature optional. So you will include the chat feature into the base `.aab` file and upload the `video call` feature as a different module on Play Store. So when the user needs the `video call` feature, it would be downloaded and added to the application at a device on demand via dynamic delivery. Even if you want the *Video feature* to be added as a paid feature to the app, you do not need to create two different versions *free* and *paid* application. App bundle and dynamic delivery. Following are a few benefits of using the Android App Bundle:

- Smaller download size.
- Optimized apk.
- On-demand app features.
- Asset-only modules (modules that contain only assets, these are mostly useful for games)
- It makes it easy to support Google Play Instant app feature. Instant Apps is a feature provided by the Play store where users can use an app or game without installing it.

NOTE: **App Bundle is a publishing format, whereas APK is the packaging format that can be installed on the device. The bundletool is the tool that builds App Bundles and converts app bundles into the different APKs for different device configurations. Bundletool is part of Android Studio, Gradle plugins, and Google Play and is available as a command-line tool.**

Introducing SafetyNet

SafetyNet helps us to protect our application against security threats, including device tampering (checks for rooted devices), malicious URLs, harmful applications, and fake users. SafetyNet is part of Google Play Services, so it required Google Play Services to be enabled and updated on the device.

It provides four basic APIs as follows.

SafetyNet Attestation API

This API checks if the device is tampered or potentially compromised. It compares the device's profile with Google-certified devices and verifies if the device or any application running on the device is Android compatible. The device is considered approved by Google if it passes the Android Compatibility Test Suits (CTS). While comparing the device with CTS standards, this Attestation API verifies the following things:

- If the application is Android incompatible or compatible.
- If the device bootloader has been unlocked or not.
- If the device is rooted or not.
- If the device is being monitored or not.
- If the device has malicious applications or not.
- If the device has unknown hardware or not.

And CTS passes when SafetyNet does not find anything.

SafetyNet Safe Browsing API

This API checks if a URL used within an application is marked by Google as malicious. To do this, the API compares URLs with the updated blacklist of threatful websites maintained by Google. If any malware or harmful codes are found within the page, a warning page will be added by SafetyNet, and the URL will be classified as a known threat.

SafetyNet reCAPTCHA API

As the name suggests, this API checks for real users and Bot by challenging captcha. And the user can continue using the application after solving the captcha.

SafetyNet Verify Apps API

This API is used to check whether the user has enabled the verify apps feature on the device and make sure that there is no harmful application running on the device. The API coordinates with the Verify Apps feature to make sure that the application's data is protected like no other apps on the device on which the app is currently running can perform any malicious actions.

So whenever security is a concern for your application, SafetyNet would be your first choice.

NOTE: **When we think about security in Android applications, there are many options available for different purposes:**

- **Custom permissions with a protection level system or signature in the manifest can be used to protect communication between your two or more applications.**

- Certificate pinning or public key pinning should be considered to implement secure communication between the Android application and your server. Almost all networking libraries provide methods to implement certificate or public key pinning. You can also consider using the "Network security configuration" provided by Android.
- Jetpack Security provides a secure way to store data into files or shared preferences.
- If data is sensitive, do not store it in external storage. If required, do not forget to encrypt the data.

Introducing Hilt

We already know about the dependency inversion principle while reading SOLID patterns in *Chapter 3: Architecture Patterns*. Let us explore more about it.

Exploring dependency injection

By following the principle of Dependency Inversion in the Android app, we make prepare a good app architecture. It helps us with the:

- Reusability of the code
- Ease of refactoring and
- Ease of testing

Figure 10.10 is an example of a **Car** and **Engine** where these two are tightly coupled:

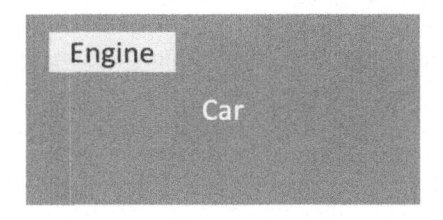

```
01.   class Car {
02.       private val engine = Engine()
03.       ...
04.   }
05.
06.   class Engine {
07.       ...
08.   }
```

Figure 10.10: When Car and Engine are tightly coupled

With the dependency injection, instead of Car creating its instance of the engine, Car receives an engine, for example, as a parameter in its constructor, as shown in *figure 10.11*:

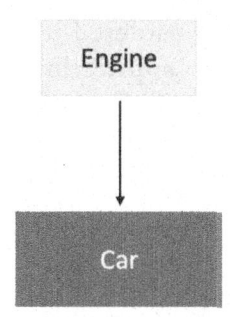

Figure 10.11: *Providing engine object from outside of Car class*

This makes the car class reusable, as it can be used with different implementations of engines, and it is also easier to test.

Manual Dependency Injection: When creating instances of classes in your project, you can exercise the dependency graph manually by satisfying the dependencies on transitive dependencies that the class requires. But doing this manually every time involves some boilerplate code and could be error-prone. See the following class, which is copied from the iosched app of Google:

```kotlin
class FeedViewModel(
    private val momentUseCase: LoadCurrentMomentUseCase,
    private val announcementsUseCase: LoadAnnouncementsUseCase,
    private val sessionsUseCase: LoadStarredAndReservedSessionsUseCase,
    private val getTimeZoneUseCase: GetTimeZoneUseCase,
    private val getConferenceStateUseCase: GetConferenceStateUseCase,
    private val timeProvider: TimeProvider,
    private val analyticsHelper: AnalyticsHelper,
    private val signInViewModelDelegate: SignInViewModelDelegate,
    private val themedActivityDelegate: ThemedActivityDelegate,
    private val snackbarMessageManager: SnackbarMessageManager
) : ViewModel(),
    FeedEventListener,
    ThemedActivityDelegate by themedActivityDelegate,
```

```
    SignInViewModelDelegate by signInViewModelDelegate {
```
}

Can you imagine the amount of code required to create **FeedViewModel** class with its dependencies and transitive dependencies? Manual dependency injection requires us to construct every class and its dependencies by hand and to use containers to reuse and manage dependencies. It is hard and repetitive, and we could easily get the dependencies wrong. So, let us see how dependency injection libraries can help us.

Understanding benefits of dependency injection solutions

Like any dependency injection library, Hilt reduces the boilerplate code of doing manual dependency, and it needs to write less code compared to other dependency injection libraries. It has the following benefits:

- Hilt is Jetpack DI solution for Android
- It is built on top of Dagger, so does everything which can be done by Dagger and more
- Removes boilerplate code via annotations
- It has tooling support
- And it has other jetpack library support

Adding dependency for Hilt

We need to add a plugin at the root **build.gradle** file, as follows:

```
buildscript {

    ...

    dependencies {

        ...

        // REPLACE 2.40.5 WITH LATEST VERSION
        classpath 'com.google.dagger:hilt-android-gradle-plugin:2.40.5'

    }

}
```

Let us add the dependency of Hilt into the **app/build.gradle** file:

…

```
plugins {
  id 'kotlin-kapt'
  id 'dagger.hilt.android.plugin'
}
```

...

```
dependencies {
    // REPLACE 2.40.5 WITH LATEST VERSION
    implementation "com.google.dagger:hilt-android:2.4.5"
    kapt "com.google.dagger:hilt-compiler:2.4.5"
}
```

Now, let us see how we can use Hilt and annotation.

Introducing annotations in Hilt

Hilt uses annotations to allow us to configure dependencies. *Table 10.1* shows Hilt annotations with uses:

Annotation	Uses
@HiltAndroidApp	It is required for all app that uses Hilt to create an Application class. So, we need to create an Application class and annotate it with @HiltAndroidApp. This annotation kicks off Hilt code generation, and it also creates a dependency container associated with the application class and the component created by this annotation will be the parent component of the app and will be available to any component: @HiltAndroidApp class BpbApplication : Application() { ... } *NOTE:* **Do not forget to add this BpbApplication class to the manifest file.**

Annotation	Uses
@AndroidEntryPoint	After providing application-level components by @HiltAndroidApp we define @AndroidEntryPoint that can be annotated in Android framework classes. It creates a dependency container for that class and populates all @Inject annotated variables: @AndroidEntryPoint class BpbActivity : AppCompatActivity() { ... }

@Inject	Annotating the constructor of a class with @Inject tells Hilt how to create an instance of that class:
	class BpbAdapter @Inject constructor(
	  private val service: BpbService
	) { ... }
	when you annotate a variable with this annotation in an @AndroidEntryPoint annotated class, Hilt injects an instance of that type into the class:
	@AndroidEntryPoint
	class BpbActivity : AppCompatActivity() {
	  @Inject lateinit var adapter: BpbAdapter
	  ...
	}
	Note that all Hilt injected variables will be available when super.onCreate() is called. In this example, we are injecting BpbAdapter into BpbActivity.

@HiltViewModel	The annotation will be used to provide instances of the ViewModel class:
	@HiltViewModel
	class BpbViewModel @Inject constructor(
	  private val adapter: BpbAdapter,
	  private val state: SavedStateHandle
	): ViewModel() { ... }

Annotation	Uses
@Module and @InstallIn	There would be some classes that cannot be constructor injected. For example, we cannot constructor-inject an interface, or we cannot constructor-inject a type that we do not own, such as a class from an external library, like Retrofit. To handle such cases, we can provide (see uses of @Provides) Hilt with binding information by using Hilt modules annotated with @Module: @InstallIn(SingletonComponent::class) @Module class BpbModule { ... } You need to annotate Hilt modules with @InstallIn to tell Hilt in which Android class the module will be used (installed in). It is kind of we scoping the binding. SingletonComponent makes binding available in the whole application. Similarly, you can use ViewModelComponent for the ViewModel, ActivityComponent for the Activity, FragmentComponent for the Fragment, and so on.

@Provides	It helps us to provide bindings for the type that cannot be constructor injected.
	
	In the following example, we are binding an object for the Retrofit service:
	
	@InstallIn(SingletonComponent::class)
	@Module
	class BpbModule {
	    @Provides
	     fun providesBpbService(
	        converterFactory: GsonConverterFactory
	    ): BpbService {
	        return Retrofit.Builder()
	            .baseUrl("https://bpb.com")
	          .addConverterFactory(converterFactory)
	            .build()
	            .create(BpbService::class.java)
	    }
	}

Annotation	Uses

@Binds	Hilt provides @Binds to bind an interface type:
	@InstallIn(SingletonComponent::class)
	@Module
	abstract class BpbModule {
	    @Binds
	     abstract fun bindsBpbService(
	        bpbServiceImpl: BpbServiceImpl
	     ): BpbService
	}
	In the preceding code, the return type is the binding type, and parameters are dependencies.
	Note that if we do not scope the type, the function body will be executed every time whenever an instance is needed.

@Singleton, @ActivityScoped See scope hierarchy for more details.	Scope annotations such as @Singleton, @ActivityScoped, @FragmentScoped, @ViewScoped, and so on are used to scope objects to a container: @Singleton class BpbAdapter @Inject constructor(private val service: BpbService) { ... } It means when we scope an object with @Singleton the same object will be provided by the container to the whole application. When we scope an object with @ActivityScoped the same object will be provided by the container for the activity, fragments inside that activity, and views being used in that activity or fragment. The following is the scope hierarchy: @Singleton ↓ ↘ @ActivityRetainedScoped @ServiceScoped ↓ ↘ @ActivityScoped @ViewModelScoped ↓ @FragmentScoped @ViewScoped ↓ @ViewScoped

Annotation	Uses
@ApplicationContext @ActivityContext	Hilt provides some qualifiers for predefined binding like @ApplicationContext @ActivityContext: @Singleton class BpbAdapter @Inject constructor(@ApplicationContext val context: Context private val service: BpbService) { ... } We can use these binding qualifiers when we need a context object, as in the preceding example.

Table 10.1: Hilt annotations and uses

So these are basic ideas about Hilt annotations that can be used in our application. Before we move to the next section, can you now write code with Hilt for the iosched app of Google, which we saw at the start of this section? Following is the code:

@HiltViewModel

class FeedViewModel @Inject constructor(

    private val momentUseCase: LoadCurrentMomentUseCase,

    private val announcementsUseCase: LoadAnnouncementsUseCase,

    private val sessionsUseCase: LoadStarredAndReservedSessionsUseCase,

    private val getTimeZoneUseCase: GetTimeZoneUseCase,

    private val getConferenceStateUseCase: GetConferenceStateUseCase,

    private val private val timeProvider: TimeProvider,

    private val analyticsHelper: AnalyticsHelper,

    private val signInViewModelDelegate: SignInViewModelDelegate,

    private val themedAmctivityDelegate: ThemedActivityDelegate,

    private val snackbarMessageManager: SnackbarMessageManager

) : ViewModel(),

    FeedEventListener,

    ThemedActivityDelegate by themedActivityDelegate,

```
SignInViewModelDelegate by signInViewModelDelegate {
```
}

In the preceding code, we have added **@HiltViewModel** and **@Inject**, that is it. Everything else will be taken care of by Hilt for you.

Writing test cases with JUnit/Robolectric

Writing a test case is equally important as writing code for your application. Tests help you to develop an application of good quality. A well-written test can also be referred to as documentation for the application.

Introducing test cases

First, we will understand why test cases are important. We write test cases to evaluate our project and identify possible bugs, missing implementations, edge cases, and so on via test cases. These test cases help in future modifications as well; for example, you can make sure that you did not break anything else (or work as expected) in the project while modifying a module or adding a module easily by running test cases. So instead of depending on manual verification of the whole app or a module, you run well-written test cases and verify your project. That is why test cases are important for any project. The following are the benefits of writing test cases:

1. Test cases ensure that features of an application are working as expected.
2. These help us to validate that our application is bug-free.
3. These test cases help us in improving the quality of the application.
4. Test cases minimize the costs of software support and maintenance.
5. Well-written test cases help other developers/testers to understand the system behavior or requirement as well.

Writing good test cases

To add a well-written test case, there are a few things that you need to follow:

1. **Name of test case**:

   To write test cases names, the following are some recommendations:
   - Test case name should include the name of the tested method (or class as well).
   - Test case names should convey a specific requirement.

- The name should include the input/state and the result for that input/state.
- The name should be written as a statement that conveys workflows and outputs.

Assuming we have a method in our application **isSeniorCitizen()** which returns true if age is equal to or more than 55, else returns **false**. The following are a few examples of naming a test case:

- **isSeniorCitizen_AgeLessThan55_False**
- **isSeniorCitizen_False_AgeLessThan55**
- **testIsNotASeniorCitizenIfAgeLessThan55**
- **IsNotASeniorCitizenIfAgeLessThan55**
- **When_AgeLessThan55_Expect_isSeniorCitizenAsFalse**

Kotlin provides us to add spaces between words for test cases. So, we can write a test case as follows as well:

```
@Test
fun `test if isSeniorCitizen returns false when age is less than 55`() {
    ...
}
```

2. **Expressive tests**:

   Most of the time, test cases written by you may be used by some other developer. So, your test cases should be more expressive and easier to understand. Remember that test cases help the new team member to get a good experience with the application.

3. **Handling of edge cases**:

   Do not write test cases just to achieve test coverage. It is very easy to achieve test coverage percentages, even without testing for edge cases. So do not write test cases only to achieve test coverage. Analyze the requirement and find out boundary cases. Add test cases for them. For example, if you are writing a method to multiply two integers, a test case should be added to check the overflow case (when the multiplication of two integers goes beyond the range of the integer).

   Writing test cases for invalid input is also a good way to write test cases. A simple example is, you are writing a method for division, then a test case must validate that method if it can handle any number divided by zero, that is, (1 ÷ 0 = undefined).

4. **Validation of expected result**:

   Each test case must validate an expected result for a given input or given the state of the application. It helps you to understand if the application is working as expected or if something is broken.

In Android, we use Junit, Espresso, or Robolectric to write test cases.

Writing local test cases using JUnit

JUnit test cases run on our local Java Virtual Machine (JVM) instead of Android devices or emulators. So, they run faster. But you cannot write the test for a method that interacts with Android framework classes.

We write Junit tests in `module_name/src/test/` like `app/src/test/` as shown in *figure 10.12*:

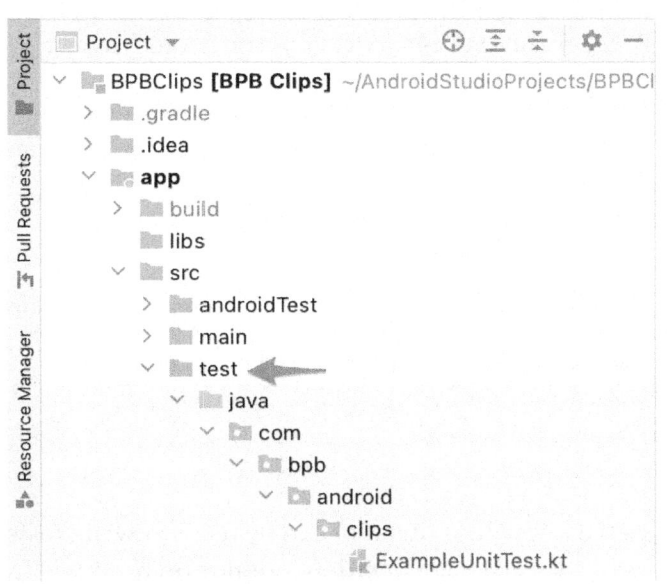

Figure 10.12: Directory to add JUnit test/local test

Following is the dependency that you need to add:

```
dependencies {

...

// JUnit 4 framework. Replace 4.13.2 with the latest version
```

```
testImplementation 'junit:junit:4.13.2'

...

}
```

Now, let us see how we can write test cases for our previous example of checking senior citizens by age. The following is the simple example code:

```
class ExampleUnitTest {

    @Test

    fun `test if isSeniorCitizen returns false when age is less than 55`() {

        assertFalse(AgeValidator.isSeniorCitizen(54))

    }


    @Test

    fun `test if isSeniorCitizen returns true when age is 55`() {

        assertTrue(AgeValidator.isSeniorCitizen(55))

    }


    @Test

    fun `test if isSeniorCitizen returns true when age is more than 55`() {

        assertTrue(AgeValidator.isSeniorCitizen(56))

    }

}
```

After reading JUnit, we knew that this tool can be used to write tests for pure Kotlin code or a method that does not have any dependency on methods from the Android framework. So how we can write tests for those methods with Android framework code? Espresso and Robolectric are the answer for it.

Introducing Espresso

Espresso is an open source UI testing framework developed by Google. We write Espresso test in the **module_name/src/androidTest/** like **app/src/androidTest /** directory, as shown in *figure 10.13*:

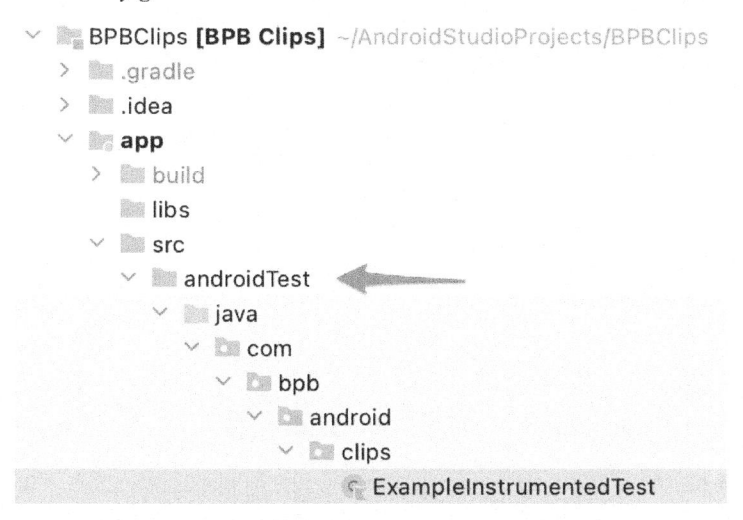

Figure 10.13: Directory to add Espresso test

We need to add dependencies in the **app/build.gradle** file as follows:

// Replace versions with latest

androidTestImplementation 'androidx.test.espresso:espresso-core:3.4.0'

androidTestImplementation 'androidx.test:runner:1.4.0'

androidTestImplementation 'androidx.test:rules:1.4.0'

Let us write Espresso test cases for an application where we show a button and text on the first screen and when the user taps on the button, it shows the second screen. The following is the code:

@RunWith(AndroidJUnit4::class)

class FirstActivityInstrumentedTest {

    @get:Rule

    val activityRule = ActivityScenarioRule(FirstActivity::class.java)

    @Test

```kotlin
fun verify_if_first_activity_launched() {
    Espresso.onView(
        ViewMatchers.withText("Hello from first activity")
    ).check(
        ViewAssertions.matches(
            ViewMatchers.isDisplayed()
        )
    )
}

@Test
fun verify_if_second_activity_launched() {
    // Press the button
    Espresso.onView(
        ViewMatchers.withId(R.id.btnShowNextActivity)
    ).perform(ViewActions.click())

    // And verify if the view from the second activity is on screen.
    Espresso.onView(ViewMatchers.withId(R.id.textview_second)).check(
        ViewAssertions.matches(
            ViewMatchers.withText(
                "Hello from second activity"
            )
        )
    )
}
}
```

In the preceding example, the first test **verify_if_first_activity_launched** checks if the first activity is visible and the second test **verify_if_second_activity_launched** checks if tapping on the button at the first activity shows the second activity.

Android Studio provides a tool to generate test cases for you. You just need to execute the flow on the device or emulator which is connected to the ADB and start recording. You can access that tool via the toolbar **Run -> Record Espresso Test**, as shown in *figure 10.14*:

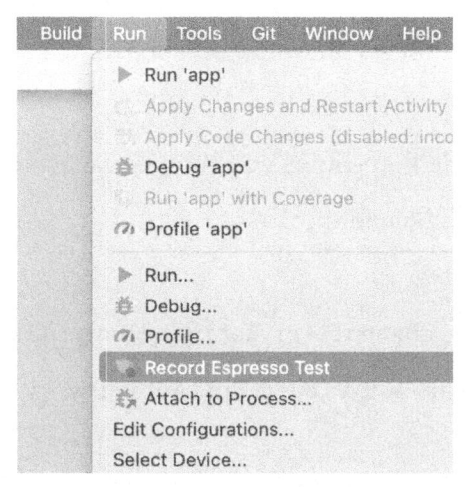

Figure 10.14: Record Espresso tests

Although it has support from Google, it has a drawback as well. Espresso requires an emulator or device connected to ADB while running test cases. We use CICD for our applications, so to execute espresso tests, an emulator or device is always needed on a remote machine where our automation server (for example, Jenkins) is running.

To resolve this dependency, the Android community and Google recommend to use Robolectric.

Introducing Robolectric

Robolectric test runs in the JVM at our system or in other words, Robolectric allows the Android applications to be tested on JVM without an emulator or real device. It makes CICD configuration easy and as tests do not require adding configurations for emulator or device. Following are the benefits of using Robolectric:

- As we read earlier, Robolectric provides a way to run our tests without launching the app on Device or Emulator, which makes it faster than other tools.

- Android components, such as Activity, Services, or even multiple build flavors can be tested using Robolectric.
- Mocking is not required while using Robolectric.

Let us see how we can add dependencies:

```
dependencies {
    // Robolectric. Update 4.3.1 with latest version
    testImplementation "org.robolectric:robolectric:4.3.1"
}
```

And following the example that shows you how you can create Robolectric tests:

```
@RunWith(RobolectricTestRunner::class)
class FirstActivityTest {
    private lateinit var controller: ActivityControllerUtil<FirstActivity>
    private lateinit var activity: FirstActivity

    @Before
    override fun setUp() {
        super.setUp()
        controller = ActivityControllerUtil.of(FirstActivity::class.java)
        activity = controller.setup().get()
    }

    @Test
    fun verify_if_second_activity_launched() {
        activity.findViewById<Button>(R.id.btnShowNextActivity).performClick()
        assertEquals(
            SecondActivity::class.java.name,
            shadowOf(activity).nextStartedActivity.component?.className
```

```
        )
    }

    @After
    fun tearDown() {
        controller.tearDown()
    }
}
```

In the preceding example, we have rewritten `verify_if_second_activity_launched` test in Robolectric. Here, you can see that we can access Android classes directly.

We read all three popular testing tools in Android. Practice them and make a habit to add test cases. They are going to help you many times. The recommendation is to use Junit and Robolectric. However, you can use Robolectric as a replacement for Junit as well; better to keep local tests in Junit. And for the classes which are Android components or depend on Android components, use Robolectric.

Best practices to follow

Following are a few best practices that you should follow while developing an Android application.

- Choose application architecture after evaluating each available architecture with your requirement. Remember that no architecture is bad till you are following coding guidelines and keeping the code clean.
- Always prefer modularization over keeping all modules in the app module. Even though you are not using the feature of the instant app or on-demand delivery, multiple modules are going to make the build time faster than a single module. Also, feature modules make your code clean and pluggable.
- Before starting the development of the application, decide design template and UI kit for your application and finalize typography, styles, and view components. It makes your task easy to design screens for the app, and you do not need to write styles, typography, and widgets again. For example, positive and negative buttons should look the same on each screen where they are being shown. So having styles for negative and positive buttons needs to apply the style only instead of writing style again and again. Keep

all these things into a separate module, so if required in the future, you can reuse that module in a different app as well.

- Define build variants for the application with respective configurations.
- While designing XML layouts, merging and including tags are your best assets. So consider developing reusable XML layouts.
- There is no best layout nor the worst layout, even in XML layout or Jetpack Compose. Your requirement/the design of the screen makes them the best suited or more optimized layout. Do not forget to evaluate the performance and optimize the layouts of your application.
- While choosing Drawables, your preference should be Vector Drawables (SVG) first. After that, 9-patch images, WebP images, and PNG can be used depending on which is the best fit.
- Configure your Gradle to increase build speed. Android provides us with well-written documentation on it at https://developer.android.com/studio/build/optimize-your-build.
- Do not log sensitive data even in DEBUG mode, and other data should be logged in to DEBUG mode only. For logging, you can use the library or create a custom class to have more control over logs.
- Writing test cases are as important as writing code for you your application. The practice has test-driven development and always measures tests using test coverage tools. Remember that do not write test cases just to achieve 100% test coverage, but also focus on the quality of tests and consider all cases and edge cases for the method which is being tested.
- Make a practice to minimize or zero Lint warnings or errors. https://developer.android.com/studio/write/lint tool helps us to find out possible code that can crash the app, deprecated code, and better options for the written code. The Lint is a very powerful tool that helps us to maintain a standard and optimized code.
- Make a practice to detect and fix memory leaks in your application. LeakCanary is the library that is going to help to find memory leaks.
- Do not push the release certificate and key on the version control system. Keep them at local and add them to an ignore list of version control, for example, the .gitignore file of git.
- SSL certificate pinning, SafetyNet, Android security library, Android KeyStore, and Network Security Configurations all solve security concerns at some level in Android. Explore them and use them in your application.

You should also follow this well-written official documentation https://developer.android.com/topic/security/best-practices.

- R8 or Proguard helps you to shrink the code or optimize the APK, and more. Refer to the *Introducing R8 and Proguard* section of *Chapter 5: Publishing the Application*.
- Integrate Google Tag Manager or Firebase to the application. Google Tag Manager helps you to understand the behavior of the user, and you can serve them better after analyzing the data collected by this tracking tool. Firebase provides tools like Remote config or experiments, which help us in the development of our application.

Android documentation provides a lot of best practices documents. The URL https://developer.android.com/s/results?q=best%20practices will let you find all those interesting and informative documentation for best practices in Android.

Third-party libraries you should know

Before going to a list of a few of the most famous and useful libraries, let us understand how you can choose the right library for your requirement.

Choosing the right Android library

Whenever you are planning to use any third-party library, you need to evaluate libraries by considering the following things

1. Check the stars or popularity of that library.
2. Check how many open issues are there and how frequent bugs are being fixed.
3. Sometimes, the number of active contributors also matters. You can check how many contributors are there and what type of quality they are adding to the library.
4. Code quality matters. Check the code and structure of the library.
5. Research the library to understand features, benefits, and limitations.
6. Make sure that you understand the license of that library.

List of a few libraries

The list of libraries is endless as Android earns huge interest from the developer community, and because of that, you can get a library for almost everything. Following are a few most used libraries in Android:

- **Retrofit** [https://square.github.io/retrofit/] is a type-safe HTTP client for Android, developed by Square.
- **OkHttp** [https://square.github.io/okhttp/] is developed by Square for sending and receiving HTTP-based network requests. It is also the underlying library for Retrofit that provides type safety for consuming REST-based APIs.
- **LeakCanary** [https://square.github.io/leakcanary/] is a memory leak detection library for Android. This is one more very good library provided by Square.

  Square developed many awesome libraries, which are being used by Android developers widely. You can find the list of other libraries at https://square.github.io/#android.
- **EasyPermissions** [https://github.com/googlesamples/easypermissions] is a wrapper library for runtime permissions. This library handles all the cases for us, and we need to write less code.
- **ThreeTen:** [https://github.com/JakeWharton/ThreeTenABP] is helpful to handle the date and time for Android. It is a backport of JSR-310, which was earlier included in Java 8 as a standard `java.time.*` package.
- **Stetho**: [https://github.com/facebook/stetho] is a debugging library that allows you to debug application data, networks, and so on.
- **Kotlin-math**: [https://github.com/romainguy/kotlin-math] provides a set of methods that makes graphics math simpler to write.
- **lottie-android**: [https://github.com/airbnb/lottie-android] Lottie is a mobile library for Android and iOS that parses Adobe After Effects animations exported as JSON with Bodymovin and renders them natively on mobile!

These are only a few important lists of libraries. Some websites maintain a list of libraries that can help you to find the best-suited library for your requirement. These https://android-arsenal.com/ and https://github.com/aritraroy/UltimateAndroidReference/blob/master/README.md two online resources are very good resources where you can find out almost any kind of library.

Conclusion

In this last chapter of the book, we learned about a few important libraries and best practices. Now, we can develop a well-structured and scalable Android application.

We learned Jetpack compose, which is a new trend in Android development. Now, you do not need to design UI using XML layouts, and you can design UI in Kotlin code only. We also learned about App bundles; we learned the benefits of App bundles as well, so next time you develop an Android application, these concepts will help you to think more about your application, and you can adopt these features.

We learned about Hilt, which is a dependency injection library. It will help us in writing clean code easily by providing dependencies automatically. We learned about SafetyNet and looked into the uses and types available in SafetyNet. While reading SafetyNet, we also read about other security things, such as certificate pinning, secure data-store, R8, and so on.

We also learned about writing a good test. We learned about Junit, Espresso, and Robolectric, and we now know when to use Robolectric or Espresso.

In the final sections, we learned some best practices to follow and some third-party libraries to develop an awesome Android application.

We reached the end of the book. Hope you find this book helpful in your Android development and that you develop some amazing applications which help the community.

Points to remember

- Libraries like Hilt and SafetyNet are those libraries that you need in almost each of your applications, so the more you get to experience, the more your application will be better.
- Even though you are not using the feature App bundle or on-demand delivery for modules, focus on modularizing the application. There are other benefits as well, like you separate the code by features, increase build time, and so on.
- Make a practice of writing tests. And do not focus on achieving 100% coverage but focus on writing good quality tests that handle each edge case as well.
- Jetpack Compose is a toolkit for building native UI using Kotlin code, but the XML layout is still there. Android does not have a plan to deprecate XML layouts as of now.

Multiple Choice Questions

1. Modularization can help us to achieve:

    A. On-demand delivery

    B. Instant app feature

C. Faster build

D. All of the above

2. To run Espresso tests, you need to run an emulator or device

   A. True

   B. False

3. Robolectric runs on local JVM and does not need a device or emulator to run?

   A. True

   B. False

4. The Row layout of Jetpack compose works like

   A. RelativeLayout

   B. FrameLayout

   C. LinearLayout

   D. LinearLayout with horizontal orientation and weight attribute

5. The main benefit of using vector drawable is image scalability. It can be scaled without loss of display quality. That is why we should use vector drawable instead of multi-sized PNG images in our application.

   A. True

   B. False

Answers

1. D
2. A
3. A
4. D
5. A

Questions

1. What are assets-only modules?
2. What is the difference between Row and Column layouts?
3. Can you list the benefits of App Bundles?
4. Why writing tests are so important?

Key Terms

- Jetpack Compose
- Row
- Column
- Box
- ConstraintLayout
- App Bundle
- .aab
- APK
- On-demand delivery
- Bundletool
- SafetyNet
- SafetyNet Attestation
- SafetyNet Safe Browsing
- SafetyNet reCAPTCHA
- SafetyNet Verify Apps
- Custom Permission
- Certificate Pinning
- Jetpack Security Lib
- Hilt
- Dependency injection
- Hilt annotations
- JUnit
- Espresso
- Robolectric
- Best practices
- Libraries

Index

A

Activity 43-45
  lifecycle 58-60
AddClipsFragment 286
add() method 55
addToBackStack() method 56
  using 57, 58
Android Application
  best practices 425-427
  creating, on Google Play
      console 229, 230
  developing 2
  publishing 232, 233
  release checklist, preparing 228
  releasing 232, 233
  settings, for paid applications 229
  setting up, on Google Play
      console 230-232
  updating, at Play Store 234
  uploading, to Play Store 228
Android build
  creating 317-322
Android build process 203
Android Game Development Kit
      (AGDK) 299
Android Jetpack 158

Android Lint 24, 25
  using 25, 26
  using, from command/terminal 26, 27
Android Studio Template
  project, creating from 2-4
android virtual device (AVD)
  creating 13-16
app bundles 404
  benefits 404-407
AppCompatActivity 45
app for Tablets
  checklist for quality, preparing 383, 384
  designing 381
  developing 381
  layout qualifiers 381
  layouts, optimizing 381-383
  tablet-specific dimensions 381
Application components 41, 42
  Activity 43-45
  broadcast receiver 48
  content provider 51
  content resolver 52
  Service 45-47
apps for Android TV
  AVD, creating 394
  developing 389-392
  Leanback support, declaring 393

apps for wearables
  AVD, creating 389
  developing 384-388
architecture patterns 89
  need for 90, 91
Awake() method 315

B

Backend-as-a-Service (BaaS) 146
  for chat application 146
backend technology
  checklist 145
  selecting 145
BestDealDataSource.kt 131
BestDealsRepository.kt 131
BestDealsUseCase.kt 135
BestDealsViewModel.kt 133-135
best practices, Android Application 425-427
Box Collider 2D 334
Box layout 401
broadcast receiver 48
  dynamic broadcast receiver 49, 50
  static broadcast receiver 48, 49
Buildbox 298
build configurations
  build types 204-207
  build variants 210
  customizations 204
  product flavors 208-210
buildTypes 19
build variants 202, 203
  configuring 210

C

CartDataSource.kt 131
CartRepository.kt 132
CartUseCase.kt 136
chat application
  backend technology, selecting 145
  chat screen, developing 183-191
  code for first screen, writing 164-166
  contacts screen, developing 177-183
  developing 141, 142

functional requirement 143
home screen, developing 173-177
login screen, developing 167-173
notifications, using 197
pricing 223
profile screen, developing 191-197
project structure 163
publishing 201, 202
screenshots, capturing 226, 227
servers 144
uploading, to Play Store 228
user flow diagrams, creating 143
checklist, for Android app release checklist
  preparing 228
clean architecture 91, 101
  benefits 102
  entities 102
  Frameworks/UI 102
  interface adapters 102
  use cases 102
ClipsDataSource.kt 260
ClipsLocalDataSource.kt 261
ClipsPagerAdapter.kt 274, 275
ClipsRemoteDataSource.kt 261, 262
ClipsRepository 264
ClipsRepository.kt 263
Column layout 401
Compose 398-400
  layouts 400
Compose project
  creating 399, 400
ConstraintLayout 402
  using 403, 404
Content provider 51
Content resolver 52
CRUD, for video sharing application
  database, creating 254-258
C# script 312
  creating 313-317
custom launcher icon
  creating 12, 13
custom view
  versus Fragment 58

D

DAO class 37
  query, running from 37, 38
Database Inspector 35
  query, running from 37, 38
  table, modifying 36, 37
  using 35, 36
databinding library 125
  using 125-128
data storage, video sharing application 248
  database 253
  files 249
  preferences 252, 253
  Preferences 251
  Room 253, 254
  Storage Access Framework (SAF) 249, 250
dimension 63-65
distributable file
  creating 220
doLogin() method
  implementing 168
DP to Pixel conversion
  with Density Bucket 65, 66

E

EasyPermissions 428
Espresso 421
  test cases, writing 421, 423
ExoPlayer 264
  dependencies 264-269

F

files, in project
  AndroidManifest.xml 6
  build.gradle 8, 9
  gradle.properties 10, 11
  gradle-wrapper.properties 10
  Java/ 7
  local.properties 12
  proguard-rules.pro 11
  res/ 7, 8
  settings.gradle 11, 12
Firebase 146
  adding, to chat application 146
Firebase Bill of Materials (BoM) 150
Firebase project
  Android application, registering with 147, 148
  configuration file, adding to Android project 148, 149
  creating 146, 147
  Firebase SDKs, adding to app 149, 150
Firebase services
  Cloud Storage 155
  Firebase Authentication 151, 152
  Firebase real-time database 153-155
  FirebaseUI 155-157
  identifying 150, 151
FixedUpdate() method 315
Fragment 52, 53
  lifecycle 61-63
  Master-Detail Flow use case 53
  showing dynamically 54, 55
  showing statically 54
  versus custom view 58

G

game development 295, 296
  ball, adding 337, 338
  ball, adding to game dynamically 349
  ball pin object, creating 341-345
  blocks, adding 334-336
  bouncing effect, adding to ball 338-340
  C# script, adding 345-349
  diamond, adding 336, 337
  duplicate blocks, adding 335
  floor, adding 331-333
  game objects, adding 330
  prefab, creating for ball 349-351
  project, creating 329, 330
  project requirement 328
  script, modifying for ball prefab usage 351-359

support, adding for multiple
    screens 359-362
  target objects, adding 334
game engine 296, 297
GameMaker Studio 2 298, 299
Google Play console
  app, creating 229, 230
  app installs, monitoring 233, 234
  app, publishing/releasing 232, 233
  app, setting up 230-232
Google Play Store developer profile
  creating 221-223
GPU overdraw 82
Gradle 17-20

H

Hello Unity project
  bricks, applying to material
    object 307-309
  bricks image file, adding 306
  bricks material object, applying to
    Cube 309, 310
  creating 301, 302
  Cube, adding to Scene 305, 306
  game objects, adding 304
  material object, adding 307
  texture, adding to Cube object 305
Hello World application
  creating 1
  running 16
Hilt 409
  annotations 412-416
  benefits 411
  dependency, adding 411, 412
  dependency injection, exploring 409-411
HomeFragment 270
HomeFragment.kt 271, 272

J

Jetpack 158
Jetpack compose 398-400
JUnit test cases
  writing 419, 420

K

Kotlin-math 428

L

LateUpdate() method 315
Layout Inspector
  using 28, 29
layouts 68
  ConstraintLayout 77-81
  FrameLayout 75, 76
  LinearLayout 68, 69
  RelativeLayout 68-71
  selecting, for design 82
  TableLayout 73, 74
layouts, in Compose
  Box 401
  Column 401
  ConstraintLayout 402
  Row 400
Layout Validator 30
LeakCanary 428
LiveData 121
Logcat 20
  filtering options 21
  tools 22, 23
logcat window
  logs, writing 23, 24
LoginActivity.kt 106-108, 121-127
LoginContract.kt 105, 106
LoginDataSource.kt 111
LoginPresenter.kt 108-110
LoginRemoteDataSource
  implementing 114
LoginRepository.kt 111, 112
LoginRequest.kt 110
LoginResponse.kt 110
LoginViewModel.kt 118, 119
lottie-android 428

M

material design
  basics 83, 84

Index

memory profiler 30
  example 32-35
  options, in profiler window 31, 32
Model View Intent (MVI) 137
Model View Presenter (MVP) 103
  advantages 115
  disadvantages 115
  model layer 103
  presenter layer 104
  view layer 104
  with code 104-114
Model View ViewModel (MVVM) 115
  advantages 129
  components and communication flow 116
  databinding library, using 125-128
  disadvantages 129
  layers 117
  UseCases 129, 130
  with code 117-124
modules 9
MutableLiveData 121

O

obfuscation 217
OkHttp 428
optimized image resource type
  Raster image 377
  selecting 377
  Vector image 379

P

Perfetto 83
playClips(...) method 278
Play Store
  app, updating 234
PNG 378
  benefits 378
  limitations 378
Pngcrush 378
pngquant 378
Preferences
  Preferences Datastore 251

Proto Datastore 251
SharedPreferences 251-253
pricing strategy 224
  free 224
  Freemium 224, 225
  paid 225
  subscription plan 225, 226
product flavors
  configuring 208-210
ProGuard 11, 213, 214
project
  creating, from Andriod
    Studio Template 2-4
  files 6

Q

qualifiers 368
  for dimensions 66, 67
  for drawables 68, 369, 370
  for layouts 67, 371
  for values 372, 373

R

R8 213, 214
  class merging 216
  code shrinking 214
  custom rules, adding 219
  dead code removal 214
  debug information, removing 216
  enabling 217
  identifiers, renaming 217
  optimization shrinking technique 214
  resource shrinking 214
  selective in-lining 215
  unused arguments removal 216
Raster image 377
  PNG 378
  WebP 378
RecyclerView 158
  classes 158
  components 159
  working 159-161

release application
  creating 220, 221
release Keystore
  creating 211-213
remove() method 56
replace() method 55
repository pattern 258
  implementing 259, 260
  package structure 260
resource directory structure 367, 368
resources, in Android application 366, 367
  qualifiers 368
  working with 373-377
Retrofit 428
Rigidbody 2D 334
Robolectric 423
  benefits 423
  test cases, writing 424, 425
role interfaces 97
Room 253
  components 254
  DAOs 254
  database class 254
  entities 254
  using 253
Row layout 400

S

SafetyNet 407
  Attestation API 407, 408
  reCAPTCHA API 408
  Safe Browsing API 408
  Verify Apps API 408
screenshots
  obtaining, for application 226, 227
screen sizes 63
  handling 66-68
server-side programming language 145
Service
  uses 45, 47
setClipData(...) method 277
setIsSender() method 189
setListeners(...) method 277

showLikes(...) method 277
Solar2D 298
SOLID principles 91
  dependency inversion principle 98-101
  interface segregation principle 96-98
  Liskov's substitution principle 95, 96
  open-closed principle 93-95
  single responsibility principle 92, 93
Splash screen 321
Square 428
staged rollout 233
Start() method 315
Stetho 428
Storage Access Framework (SAF) 249, 250
Structured Query language (SQL) 145
Systrace 83

T

TabLayout 161, 162
templates 5, 6
terms, in Unity
  Asset 312
  Colliders 311
  component 311
  GameObject 311
  material 310
  packages 310
  Prefab 312
  Renderer 311
  RigidBody 311
  scene 311
  Screen Space 312
  script 311
  SerializeField 312
  Transform 312
  World Space 312
test cases 417
  benefits 417
  writing 417-419
  writing, with JUnit 417-420
  writing, with Robolectric 417
third-party libraries
  EasyPermissions 428

Kotlin-math 428
LeakCanary 428
lottie-android 428
OkHttp 428
Retrofit 428
selection considerations 427
Square 428
Stetho 428
ThreeTen 428
TinyPNG 378
TV application
  AVD, creating 394
  developing 389-392
  Leanback support, declaring 393

U

Unity 297-299
  installing 299-301
  terms 310
  workspace 303, 304
Unreal engine 298
Update() method 315

V

Vector drawable
  benefits 379
  creating 379
  definition 379
  limitations 380
  reference 380
Vector image 379
video sharing application 241
  add clips screen, developing 284-291
  BottomNavigationView 244-248
  comment feature, implementing on clips 283
  CRUD, creating for 254
  data storage 248
  functional requirement, obtaining 241
  home screen, developing 269-278
  likes feature, implementing on clips 278-281
  material UI components 244
  project structure 269
  share feature, implementing for clips 281, 282
  user flow diagram, creating 242, 243
View 52, 53
ViewGroup 68
View Interactor Presenter Entity Router (VIPER) 137
ViewPager 161, 162

W

wearable application
  AVD, creating 389
  developing 384-388
WebP 378
  benefits 378, 379
  URL 379

Made in the USA
Las Vegas, NV
30 April 2023